THE
GOD
WHO SAVES

THE
GOD
WHO SAVES

An Introduction to the Message of the Old Testament

GLENN PEMBERTON

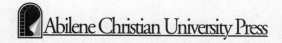

Abilene Christian University Press

THE GOD WHO SAVES

An Introduction to the Message of the Old Testament

ACU PRESS

Copyright © 2015 by Glenn Pemberton | ISBN 978-0-89112-482-5

Printed in the United States of America | ALL RIGHTS RESERVED

For information contact:
Abilene Christian University Press, ACU Box 29138, Abilene, Texas 79699
1-877-816-4455 | www.acupressbooks.com

15 16 17 18 19 20 / 7 6 5 4 3 2 1

For Our Parents

Cotton and Peggy Pemberton

and

Ken and Retha Kennamer

Table of Contents

Abbreviations

General Abbreviations

c.—century
ca.—circa
cf.—*confer*, compare
e.g.—*exempli gratia*, for example
et al.—*et alii,* and others

etc.—*et cetera,* and so forth, and the rest
ibid.—*ibidem*, in the same place
i.e.—*id est*, that is
lit.—literally
n.b.—*nota bene*, note carefully

The Books of the Old Testament

Genesis	Gen	Song of Songs	Song
Exodus	Exod	Isaiah	Isa
Leviticus	Lev	Jeremiah	Jer
Numbers	Num	Lamentations	Lam
Deuteronomy	Deut	Ezekiel	Ezek
Joshua	Josh	Daniel	Dan
Judges	Judg	Hosea	Hos
Ruth	Ruth	Joel	Joel
1–2 Samuel	1–2 Sam	Amos	Amos
1–2 Kings	1–2 Kgs	Obadiah	Obad
1–2 Chronicles	1–2 Chr	Jonah	Jonah
Ezra	Ezra	Micah	Mic
Nehemiah	Neh	Nahum	Nah
Esther	Esth	Habakkuk	Hab
Job	Job	Zephaniah	Zeph
Psalms	Ps or Pss	Haggai	Hag
Proverbs	Prov	Zechariah	Zech
Ecclesiastes	Eccl	Malachi	Mal

The Books of the New Testament

Matthew	Matt	1–2 Thessalonians	1–2 Thess
Mark	Mark	1–2 Timothy	1–2 Tim
Luke	Luke	Titus	Titus
John	John	Philemon	Phlm
Acts	Acts	Hebrews	Heb
Romans	Rom	James	James
1–2 Corinthians	1–2 Cor	1–2 Peter	1–2 Pet
Galatians	Gal	1–2–3 John	1–2–3 John
Ephesians	Eph	Jude	Jude
Philippians	Phil	Revelation	Rev
Colossians	Col		

Translations of the Bible
or Hebrew Scriptures

ASV—American Standard Version
CEB—Common English Bible
CEV—Common English Version
ERV—Easy-to-Read Version
ESV—English Standard Version
HCSB—Holman Christian Standard Bible
JB—Jerusalem Bible
KJV—King James Version
LB—The Living Bible
MSG—The Message
MLB—Modern Language Bible
NAB—New American Bible
NABR—New American Bible,
  Revised Edition
NASB—New American Standard Bible
NAV—New American Version

NCV—New Century Version
NEB—New English Bible
NIV—New International Version
NIVI—NIV, Inclusive Language Edition
NJB—New Jerusalem Bible
NJPS—New Jewish Publication Society
  Translation
NKJV—New King James Version
NLT—New Living Translation
NRSV—New Revised Standard Version
REB—Revised English Bible
RSV—Revised Standard Version
TEV—Today's English Version
  (= Good News Bible)
TNIV—Today's New International Version

For the Study of the Old Testament

ANE—Ancient Near East
BCE—Before Common Era
CE—Common Era
ch(s).—chapter(s)
Dtn—Deuteronomic (History; writer of
  Deuteronomy-2 Kings)
Dtr—Deuteronomistic (History; writer of
  Deuteronomy-2 Kings); also called the
  Deuteronomist
Ham.—Hammurabi
HB—Hebrew Bible
Heb.—Hebrew
JBL—*Journal of Biblical Literature*
JSOT—*Journal for the Study of the Old
  Testament*

JSOTSup—*Journal for the Study of the Old
  Testament Supplement Series*
LXX—Septuagint (Greek Version of
  Hebrew Bible)
MT—Masoretic Text
NT—New Testament
OT—Old Testament
SBL—Society of Biblical Literature
SBLDS—Society of Biblical Literature
Dissertation Series
TANAK—Torah, Nebi'im, Ketubim
  (Jewish Bible)
v(v).—verse(s)

List of Figures

List of Tables

Acknowledgments

resisted this project for over fifteen years, each year skimming the pages of excellent introductions designed for graduate students or for exceptional undergraduates, both with extraordinary motivation to learn and far more than a beginner's knowledge of the text. Not the world in which I or many of my colleagues live: a life in colleges or universities that require a course on the Old Testament (OT), usually in the student's Freshman or Sophomore year. Here the teacher often gets only one semester to transform attitudes toward this three-fourths of the Christian Bible and the God to whom this text testifies; and here the student is as likely to be uninterested as they are interested. Finally, the encouragement of my department chair, Dr. Rodney Ashlock, and even more so, my spouse, Dr. Dana Pemberton, won the day. At first it appeared that the project would be like any other book, and then (I'm not sure exactly when) I began to realize that I had agreed to a project like none other in my experience.

A project designed specifically for the classroom changes everything for the writer. Consequently, I have sought the help of many colleagues in this project—scholars and writers who have provided enriching ideas, caught me when I stumbled, and graciously given of their time to make this book far better than if I had walked alone. Several colleagues took a draft of this book out for a test flight with their students in the Fall of 2014: Dr. Charles Stephenson (Chair of the Department of Biblical Studies, Lubbock Christian University), Dr. Rodney Ashlock (Chair of the Department of Bible, Missions, and Ministry, Abilene Christian University [ACU]), Dr. Kilnam Cha (Assistant Professor of Bible, ACU), and Noemi Palomares-Kern (Instructor of Bible, ACU). A second team participated in a round-table discussion of the manuscript at the annual meeting of the Society of Biblical Literature and American Academy of Religion in San Diego (2014): Dr. Marty Michelson (Professor of Old Testament, Southern Nazarene University), Dr. Charles Rix (Associate Professor of Bible, Oklahoma Christian University), Dr. Kevin Youngblood (Professor of Old Testament, Harding University), and Dr. Chris Heard (Associate Professor of Religion, Pepperdine University), along with some of the test pilots already mentioned. In addition to these, others visited with me privately: Dr. John Jackson (Associate Professor of Bible and Humanities, Milligan College), Dr. Melinda Thompson (Assistant Professor of Old Testament, ACU, Graduate School of Theology), Dr. Curt Niccum (Professor of New Testament, ACU), and Dr. Tim Sensing (Associate Dean, ACU, Graduate School of Theology). Finally, a third group of colleagues from ACU in disciplines other than Theology read the manuscript and engaged in lively conversation each month during the Fall semester of 2014: Dr. Jennifer Shewmaker (Associate Professor of Psychology), Dr. Jim Nichols (Professor of Biology), Dr. Monty Lynn (Professor of Management), Dr. Stephanie Hamm (Assistant Professor of Social Work), Dr. Jonathan Camp (Assistant Professor of Communication), Dr. Lesa Breeding (Former Director of the Adams Center and former Dean of the College of Education and Human Services), Dr. Jessica Smith (Associate Professor of Journalism and Mass Communication), and Dr. Greg Powell (Professor of Chemistry). My thanks to David Christianson and the Adams Center for Teaching and Learning for hosting these conversations. To all of these colleagues (and their students) I express my gratitude for every observation, question, correction, and challenge that helped turn the manuscript into a better textbook.

Those who may have read *Hurting with God* (ACU Press, 2012) or *After Lament* (ACU Press, 2014) are aware of my personal journey through chronic pain with Complex Regional Pain Syndrome (CRPS; RSD). Because of my health challenges, I am also grateful for the wisdom and dedication of the medical team in my corner. These professionals keep me in the fight and, when needed, they do not hesitate to step into the ring and fight on my behalf: Robbie Cooksey, DO; B. Corey Brown, DPM; Gary L. Heath, MD; Shona S. Preston, FNP, BC; Daniel Vaughan, MD; Steven Brown, MD; and Larry Norsworthy, PhD, LCP, BCPM. May God bless you.

Two capable graduate students have assisted me over the past two years. First, Joe Ross, a graduate of Oklahoma State University, read early drafts with an attentive eye to both detail and the broader picture of what works for students. To thank Joe I am obliged to say—*ride 'em Cowboys, go orange and black!* Second, Kipp Swinney, a graduate of ACU, kept me afloat during the Fall of 2014 and the period of final editing in the Spring of 2015. Kipp has worked on secondary materials for teachers, in addition to checking references, compiling bibliographies, and numerous other details. So, to thank Kipp, I am obliged to say—*Go purple and white!*

This is my third book with ACU Press and its skilled staff. Dr. Leonard Allen, director of the Press, was a strong early supporter of this project until his departure to Lipscomb University (as Dean of the College of Bible and Ministry). Interim director, Duane Anderson, seamlessly continued the Press's support, along with his own personal belief in me and in the project. His leadership enabled us to move the manuscript through pilot testing and peer review, investing necessary resources to gain the feedback we needed to make the final product better. I also have special appreciation for Mary Hardegree, along with Lettie Morrow and her staff, who turned the manuscript into a presentable form and brought together all the moving parts to produce the hundreds of pre-publication "books" for the pilot study and peer reviews. I have also been fortunate to work once again with Robyn Burwell, my editor and project manager, who was responsible for bringing this project to its conclusion. For all the answers to all the questions, and all the ways you push me to be a better writer, thank you.

Every page I write has a first reader who tells me the truth, even when I may not want to hear it. This woman creates physical space for me to write and adapts her world to the rhythm of my putting words on paper and then typing them onto the big white screen. Without her I would not have found new life in words and sentences. Neither of us foresaw the number of hours, the days and nights this project would consume. So for her patience during all those days and nights when I was lost in a world of my own, for her unflinching support, and her belief in this book—thank you, Dana. You are the great surprise and love of my life.

Together we dedicate this book to our parents: Dana's father and mother, Dr. Ken and Retha Kennamer, and my father and mother, Cotton and Peggy Pemberton. For the faith you passed to us, and all you have done to form us into Christ-followers, we thank you. It is our honor to dedicate to you this book about a God of unfailing love. I grieve that my mother died suddenly in September 2014. She had, thankfully, seen the pre-publication draft with its dedication page. I love you and I miss you, Mom.

To the **Instructor**

During the process of peer review and pilot testing, I learned one absolute truth, perhaps two: (1) every instructor has his or her own way of teaching this course, and (2) we are all looking for something a little different in the ideal textbook. So, I have done my best to provide an approach that has worked well in my classes, and tried to listen carefully to other instructors here at ACU and elsewhere so that I provide material that will be helpful to many classes and styles, not just my own. Before you begin, or as you consider course adoption, in all fairness I want to make you aware of what this text does and does not attempt to do:

- I write for undergraduate students, though I hope older students also find benefit in the text. My primary audience is the 18- to 20-year-old student who comes to a university-wide required course on the Old Testament. Some are eager to learn, others less so, and more than a few resent the requirement. So I do not assume the student is interested in what you and I find fascinating. As you know, here we must earn our right to speak and be heard.
- This is not a survey of the Old Testament. From the beginning of the project it was never my intention to offer an introduction to the Old Testament that included every book. The plan is to build a basic framework and provide enough instruction in reading the biblical texts that a student will be able to return alone and confidently read the books we left aside.

1

- Although I follow the narrative order of the Hebrew Bible and try with all my might to help students make the journey in time and space to read these texts from the perspective of ancient Israel, I cannot escape my own religious commitment to the Christian tradition. I do not, however, write an introduction to the message of the Old Testament with every chapter pointing toward the Messiah. The message is so much more complex and richer than any one theme, even the coming Messiah.

With these assumptions, objectives, and perspective in mind, allow me to share just a little more about the chapters and materials available to you upon request:

- The maps, figures, and tables, as well as other supporting materials (sample syllabi, course schedules, quizzes, and exams), are available to you at no additional cost. We do, however, try our best to keep the student on the fourth row, seat eleven from financing college by tapping into an extra source of income. So if you adopt the textbook, please contact ACU Press via email, and we will conduct our due-diligence before directing you to the secret place inside the ACU Press vault. If it has been some time since you adopted the book and are re-adopting, you will need to contact ACU Press again for authorization.
- The book provides fifteen chapters so that you may ideally cover one chapter a week or a little more (the length of many academic semesters). The chapters are short so that students have time to read from the primary source: Scripture.
- The beginning of each chapter provides: (1) Two or more biblical reading assignments so that you may decide which to assign for the next class session. (2) The definition of key terms that are used in the chapter (then denoted by **bold grey type** the first time they appear in the chapter). These terms may also appear later but are not repeated in the key terms for those chapters. All key terms are gathered in the glossary for easy reference.
- In each chapter, among the tables and figures, are sections entitled "Texts in Conversation" and "The Message of the Old Testament." In "Texts in Conversation," I bring together different voices on an important topic, e.g., (1) the Deuteronomistic Theology in conversation with the death of Josiah, and the Books of Job and Ecclesiastes; or (2) the ban against marriage to non-Israelites in conversation with the Books of Ruth and Esther—along with Nehemiah's revival. In these sections, I want the student to hear the plurality and inner conversation of the Old Testament. In the "The Message of the Old Testament," I draw attention to many different ideas about God and faith to which the Old Testament testifies, e.g., (1) the two perspectives on God from Genesis 1 and 2; or (2) the Lord's two-sided revelation in Exodus 34. Much like the "Texts in Conversation," these sections show the student the many "Messages" of the Old Testament.
- The end of each chapter includes: (1) "To Discuss"—discussion questions based on the content of the chapter and the assigned biblical texts. (2) "To Know"—a list of key persons, places, and events. It poses questions for you to review and select from for the students to learn. If you assign additional "To Know" items, I would appreciate your sharing these with me for possible inclusion in future editions. (3) "Dig Deeper"—a list of topics for

further research, most of which are interdisciplinary in nature. Any of these topics could work for an individual or group term project. (4) "For Further Reading"—a list of books, articles, and other resources for students who may be interested in issues or topics the chapter raises.

- Material in the appendices is for optional use. In my classes, I choose to open with Appendix I before beginning Chapter One. The design allows you to use or not use this material at your discretion. I recognize that many other topics could have been added. At least for now, I have left these topics for you to present as you see fit.

- You may also want to say a few words about Chapter One before assigning it for reading (e.g., that it begins with ancient Near Eastern materials, not the Bible), or you might choose to say nothing and let the students be surprised by an Old Testament text book that begins with ancient mythology—especially those who have heard Genesis 1–2 all their lives, but probably not "The Epic of Creation." Reading common material, unfamiliar to students who have grown up at church and unfamiliar to students who have never gone to church, may provide an experience that sends both groups tumbling back into the ancient Near East *together*, suddenly united in their trek.

I hope these brief points help orient you toward what is in this textbook. I also hope that you will not hesitate to contact me and share your experience with the book, including suggestions for future editions (if we are blessed to produce a textbook that teachers find genuinely helpful).

Glenn Pemberton
Abilene, Texas
July 2015

To the **Student**

Take a deep breath and prepare to immerse yourself in the wonder and power of the Old Testament. In the pages that follow, we will read of scandals, intrigue, comedy (yes, even good jokes), dysfunctional families, and a people struggling to be faithful to God. In other words, prepare to read about people much like us. But to understand these people and their God, we must travel back in time to a place far away and long ago. On our journey, we will meet a God who wants to bless these people—people who just don't understand a God who transcends both ethnic and national boundaries (and this is just the beginning of what will surprise them). We will follow their story from beginning to end, along the way meeting some who will enter and encourage their lives for a time (e.g., prophets), and meeting others who will challenge their confidence and hopes in God (my thanks to Dr. Kathy Armistead for these words to describe what is to come).

Each chapter in this book begins with a glossary of key terms and ends with discussion questions ("To Discuss"), a study guide ("To Know"), potential research topics ("To Dig Deeper"), and suggestions "For Further Reading." As a textbook on the Old Testament, one purpose of *The God Who Saves* is to supplement your reading of the Bible with information that will help you make the leap back in time so that you may read and better understand this ancient text. A second purpose is to challenge you to think deeply about the biblical texts by presenting readings you may not have heard before and with which you may disagree. Consequently, if at the end of reading several pages you say to yourself, "I've never heard of this before," or even, "I disagree with these claims," then this textbook will have achieved its goal. My hope is that you will rise to the challenge and think critically about why you disagree before you dismiss the idea as wrong or crazy.

My hope is that as you read, you will discover that understanding the Old Testament is not as difficult as so many people claim. My hope is that as you read, you will begin to fall in love with this half of the Christian Bible and its testimony to the life of faith. And my hope, most of all, is that through the testimony of these ancient books, you will begin a lifelong love affair with the God to whom they testify.

Glenn Pemberton
Abilene, Texas
July 2015

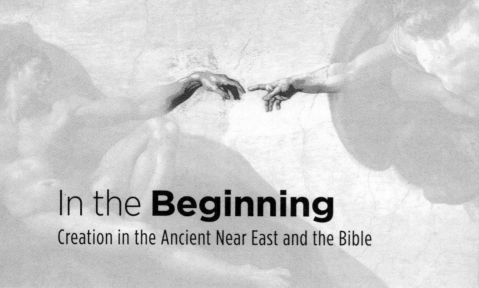

In the **Beginning**
Creation in the Ancient Near East and the Bible

1

In the beginning, before the skies above or the earth below existed, Father Apsu (fresh water) and Mother Tiamat (salt water) gave birth to children, who became the parents of Anshar (the older sky god) and Kishar (the earth goddess). Anshar's firstborn son was Anu (the sky god); Anu also fathered a son in his likeness, who was superior to his ancestors in wisdom and strength. Among the gods there was none who rivaled Anu's son.

At that time, the younger gods would gather together at the home of the gods and make a lot of noise. Father Apsu tried to get them to settle down and be quiet, but it was of no use. And even though neither Apsu nor Tiamat were able to sleep or get any rest because of these young gods, Tiamat refused to do anything to them. But Apsu, on the other hand, called upon his advisor, and together they went to discuss this terrible situation with Tiamat. Apsu stated his position loud and clear, "Their ways are intolerable to me. I cannot rest during the day and I cannot sleep at night. So I will destroy them and be rid of them, so we can sleep."

When Tiamat heard this, she was furious and shouted at her lover, "How could we destroy what we ourselves created? Even though their ways are so grievous, we should be patient with them." Apsu's advisor, however, sided with his plan to destroy the gods, his own children and grandchildren. But everything they plotted was reported to the younger gods, who listened carefully, and ironically, fell silent.

One day, Ea (the god of wisdom and magic) took action. He made a clever spell and poured it on Apsu as he was sleeping so that he went

READING ASSIGNMENTS
JOB 38
PSALM 33, 74, 104
PROVERBS 8
GENESIS 1–2

KEY TERMS

Ancient Near East: the land area roughly equivalent to nations from modern Egypt on the West to Iran in the East

Cosmogony: a story of the origins of the world and/or the universe

Enuma Elish: the opening words of the Babylonian creation myth "The Epic of Creation," often used as title of this story

Etiology: a story of how something began, e.g., how did the practice of marriage begin?

Genre: the type or category of a written work, e.g., poem, novel, myth, or history

Israel: a family chosen by God to become a mighty nation and to bless the world

Leviathan: a mythological sea serpent, often represents chaotic forces that stand against life

Mace: a club for combat that has one larger end, often laced with metal spikes

Tablet of Destinies: a tablet upon which the future is written; the god who holds this tablet has the authority to set laws and decree what will happen in the future

into a deep sleep; he also put Apsu's advisor into a daze. Then Ea held Apsu down, killed him, removed his crown, and took his counselor captive by a nose rope. Ea built a triumphal city over the body of Apsu; he established his private quarters there so that he and his lover coud live in splendor. Ea then fathered Marduk—a powerful god, superior in every way. He had four eyes to perceive everything, four enormous ears, and when he spoke, fire blazed from his mouth. His father created the four winds and put them in Marduk's hand, saying, "My son, let them play!" Marduk was the majesty of the gods.

Meanwhile, although Tiamat was enraged over the murder of her lover, she sat mute. Finally, the older gods rallied to her side and complained that because she had done nothing to avenge Apsu's murder, Ea had created four winds—winds that make so much noise, now they cannot rest. They begged her:

> Are you not a mother? You heave restlessly
> But what about us, who cannot rest? Don't you love us?
> Our grip is slack, and our eyes are sunken.
> Remove the yoke of us restless ones, and let us sleep!
> Set up a battle cry and avenge them!

Tiamat listened and was stirred into action by their words. So with these gods crowding around her, she prepared for war against those responsible for Apsu's death and all those in open rebellion against her, making so much noise that neither she nor the older gods could rest. She created ferocious beasts and merciless and powerful weapons; and she promoted Kingu to lead her army, giving him the **Tablet of Destinies**.

Ea heard the report about Tiamat's actions and was dumbfounded; he went to his father, Anshar, and told him everything that Tiamat was planning:

> Father, Tiamat who bore us is rejecting us!
> She has convened an assembly and is raging out of control.
> The gods have turned to her, all of them.
> Even those whom you begot have gone over to her side . . .

Ea described the creatures Tiamat had prepared for battle and Kingu's promotion to lead the army and carry the Tablet of Destinies. His father listened carefully and spoke with a weak voice: "You killed Apsu, so you must be the one to declare war and face Tiamat. Where else will we find someone to face Tiamat?" So Ea went, only to retreat in fear. Then his brother Anu went to calm Tiamat, only to retreat in fear. Tiamat would not be pacified.

So the assembly of gods came together again. They all sat silently, and then spoke as one: "Will no other god come forward? Is our fate fixed? Will no one go out to face Tiamat?" Then Ea called out from his dwelling place, "Anshar, father of the great gods, what about your grandson, the one who rushes into battle: Marduk the Hero?"

Anshar sent for Marduk and was glad to see his grandson now grown to maturity, but hesitant to send him to face Tiamat. "Don't you realize that it will be Tiamat, a woman, who will advance against you?"

Marduk answered, "Anshar, my creator, rejoice and be glad! You will soon set your foot upon the neck of Tiamat in victory!"

So Anshar said, "Then go, son, knowing all wisdom. Defeat Tiamat with your spell."

Marduk was glad and spoke to the gods,

> If indeed I am to be your champion,
> If I am to defeat Tiamat and save your lives,
> Convene the council, and name a special reward,
> Let my word establish fates instead of you!
> Whatever I create shall never be altered!
> The decree of my lips will never be revoked, never changed!

Quickly, the gods accepted what Marduk proposed. They decreed a reward for Marduk, their champion, and built a princely shrine for him (Babylon), where he took up residence. They declared that from that day forward, Marduk's command would never be altered. His word would be law: "We hereby give you sovereignty over the whole universe." They proclaimed, "Marduk is King!"

So Marduk prepared his weapons for battle against Tiamat. He made a bow with a feathered arrow and slung them over his shoulder, took a **mace** in his right hand, and made a net to capture Tiamat. Marduk then marshaled the whirlwind and the four winds: South, North, East, and West. He created the evil wind, the tempest, and the whirlwind. Then he

> . . . released the winds which he had created, seven of them.
> They advanced behind him to make turmoil inside Tiamat.
> The Lord raised the flood-weapon, his great weapon,
> And mounted the frightful, unfaceable storm-chariot.

Meanwhile, Tiamat, in the form of a sea serpent, was raging out of control. As Marduk came near he sent a message detailing her offenses and the wrongs she had done against the gods: her decision to kill the gods just because they made so much noise; the appointment of Kingu, giving him the Tablet of Destinies that is not rightfully his, and charging her as the true rebel against the gods. So Marduk said, "Let you and I do single combat."

When Tiamat heard all this, she went wild, lost her temper, and screamed in passion. They came face to face (see Figure 1.1). Marduk spread his net to encircle Tiamat, while she tried to cast a spell. He sent the evil wind into her face and she opened her mouth to swallow it, but she was unable. Marduk kept sending powerful winds so that her mouth opened wide and her belly inflated. He then shot the arrow into her belly so that she exploded, popping open and dying. Marduk threw down her corpse and stood on top of her. All the gods marching behind

Figure 1.1. Tiamat and Marduk in Battle

her turned to run, but they were surrounded by Marduk's army, unable to escape.

Marduk trampled on Tiamat's body and smashed her skull with his mace. He rested, inspecting her corpse, and then split her body in half. One half he put up to form the sky, putting a bolt in place to hold it. The other half of Tiamat's body Marduk laid down as the earth. He made the Tigris and Euphrates come out of her eyes and piled up mountains from her udder.

The gods were elated and proclaimed Marduk king. He decided to make himself a luxurious dwelling on earth, a place for the assembly of gods and for his own resting place. Marduk spoke, "I hereby name it Babylon, the home of the great gods, the center of religion."

After some time, when the gods were weary of the tiresome work of digging and clearing the canals of the Tigris and Euphrates, Marduk decided to work a miracle:

> Let me put blood together, and make bones too.
> Let me set up primeval man: Man shall be his name.
> Let me create a primeval man.
> The work of the gods shall be imposed on him,
>   and so they shall be at leisure.
> Let me change the ways of the gods miraculously,
>   so they are gathered as one, yet divided in two.

The gods loved the idea and proposed that Kingu should die and his blood used, since he incited Tiamat into war. So Marduk "created mankind from his blood, imposed the work of the gods on man and released the gods from it." [1]

Creation in the Bible

With awareness of "The Epic of Creation" (or "*Enuma Elish*"), one of the most well-known stories of creation in the **ancient Near East**, we are better prepared to read the biblical texts about creation alongside those for whom they were originally written. Our task is to travel back in time, insofar as that as possible, and read the text on its own terms—instead of dragging the Old Testament into the twenty-first century—and reading it as a modern publication. Such time travel is not easy, but critical if we are to be competent readers and interpreters of the biblical text. After all, **Israel**'s claim is that the LORD entered her culture, with all her disturbing practices and attitudes, in order to make himself known. So if we are going to understand what the LORD did and who he is, then we too need to enter Israel's world.

---

[1] This story of creation, "The Epic of Creation," is summarized from Stephanie Dalley, *Myths from Mesopotamia* (Oxford: Oxford University Press, 1989), 233–262; Victor Matthews and Don Benjamin, *Old Testament Parallels: Laws and Stories from the Ancient Near East*. Rev. and exp. 2d ed. (New York: Paulist Press, 1997), 9–18; and Michael Coogan, *A Reader of Ancient Near Eastern Texts: Sources for the Old Testament* (New York: Oxford University Press, 2013), 9–14.

Now that we, with Israel, are aware of the "Epic of Creation" and its claims about King Marduk's conquest over the serpent Tiamat, we are in a better position to read biblical texts such as Psalm 74.

> Yet God has been my king from ancient days—
>> God, who makes salvation happen in the heart of the earth!
>>> You split the sea with your power.
>>> You shattered the heads of the sea monsters on the water.
>>> You crushed Leviathan's heads.
>>> You gave it to the desert dwellers for food!
>>> You split open springs and streams;
>>> you made strong-flowing rivers dry right up.
>>> The day belongs to you! The night too!
>>> *You established* both the moon and the sun.
>>> *You set all the boundaries* of the earth in place.
>>> Summer and winter? *You made them!* (Ps 74:12–17, emphasis mine)[2]

For those with some familiarity with the Bible, Psalm 74 may sound like the story of the great flood, or even the exodus from Egypt. These ideas are, in fact, present in the text. Nonetheless, creation is the focal point of Psalm 74, as verses 16–17 make clear (see the italics above). With the ancient readers, we may also detect strong echoes from "The Epic of Creation" in verses 12–15. Like Marduk, the Creator God "split the sea . . . shattered the heads of the sea monsters . . . crushed **Leviathan**'s heads . . . [and] split open springs." But the poet asserts that without question it was Israel's God who defeated the sea monster Leviathan (a sea serpent like Tiamat). Israel's God is the true Creator and King (74:12), not Marduk.

Job 38:4–11 also uses imagery in common with "The Epic of Creation" to describe God's work. God speaks to Job:

> Where were you when I laid the earth's foundations?
>> Tell me if you know.
> Who set its measurements? Surely you know.
>> Who stretched a measuring tape on it?
> On what were its footings sunk;
>> who laid its cornerstone,
>> while the morning stars sang in unison
>>> and all the divine beings shouted?
> Who enclosed the Sea behind doors
>> when it burst forth from the womb,
>> when I made the clouds its garment,

---

[2]Unless otherwise indicated, all biblical quotations are from the Common English Bible (CEB) translation.

> the dense clouds its wrap,
>> when I imposed my limit for it,
>>> put on a bar and doors
>> and said, "You may come this far, no farther;
>>> here your proud waves stop"?

God describes the birth of the sea as an event that posed no threat to the Lord. Instead, the Lord swaddles the infant sea with the clouds and then set limits for how far the sea may come on dry ground (see also Job 26:12–13). Even more striking—and demeaning of Babylon's serpent, Tiamat—the writer in Psalm 104 describes the creation of living things in the sea and "Leviathan, which you made, plays in it!" (104:26). The fearsome serpent of Babylon has become nothing more than a plaything, God's giant rubber duck in the sea.

Other texts in the Old Testament emphasize a variety of messages about creation and the Creator. To continue with Psalm 104, this poem elaborates the grandeur of creation and the Lord's ongoing support of nature. The Lord makes springs gush out in the valleys (104:10). The Lord waters the mountains (104:13), makes the grass grow (104:14), makes darkness come (104:20), and provides food for all living things (104:27–28). In other words, the Lord is responsible for the ongoing welfare of creation; if the Lord were to pull away, creation would collapse.

In Psalm 33, the emphasis is placed on the Lord's ongoing intervention in human affairs. After a brief description of creation (33:6–9), the writer speaks of the Lord who "overrules what the nations plan; he frustrates what the peoples intend to do" (33:10). The Lord looks down from heaven, from where he watches all humanity; he sees the human tendency to depend on military power for self-confidence, stability, and victory (33:13–17). But the Lord watches over those who fear him and delivers them from death in famine (33:18–19). So, the psalmist concludes, "We put our hope in the Lord. He is our help and our shield. Our heart rejoices in God because we trust his holy name. Lord, let your faithful love surround us because we wait for you" (33:20–22; see also Ps 89:9–10; Isa 27:1, 51:9–10).

Finally, Proverbs 8 wins the prize for the most unusual description of creation in the Old Testament. Here, the concept of wisdom is personified as a woman (8:1–21; see also 4:4–9 and 9:1–6). To be more precise, in Proverbs 8, Wisdom is a baby girl—born of God before the creation of the world (8:22–26). Consequently, when "take your daughter to work day" came around, young Wisdom went and watched as her Father made the sky firm, set the limits of the sea, and marked out the foundations of the earth (8:27–29). And while her Father was at work, young Wisdom was "beside him, as a master of crafts" (8:30a), or perhaps better translated, "I was like a child by his side" (NCV, see also ERV, KJV). The second translation, which seems to fit the context better, pictures young Wisdom dancing and playing in the new world, with special delight in humans (8:30–31). At least one purpose for this vivid personification is to stress that Woman Wisdom is a reliable guide to life because she saw how the world was created and understands how it works (8:32–36).

Creation in Genesis 1:1–2:3

The more famous stories of creation come from the opening chapters of Genesis, the first book of the Bible. Here we find two stories that stress different ideas about creation and the Creator—stories written with full awareness of the "Epic of Creation" and other competing creation stories from other cultures. It is crucial for us to remember that in the ancient Near East, everyone believed in creation and a Creator God or gods; the question of their day was not between creation and evolution or creation and science. Their questions were scientific to them: Which god created the world, what is this god like, what is the nature of creation, and what is my place in the world? With this in mind, read the magnificent story of creation from Genesis 1:1–2:3 (author's translation).

1:1-2 When God began to create
    the sky and the earth,
the earth was a wasteless nothing,
    darkness was over the deep sea (*tehom*),
    and a mighty wind blew across the water.

Day One
1:3-5 Then God said, "Let there be light,"
    and there was light.
God saw that the light was good.

So God divided between the light and
    the darkness;
    God called the light, "day,"
    and called the darkness, "night."

There was evening and morning,
    one day.

Day Two
1:6-8 Then God said, "Let there be a dome in
    the waters,
    and let it separate the waters from waters."

So God made the dome
    and he divided the waters below the dome,
    from the waters above the dome.
And so it was.

God called the dome, "sky."

There was evening and morning,
    a second day.

Day Three
1:9-13 Then God said, "Let the water below the sky
    gather to one place so dry land will appear."
And so it was.

God called the dry land "earth,"
    and the gathered waters he called "seas."
God saw that it was good.

Then God said, "Let the earth sprout plants,
    seed-bearing plants,
    fruit trees of every kind on earth,
    bearing fruit with seeds."
And so it was.

So the earth produced plants
    seed-bearing plants of every kind,
and trees of every kind bearing fruit with seeds."
God saw that it was good.

There was evening and morning,
    a third day.

Day Four
1:14-19 Then God said, "Let there be light-bearers in
    the sky-dome
    to divide between the day and the night.
They will mark signs and seasons, days,
    and years.
    They will be lights in the sky-dome to give
    light on the earth.
And so it was.

God made two lights:
> the sun to rule the day,
> and moon and the stars to rule the night.

God put them in the sky-dome
> to give light on the earth,
> to rule over the day and night,
> and to divide the light and darkness.

God saw that it was good.

There was evening and morning,
> a fourth day.

Day Five

1:20–23 Then God said, "Let the seas swarm with life,
> and let birds fly above the earth, across the
> sky-dome."

So God created the great sea monsters (*Tannim*),
> and every species of life that swarms in
> the waters,
> and every species of flying birds.

God saw that it was good.

And God blessed them saying, "Be fruitful and
> multiply
> and fill the water in the seas,
> and may the birds multiply on earth."

There was evening and morning,
> a fifth day.

Day Six

1:24–31 Then God said, "Let the earth produce
> every species of living creature:
> domesticated animals, creeping things,
> and wild animals of every kind."

And so it was.

So God made wild animals of every kind,
> and domesticated animals of every kind,
> and every thing that creeps on the land.

God saw that it was good.

Then God said, "Let us make a human (*adam*)
> in our image and likeness.

And they will rule over the fish of the sea
> and over the birds of the sky

and over the domesticated animals and over all
> the earth,

and over all the creepings things on the earth.

So God created humanity (*adam*) in his likeness;
in his image God created humanity:
> male and female, he created them.

And God blessed them and God said to them,
> "Be fruitful and multiply,
> fill the earth and take charge of it.
> Rule the fish of the sea and the birds of
> the sky,
> and all wild animals that creep on the earth."

Then God said, "Look, I have given you every
> green plant
> producing seed which is on the face of all
> the earth,
> and every tree which produces fruit;
> they will be your food.

And for every wild animal of the earth
> and for every bird of the sky,
> and for every creeping thing on the earth.
> in which there is life-breath—
> all the green plants for food.

And so it was.

God saw all that he made,
> and look—it was *very good*.

There was evening and morning,
> a sixth day.

Day Seven

2:1–3 The sky and the earth
> and everything in them were finished.

So on the seventh day God finished his work,
> and he rested on the seventh day from all
> his work.

Then God blessed the seventh day and declared it
> a holy day,
> because on it he rested from all his work of
> creating
> which God had done.

There is no lack of topics for discussion from Genesis 1:1–2:3. From the translation of the opening lines—"When God began to create the heavens and the earth—the earth was without shape or form, it was dark over the deep sea . . ." (CEB, see also NJPS, NRSV) or "In the beginning God created the heavens and the earth. The earth was formless and empty, and darkness covered deep waters . . ." (NLT, see also JB, NASB, NIV, TNIV)—to where the story concludes—in 2:3 or 2:4. And with only a little exaggeration we may say every line between these points raises one or more questions, some we may answer and others that defy research. There is some merit to the observation that when we become frustrated with a text because it refuses to answer our questions, we may need to ask if we have misidentified the text's **genre**. Perhaps nothing frustrates a reader more than trying to read one genre as if it were another: to read a novel as if it were nonfiction or a cookbook as if it were a poem.

For the sake of our analysis, we raise only five questions of this creation story that should help us unpack what the poem is trying to say about God and the world. These questions may be best represented by a simple chart (see Table 1.1).

CREATION IN GENESIS 1:1–2:3	
What is the...	
1. Literary Style?	The story has a rhythmic, poetic quality created by an economy of words, parallelism (tight relationship of lines), and repetition. Thus, unlike most English versions, my translation keeps the poetry intact.
2. Scope or Scale?	The scope or scale of creation is universal, all-encompassing, from basset hounds to Professors of Old Testament, from an amoeba to a galaxy.
3. Term for God?	The term used to refer to the creator is the common Hebrew word for god/God (*Elohim*).
4. Order of Creation?	Creation takes place in an orderly process that gives the impression of intentionality from beginning to end (see further discussion below)
5. Manner of Creation?	God is at some distance from creation and so creates by the spoken word, like a king who issues orders that are immediately obeyed and carried out.

Table 1.1. Creation in Genesis 1:1–2:3

The fourth question, regarding the order of creation, requires more consideration (to assist with this process, complete Table 1.2). Israel's God begins with three days of bringing the chaotic waters under control. First, God establishes light and fixes a division between light and darkness to form the most fundamental element of human life: time—the basic unit of time, a day (beginning with evening and ending as day light fades). Second, God separates the waters above from the waters below, holding the waters above back with a translucent dome or bowl ("sky dome" in my translation, "firmament" in older translations). By this restraint of water God creates the sky and the seas, with the sky naturally taking a blue color because of the water behind the bowl. Third, God further pulls back the seas to expose the dry land beneath. By command, God fixes a boundary so that dry land is insured from water taking over, as it had at the beginning of creation; then, in addition to dry land, God commands all types of vegetation and trees to sprout. By these actions the Lord establishes three basic environments for other objects and living beings to fill on corresponding days: (1) time/light, (2) sky and sea, and (3) dry land.

The next three days parallel the first three. On day four, God creates objects to carry or reflect the light created on day one—sun, moon, and stars—to provide light and to "mark signs and seasons, days, and years" (1:14–19). On day five, God makes birds to fill the sky and fish to fill the seas, environments created on day two (1:20–23). Then, on day six, God creates land animals (wild and domesticated) and then humans to live on the dry ground exposed on day three (1:24–31). Finally, on the seventh day, God "rests" from all the work he had done (2:2). Here is a concept that often suffers from the lack of time travel. We are apt to think that "rest" indicates a God weary from work and in need of physical rest. In the ancient Near East, however, in a story like this, "rest" has royal overtones. Just as Genesis 1 has presented God as King, in the ancient Near East kings "rest" over lands they have conquered. In other words, to rest means to reign over. Thus, on the seventh day, God takes the throne to reign over all creation.

THE ORDER OF CREATION IN GENESIS 1:1–2:3				
Environment			**Filling the Environment**	
Day 1	"Space" Light/darkness	→	Day 4	Light carriers: sun, moon, stars to mark seasons, days, and years
Day 2		→	Day 5	
Day 3		→	Day 6	

Table 1.2. The Order of Creation in Genesis 1:1–2:3 (Blank)

Many modern readers are distressed by the ways in which Genesis 1 fails to measure up to modern science. And indeed, Genesis 1 is not modern scientific literature, nor should we ask or demand that it be—dragging an ancient text, kicking and screaming, into the twenty-first century. Once again, a better reading strategy is for us to read from the perspective of the ancient reader, insofar as we are able to manage such time travel. Everyone in the ancient Near East believes in creation and holds a view of the cosmos similar to that in Genesis 1 (see Figure 1.2). Thus, in Genesis 1:1–2:3, one claim the writer makes is that the Creator is a powerful King who brought the primeval chaotic waters under control with simple commands.

A second example of our struggle with the theological nature of this text in its ancient context comes from day one:

> Then God said, "Let there be light,"
> and there was light.
> God saw that the light was good.

> So God divided between the light and the darkness;
>> God called the light, 'day'
>> and called the darkness, 'night.'
>
> There was evening and morning,
>> one day. (1:3–5, my translation)

The modern question is obvious: How can there be light before the sun or stars are created (on day 4)? Scientifically, the hypothesis is impossible. But theologically, consider the countries with whom the ancient Israelites interacted: nations with different claims about creation, the gods, and the sun. Viewed from this theological perspective, the writer appears to recognize and dismiss Egyptian claims for Ra or Atum Ra, the sun god. Some Egyptians worshiped Ra as the creator god who spoke all forms of life into existence by saying their name. But according to Genesis 1, Ra is neither the creator god, nor is Ra or the sun necessary to create light or warmth. The God of Israel can speak light into existence without the sun or Ra; in fact, the sun is merely one of many created objects. Not a god.

In a pre-scientific world where all people believe in creation, the issue is neither creation versus evolution, nor are the writers and readers particularly concerned about a literal scientific account of how creation took place (this is our interest, not theirs). In fact, had God tried to teach modern physics to the ancient reader, not only would the reader be totally lost, but the reader would likely dismiss the scientific account as crazy talk. So instead, God enters the culture of the ancient Near East in order to introduce himself to Israel and her world. God models what we know to be the best strategy of missionaries: work in and through culture, not above or around culture.

So, based on Genesis 1, what is the God of Israel—this Creator God—like? Let me begin a list for you to continue. The God of Genesis 1 is:

- a powerful God, able to speak creation into existence.
- a Creator without conflict or challenge from other gods; this God does not create as the result of a fight or struggle for power.
- a God with a plan from beginning to end; this God knew what he would do on day six when he began on day one.

Taken together, these observations lead us to at least one conclusion: Israel's God is a great and powerful King. I hope my observations and conclusion are only the beginning of a vigorous discussion about the God to whom Genesis 1 testifies.

Creation in Genesis 2:4–25

The second creation story in Genesis differs significantly from the first. Many readers may, however, choose to read Genesis 2 as a close-up of the last day or two of the creation story in Genesis 1 and harmonize all apparent conflicts. Such attempts to harmonize the two stories assume the two creation stories in Genesis are, in fact, one story. Thus, the stories must agree in every detail,

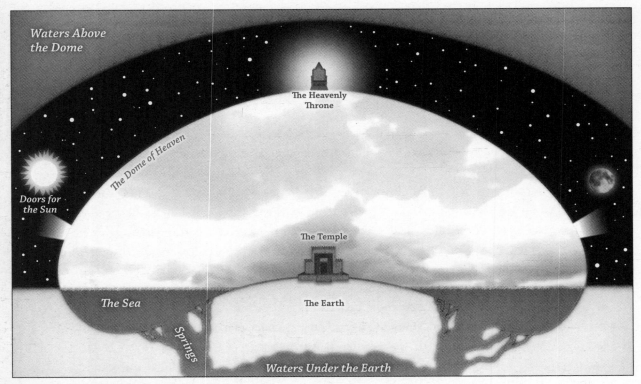

Figure 1.2. An Ancient Near Eastern Model of the Cosmos

with primacy given to the first account. Such a reading is supported by many people of faith; here, however, I will read Genesis 2:4–25 as a distinct and different story. We have already seen that the Old Testament describes creation in many different ways, from smashing the heads of a sea serpent (Ps 74:13–14), swaddling newborn seas like a baby (Job 38:4–8), and taking daughter Wisdom along to watch her Father at work (Prov 8:22–31). The Bible is comfortable with the presence of many different voices speaking from a wide variety of perspectives (see Texts in Conversation below). Consequently, it does not seem necessary to force Genesis 2 into harmony with Genesis 1 as if the Old Testament had only one creation story. More important, such a move may very well cause us to miss the distinct claims about the Creator and creation that Genesis 2 tries to convey.

In Genesis 2, the second story begins with barren ground, no plants growing for two reasons: (1) the LORD God (a new, more personal name; see Chapter Four) has not yet caused rain on the earth, and (2) there was no human to work the ground (2:5). The differences from Genesis 1 are immediately clear: in Genesis 1 when the dry ground appears on day three, vegetation of all sorts begins to grow (1:12). But not in chapter 2. Here, the land is barren, awaiting the appearance of rain and humans.

So in need of a human, like a potter the LORD God forms a human (Heb. *adam*) from the ground (Heb. *adamah*). The word play gives us the name *Adam,* which means something along the lines of "dirt," "taken from dirt," or simply "dirt-clod." Like a paramedic, with a little CPR the LORD God blows life-giving air into the human so that the dirt-clod "came to life" (2:7), an act that does not occur until the highpoint of all creation in Genesis 1. But now in Genesis 2, with an irrigation system in place to remedy the lack of rain (2:6, similar to the irrigation systems of the Egyptians and Babylonians) and a human ready to work, like a gardener the LORD God plants an incredible garden with every beautiful tree and every plant that produces food—along with the tree of life and the tree of the knowledge of good and evil (see discussion in Chapter Two).

Texts in Conversation

The distinct stories in Genesis 1:1–2:3 and Genesis 2:4–25 are the first of many texts read best when kept in dialogue with one another. They are not the first skirmish between irreconcilible positions over how creation occurred, or the mark of a terrible editor who cannot see the differences. Quite the opposite. Genesis 1 and 2 bear the marks of a master writer who brings divergent stories about creation into conversation with one another. An opening bell that foreshadows what is to come—not a narrative with clean-cut edges, rough spots sanded smooth, and contradictory viewpoints harmonized. No, instead, one way the Old Testament achieves depth is by including diverse voices and polyphonic perspectives that rise together into a symphony of witnesses to Israel's God and what it means to live by faith in this God. The message of the Old Testament cannot be limited to a single idea any more than Israel's God can be described from one perspective. Israel's God is both the Supreme King of the universe, who tolerates no rival, and close friend who is emotionally aware that Adam is lonely (God alone is not enough for him, Adam also needs a companion of flesh and blood). Israel's God possesses all power, only needing to speak the word and it is done. The LORD God is also personally involved, forming like a potter, planting like a gardener, and cleaning the dirt from beneath his nails at the end of the day. This feature of the text is no accident, but the result of allowing the two perspectives to stand side by side, with all the dissonance and harmony they create. With Genesis 1 and 2 introducing the Old Testament, we can be sure we are in for an amazing rollercoaster ride.

The LORD puts the human in the garden with the vocation of tending and keeping the garden (2:15). But no sooner is the human in the garden than a problem emerges. The LORD God realizes Adam is lonely and that it is not good for him to be alone. So the LORD God determines to resolve Adam's problem by making something or someone who will be a suitable partner-helper, "that is perfect for him" (2:18). These terms do not suggest that the LORD is going to make someone Adam can boss around or that Adam will be higher on some hierarchical scale. God is described as "our help" (Ps 33:20 et al.), and "my help" (Ps 70:5 et al.); we would never think that, as a result, we are in a position over or above God. Instead, the idea is to make someone who will be a companion, working alongside and fulfilling Adam's need for relationship. And so the LORD God begins to make animals and bring them to the man for evaluation and for a name (CEB, NRSV, NJPS, JB, NLT; cf. NIV, KJV).

The human, however, is picky and does not identify any animal suitable as a partner-helper (Gen 2:20). The LORD God also recognizes the failure of the experiment and the human's continued loneliness. So, like a surgeon, the LORD God puts Adam into a deep sleep to remove a rib (2:21) from which the LORD builds a woman, and then brings her to the man (2:22). At this point, at the moment he lays eyes on the woman, it is love at first sight. The man speaks in ecstasy:

> This one finally is bone from my bones
> > and flesh from my flesh.
> She will be called a woman (Heb. *ishshah*)
> > because from a man (Heb. *ish*) she was taken. (Gen 2:23)

Or, as translated by Peterson:

> Finally! Bone of my bone,
> > flesh of my flesh!
> Name her Woman
> > for she was made from Man. (2:23 MSG)

The LORD God not only provided the right partner-helper, the LORD God knocked the ball out of the garden! Consequently, the text turns to an **etiology** for marriage. This story explains why a man leaves his parents to "cling" to his wife and how they become one flesh—reuniting the missing rib in their common life. And their relationship is such that they have no shame in their nakedness (2:25). This original marriage was the ideal: no shame, no hierarchy, or patriarchy. But a couple who are in every way *one flesh*.

Many features of this creation story merit our attention, especially in contrast to what we see from the questions put to Genesis 1:

CREATION IN GENESIS 2:4–25	
What is the . . .	
1. Literary Style?	This story is, in fact, a story—a narrative with dialogue, characters, and a plot—unlike the poetry of Genesis 1.
2. Scope or Scale?	The scope or scale of creation is limited to the land.
3. Term for God?	The name of the deity is LORD God; "LORD" with all capital letters represents the personal name of God, which will be revealed to Moses at the burning bush (Exod 3).
4. Order of Creation?	The LORD creates as needs arise. The LORD is especially aware of and attentive to human need.
5. Manner of Creation?	The LORD gets his hands dirty: planting a garden, forming a human (like a potter), making animals, and performing surgery to make a woman.

Table 1.3. Creation in Genesis 2:4–25

In ways impossible for Genesis 1 to express, Genesis 2 tells the reader of a personal God, with a personal name, personally forming humans from the humus, and establishing an intimate relationship. The LORD is driven by human need, not by a predetermined schedule. Nothing is more important to this God than the human, and the relationship of the human to God.

Relationships are, in fact, especially important in the narrative of Genesis 2. Four relationships are established (created) that are critical for the book of Genesis (and beyond):

1. A God/human relationship that is thriving. Anytime the human is in genuine need (e.g., lonely), the LORD responds with help. There is no hint of a conflict.
2. A human/land or ecosystem relationship is also thriving. The humans are tending to the garden, and, in response, the garden provides ample food for the humans.
3. A human/animal relationship also comes into existence and from what we can see, the relationship is harmonious. The humans have named the animals, an act that may suggest authority over the animals. But the humans are not eating animals, nor are the animals attempting to eat the humans; such aggression will not begin until after Genesis 9:3–4.
4. A male/female relationship has been established as the climax of the story, and their relationship is wonderful. The male has exclaimed in ecstasy that the woman is the perfect creation to be his partner-helper. They are unashamed of their nakedness, and there is no hint of patriarchy or the male acting in a dominate role. Like all of the relationships established in Genesis 2, their relationship is perfect.

These are hardly all the observations to be made about Genesis 2 and its witness to creation and the Creator. But again, I hope it is at least a good place to start a spirited discussion.

Conclusion

As I have pointed out, the two stories in Genesis are different from one another in significant ways, a feature that could hardly be accidental or a mistake at the very beginning of Genesis. The challenge for us is not to find a way to force these two stories into harmony at every point, but to understand why an ancient writer or editor would begin a book with two such different stories. What is the writer trying to tell us about God?

A modern analogy from the world of art may be helpful. One feature of Cubism made famous by Pablo Picasso and Georges Braque is the use of multiple perspectives in a single work of art (of course, Cubism is much more complex than this one feature). As a consequence, their art often looks strange, to state the case mildly. But to some extent, this feature of multiple perspectives is what we find in Genesis 1 and 2. It is as if the writer or editor is confessing that no one story can possibly capture the creation or Creator—what Israel's God is like. On the one hand, Israel's God is a distant and powerful king; but on the other hand, Israel's God is also close and attentive to every human need. Or again, on the one hand, Israel's God operates according to a clear plan from start to finish; but on yet the other hand, Israel's God operates in response to human need. The two pictures of the Creator are different because there is no way that a single story about creation could possibly suffice. Israel's God is more complex and multidimensional than a single story allows. So, the editor stacks two stories on top of one another to make a claim about Israel's God and to issue a strong warning to us as we begin to read this text. The God with whom we will deal in the following chapters cannot be trapped and contained in a box or be understood based on any single story. Israel's God is too complex.

An old definition of heresy is "truth out of balance." The challenge of Genesis 1 and 2 is to hold both portraits of God together, to keep all of the different images and claims—here and elsewhere in the Old Testament. The truth is in the combination, not the separation. The God of Israel is both cosmic King and personal friend, a God with a plan and a God who attends to human need, a God who rests (reigns) over creation and a God who has empowered humans to be co-regents—to reign with God. Consequently, it takes not one—or even two—stories about creation to describe the Creator God, it takes many different perspectives in the Old

Figure 1.3. Portrait of Pablo Picasso (Juan Gris)

Testament to even begin to describe the God with whom we live and with whom we will deal in the text before us. In fact, it takes more text than we can cover in a semester, more ideas than we can comprehend in a lifetime.

To Discuss

1. Consider further similarities and differences between the biblical stories of creation and "The Epic of Creation"? What significance or conclusions do you draw from these similarities and differences?

2. Which portrait of the Creator in the Old Testament are you most drawn to? Why are you drawn to this portrait? What challenge(s) do the other stories of creation present for you?

3. Ancient societies developed cosmogonies or creation stories in order to explain their world and their place in the world. Based on Genesis 1 and 2, what is Israel claiming about her world and the role of humans?

4. List the many different roles the Lord God plays in Genesis 1 and 2. What does each role reveal or teach us about God? What do you make of such a large number of descriptors? Do any of these descriptions raise questions for you?

5. For what purposes does God create humans in Genesis 1 and 2? (Be careful to base your answer on what the text actually says or suggests.) What have you often heard about the purpose for which God created humans? Do Genesis 1 and 2 or any of the other creation texts support these claims? Why do you think God created people?

6. How does the picture of marriage in Genesis 2 differ from cultural practices or views in your society? Are the differences good or bad? What might Genesis 2 be saying to us about marriage?

7. What is the best way to identify the interhuman relationship established in Genesis 2: male/female, human/human, or some other description? Why? What difference may our words potentially make?

8. How has this chapter challenged what you may have previously thought? What new questions does this chapter raise for you?

To Know

Please Note: *This chapter is different from coming chapters in that it contains most of the required biblical reading in the chapter itself. Even so, here and especially in Chapters Two through Fifteen, you must read the assigned biblical texts in order to know and be prepared to discuss the assigned material. Reading only this chapter will not prepare you for class discussion, quizzes, or exams.*

1. The significance of the following in this chapter:

    Adam   Leviathan
    Apsu   Marduk
    Babylon   Ra
    Ea   Tiamat
    Eden   Woman Wisdom
    Eye

2. The order of creation in Genesis 1 and Genesis 2, and what the order teaches about the Creator and the creation. How God is portrayed in each story. Describe what happens to our understanding of God when we permit Genesis 1 and 2 to contain two distinct stories.

3. The other descriptions of creation in assigned texts and what each claims about the Creator: Psalm 33, Psalm 74, Psalm 104, Proverbs 8.

4. The basic storyline of "The Epic of Creation," creation in Genesis 1, and creation in Genesis 2. The only names you need to know are listed above. The student should know these stories well enough to retell each one and to compare and contrast them (not simply repeating what the chapter says about them).

5. The four relationships established in Genesis 2. Describe whether these relationships are working as well as intended.

6. The specific claims that Genesis 1 or 2 might make against Babylonian or Egyptian beliefs. (Again, the student should be able to say more than what this chapter claims.)

To Dig Deeper: Research Topics

1. If your own society were to develop a **cosmogony** or creation story to explain your world and the role of humans, what might that story say? What key issues or ideas would your story address? Write a cosmogony or creation myth for your society.

2. Find another cosmogony from the ancient Near East or elsewhere (e.g., Egyptian or Native American) and analyze the story. What does it teach about creation, the Creator, and humanity? Why?

3. Investigate an artistic depiction of creation. What influenced the artist to present creation as he or she did?

4. Many children's books retell the story of creation, such as James Weldon Johnson's *The Creation*, illustrated by Carla Golembe (Little Brown, 1993). Compare the way three or more of these books retell the story of creation. Investigate why the authors and illustrators move in the directions they have chosen.

5. Many specific questions are raised about statements, objects, or other matters in Genesis 1 or 2 (e.g., the meaning of human creation in the "likeness" or "image" of God, or the use of the plural "let us make" in 1:26 and elsewhere). Select one question for a research paper and/or presentation to your class.

For Further Reading

Coogan, Michael D. *A Reader of Ancient Near Eastern Texts: Sources for the Study of the Old Testament*. New York: Oxford University Press, 2013.

Dalley, Stephanie. *Myths from Mesopotamia: Creation, the Flood, Gilgamesh, and Others*. Oxford: Oxford University Press, 1989.

Matthews, Victor Harold, and Don C. Benjamin. *Old Testament Parallels: Laws and Stories from the Ancient Near East*. Rev. and exp. 2d ed. New York: Paulist Press, 1997.

Pritchard, James B., ed. *The Ancient Near East in Pictures Relating to the Old Testament*. 2d ed. with suppl. Princeton: Princeton University Press, 1969.

———. *Ancient Near Eastern Texts Relating to the Old Testament*. 3d ed. Princeton: Princeton University Press, 1969.

Taylor, Barbara Brown. *The Luminous Web: Essays on Science and Religion*. Washington, DC: Cowley Publications, 2000.

The following two lengthy and expensive volumes by Pritchard (above)
may also be purchased in smaller versions:

Pritchard, James B., ed. *The Ancient Near East, Volume 1: An Anthology of Texts and Pictures*. Princeton: Princeton University Press, 1973.

———. *The Ancient Near East, Volume 2: A New Anthology of Texts and Pictures*. Princeton: Princeton University Press, 1976.

A **Good** Creation Gone Wrong
Humans Take Control

2

The "Epic of Gilgamesh" is a better known story to many than the "Epic of Creation," and is equally important for our effort to get back to ancient Israel's world. Picking up in the middle of the story, our hero Gilgamesh has turned away the advances of the goddess Ishtar, pointing out to her that every lover who has ever fallen for her has come to a grisly end. Furious, Ishtar goes to heaven and weeps before her father, complaining of Gilgamesh's actions: "Father, Gilgamesh has shamed me again and again! Gilgamesh spelled out to me my dishonor and my disgrace."

Ishtar requests that the Bull of Heaven go strike down Gilgamesh for shaming her. Her father is reluctant, but eventually Ishtar talks him into giving her what she wants—thus we're introduced to the first spoiled goddess. Under her direction the Bull of Heaven charges for Enkidu (Gilgamesh's best friend) and Gilgamesh, and after a moment of self-reflection on their prideful actions, Enkidu kills the Bull of Heaven. They pull the Bull's intestines out and set them before the sun god, and worship him.

Ishtar goes ballistic with rage, hurling curses at the two friends. Enkidu listens and, when he has heard enough, pulls out the Bull of Heaven's shoulder and slaps Ishtar in the face. He then says, "If it were possible, I would hang the intestines on your arms." A terrific insult, but probably not Enkidu's wisest choice of words, especially considering Ishtar's father is a powerful god.

READING ASSIGNMENTS
GENESIS 3

GENESIS 4–11

DEUTERONOMY 15, 21, 24

KEY TERMS
Covenant: an agreement between two parties, whether they are nations (e.g., a treaty), or individuals (e.g., marriage), that sets expectations, promises for obedience, and curses for disobedience

Glean: to pick up leftover crops after the harvest or pick fruit left on the vine

Grace: a gift, or kind and loving treatment instead of punishment

Patriarchy/Patriarchal: a family system in which the father controls and leads the family

Pentateuch: the first five books in the Old Testament, also called the Torah or Law

Theology: literally "words or talk about God," thus, our speech about God or life with God

Figure 2.1. Relief of Gilgamesh Mastering a Lion. From the throne room of the palace of Sargon II, 713–706 BCE

That night, Enkidu had a vision of the heavenly council of gods deciding what to do about the killing of the Bull of Heaven. Their decision is clear: Enkidu must die. The next day, Enkidu tells his friend Gilgamesh about his fate, and immediately Enkidu falls ill. He lays in bed growing weaker and weaker until finally, he dies.

Gilgamesh does not take Enkidu's death well. He refuses to accept that Enkidu is dead for days, until finally a worm falls out of his decomposing body. Our hero, faced with his friend's death, develops a pathological fear of his own mortality and begins a quest to find eternal life. In his search, Gilgamesh learns of the existence of a couple, mere humans, upon whom the gods have lavished eternal life. Unfortunately, this couple now lives on the other side of the sea—a perilous journey no human has ever taken.

It is no easy task, but Gilgamesh convinces a sailor to take him across the sea. He quickly builds a boat according to the sailor's expert instructions and they set sail. After a month and a half, they come to lethal waters, which require the use of one log push pole after another. Just as they use their final log pole, they reach the man Utnapishtam (Ut-na-pish-tam) and his wife.

Gilgamesh tells his whole story to Utnapishtam, about his friend Enkidu and his death, his refusal to bury Enkidu until the worm fell out of his nose, and his quest to find eternal life. Utnapishtam responds, but it is not what Gigamesh wants to hear: death is inevitable for mortals.

"But if that is the case," Gilgamesh asks, "how have you come to have eternal life?"

Utnapishtam, hesitantly, begins to tell Gilgamesh his story.

Long ago, the gods decided that there should be a great flood, and they made each god take an oath so that no human might know and escape. Ea, a wise and far-sighted god who recognized the consequences of killing all humans, took the oath but then spoke to the reed hut in which I, his devoted follower, lived. He said, "Reed hut, Reed hut . . . dismantle your house, build a boat. Leave possessions, search out living things. . . . Put aboard the seed of all living things. The boat that you are to build shall have dimensions in proportion, her width and length shall be in harmony; 120 cubits by 120 cubits."

I was obedient, explaining to neighbors that the god of the city was angry with me, so I must move to be with my master, Ea. Many workers came to help in the boat's massive construction. The boat was ten poles high, with between six and nine decks. I launched her and loaded everything I needed to reestablish civilization: silver, gold, seeds, all my kin, cattle, wild animals, and all kinds of craftsmen.

A tremendous storm came, destroying everything. Even the gods were afraid of the storm and withdrew to heaven, where they cowered like dogs. Ishtar screamed in regret, "How could I have spoken such evil in the god's assembly?" The gods sat weeping.

For six days and seven nights, the storm raged; on the seventh day, the sea became calm. I opened a porthole and light fell on my face. I bent down and wept. I looked out and saw land emerging everywhere; the boat landed on Mount Nimush. I waited six days and on the seventh day I sent out a dove, but it came back. I released a swallow, but it came back. I released a raven; it did not return. Then I opened up the boat and made a sacrifice. The gods smelled the sacrifice, and, starving, gathered like hungry flies to consume the food I offered.

But when Ellil (or Illil, the head of the younger generation of gods) saw the boat, he was furious, "No human should have lived through the destruction. Who other than Ea would have done such a thing?"

Ea spoke, "You are supposed to be the wisest of the gods. How could you impose the flood? Punish the sinner for his sin; punish the criminal for his crime. But not this! Instead of a flood, reduce human population with a lion, a wolf, a famine, or such. I did not break the vow and disclose the secret of the great gods. I just showed his hut a dream."

So Ellil came down and took me and my wife, touched our foreheads, and blessed us. He said, "Until now, Utnapishtam and his wife were mortal, but from now on they shall be like gods and dwell far away at the mouth of the rivers."

"So, Gilgamesh, who can gather the gods on your behalf so that you may find eternal life? To do this, first you must not sleep for six days and seven nights."

At this, Gilgamesh immediately fell asleep and slept for six days; so much for that option. So Utnapishtam and his wife prepared the sailor and his boat to go home. But when Gilgamesh awoke and was about to leave, Utnapishtam told Gilgamesh of a secret plant at the bottom of the sea that gives eternal life. Gilgamesh immediately tied heavy stones to his feet and dove to the bottom of the sea, got the life-giving plant, and set sail for home.

Figure 2.2. The Flood Tablet from the "Epic of Gilgamesh." Photograph by Mike Peel (www.mikepeel.net).

On their way, they came to a pool of calm, cool water in which Gilgamesh went to wash. But as he washed, a snake smelled the fragrance of the plant. It came up silently and carried off the plant. As it went, the snake shed its scaly skin, renewing its life. When Gilgamesh discovered his loss, he sat down and wept. [1]

Genesis 3–11

Just as Israel was well acquainted with the "Epic of Creation," so was Israel aware of the "Epic of Gilgamesh," a tale far older than any of Israel's literature. In fact, a fragment from the Gilgamesh epic has been recovered from Megiddo, a town sixteen miles inland from the Mediterranean Sea and fifty-five miles north of Jerusalem.

The Tree of Knowledge

Many want to know more about the tree of knowledge of good and evil. What did this tree offer? What did Eve and Adam gain by eating from the tree? And why did God put the tree in the garden in the first place?

The most important thing about the tree, however, is not what it did for Eve or Adam, but what it does in the story—and what it means for creation. The presence of the tree tells us that human choice is built into the fabric of creation. So whether it be a tree with knowledge, a forbidden stone, or millions of dollars, the LORD's world gives humans a choice—to trust the Creator or trust themselves.

Adam and Eve

Genesis 3 continues the story begun in chapter 2, playing upon key features of its account of creation. First, in Genesis 2, God made two special trees and put them in the middle of the garden: the tree of the knowledge of good and evil and the tree of life (2:9). God says nothing about the tree of life, but as for the tree of knowledge of good and evil the LORD gives specific instructions: "don't eat from the tree . . . because on the day you eat from it, you will die!" (2:17). Genesis 3 records their failure to obey and their exile from Eden. Like Gilgamesh, the couple loses their chance to eat fruit and live forever. Second, Genesis 3 chronicles the demise of the four harmonious relationships established in Genesis 2:

1. God and humans
2. Humans and the ecosystem
3. Humans and animals
4. Male and female

Believers who read Genesis 3 often come away with radically different conclusions as to the chapter's theme. Most Judeo-Christian interpreters regard the story as the beginning of sin and the "Fall" of humanity from relationship with God. Other readers, however, point out that the word "sin" does not occur until chapter 4. So they read chapter 3 as the story of human maturation or coming of age. In other words, what the couple does is not sinful or against God. Instead, they grow up—making decisions for themselves, for which there are natural consequences—just as God and every parent expect for their children. If you pull the cat's

---

[1] "The Epic of Gilgamesh" is summarized with citations from Stephanie Dalley, *Myths from Mesopotamia* (Oxford: Oxford University Press, 1989), 77–120.

ears, you are going to get scratched. So it is possible to read Genesis 3 in the same way. However, God's direct command (2:17), the couple's violation of that command (3:6), and God's response (3:8–19) are strong evidence that Genesis 3 is the story of sin entering the world—a story that occurs not only in Genesis 3, but that has been repeated over and over again throughout human history. Genesis 3 is our story. So, because of its importance for Eve and Adam, ancient Israel, and our lives, we will work carefully through this text.

The snake subtly tempts the woman, first with an outlandish question, "Did God really say that you shouldn't eat from any tree in the garden?" (3:1). Between the lines, the snake implies other ideas and questions: *What kind of God would put you in such a beautiful place with so much great food to eat and then tell you that you could not eat any of it?* A claim the woman corrects: "We may eat the fruit of the garden's trees but not the fruit of the tree in the middle of the garden. God said, 'Don't eat from it, and don't touch it, or you will die'" (3:2b–3).

The snake's first question, however, has introduced a subtle skepticism: *What kind of God would make such an irrational demand?* Though the woman answers correctly, the snake has already planted a seed of doubt about the LORD God's goodness. So now the snake goes for the kill with a direct accusation: "You won't die! God knows that on the day you eat from it, you will see clearly and you will be like God, knowing good and evil" (3:4–5). Again, between the lines but with far less subtlty, the snake asserts: *The LORD God is lying to you! God knows that if you eat of the fruit, you will become like God—like him. God is holding you back; he cannot be trusted with your life. So if you really want to live your life to the fullest, then you have to take it into your own hands—trust yourself. God is only looking out for God; you had better start looking out for yourself, or no one will.*

This temptation is the essence of every temptation and the allure of every sin: *You cannot trust God to do or say what is in your best interest so you must decide; you must act. Trust yourself, not God.* So the woman goes to the tree and considers the snake's claim: she saw that it looked good for eating . . . she saw it was beautiful . . . she considered that the tree could make a person wise . . . so she took some of its fruit . . . and she ate it . . . then she gave some to Adam *who was with her* . . . and he ate (3:6). All of the verbs, stacked one on the other, suggest a process over an indefinite period of time.

In response to their decision and action, two types of consequences occur: immediate consequences and secondary, spoken consequences. The immediate consequences seem to occur as 'natural outcomes' of the couple's action. For example, the couple immediately recognizes their nakedness and realizes a sense of shame, without anyone telling them they are naked or that they should be ashamed—it just happens. Next, when the LORD comes to take an afternoon walk in the garden, the humans hide from God (suggestive that they normally walked along with him). The LORD begins to ask questions: *Where are you? Have you eaten from the forbidden tree?* At this point, the male responds with an excuse: "the woman *you gave me*, she gave me some fruit" (3:12, emphasis mine). The woman, for her part, continues the blame game: "the snake tricked me" (3:13; implying, *the snake that you made*), it made me do it. The good relationships established in Genesis 2 are crashing faster than a twenty car wreck at the Indianapolis 500; car parts are flying everywhere. And all of these consequences are occurring without God speaking to impose any punishment. The decision to take control of life has tragically caused life to spin out of control.

Secondary consequences, spoken by God, come next. First, God curses the snake to crawl on its belly and eat dust, which may be an etiology for why snakes slither on the ground instead of walk. Or, the curse may be figurative; crawling on one's belly and eating dust are images of shame. So it may be a way of saying the snake will now live a life of constant humiliation. Next, the LORD explains that there will be hostility and an ongoing fight between the descendants of the serpent and those of the woman (3:15). Again, this may be an etiology for why people don't like snakes and snakes don't like humans; humans kick at snakes while snakes strike out at people. In the long history of interpretation, however, many Christian writers have concluded that Genesis 3:15 is the first prediction of the coming of Jesus to defeat the serpent (the devil). While possible, there are at least two problems with such a reading: (1) The action verbs are the same ("strike"); the text does not suggest a defeat of the serpent, but rather an ongoing and unresolved fight between humans and snakes. (2) This Christian interpretation of Genesis 3:15 did not appear until the second century, in the writings of the Church Father Irenaus; the New Testament does not mention Genesis 3:15 as a prediction of Jesus.

The second spoken consequence is directed toward the woman and raises tremendous questions that directly influence our lives today (3:16). First, note carefully that the LORD does not curse the woman. In fact, it is questionable whether the LORD declares punishments or describes what the woman has brought on herself. The difference between these two readings may seem slight, but is in fact enormous. If it is a declaration of punishment, the punishment is decided by God and humans have no business lessening it or taking it away (e.g., through drugs during labor to deliver a child). If it is a description of a problem, the problem is to be solved and overcome with the LORD's help. With these two possibilities in mind, consider the LORD's statements. First, the woman will have "increased pains in childbirth" (so it is in the NIV, NRSV, and most other English translations). Phyllis Trible, however, has convincingly argued that the Hebrew text may also be read as, "I will greatly multiply your pain and your childbearing, in pain you will bring forth children."[2] In other words, the increase is in the number of pregnancies and painful childbirths. Her pain increases, but only because "the more she gives birth, the more her pain increases."[3] God mentions this consequence because God knows that outside the garden, for the human race to survive, women must face multiple pregnancies and painful childbirths, and this is dangerous—a leading cause of death for young women in the ancient Near East. In the context of Genesis 3 and Israel's culture, Trible's reading is strong. God's words address the realities of life the woman has brought on herself because she trusted herself rather than God. Infant mortality rates were high, and few babies would reach adulthood. Consistent with this reading, and despite the dangers of pregnancy, the woman will desire sexual intercourse with her husband; and even if a woman does not desire intercourse, "your husband . . . he will rule over

[2] Phyllis Trible, *God and the Rhetoric of Sexuality: Overtures to Biblical Theology* (Philadelphia: Fortress Press, 1978), 127.
[3] Ibid.

you" (3:16). The male's sex drive will insure that the woman faces the painful danger of multiple childbirths. Thus, in its context, the statement "he will rule over you" does not give husbands or men authority over women in every area of life; this statement describes sexual life of ancient Near Eastern couples and the pain women will face in giving birth so often and in watching so many of their children die. Life outside of the idyllic garden will be harsh.

The third spoken consequence is directed toward the man. Here, God describes what life is going to be like for the man outside the garden. (This supports reading the statement to the woman in the same way, as a description of what is to come rather than a pronouncement of God's punishment.) Instead of the vocation of tending to a garden (2:15), the ground will be cursed—not the man (3:17). Consequently, the man's task of producing food will come through hard work "by the sweat of your face" (3:19), until the human (Heb. *adam*) dies and returns to the humus (Heb. *adamah*).

Finally, concerned that the humans will eat from the tree of life and live forever, the LORD sets a heavenly guard across the entrance to the garden so the humans are unable to return to Eden. Some things are worse than death, especially an eternal life separated from God. We can never go back to Eden—a time of innocence and intimacy with God. Yet, out of concern for the difficult conditions of their new life, the LORD makes sturdy clothes for them out of animal skins (3:21). Despite the problems they have created for themselves because they rejected God, God acts in **Grace**: God provides for their needs, even though they generated these needs by their own actions.

Genesis 4–11

Genesis 4–11 chronicles the growth of sin from a single couple (Eve and Adam) to all humanity through three major stories (and other minor stories) stitched together by geneaologies:[4] (1) Cain and Abel (4:1–16), (2) the Generation of Noah (and the flood; 6:1–9:29), and (3) the Great Migration East (and the Tower of Babel; 11:1–9). Although a mixture of both simple and complex narratives, one way to uncover the major themes shared and developed by these stories is to ask the same three questions of each story: (1) What is the sin(s)—the heart problem that led to an external action? (2) What are the consequences of the sin? (3) In what ways does God help those caught up by sin? The chart below will bring this information together for further analysis, including the story of Eve and Adam (for review):

Cain and Abel

The first story involves three characters: Cain (a farmer), Abel (a herdsman), and the LORD (4:1–16). A problem arises when God accepts Abel's offering of an animal sacrifice, but does not like Cain's offering of his crops. Our question is the same as Cain's: Why does the LORD accept Abel's offering but not Cain's? Cain wants to know, because from where he stands it looks like

---

[4]On the fantastic ages of the people in these genealogies, see Appendix III: "The Millenials: Genesis 1–11" and "Would You Like to Be a Thousand and Three?"

the Lord is playing favorites—accepting Abel's gift, while rejecting his own. We want to know if the Lord is fair. Cain doesn't understand, nor do we. Despite many efforts to explain and justify the Lord's actions, the text itself is silent on the issue, indifferent except to say Abel gave "his flock's oldest offspring" (4:4). But what is Cain to do? He's a farmer, not a herdsman. For Cain, the rejection is personal and eats on him; he is angry at the Lord and his brother, an internal heart problem that leads him to the premeditated murder of his brother (4:8).

	The Growing Problem of Sin Genesis 3–11			
Story	Sin		Consequences	God's Grace
	Heart Problem	External Action		
Eve & Adam				
Cain & Abel				
Noah's Generation				
The Great Migration East				

Table 2.1. The Growing Problem of Sin in Genesis 3–11 (Blank)

Like the story of Eve and Adam, God enters the narrative through questions, not because God is unaware, but because God wants Cain to face his actions and recognize what he has done—a first step toward healing. Cain, however, is like his parents and refuses to confess. Instead, he chooses a sarcastic reply, "Am I my brother's guardian?" to which God responds with the worst news a farmer could hear—the blood-stained ground will no longer produce food for him (4:11–12). So his way of life must change from that of a settled farmer to a wanderer who gathers food wherever it may be found, a wanderer who must leave the protection of his family—the only security a person has in the ancient Near East. Cain's next statement reveals how much we don't know about creation and the ancient world, further evidence that the purpose of Genesis 1–3 is not to provide scientific or comprehensive history. Cain expresses fear for his life, "Anyone who finds me will kill me" (4:14). Many other people live in Cain's world—people whose origins the writer of Genesis has no interest in explaining. Instead, Cain knows that without family protection, someone will kill him. So in another act of grace, God gives Cain a protective mark so that everyone who sees Cain will be too afraid to hurt him (yet another detail the writer has no interest in explaining).

Noah's Generation

The next major story I leave primarily to your reading of the biblical text. Here, I only draw attention to a few key ideas, beginning with the double introduction to the story. First, Genesis 6:1–4 describes a strange situation in which the "sons of God" are marrying the "daughters of humans" (NRSV); a practice the writer (and God) find deplorable. Precisely what is happening, however, is far from clear (a good project for "Digging Deeper"). Of the many possibilities, it seems most likely that the "sons of God" are some type of divine beings (angels?) taking/sleeping with human women and producing a race of demi-gods, the Nephilim. Thus, the problem of sin has grown beyond merely a human problem, a serious development in the history of sin.

The second introduction to the story is equally grave, completing the picture of sin growing from one family to everyone, everywhere, and the depth of sin growing from one act to a constant state of the heart.

> The LORD saw that humanity had become thoroughly evil on the earth, and that every idea their minds thought up was always completely evil. . . . God saw that the earth was corrupt, because all creatures behaved corruptly on the earth. God said to Noah, "The end has come for all creatures, since they have filled the earth with violence . . . " (Gen 6:5, 12–13a)

Only four chapters away, we are far from the world of Genesis 1–2, where God looked at creation and proclaimed it to be "very good" (1:31). Now, God looks and sees that the human heart is totally corrupt and the earth is filled with violence (6:11). And, in a shocking revelation, we see inside God's heart:

> The LORD regretted making human beings on the earth, and he was heartbroken. . . . "I regret I ever made them." (6:6, 7b)

What is a heartbroken God to do with a good creation gone so terribly wrong? The expulsion and correction of Eve and Adam and the exile of Cain have not solved the problem. So God makes a radical decision—to reverse creation, to undo what had been done to bring order to the chaotic waters and start over again. Maybe a reboot of creation will get rid of sin and solve the problem. So God opens the windows in the sky-dome holding back the water above and opens the floodgates holding back the water below dry land (7:11; see Figure 1.2 in Chapter One)—and the water pours in.

God's plan, however, is not to create as was done the first time. Instead, similar to the "Epic of Gilgamesh," God chooses a righteous man, Noah, to build a ship to carry life in order to replenish the earth once the chaotic waters have done their work and destroyed all life. Once God is satisfied with the destruction, God starts over. A mighty wind blows across the water just as the first time (8:1; cf. 1:2), the beginning of pushing the waters back into their place. In time, Noah is able to open the ark and let out the animals. He offers a sacrifice to God, a "pleasing scent" to the LORD (8:21), but not an aroma that causes God to act like a starved insect.

Most important, the biblical text describes a realization and promise on God's part:

> I will not curse the fertile land anymore because of human beings since the ideas of the human mind are evil from their youth. I will never again destroy every living thing as I have done. (8:21)

God recognizes that floods—or any other form of destroying the world to start over again—don't work because the problem is the human heart—human attitudes, thoughts, and desires. So the LORD establishes the first of several covenants we will see in the Old Testament.

The LORD makes a **covenant** with all creation: "with you [Noah], with your descendants, and with every living being with you" (9:8–10). The form of ancient covenants can be quite complex, but the covenant in Genesis 9 is reduced to its most essential form and is easy to lay out in chart form.

ELEMENTS OF THE COVENANT	THE TWO SIDES AND VARIABLES	
Persons or Participants Entering the Covenant	**God**	**Noah, his descendants, and every living being (9:9–10)**
Promises, Conditions, Expectations, or Stipulations	Not destroy all life by flood again, not destroy the earth (9:11)	
The Sign or Reminder of the Covenant	God hangs his "bow" in the sky (9:12–16)	
Duration of the Covenant Agreement	God promises for all time: "never again" (9:11)	

Table 2.2. The Post-Flood Covenant

This covenant is entirely one-sided: God makes the promises, God sets the sign by which he will remember his promises (hanging his hunting bow in the sky, what we see as a rainbow, for a reminder that he will not attack the earth in the future), and God sets the duration, all while humans do nothing. In fact, humans are no more responsible for keeping any promise or upholding any expectation than a lion is expected not to eat the weakest member of a herd. Unilateral and one-sided, God pledges himself to the world with no requirement from the other side. Why? No requirement from the animals is understandable, but humans? The answer or reason lays only a few verses back in the story. Do you remember? Humans, God has "learned," are incapable of keeping any covenant at any time with God or anyone else. The human heart is broken (8:21). So if God should put any requirement on the human side of the ledger, the covenant would be a joke. The Lord would hit the reboot switch over and over again, but the problem would never be fixed—because the human heart remains the same. So if there is to be any movement toward a real solution, God is going to have to hang up his bow and cease hostilities while something else is worked out. A conclusion verified by the last scene of Noah's story in which one of his sons, Ham, "saw his father naked" (9:22) while Noah is passed out drunk. Ham's offense is unclear;

suggestions include breaking a cultural taboo by seeing his father naked and inappropriately boasting about it to his brothers, or that "to see the nakedness of" (NRSV) is a technical phrase to denote sexual intercourse (see Lev 18). An interpretation that makes sense of the phrase, "When Noah awoke from his wine, he discovered what his youngest son *had done to him*" (Gen 9:24, emphasis mine). Whatever happened, it is obvious that wiping out humans to start over again has not and will not solve the sin problem; even the best of families is plagued by sin.

The Great Migration East

The last major story of Genesis 4–11 further confirms the failure of the flood. A large group of people migrate to "a valley in the land of Shinar" (11:2)—the land of Babylon in the ancient world. Here they are anxious about being scattered across the face of the earth (9:1). Instead, they want to "make a name for ourselves;" in other words, they want to "become famous" by using available technology to build a tower (a Ziggurat, see Figure 2.3) to the heavens (11:4). Their ambition parallels the *first* story of humans; Eve and Adam wanted to become like gods. A tower—the Tower of Babel—with its top in the heavens would provide humans access into the realm of the divine, giving them a place from which they could access the heavens and the gods. Genesis 11 has brought us back full circle to the beginning in Genesis 3.

In response, and with irony, the text explains that God has to come down to see this tower; the tower is hardly a threat to God. And yet God is concerned about what the common language of these people might enable them to do. So God mixes up their language. They do make a name for themselves, but it is "Babel"—a theological and political commentary on Babylon with its many ziggurats that ascend into the sky. These are the temples where they believe the gods come down to do their work on earth (see Gen 28:11–17).

Figure 2.3. A Restored Ziggurat

Sin in the Old Testament

Listening to a Second Voice

Before we continue our trek into Genesis 12 to discover what Israel's God will do about the problem of sin, we need to step away from Genesis for a moment and take a more complete case history of sin, from a different perspective and another voice in the conversation. From Genesis 1–11, we have learned that sin is like a disease—a deadly malfunction of the human heart running rampant throughout the world, infecting every generation. We have also learned this heart disease (our trust of God replaced by a self-centered trust) eventually shows its presence through external symptoms; and, left untreated, self-centered trust will sooner or later lead to our death—a metaphorical living death.

Now we turn to the Book of Deuteronomy—the final book in the **Pentateuch**—its special concern for sin within a community, and what happens to the poor and marginalized when a community is infected by self-centered trust.

First Finding: Self-Centeredness and Disregard for Others

Our first finding in Deuteronomy is that sin moves beyond simple self-centeredness to a dangerous disregard of others, especially those who live on the margins of society. To explain, if we were to represent society with a circle, at the center would be wealth, power, legal rights, and other desirable benefits that give a person security and social standing. The further away a person moves from these advantages—and the center—the more they become marginalized, living on the edges of society (see Figure 2.4). And the more marginalized a person becomes, the easier it becomes for others with social standing to mistreat and take advantage of them because they have no power, no rights, and no one who will stand up for them.

In Deuteronomy, those most often caught on the margins of ancient Israel (and other societies, both ancient and modern) are the poor, widows and women in general, orphans, indentured servants, and foreigners or outsiders. Deuteronomy insists that instead of mistreating others—which grows out of a self-centered heart—God's people should develop a heart that loves and therefore tries to help those at risk on the margins. So, to take a few examples, God's people should love the poor, which on a practical level means not to be tight-fisted with loans to help them (Deut 15:7–11). Collateral for loans is appropriate, but it is unthinkable to take a person's working tools as collateral (24:6), or to take and keep their only cloak in which they may sleep (24:12–13). In addition, when collecting collateral the wealthy should not storm into a poor person's house to collect the goods, thereby also taking their dignity and honor; instead, they should wait at the door for the collateral to be brought out to them (24:10–11). The poor should be paid at the end of every workday—it may be the only way they have to purchase food for their family for that day (24:14–15). And during the harvest, some of the grain or grapes should be intentionally left behind for the poor to **glean** or pick up behind the workers (24:19–22).

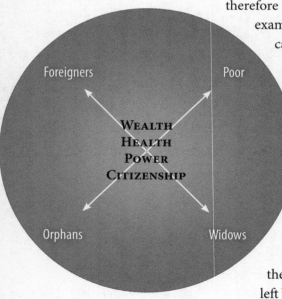

Figure 2.4. Life on the Margins of Society

Foreigners

Poor

WEALTH
HEALTH
POWER
CITIZENSHIP

Orphans

Widows

If a person falls into such debt that he or she must sell himself or herself or another family member to the debtor, the term of indentured service may last no longer than seven years (15:1–2). And when the debt-slave completes his or her service, the master must set them free and provide enough goods for a strong fresh start (15:12–18). In other words, it would be very easy for the

The Message of the Old Testament

Israel had a unique way of doing **theology**, i.e., thinking and talking about God, God's ways, and living with God. They would do so with, *Let me tell you a story . . .* or what researchers call Narrative Theology. Want to know what the LORD is like? *Let me tell you a story . . .* Want to know more? *Let me tell you another story . . .* What does it mean to live by faith in the LORD? *Let me tell you a story . . .* Stories can be fun to tell, easy to remember (even for an exam), stir our imaginations, and include odd details that fascinate us, though apparently not the storyteller, who doesn't pause to explain. And stories can carry profound insights about the LORD: a powerful wise King who speaks and light appears, speaks again and chaotic waters are brought under control (Gen 1); or a God who is closer than your best friend—passionately seeking relationship with the humans he made, tuned in to every need, and resolved to fix what is not good (Gen 2).

Genesis 1–11 is powerful Narrative Theology, introducing us to the way God intended for human life to work and explaining why our world does not look like the Garden of Eden. Through these stories, we have learned about the nature of sin and about God's commitment to pursue relationship with us, even when we decide God is not trustworthy and we trust ourselves. God will do whatever it takes to win back our hearts, but God will not force us—the decision for relationship is ours. All these "Messages" and so many more, all from stories we may read and reread, then read again—reflecting and thinking. So take a moment before you get to class and reconsider these stories you may have known from childhood. Now, as an adult, what do you see? What do you learn about God? About your life with God? What new questions do you have about God? For God?

wealthy to keep the poor in a state of perpetual indentured service; sending a servant away with nothing guarantees that they will end up in debt service again. So, Deuteronomy makes it clear that God's people must not take advantage of the poor who live on the margins of society. Instead, God's people should act in ways to help break the cycle of poverty: to love and act as God loves. To do otherwise demonstrates a heart infected with selfishness.

A second example from Deuteronomy about those living on the margins has to do with women, and especially widows. Because of Israel's **patriarchal** society, women generally depended on a relationship to a man, typically her husband and/or sons, for their well-being. Regretfully, sometimes women found themselves in less than this "ideal" circumstance. So Deuteronomy gives legislation to provide some protection or dignity to women far out on the margins, e.g., women taken in battle (21:10–14), women involved in polygamy (21:15–17), and women whose husbands die without leaving a male heir (25:5–10). The situation for women in all of these circumstances was difficult, and it may be argued that Deuteronomy doesn't do enough to help them. It does, however, at least begin to take steps in the right direction for these women.

The same is true for the laws pertaining to divorce, in which Deuteronomy's primary concern is the welfare of the woman (Deut 24:1–4). If a man has married and finds something objectionable about his wife—whatever this might be (arguments have ranged from burning his toast to sleeping with another man)—and he divorces her, then the man must write a certificate of divorce and put it in her hand. He may then send her out. He is not permitted to throw her out without divorce papers: the papers allow her to remarry. Otherwise, without the possibility of remarriage, her future is bleak, with prostitution her most likely means of survival. Again, from our perspective, the law may not be perfect or the most helpful thing for women, but the law does start the work toward helping those who are most threatened by living on the margins of society.

Second Finding: Love the LORD and Obey for Your Well-being

It is one-sided and maybe misleading to only listen to and talk about the ways the human heart becomes corrupt, and what God dislikes and consequently forbids, without talking about what God wants us to become. By leaving out this half of the picture we are apt to support the myopic view that either the God of the Old Testament is a legalistic God who makes unreasonable demands just so he can condemn people, or that the Old Testament is just about a bunch of laws and rules. So let's close this chapter by acknowledging another voice from Deuteronomy, a voice that insists that the LORD is nothing like such a caricature. What does the LORD want us to become? What is best for us? The answer is simple. The LORD asks for love, trust, and devotion.

> Israel, listen! Our God is the LORD! Only the LORD!
> Love the LORD your God with all your heart, all your being, and all your strength.
> These words that I am commanding you today must always be on your minds.
> (Deut 6:4–6)

In another similar text, the writer asks,

> Now in light of all that, Israel, what does the LORD your God ask of you? Only this:
> to revere the LORD your God by walking in all his ways, by loving him, by serving
> the LORD your God with all your heart and being, and by keeping the LORD's
> commandments and his regulations I'm commanding you right now. It's for your own
> good! . . . He enacts justice for orphans and widows, and he loves immigrants, giving
> them food and clothing. That means you must also love immigrants because you were
> immigrants in Egypt. Revere the LORD your God, serve him, cling to him, swear by
> his name alone! (Deut 10:12–13, 18–20)

What the LORD wants more than anything is for people to be like him, to love those on the margins because he loves those on the margins. Sin is a prevalent problem throughout the Old Testament. But sin is nothing more than a failure to love other people—especially those with no one to love them—and a failure to love the LORD, trusting that the LORD loves us and would only give instructions or laws that are for our best interest or the best interest of those we are to love.

Conclusions

To be sure, sin is a prevalent and dangerous problem throughout the Old Testament and today. Sin is a matter of a sick heart: a heart that has turned inward, from trust in God to trust in self, and a heart that cares only about self (selfishness), without concern for the harm or even violence done to those with no way to fight back. Viewed in this way, it is much more difficult to cast judgment on ancient Israel for her failures while we excuse ourselves for practices that hurt others. Or worse, proclaim judgment against a legalistic God of the Old Testament, without considering the things we do that hurt people on the margins of our societies. Without a cure, the illness that affects our heart will advance, take control of our lives, and kill us. What God can, or will, do to help us is an open question as we look toward Genesis 12 and the rest of the Old Testament.

To Discuss

Note: In no case is the material in the textbook sufficient for full engagement with the discussion questions. **You must read the biblical text.** *Answers parroted (copied) from the chapter are insufficient.*

1. Compare the story of Utnapishtam in the "Epic of Gilgamesh" to the story of the great flood in Genesis. In what ways are the stories similar or different? Analyze what you find. What do the differences or similarities indicate about the societies from whom these texts come? What about the depiction of God or the gods in each story?

2. Reread Genesis 3:6–7. At what point do you think the woman (and/or man) sinned? Why? Support your answer with good evidence and/or arguments. What's the problem with this discussion question?

3. God's initial response to Eve and Adam is to ask what appear to be dumb questions: *Where are you? Who told you that you were naked? Have you eaten of the fruit? What is this you have done?* Why is God asking these questions? Does God not know? Or if God knows, then why the questions? What does this teach you about God's first response to sin?

4. Students often ask me whether God knows everything in Genesis 1–11, or he is learning on the job. What features of the text make it sound as if God is learning as time progresses? Consider the necessity of using human language to describe God; what is bound to happen in our descriptions?

5. Do you think Genesis 3 is a story of human maturation (growing up) or of sin and the Fall? What evidence supports your position? Since the term "sin" is used in Genesis 4, does your position on Genesis 3 make a difference? If so, what is the significance of the position you take on Genesis 3?

6. In your experience, how have we applied God's statement to the woman (3:16)? Have we viewed it as a punishment that must be enforced? Have we viewed it as a description of consequences or problems to fix or overcome with God's help? How have we applied God's statement to the man (3:17–19)? Have we been consistent in our interpretation of these two statements? Why or why not?

7. What groups of people are most often on the margins of your society? Why? What goods or accomplishments are at the center of your society? Who are the people most likely to have access to these goods? What are the most common ways in which marginalized people are taken advantage of or harmed?

8. Given the discussion of the Flood Story and other narratives in Genesis 3–11, how many common questions about these events would you say are essentially irrelevant questions? Why? What new relevant questions has the text raised for you?

To Know

The student should know or be able to do the following tasks:

1. Know the significance of the following in the assigned chapters:

Abel	Ham
Adam	Ishtar
Babel	Japheth
Cain	Noah
Covenant (concept and definition)	Seth
Ea	Shem
Eve	Snake
Enkidu	Tree of knowledge (purpose)
Gilgamesh	Utnapishtam

2. Retell the story of Gilgamesh (from the information given in the chapter). What is Gilgamesh's mission? Why? What does he discover?

3. Retell each of the major stories of sin (with fair detail) from Genesis 3–11.

4. Identify and explain the immediate and secondary consequences for sin in Genesis 3.

5. Describe the guidelines given to Israel regarding the treatment of the poor in Ancient Israel. What principles undergird or support these guidelines?

6. Complete the chart on page 34, "The Growing Problem of Sin in Genesis 3–11."

To Dig Deeper: Research Topics

1. Find out what people or institutions in your community work to break the cycle of poverty. Interview them using these and other questions: What do they do? What are their greatest frustrations? What do they identify as the factors or practices that tend to keep the cycle of poverty in place? What can a college student do (now) to side with the poor and disadvantaged?

2. Research the stories of great floods in the literature of diverse cultures. Analyze the purposes of these tales. How do the narratives and their purposes compare to that of the Bible?

3. The conflict between Cain (the farmer) and Abel (the herdsman/rancher) is common in the history of many cultures (including that of the American West). Explore this theme in history and/or literature. How do your findings interact with or provide insight into the story of Cain and Abel?

4. Select a text or topic of particular interest to you for a research paper or report to the class. After your research, do you find that the questions that drew you to the topic or text answerable; are you able to reach some resolution? If not, why do think this is so? Topics might include one of the following common texts/issues:

    a. Who are the "sons of God" and the "daughters of men" and what are they doing (Gen 6:1–4)?

    b. What is the "tree of knowledge of good and evil"? What does it give? (Gen 2:9, 3:1–7)?

    c. What is the meaning of Genesis 3:15? Is this text a prediction of the coming of Jesus?

    d. What is the meaning of the Lord's words to Eve (Gen 3:16)?

    e. What does Ham do to make Noah furious? Why does Noah curse Ham's son (Gen 9:20–27)?

5. One or more of the Discussion Questions for this chapter might be an appropriate research topic (consult your instructor).

6. View the film *Noah* (Paramount, 2014) starring Russell Crowe as Noah. Analyze the film in view of the reasons for and purpose(s) of the flood in Genesis. Do not compare how closely the script follows the biblical story in its details. What do you find?

For Further Reading

Baker, David L. *Tight Fists or Open Hands? Wealth and Poverty in Old Testament Law*. Grand Rapids: Eerdmans, 2009.

Coogan, Michael D. *A Reader of Ancient Near Eastern Texts: Sources for the Study of the Old Testament*. New York: Oxford University Press, 2013. For a complete text of Gilgamesh.

Krugel, James L. *The Bible as It Was*. Cambridge, Mass.: Belknap Press of Harvard University Press, 1997. A fascinating review of ancient Jewish interpretation of the Pentateuch.

Trible, Phyllis. *God and the Rhetoric of Sexuality*. Overtures to Biblical Theology. Philadelphia: Fortress Press, 1978.

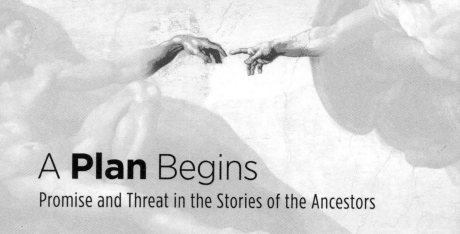

A **Plan** Begins
Promise and Threat in the Stories of the Ancestors

3

The end of Genesis 11 is like the end of *The Hunger Games*[1] or *The Bourne Identity*.[2] These books or movies (or biblical chapters) have begun a story and set up fundamental issues that await resolution in future installments. *The Hunger Games* begins Katniss Everdeen's quest, continued in *Catching Fire*, and concluded in *Mockingjay*. *The Bourne Identity* begins Jason Bourne's efforts to recover his true identity (and stay alive in the process), continued in *The Bourne Supremacy*, and *The Bourne Ultimatum*. We know matters must certainly turn out well for our heroes; after all, we know that neither Hollywood nor Scholastic Press are about to kill off our heroes and walk away from the money to be made in sequels. Nonetheless, at the end of the first installments of *The Hunger Games* and *The Bourne Identity*, we are unsure how matters will turn out.

In the same way, by the end of Genesis 11, we know the fundamental issues that need resolution—and we know things must generally turn out well because we have over a thousand pages still to read in our Old Testament. What we don't know is how God will respond to a good creation that has stabbed its creator in the back. Genesis 1–11 has demonstrated that sin is fundamentally a problem within the human heart, the choice to take life into our own hands and trust ourselves

READING ASSIGNMENTS
GENESIS 12–13, 15–18, 20–22
GENESIS 26–35
GENESIS 37–46, 49:29–50:26

KEY TERMS
Birthright: the inheritance typically given to the firstborn son, twice the amount given to other sons
Chaldeans: southern land area between the Tigris and Euphrates rivers, often associated with Babylon
Circumcision: the removal of the foreskin from a man's penis
Mesopotamia: the land between the Tigris and Euphrates rivers
Motif: a recurring idea or theme in a literary work

---

[1] Suzanne Collins, *Hunger Games* (New York: Scholastic, 2008); Film, Lions Gate Entertainment, 2012).

[2] Robert Ludlum, *The Bourne Identity* (New York: Richard Marek Publishers, 1980); Film, Universal Pictures, 2002).

rather than trust God. And this problem, we have learned, cannot be remedied by correction and expulsion (Eve and Adam), exile (Cain), wiping out creation and starting over again (Noah), or confusing and scattering humans (the Tower of Babel). But we have also learned our hero (God) is not about to walk away from the problems humans created when they turned their backs on him; Israel's God is determined to do whatever he can do (within a world created to include free choice), to bring creation and his people—*all people*—back to himself. How the Lord will do this is the underlying **motif** in the stories about Israel's ancestors. For the sake of simplicity, these stories may be viewed as six stages (in Genesis) in which God develops the plan to reach the world through this one family. In the first stage, the Lord will introduce the plan through six episodes of promise-making.

The Promises

Stage One: Abram and Sarai

No one could ever have guessed what the Lord would choose to do next. Instead of a power play or some highly visible move, the Lord chooses two people who live in southern **Mesopotamia** and worship other gods: Sarai and Abram (Josh 24:2). To this otherwise unknown couple, the Lord makes a series of promises, starting with the opening words of Genesis 12:

> The Lord said to Abram, "Leave your land, your family, and your father's household for the land that I will show you. I will make of you a great nation and will bless you. I will make your name respected, and you will be a blessing.
>
> I will bless those who bless you,
>
> those who curse you I will curse;
>
> all the families of the earth
>
> will be blessed because of you." (12:1–3)

Perhaps more surprising than God's decision to work through one family is Abram and Sarai's decision to play along. They leave their homeland, and when they arrive in the land of Canaan (see Figure 3.1), the Lord makes another promise: "I give this land to your descendants" (12:7). So we go to the first episode.

Episode One. Within this initial episode, the Lord has made four fundamental and essential promises (12:1–9):

- I will make you into a great nation (a promise of many descendants).
- I will give you the land of Canaan (land necessary for a great nation).
- I will be your God (implicit at this time, soon to be explicit).
- I will bless the world through you.

In the stories about Abram and Sarai that follow, God reiterates, elaborates, and clarifies these four promises in no less than five additional promise episodes (for a total of six episodes) in this first stage of Genesis.

Episode Two. In the second episode of promises, Abram and Sarai have returned from a memorable trip to Egypt (12:10–20) and have become so wealthy in cattle (among other things) that it has become necessary for the uncle (Abram) and nephew (Lot) to separate (13:1–13). So Abram gives Lot his choice of where to live (13:8–9), after which the LORD affirms that it will be Sarai and Abram's family who will inherit all the land around them:

> After Lot separated from him, the LORD said to Abram, "From the place where you are standing, look up and gaze to the north, south, east, and west, because all the land that you see I give you and your descendants forever. I will make your descendants like the dust of the earth. If someone could count the bits of dust on the earth, then they could also count your descendants. Stand up and walk around through the length and breadth of the land because I am giving it to you." (13:13–17)

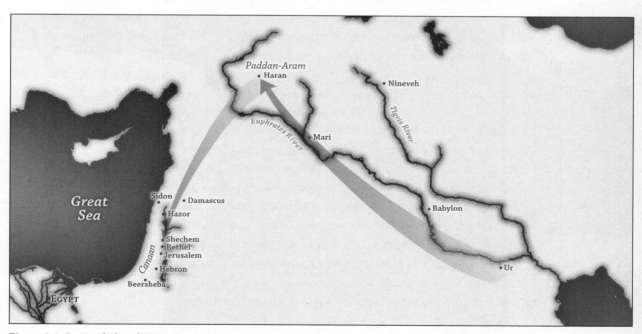

Figure 3.1. Sarai and Abram's Migration to Canaan

In addition to confirming the land promise, new to God's commitments in this encounter is the metaphor of dust to capture the size that Sarai and Abram's family will eventually become: more numerous than the dust in all the deserts of the world (or, even more, the dust behind the books on my bookshelves).

Episode Three. The third episode begins with a simple affirmation from the LORD: "Don't be afraid, Abram, I am your protector; your reward will be very great" (15:1). This commitment

Laws Pertaining to Women in the Ancient Near East

Discoveries and advances in translating texts from the ancient Near East provide us with new insights that scholars one hundred years ago would have died to know (well, I suppose they are dead now and know). Survivng records now give us insight into what had been a lost world. Perhaps the most important insight learned is that social and legal practices regarding women were not the same, but varied to extremes across the time and geographical expanse of the ancient Near East. For example, if a woman could veto living in any one time period and place, without doubt it would be the Middle (ca. 1360–1050 BCE) and Late Assyria kingdoms (ca. 934–612 BCE; as a reference point, the united state of Israel will begin in ca. 1040 BCE). Most Assyrian women were reduced to the status of property or sex objects in a male-dominated world. Women married in a transaction that looked like the sale of goods and were treated as such: a woman became their husband's legal property, with her primary task being to have children.

In ancient Sumer (ca. 3000–1750 BCE) and Old Assyria I (ca. 2000–1800 BCE), women enjoyed a much higher standing. For example, in Sumer, cities were ruled by assemblies of men and women, women had legal rights and could go to court to defend their rights, and considerable evidence demonstrates that women worked outside the household as weavers, spinners, and potters—though men earned two to three times as much as women in the same or similar job (I suppose some practices started long ago and have yet to change). Though we do not know when Abram and Sarai migrated (historical estimates range from ca. 2100–1800 BCE, if the historicity of the narratives is accepted; a question beyond our work), Ur, the city that was their home before they left, was one of the principal city-states in Sumer. In Old Assyria, a strong middle class developed, in which a minority of women were literate professionals who ran international trading companies. Women could hold religious offices, be a party to a lawsuit (through a representative), and could be entitled to a share of her father's property. In marriage, women had almost equal rights as men, though the need to bear children was still great. In fact, if a primary wife did not bear a child within the first two years of marriage, she would purchase a slave woman to be a surrogate and bear children for her husband. Written records about women, of course, come primarily from the urban upper classes, not from the lives of women out in the fields and agrarian villages.[3]

spurs Abram to raise some rather obvious questions about the LORD's plan. So a pattern emerges: the LORD makes an assertion, Abram raises an objection, the LORD confirms his promise, and then the two reach a resolution. Thus:

[3]Information summarized from Elisabeth Meier Tetlow, *Women, Crime, and Punishment in Ancient Law and Society, Volume 1: The Ancient Near East* (New York: Bloomsbury Academic, Continuum, 2005).

- Assertion: "Your reward will be very great." (15:1)
- Objection: Without a child of our own, the head servant of my household will become my heir. (15:2–3)
- Confirmation: "He brought Abram outside and said, 'Look up at the sky and count the stars if you think you can count them.' He continued, 'This is how many children you will have.'" (15:5)
- Resolution: "And he believed the LORD; and the LORD reckoned it to him as righteousness." (15:6 NIV)

While this first part of the encounter focuses on descendants, the second half of the episode concerns the land.

- Assertion: "I am the LORD, who brought you out of Ur of the **Chaldeans** to give you this land as your possession." (15:7)
- Objection: How can I know that I will possess it? (15:8)
- Affirmation: The LORD invites Abram into an ancient form of a solemn oath (another type of covenant). Abram brings selected animals, cuts them in half, and arranges them in such a way that each party to the agreement could walk between the pieces; a somber way to swear that if I do not keep my word, may I become like these animals. Except, in this case, only God passes between the animals (15:17), because God alone is making a legally binding commitment to Abram:

> Then the LORD said to Abram, "Have no doubt that your descendants will live as immigrants in a land that isn't their own, where they will be oppressed slaves for four hundred years. But after I punish the nation they serve, they will leave it with great wealth. . . . That day the LORD cut a covenant with Abram: "To your descendants I give this land, from Egypt's river to the great Euphrates . . ." (15:13–14, 18)

The legal agreement affirms and resolves the matter for Abram. After his death, his descendants will one day take possession of the land (and be a mighty nation). It's as if in a legal court, God raises his hand and swears, "So help me, God," or "So help me, Me."

Fourth Episode. After a bungled attempt to take matters into their own hands by using Hagar as a surrogate mother (16:1–3), causing unexpected problems (16:4–16), the fourth episode of promise-making comes from the LORD in another form of legal contract—a covenant—with both Abram and Sarai. The LORD challenges Abram, "Walk with me and be trustworthy" (17:1b) and reassures him in response, "I will make a covenant between us and I will give you many, many descendants" (17:2). In humility, Abram bows to the ground as the LORD continues—*this is my covenant with you:*

1. I will make you exceptionally fruitful, so that many nations and kings come from you. Your name will no longer be Abram, but Abraham.[4]
2. I will establish my covenant between me and you and all your offspring to always be your God.
3. I will give you, and your offspring after you, the land where you are now an alien— all the land of Canaan. (17:4–8)

The Lord *explains that from this point forward, every male in Abraham's family will be* **circumcised** as a memorable sign of the covenant (17:9–14). Then the Lord continues, turning his attention to Abraham's wife:

> God said to Abraham, "As for your wife Sarai, you will no longer call her Sarai. Her name will now be Sarah. I will bless her and even give you a son from her. I will bless her so that she will become nations, and kings of peoples will come from her." (17:15–16)

By this time the enterprise has become more than a little crazy to Abraham, and he falls down, not in worship, but laughing: "Can a 100-year-old man become a father, or Sarah, a 90-year-old woman, have a child?" (17:17). The whole thing is ridiculous, bizarre—crazier than . . . well, what could be crazier than two people from the local nursing home *nursing a baby*? So the newly named Abraham laughs, rolling around on the floor, and the Lord just steps over him to confirm his word. God tells Abraham his wife will give birth to a son who will be named "laughter" (Isaac), and that God will continue the covenant with him and all who follow (17:19, 21).

Episode Five. The fifth episode of promise occurs in conjunction with the story of the downfall of Sodom and Gommorah (Gen 18–19). What initially appears to be three men going to Sodom are actually two angels with the Lord. While Sarah and Abraham extend hospitality to them, during the meal one of the "men" declares, "I will return to you next year, and your wife Sarah shall have a son!" (18:10 njps). Sarah listens from around the corner and laughs to herself thinking, "Now that I am withered, am I to have enjoyment—with my husband so old?" (18:12 njps). Her inner dialogue identifies the absurdity of the promise: she is too old, beyond menopause—*and*—Abraham is too old (and without medicine for getting up to the task). Nothing is happening between this couple—*nothing*. If you were Sarah, you would laugh too.

The "man" asks Abraham why Sarah is laughing—a charge she denies—and then asks the question that stands at the center for all these stories and for God's plan:

> "Is anything too difficult for the Lord?" (18:14a ceb)
> or, "Is anything too wonderful for the Lord?" (18:14a njps)

---

[4] The name changes from Abram to Abraham ("ancestor of a multitude") and Sarai to Sarah ("princess"), denoting the greater roles this couple will play in the formation of the nation.

Our heroes understandably have trouble believing that this God, who called them away from home so many years ago, is capable of making good on his promises. So they face a question similar to the one Eve and Adam faced: Will they trust the God who called them, or, lacking trust, take matters into their own hands?

And then, just when the idea could not be more absurd, the LORD takes note of Sarah and she becomes pregnant (21:1–12). Little wonder that the child is named "Isaac," meaning "laughter" or "he laughs" or perhaps even "laughing boy," because everyone in this story is laughing—not just smiling or chuckling, but fall down, roll around, can't-catch-your-breath laughing—more than you can ever remember. Who would have thought it possible? And that is the point (18:14a; 21:7). No one, then or now, would ever imagine such a thing; only God could and only God did.

Episode Six. The sixth and final episode of promise to Abraham is the only event that could possibly be crazier than the birth of "Laughter" and the only story of the six that has its own name: the *Akedah* ("the Binding," taken from the Hebrew verb *aqd* or *akd* — "to bind" Isaac). The LORD tells Abraham to take Isaac and sacrifice him back to God, which Abraham immediately sets out to do (22:1–19). Stunning. What kind of God is this—a God who plays fast and loose with ethics, as long as it suits him? What kind of God asks a father to kill his son? And what kind of father is ready to kill his son because "God told me to"? (Most, if not all, of them are locked safely away in their mental institutions.) What kind of man is Abraham—willing to sell out (or kill) anyone in the family, as long as he is safe? Every indicator in the narrative suggests—confirms—Abraham is going to go through with it. He is going to slit his son's throat on a sacrificial altar. "Stop!" At the last second, God stops the absurdity. Isaac walks (runs?) away, while the LORD makes his final commitment to Abraham:

> I give my word as the LORD that because you did this and didn't hold back your son, your only son, I will bless you richly and I will give you countless descendants, as many as the stars in the sky and as the grains of sand on the seashore. They will conquer their enemies' cities. All the nations of the earth will be blessed because of your descendants, because you obeyed me. (22:16–18)

The LORD will work through this one son to do everything he has promised Sarah and Abraham, which leads to the second stage of the promises.

Stage Two: Isaac and Rebekah

By necessity, the narrative escorts old players off the stage while introducing new faces. Sarah and Abraham die (23:1–20; 25:1–11), finding rest in the only piece of land that now belongs to the family—a tomb in the field of Ephron in Machpelah. Oddly, however, despite all the build-up leading to his birth, once Isaac is on stage, he plays only a brief supporting role to either his father or his twin sons.

Most importantly, Isaac and his wife Rebekah receive the same promises that God had made to Abraham and Sarah (26:2–5):

- I will make your offspring numerous as the stars of heaven.
- I will give your descendants all these lands.
- I will be with you (implied: I will be your God).
- I will bless the world through your offspring.

The promises do not die with Abraham and Sarah; instead, the LORD's commitment and promises to the family continue to the next generation, and will continue to do so until God lives up to his word.

As for Isaac, his story turns to the question of which of his and Rebekah's twin sons will be the carrier of God's promises: Esau (the firstborn) or Jacob. And, in another move that no one could have predicted, the winner is a man who is a self-centered liar, cheat, and first-class manipulator: Jacob.

Stage Three: Jacob—Getting the Promises

Though he is the youngest, Jacob is twice blessed as the firstborn by his father, Isaac (after taking advantage of his older brother to get his **birthright**, 25:27–34). In the first scene, Jacob dupes his father, with an assist from his mother (who loves him most). Isaac is suspicious, but Jacob, the son standing before him, assures his blind father that he is his firstborn, Esau (who is Isaac's favorite; this family, with its favoritism and win-at-all-costs attitude could have made a therapist rich). Consequently, Isaac inadvertently grants Jacob the blessing of the firstborn:

> May God give you
> > showers from the sky,
> > olive oil from the earth,
> > plenty of grain and new wine.
> May the nations serve you,
> > may peoples bow down to you.
> *Be the most powerful man among your brothers,*
> > *and may your mother's sons bow down to you.*
> > Those who curse you will be cursed,
> > and those who bless you will be blessed.
> > > (27:28–29, emphasis mine)

In the second scene, Isaac is aware of his son's identity and how Jacob has mistreated him and his brother. Nonetheless, he has given his word, and in his world, your word is irrevocable. The destiny of the family with its God is most important. So before sending Jacob away to get a wife from the family in Haran (and for Jacob to save his life from Esau's plan to kill him), Isaac speaks to Jacob again:

> God Almighty will bless you, make you fertile, and give you many descendants so
> that you will become a large group of peoples. He will give you and your descendants

Abraham's blessing so that you will own the land in which you are now immigrants, the land God gave to Abraham. (28:3–4).

Inexplicably, God also accepts Jacob—the liar, cheat, and swindler—as the man who will lead this family into the next crucial phase of its development. Headed back to his mother's family in Paddan Aram, and on the run from his brother, Jacob stops for the night at Bethel, unaware that he has stumbled onto a gateway into the heavens—a genuine portal (what the people were trying to build at Babel, 11:1–9). In a dream, Jacob sees angels coming and going from heaven and the LORD confirms what Isaac has told Jacob:

> Suddenly the LORD was standing on it and saying, "I am the LORD, the God of your father Abraham and the God of Isaac. I will give you and your descendants the land on which you are lying. Your descendants will become like the dust of the earth; you will spread out to the west, east, north, and south. Every family of earth will be blessed because of you and your descendants. I am with you now, I will protect you everywhere you go, and I will bring you back to this land. I will not leave you until I have done everything that I have promised you." (28:13–15)

Together, the LORD and Isaac have assured Jacob of the same four fundamental commitments the LORD has made to the family:

- I will give you many offspring ("like the dust of the earth").
- I will give you the land (you will spread out in every direction).
- I will be your God ("I will not leave you until I have done everything I have promised").
- I will bless the world through you ("Every family of earth will be blessed because of you and your descendants").

We have good reason to wonder how the LORD will bless other families through Jacob when he has been anything but a blessing to his own family. And while anyone else would be honored to accept the LORD's gifts and commitments, especially someone with Jacob's track record, Jacob sees another opportunity to get what he wants and stamps a giant *"if"* over everything God has said. *If*, and only if, the LORD will do what he promises *and* brings Jacob back home to his father's house safely, *then*, and only then, will Jacob let the LORD be his God. But the LORD has to pay up first (28:20–22).

Stage Four: Jacob—Life away from Home

For the twenty years or so that he is away from home, Jacob lives with his uncle Laban (his mother Rebekah's brother) in Haran, on the Euphrates River (see Figure 3.2). During this time, two notable developments occur in Jacob's life and in God's promises to the family. First, Jacob comes to have a large family before leaving Laban: eleven sons, along with one named daughter (Dinah), among

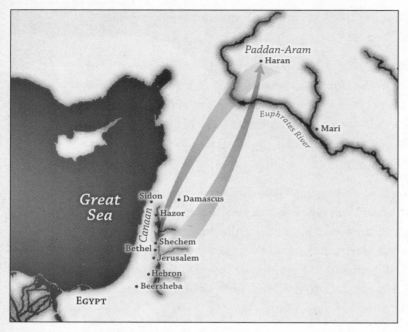

Figure 3.2. Jacob's Travel to Paddan-Aram and Back

many other daughters—unnamed and unmentioned in a man's world.[5] How Jacob comes to have all these children is the first special interest of the writer (29:1–30:24). The question, "Where do babies come from?" is trumped by a different question: How does Jacob come to have two wives and their two maid servants doing all they can to give Jacob sons?

First, our deceptive trickster, Jacob, is himself deceived and tricked by Laban, his new father-in-law. After working seven years to pay the bride's price for the woman who stole his heart (Rachel), on Jacob's wedding night Laban slips his oldest daughter Leah between the sheets. The next morning, Jacob wakes up and, with a magnificent understatement, the writer speaks from Jacob's perspective and says, *"There she was—Leah!"* (29:25a) How did he not know? How *could* he not know? Jacob protests, but it is too late. Laban provides an excuse, whether true or not, and offers Jacob a deal: Finish the bridal week for Leah, then marry Rachel and work seven more years to pay the debt for her (29:27). Bested by Laban, Jacob takes the deal—in love with Rachel, but stuck with Leah.

What happens next is better—or perhaps worse—than any reality television series. The two sisters begin a baby-bearing contest for Jacob's affection. Leah, the unloved wife, only wants her husbands' love, as evidenced by the names she gives her first four sons:

- Reuben—"The LORD saw my harsh treatment, and now my husband will love me." (29:32)
- Simeon—"The LORD heard that I was unloved, so he gave me this son too." (29:33)
- Levi—"Now this time my husband will embrace me, since I have given birth to three sons for him." (29:34)
- Judah—"This time I will praise the LORD" (29:35)

Meanwhile, Rachel becomes alarmed by how many sons Leah is producing and how far behind she is falling, unable to get pregnant. So, feeling desperate, Rachel takes her servant Bilhah and

---

[5]During his time with Laban, Jacob has eleven sons. Benjamin (the twelfth son) is born after he leaves Laban and is back in the land promised to his family (Gen 35:16–20). Much later, Jacob also adopts Joseph's two sons, Ephraim (the thirteenth son) and Manasseh (the fourteenth son, Gen 48:5). So, in time, Jacob comes to have a total of fourteen sons.

puts her in Jacob's bed, in order to get surrogate children through her (recall Sarah and Hagar?). So Rachel begins to give sons to Jacob through Bilhah:

- Dan—"God has judged in my favor, heard my voice, and given me a son." (30:6)
- Naphtali—"I competed fiercely with my sister, and now I've won." (30:8)

When Leah realizes she is no longer getting pregnant, she copies her sister and puts her maid Zilpah in bed with Jacob (Jacob, of course, makes no objection to all these arrangements). So, Zilpah begins to produce sons:

- Gad—"What good luck!" (30:11)
- Asher—"I'm happy now because women call me happy." (30:13)

Then, with a night of sex purchased by an aphrodisiac (mandrakes), Rachel allows Leah to sleep with Jacob (we take note of who is in charge of where and with whom Jacob sleeps). Leah bears a fifth and later a sixth son, at this point finally accepting that Jacob will never love her.

- Issachar—"God gave me what I paid for, what I deserved for giving my servant to my husband." (30:18)
- Zebulun—"God has given me a wonderful gift. Now my husband will honor me since I've borne him six sons." (30:20)

God finally enables Rachel to get pregnant, presenting Jacob with his eleventh son, but her first. She gives the child a name that makes it clear she is not satisfied with one son. In essence Joseph's name means something like, "Give me another."

- Joseph—"May the LORD give me another son." (30:24)

So, through a totally dysfunctional marriage to two sisters (his cousins, no less), Jacob becomes the ancestor who starts the family down the road to becoming a great people.

The second notable development in Jacob's life is the enormous wealth he acquires, all at the expense of his father-in-law, Laban. Having paid for both wives, Jacob is eager to go back home to his own family, but Laban doesn't want him to leave. Aware of the LORD's blessing through Jacob, Laban strikes another deal with Jacob, and cheats Jacob at the outset (30:27–36)—a trick that Jacob trumps with his own (30:37–42). And however it worked—through selective breeding, black magic, or the LORD's blessing—it worked; Jacob "became very, very rich: he owned large flocks, female and male servants, camels, and donkeys" (30:43).

Jacob has become a success that Laban's sons cannot overlook; he is taking everything that would otherwise become their inheritance (31:1). And, anything but a fool, Jacob is aware that the time has come to leave Laban; but he also knows that Laban will never let him go with all his wealth, wives, and grandchildren. So our trickster executes one more plan: get at least a three-day head start and hope his father-in-law doesn't catch-up.

Stage Five: Jacob—Coming Home Again

So far, Jacob's strategy for dealing with his problems has been to run. But as Jacob leaves for home, he must face the people and the conflicts from which he ran away. One simple way to capture these conflicts and their resolutions is by constructing another simple chart. The first column identifies the people with whom Jacob has a conflict, the second describes the conflict, and the third explains how the conflict is resolved:

JACOB'S RETURN HOME		
Jacob's Conflicts	**The Conflict**	**The Resolution**
1. Laban		
2. Esau		
3. God		

Table 3.1. Jacob's Return Home

1. Laban. Jacob ran from Laban, but after ten days, Laban caught up to him. Jacob's trouble with Laban has to do with several issues: his wealth, Laban's daughters, the grandchildren, and—to Jacob's surprise—small family gods that Rachel stole (but craftily hid, 31:32–35). After Laban is

The night before Jacob faces his brother—and before he comes back to the homeland promised to his father and grandfather (and to him)—Jacob is alone when a man attacks him and "wrestled with him until dawn broke" (Gen 32:24). In one of the most mysterious texts in the Old Testament, Jacob wrestles with this "man" all night long, and whoever this "man" is—*an angel, God, Esau, just a man*—though he inflicts a serious injury, he is unable to defeat Jacob. The episode is the pinnacle or epitome of Jacob's life-story: all his life he has been a man who struggles with everyone (Esau, Isaac, God, Laban, Laban's sons). And no matter what it may cost him or how long it may take, Jacob never gives up until he gets what he wants. Based on the name Jacob gives the place, it is clear he believes that his struggle has been with God (Peniel, face of God). He has seen the face of God and lived (32:30).

Even with this terrifying night and Esau's forgiveness the next day, it is difficult to tell if Jacob is a changed man. Our decision on this matter depends on how we read Jacob's prayer from the day before (32:9–12; is Jacob still trying to manipulate God to get what he wants or is he sincere?) and how we read Jacob's words and actions to Esau (33:12–17; is he still a liar?). Readers disagree. It would be great to say that Jacob is a changed man when he comes home, but is he really?

unable to find his gods, he and Jacob resolve their differences through a covenant. The covenant is a bi-partisan, non-aggression treaty that sets a boundary between the two men and sets conditions on Jacob's treatment of his wives, Laban's daughters. Laban gives the speech commonly recited by fathers who are about to see their daughter marry a young fellow: *you better treat her well or else* (31:43–54).

Figure 3.3. "The Journey." Gouache on paper by Jack Maxwell. Jacob as he walks away, limping for the rest of his life.

2. *Esau*. Jacob also ran from his brother, who was ready to kill Jacob some twenty years ago (27:41). As Jacob travels home, he sends messengers ahead to Esau, and the messengers return with a report—*there are four hundred men coming with Esau to meet you* (32:3–6). Jacob is terrified, deducing the only meaning he or we can imagine: Esau is coming with a small army to kill him (32:7). So the deceptive trickster sets to work again, dividing the women and children, setting them in order of importance, and sending one gift after another to Esau (32:8–21; 33:1–2). The next day, after a strange night of wrestling (32:22–32), Jacob faces his brother and walks ahead of the women and children. Jacob bows to the ground when Esau comes running toward Jacob (33:3). And after a dramatic pause, Esau "threw his arms around his neck, kissed him, and they wept" (33:4). Esau forgives his brother. The brothers talk, with Jacob still not entirely truthful (33:13–14, 17). Nonetheless, another conflict is resolved in Jacob's life, leaving the most important struggle for last.

3. *God*. When Jacob was on the run all those years ago, he had a remarkable vision and an even more remarkable conversation with God (28:12–22). True to his character, Jacob was not willing to buy into the Lord's plan so quickly, so he cut a deal with God. He promised that if God would do everything he promised—and blessed his journey and brought him home safely—then Jacob would let the Lord be his God.

The Lord has lived up to the agreement, a point Jacob has noticed (31:5, 42). But on his first arrival in the land, Jacob's response to his promise is ambiguous and depends on the sincerity we grant his prayer before he meets Esau (32:9–12), what we make of the strange night of wrestling (32:22–32), and his initial actions after his return (33:18–20). Perhaps it is all this ambiguity that causes God to call Jacob's bluff and summon him back to Bethel (35:1); and, to his credit, Jacob recognizes what God intends for him to do. Jacob calls for the family to hand over all the other gods they are carrying and Jacob hides them under an oak tree, rather than burning them (35:2–4; perhaps there was a drought and a burn-ban in effect? Or maybe you can never be sure if you might need those gods again?). Then, he goes back to Bethel to resume a conversation and a commitment he cut short years ago (35:5–15). But this time, there are no deals to be made; only worship follows God's promises.

Stage Six: Joseph—The Move to Egypt

With Jacob's homecoming, the story takes a decisive turn—in direction and in type. In direction, the story turns toward Egypt and to how the family comes to live in Egypt. In type, the story takes on a different quality, shifting away from stacking short stories about the ancestors, one upon another, to a more complex literary style. The narrative becomes more interconnected with foreshadowing (e.g., the dreams), character development (e.g., watch for Judah and Joseph), and consistent motifs (e.g., watch for Joseph losing and gaining articles of clothing). Finally, the story—in literary terms, much more of a novella—may be mapped through the motif of the houses in which Joseph enters, why he rises to prominence, and the cause for his collapse into another house.

Figure 3.4. "Jacob's Dream." Bronze sculpture by Jack Maxwell on the campus of Abilene Christian University

House One. Joseph begins, obviously, in his father Jacob's (Israel's) house as the eleventh son. And yet Joseph rises in Jacob's house because he is the firstborn of Jacob's favorite wife (recently deceased, 35:16–21). Jacob's family dysfunction, however, refuses to die; he still plays favorites despite the troubles his actions bring, especially to his favored choices. For his part, Joseph demonstrates all the qualities of a spoiled brat. True or false, he brings bad reports about his brothers. He is delighted to tell them about dreams that have obvious meanings of his future grandeur and their bowing to him, especially when he knows that his dreams will infuriate them. After he does this for the second time, even his father scolds him, though he also takes careful note of what Joseph says (37:10). Joseph's only mistake was thinking his dad's protection would keep him safe when he was far away and alone with his brothers. This miscalculation almost cost Joseph his life; instead, he loses his first cloak and his standing in House One.

House Two. Joseph soon finds himself in Egypt as a servant to Potiphar, a high official in Pharaoh's government (39:1). Once again, Joseph rises to a position of prominence in the house, though for different reasons than favoritism. Potiphar recognizes the Lord's blessing on his house, on account of Joseph (39:2–3, 5). His fall from Potiphar's house also comes for different reasons: Joseph's integrity and commitment to his God (and Potiphar) keep him from going to bed with his master's wife (39:9). But again, he loses his cloak and his house on the basis of trumped up charges of attempted rape (39:11–20). We see little to nothing about Joseph and the Lord in these chapters. If Joseph held faith, he must have wondered if God was really with him or not? Or if the dreams (taken seriously in his culture) God gave him were just a bad joke.

House Three. Joseph hits rock bottom in "The Big House"—a jail for political prisoners (39:21). And yet, once again Joseph rises to prominence—not necessarily for his character, but because the Lord was with him and blessed whatever he did (39:21–23). At first, it appears that

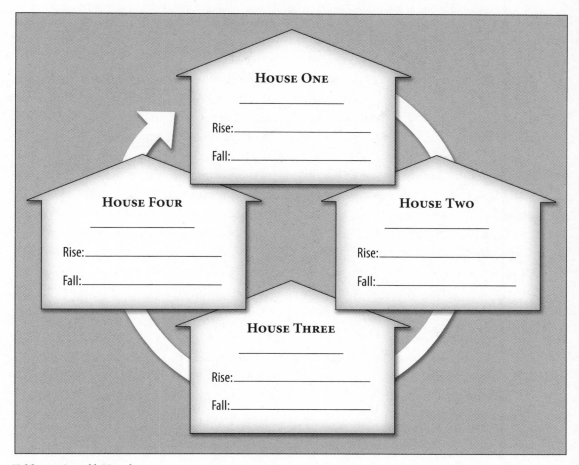

Table 3.2. Joseph's Travels

Joseph's stay in jail will be short, until he is used and then conveniently forgotten by Pharaoh's chief cupbearer (40:1–23). Not until a national crisis erupts two years later and Pharaoh is disturbed by his dreams does the cupbearer confess his failure and call for Joseph (41:1–13). Joseph emerges from jail with another new set of clothes (41:14–15) and comes into Pharaoh's house—and has a meteoric rise to power (41:16–49).

House Four. Only thirty years old when he enters Pharaoh's service (41:46), Joseph has spent some thirteen years in Egypt (39:2). Before he turns 37, we gain an insight into his character through the birth and naming of his two sons: Manasseh, because "God has helped me forget all of my troubles and everyone in my father's household" (41:51), and Ephraim, "God has given me children in the land where I've been treated harshly" (41:52). Only now, finally, he has been able to forget his family back in Canaan and come to terms with all that has happened in his life. Now the story has set Joseph and the reader up for his brother's sudden reappearance in his life, bowing before Joseph and asking for life—for food (42:1–9). Joseph's response to his brothers on this occasion and on their second trip is cause for discussion: Why does he treat his brothers so roughly? Does he have some plan in mind or is he simply getting revenge for the way they treated him? Or if he has a plan, what is it? After all, if all he wants is to bring his father and brother Benjamin to Egypt, Joseph could do that with a snap of his powerful fingers, so why all the posturing (42:1–28; 43:1–34)?

Whether or not Joseph has a plan, the climactic scenes in the drama demonstrate significant personal growth by two of Israel's most important ancestors: Joseph (whose family will become the largest group/tribe in the future nation of northern Israel) and Judah (whose family will become the future nation of southern Judah). At the beginning of Joseph's story, it was Judah who proposed making some profit off Joseph by selling him (37:26–28). But now, it is Judah who puts himself and his family on the line to take Benjamin back to Egypt, as Joseph demanded (43:1–10). And when Joseph sets the brothers up so that they have the opportunity to be rid of Benjamin, their dad's next favorite son, rather than walking away, Judah steps up and offers his life in exchange for Benjamin (44:18–34). Whatever Joseph may have planned, the writer shows us Judah's tremendous growth into a family leader.

But Judah is not the only person who demonstrates growth in this story; Joseph, the brat who loved to rub his brother's faces into his favored position, now sees himself in a new light. He now understands that his life is not all about himself, but a part of God's plan to save the family and the surrounding countries. Now Joseph can say to his brothers:

> . . . don't be upset and don't be angry with yourselves that you sold me here. Actually, God sent me before you to save lives. . . . You didn't send me here; it was God who made me a father to Pharaoh, master of his entire household, and ruler of the whole land of Egypt. (45:5, 8)

He has also grown, even if old family dysfunctions are still alive and well (see 45:22, 24).

Return to House One. Finally, as Joseph re-enters his father's house, there are two other ways in which the Joseph novella and the end of Genesis differ from the ancestor stories in Genesis 12–36: (1) the emphasis on promises virtually disappears, along with (2) God. I emphasize *virtually*, because God and the promises are present in the Joseph novella, just in a different fashion than before.

Conclusion

God is present, although not appearing as a human or speaking in so many visions as in Genesis 12–36. Instead, we learn that God is working behind the scenes in such ways that the reader (and Joseph) must discern the LORD's work. Thus, the writer recognizes that God is working in Joseph's life when he is with Potiphar (39:2–3, 5), during his time in jail (38:21–23), and implicitly in Joseph's work with Pharaoh. And Joseph is able to see God's work without a vision or direct revelation from the LORD, though only in retrospect (45:5–8; 50:19–21, 24–25). God is at work in the world, but perhaps more like we experience God's involvement—with a need to discern God's hand in events, often times well after the event itself is past.

The promises are also still alive and well, though we must pay closer attention to see them. For example, before Jacob leaves Canaan—the land of promise—to go to Egypt, God appears to him in a vision and reassures him that the land promise still stands, even if he leaves the land:

> God said to Israel in a vision at night, "Jacob! Jacob!" and he said, "I'm here." He said, "I am El, your father's God. Don't be afraid to go down to Egypt because I will make a great nation of you there. I will go down to Egypt with you, and I promise to bring you out again. Joseph will close your eyes when you die." (46:2–4)

So, while the family may come to live in the land of Goshen, Jacob insists that the family bury him back in Canaan (47:29–31), which they do (49:29–50:14). What's more, Joseph also insists that his body (bones) be taken back to Canaan (50:24–25). Why? Because no matter where you may move, people want to be buried *back home*. Egypt is not home, no matter how long they may live there; the land God promised is their real home.

Along with the promise of land, the promises of a mighty nation with numerous descendants still holds. In fact, of all the promises, this one appears to be gaining the most traction at the end of Genesis. In total, the members of Israel's house who made the trip to Egypt was seventy—not counting daughters-in-law (46:26–27). Goshen, however, was like a greenhouse for reproducing. Notice the writer's language: "Thus Israel settled in the land of Egypt, in the region of Goshen; and they gained possessions in it, *and were fruitful and multiplied exceedingly*" (47:27 NRSV, emphasis mine). The family is hardly a great nation yet, but they seem to be doing all they can to increase in size.

The final two promises are more obscure and debatable. To what extent is God blessing the world through Israel's family? Arguments can be made in favor of Joseph (feeding all who came), but also against him. He takes everything from those who are starving, even their land, into the possession of Pharaoh and the government (47:13–26). Jacob may formally bless Pharaoh or not (47:7–10). But as often as the family blesses those around them, they also seem to bring trouble. Regardless, God's intended blessing is not yet complete at the end of Genesis.

To what extent the LORD is the God of Israel may also be argued. Joseph acknowledges that dream interpretations belong to God or perhaps *the gods* (40:8; 41:16, 25, 28, 32), and he is also unclear about which god is his master; he marries the daughter of an Egyptian priest (41:50). So we need to exercise caution with all the God talk; everyone in Egypt and Israel believes in the gods, but which god/God they hold to be their god/God is not so clear.

So the first book of the Old Testament comes to a conclusion—with a beautiful but broken creation, a loving and determined Creator, the choice of one wildly dysfunctional family, and promises to reclaim creation and the people the LORD loves—*all people*. But as we pause for a station break before we turn the page to the next book, it is fair to say, *we've not seen anything yet!*

To Discuss

1. Why do you think the promises are so frequently repeated to Abraham and Sarah in the text? What challenges did they face in believing the promises?

2. Compile a list of the occasions when Abraham and Sarah most trusted the LORD, and a separate list of the occasions when they lacked trust. What behavior followed when they trusted? What behavior followed when they failed to trust? When is their trust or doubt ambiguous? What consequences follow when they either trust or doubt?

3. Genesis 22, the *Akedah* (binding of Isaac), stirs the imagination in many ways. Consider the following questions: Do you think God is serious in his request for Abraham to sacrifice Isaac? Do you think Abraham is serious in his resolve to follow through with the sacrifice? How do you think the event changes Isaac's relationship to his father? With God? What other questions come to your mind?

4. Considering all the difficulties posed by Abram and Sarai's family over the years, why do you think the LORD selected their family? Later texts claim that their family was not especially large (Deut 7:7–8), good (Deut 9:4–5), or powerful (Deut 8:12–14). So why do you think God chose them?

5. Why do you think God accepts Jacob's bargain and puts up with the way he treats the people in his life? What does this teach you about God? What questions about God does this raise for you?

6. Genesis 32:22–32, Jacob's nighttime wrestling also stirs the imagination. Who do you think Jacob is wrestling? What does Jacob think? Why are they wrestling? How does this episode epitomize Jacob's life? What other questions does the story raise for you?

7. What do you think about Joseph? Was he really a brat when he was young? What kind of relationship does Joseph have with the LORD? (You must be able to back up your ideas with solid evidence from the text.) In what ways does Joseph grow?

To Know

1. The significance of the following in this chapter:

Abimelech	Ishmael	Rachel
Abraham	Jacob	Rebekah
Benjamin	Joseph	Reuben
Bethel	Judah	Sarah
Bilhah	Laban	Sign of the Covenant
Dinah	Leah	(Gen 17)
Ephraim	Lot	Sodom
Esau	Manasseh	The Baker
Goshen	Pharaoh's dreams	The Cupbearer
Hagar	(and their meaning)	The silver cup
Isaac	Potipher	Zilpah

2. The four fundamental promises the LORD made to Abraham and Sarah and their family.

3. The most common threats to the promises God makes to the family(s).

4. The status of each promise at the end of the Book of Genesis.

5. How Jacob gets the birthright from his brother, Esau. How he gets the blessing from his father.

6. What happens to Jacob at Bethel when he is running away from home? What two significant things happen in his life while he is away from home? How?

7. Be able to complete the chart on page 61 and identify the houses through which Joseph moves.

8. Locate the following on a map (see Figures 3.1 and 3.2): Ur, Paddan-Aram, Haran, Euphrates River, Tigris River, Canaan, Great Sea, Egypt, and Bethel.

To Dig Deeper: Research Topics

1. Genesis 12–39 frequently deals with the problem of infertility and the personal and societal pressure on women to bear children, especially sons. Consider the same issues from a modern perspective. What pressures exist? Where do these pressures come from?

2. Read, compare, and contrast two stories from the ancient Near East to the story of Joseph: "Aqhat" (see Coogan, 52–56) and "The Tale of Two Brothers" (see Coogan, 58–63). What insights does this comparative literature provide? What questions does the literature raise?

3. Identify the recurring family dysfunctions about the ancestors in the stories. Use insights from modern family studies to analyze what is happening in the family and why.

4. Consider further the cause for the LORD's alarm over Sodom and Gomorrah (Gen 19). Why is Lot so concerned that the visitors not spend the night in the town center? What threats do the men of the town make? Consider Lot's actions carefully; analyze his behavior. Does this seem fair? Now read Ezekiel 16:49. How does this text reshape your understanding of the story in Genesis?

5. The binding of Isaac (Gen 22, The Akedah) raises numerous questions about God. Do you think God was serious in his request? Do you think Abraham believed God intended for him to carry out this command? Do you think it was ethical for God to ask Abraham to sacrifice his son? Read Leviticus 20:1–4. What questions does the Leviticus text raise?

6. Is God fair to Cain? Why or why not? (Your instructor will determine to what degree you may appeal to texts beyond Genesis 4, or if you must decide only on the basis of what you have read to this point.) How does God respond to Cain's actions (i.e., what are God's first words)? Why?

For Further Reading

Coogan, Michael D. *A Reader of Ancient Near Eastern Texts: Sources for the Study of the Old Testament*. New York: Oxford University Press, 2013.

Dalley, Stephanie. *Myths from Mesopotamia: Creation, the Flood, Gilgamesh, and Others*. New York: Oxford University Press, 1989.

Matthews, Victor Harold, and Don C. Benjamin. *Old Testament Parallels: Laws and Stories from the Ancient Near East*. Rev. and exp. 2d ed. New York: Paulist Press, 1997.

Pritchard, James, ed. *Ancient Near Eastern Texts Relating to the Old Testament*, 3d ed. Princeton: Princeton University Press, 1969.

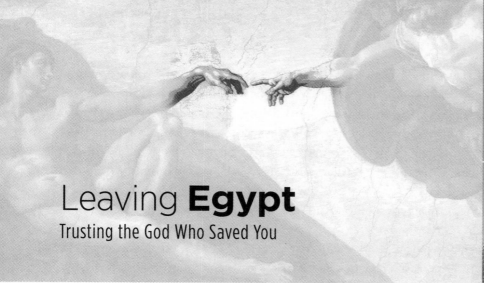

Leaving **Egypt**
Trusting the God Who Saved You

4

Beautifully you appear from the horizon of heaven,
    O living Aten who initiates life.
For you are risen from the eastern horizon
    and have filled every land with your beauty.
For you are fair, great, dazzling,
    and high over every land,
and your rays enclose the lands
    to the limit of all you have made.
For you are Re [the sun god], having reached their limit
    and subdued them for your beloved son [the Pharaoh];
for although you are far away, your rays are
    upon the earth and you are perceived.
        —opening lines from "Great Hymn to the Aten"[1]

READING ASSIGNMENTS
EXODUS 1–4
EXODUS 5–12
EXODUS 13–19, PSALM 105

KEY TERMS
Israelites: members of the family or nation of Israel (descended from Jacob/Israel)
Hebrews: members of the nation of Israel whose native language is Hebrew
Midwives: women trained to deliver babies
Pogrom: an organized massacre of helpless people (often Israelites or Jews)

Welcome to Egypt. Local time is somewhere around three thousand or more years ago, during an *in-between time.* Not yet this, but soon no longer that, either. The LORD had promised Abraham that his descendants would take possession of the land of Canaan, but the LORD also warned Abraham that before this settlement took place, his heirs

---

[1] William Murnane, trans., "Great Hymn to the Aten," in *A Reader of Ancient Near Eastern Texts: Sources for the Study of the Old Testament* (New York: Oxford University Press, 2013), 125.

would be victimized as slaves in a foreign land (Gen 15:13). Only after a long passage of time would God make good on the land promise; we have come just in time to see God at work again.

Quite a long passage of time occurs between the final chapter of Genesis and the first chapter of Exodus. At the end of Genesis, the family, now collectively known as "Israel" or "**Israelites**," had moved to Egypt and was beginning to grow (47:27). At the beginning of Exodus, Israel is still in Egypt—experiencing astronomical growth (Exod. 1:7). What God had promised Abraham and Sarah is happening. The small family is on its way to becoming a mighty nation—with one significant problem: Israel is in Egypt, not the land of promise. And growing too large in the wrong place spells trouble.

While Israel has been growing, a new king has risen in Egypt (1:8), probably meaning the rise of a new dynasty. And the pharaoh of this new dynasty knows nothing about how Joseph saved Egypt. Instead, this pharaoh sees the growing presence of Israel in Egypt as a potential threat to the throne and native rule (1:10). So he initiates a planned series of attempts to bring, and keep, Israel under control.

First Plan: Pharaoh begins a secretive operation to work the Israelites so hard that they would stop multiplying. We might call it the "Honey, I'm too tired tonight" strategy (1:11); and as reasonable as it seems, it backfires. As the writer puts it, "the more they were oppressed, the more they grew and spread" (1:12). In this case, harder work = more sex. And when Pharaoh realizes that his first strategy is not working, he imposes ruthless brutality on the workers and turns to another plan (1:12–14).

Second Plan: Pharaoh summons the **midwives** to the **Hebrew** (Israelite) women and tells them to kill every male baby before he reaches his mother's arms (1:15–16). For the plan to work, the midwives must fear Pharaoh, the plan has to be kept top secret, and the midwives must invent causes for why the baby boy dies at birth. But this strategy also fails: the midwives fear the LORD more than they fear Pharaoh (1:17) and they invent a story when Pharaoh calls them to account for their failure. Finally, Pharaoh is done with secretive plans and turns to a Final Solution.

Third Plan: Pharaoh orders all of his people to kill every Israelite baby boy they discover, throwing the infant into the Nile. Pharaoh's **pogrom** is all too familiar to us in a post-Holocaust world. Thank God, it is women who once again spoil his plans.

So, within the first paragraphs of the Book of Exodus, we find the people God has chosen—and through whom God plans to bless the rest of the world—in desperate need of God's saving power, or they will die.

The first half of Exodus (1–18), then, is about the rescue of God's chosen people from slavery in Egypt and moving them a safe distance from Egypt, where they will make their own commitment to be God's people. It is not possible for us to cover every chapter and verse in the text; instead, depending on the student to read assigned material, we will focus on key issues or themes:

I. Preparing a Leader: Moses (Exod 2)
II. Calling a Leader into Service (Exod 3–4)
III. Initial Failure (Exod 5–6)
IV. The Purpose of the Ten Plagues

V. The Fight with Pharaoh (Exod 7–13)

VI. Learning to Trust the Lord (Exod 14–18)

1. Preparing a Leader: Moses (Exodus 2)

Moses comes on stage in no special way, but once on stage he becomes the co-star (along with God) of the Pentateuch. And yet our reading should exercise caution not to read what we have seen from Hollywood or Disney into the text. Moses is not "The Prince of Egypt," nor is he locked in a battle with an older brother to determine who will become the next pharaoh. He is one of an unknown number of Israelite baby boys who slips through Pharaoh's net, saved by wise women: (1) his mother literally obeys Pharaoh's directive and puts Moses in the river, but floating in a basket near where one of Pharaoh's daughters bathes; (2) Pharaoh's daughter discovers Moses and appears to understand the situation, especially when Moses' sister steps forward and offers to find a woman who would be glad take the baby home and nurse him. It is difficult to believe that Pharaoh's daughter doesn't know what Moses' mother and sister are up to. So, once again, for all his fanatical rules—weak, powerless women in his kingdom upset Pharaoh's plans.

So Moses survives Pharaoh's pogrom and grows up at home, at least past the age of weaning (2:10; 4–5 years or longer). When he does finally come to the royal house, the writer exhibits no interest in what privileges, if any, come to Moses. Instead, the object of concern is Moses' heart—as it is revealed by his actions. Three stories combine to tell us what we most need to know about Israel's future leader:

- Story One. Moses steps in to stop an Egyptian from beating a Hebrew and secretly kills the Egyptian (2:12).
- Story Two. Moses attempts to break up a fight between two **Hebrews** by appealing to the man in the wrong (2:13). In so doing, he discovers the word is out about his murder of the Egyptian and that his efforts to help his people are not appreciated (foreshadowing the rocky relationship he will have with the Israelites all his life, 2:14).
- Story Three. Even on the run in Midian (see Figure 4.1), Moses steps in to defend women from mistreatment by male herdsmen (2:16–17), and in the process gains a wife (2:18–22).

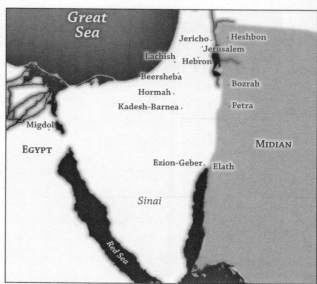

Figure 4.1. The Land of Midian

So, while we might infer many benefits to Moses because of his adoption and want to know about his life so near the seat of Egyptian power, for the writer, only one thing really matters: Moses has a heart of compassion for people who are oppressed and is willing to risk taking action to help the mistreated. The only question that remains is whether the God who made a covenant with Abraham and Sarah is like Moses. And is he going to do something to help his people and keep his promises. The answer is an unequivocal yes (2:23–25).

II. Calling a Leader to Service (Exodus 3–4)

We know from the movies that Moses will become the great leader of the Israelites; though, at the moment, he is far away from Egypt with no intention of ever going back. Just how uninterested he is in returning and how determined he is to live a settled life a safe distance from Egypt becomes clear with a close reading of Exodus 3–4. Before the LORD can get the Israelites out of Egypt, he must first get Moses back in Egypt.

The first task is to get Moses' attention so that a conversation and commission are possible; so, the LORD sets a bush on fire and keeps it burning until (and beyond) Moses decides to check out the bush. As Moses gets close, God speaks to him from the burning bush, starting with his name: "Moses, Moses," and then telling Moses to get his filthy sandals off God's holy ground before offering a formal introduction: "I am the God of your father, the God of Abraham, the God of Isaac and the God of Jacob" (3:6 NIV). Now, our hero, who was so anxious to see the bush, is barefoot on holy ground, face down, and afraid that he might catch a glimpse of this God and die on the spot.

The LORD has Moses just where he wants him and begins a speech that will rock Moses' world. The LORD explains that he knows all about what is happening back in Egypt. He has heard the outcry of despair, he knows about his people's suffering, and he has come down to rescue them from the Egyptians and take them to the land of promise (3:7–9). Personally, if I were Moses, I would wonder at least two things: First, where has this God been the past forty years? Moses knew about these problems years ago and tried to help; where was this God-in-a-bush then? And second, everything this God is saying is wonderful news, but why are you telling me? If you know all about this trouble and have come down to keep your promises, then go to it! You don't need to tell me or ask my permission.

Then the LORD drops the big news:

> So get going. *I'm sending you* to Pharaoh *to bring my people*,
> the Israelites, *out of Egypt.* (3:10, emphasis mine)

Now, suddenly, everything makes sense—the burning bush, the holy ground, God-in-a-bush. It was all a set up! But Moses is not about to sign on for this mission—this death-trap; going back to Egypt is a bad idea for more reasons than even a God-in-a-bush can imagine. So, the first of many arguments between Moses and God begins—the first time they meet:

1. Moses asks: "Who am I" to carry out such an assignment (3:11)? To which the LORD says, "I'll be with you" (3:12); in other words, roughly stated, God says it doesn't matter who Moses is, what experience he may have, or what training he might have for leading people through the wilderness. The only thing that matters is that the LORD will be with Moses (3:12).

2. Moses asks: Who are you? If the issue is not who Moses is or what he is able to do, but that this God will be with him, then Moses needs to know who this God is; more specifically, *What is your name* (3:13)?

The answer that comes back is difficult to understand in Hebrew, and even more difficult to translate into English. Eventually, God tells Moses to say that "the LORD" has sent me to you: "This is my name forever" (3:15). Three observations about God's name must suffice for now: (1) Most scholars agree that the name of God (YHWH) is somehow related to the verb "to be" (Heb. *hyh*), though precisely how it relates and what it means is beyond agreement. (2) In Hebrew, the name of God consists of four consonants: *yhwh*. The vowels are less certain, due to a long history of not pronouncing the name of God so as not to show any possible disrespect to God's name. Instead, the practice arose of substituting another Hebrew term ("lord" or "master") when reading the Hebrew text. Consequently, we can only give our best educated guess as to the full name given to Moses: *Yahweh* (with the German "w" pronounced as a "v"). (3) In English Bibles, the tradition of not pronouncing the name of God continues by translating the name of God as "the LORD"—notice all the small capital letters. Thus, any time we read the word "LORD" in the Old Testament, we are actually reading the name of God, *Yahweh*.

3. Moses raises a third concern: What if the Israelites don't believe me? After all, what would you think of a man who came to tell you about a God-in-a-bush who spoke to him in the desert, claiming to be the God of their ancestors, and announcing that he was there to lead you to the promised land? So, the LORD provides three signs to prove his identity and mission: (a) his staff turns to a snake and then back into a staff, (b) his hand turns diseased (leprous) and then turns back clean, and (c) when he pours water on the ground it turns to blood. Armed with these signs, the LORD expects Moses to leave for Egypt.

4. But Moses still refuses to go. It doesn't matter that God will be with him, that he knows the name of Israel's God, or that he has signs to prove that the LORD has sent him. *Moses doesn't want to go back to Egypt.* So he claims: "I've never been able to speak well, not yesterday, not the day before, and certainly not now since you've been talking to your servant. I have a slow mouth and a thick tongue" (4:10). He is not eloquent, or perhaps has some speech impediment that makes him a poor choice for the kind of political rhetoric necessary to deal with Pharaoh and his royal court. A good excuse, except for one small detail: the LORD made Moses and his mouth and knows how well he can speak (4:11). Moses is missing the point, and the LORD is getting frustrated. It doesn't matter what Moses can or cannot do, the LORD will be with him. Perhaps we should cut Moses a break; what this God-in-a-bush is asking him to do is crazy. Go tell the ruler of a superpower to let a bunch of slaves go free? If Moses agreed without an argument, we would question his sanity. But at this point, if Moses argues with Pharaoh as well as he does with the LORD, the Israelites should start packing their bags. He is great at arguing for what he wants, or doesn't want.

5. Finally, Moses lays his cards on the table: "Please my Lord, just send someone else" (4:13). *Moses has no intention of going back to Egypt.* The LORD can send someone else. Now the LORD has reached the end of his patience with Moses; his anger flares and his tone undoubtedly changes. No more give and take; no more dialogue. The LORD knows Aaron is on his way to see

Moses, and Aaron can speak fluently; so Moses can take Aaron back to Egypt to help negotiate for Israel's release. No matter what Moses may say, God is finished with Moses's objections: "Take this shepherd's rod with you too so that you can do the signs" (4:17) and go!

With no other choice than to go back to Egypt, and at the same time warned that Pharaoh will not cooperate, Moses, his wife Zipporah, and their sons begin the journey (4:18–23).

After the LORD tries to kill Moses one night on his way to Egypt (4:24–26)—*I warned you, this is a wild and crazy text*—the LORD sends Aaron to meet Moses. Moses briefs his brother about God's commission and the signs he can now do, and the next thing we know, our small troop is back in Egypt where they gather the Israelite leaders ("elders"), tell them God's plans, and show them the signs (4:29–31). The people believe, even bowing in worship when they hear that God has noticed their condition and plans to help (4:31).

III. Initial Failure (Exodus 5–6)

At their first meeting, Pharaoh is unimpressed with Moses and Aaron; his opening words set the tone and direction for all that is about to unfold: "Who is this LORD whom I'm supposed to obey by letting Israel go? I don't know this LORD, and I certainly won't let Israel go" (5:2). Pharaoh does not know Yahweh, so why should he listen to Moses?

What follows may be described in various ways: a ten-lesson correspondence course on who the LORD is; a television mini-series on how the LORD is greater than the gods of Egypt; or—my favorite—a ten-round super-heavyweight championship fight, the winner takes all of Israel. On one side are the gods of Egypt, represented by Pharaoh and the Egyptian magicians; on the other side is the LORD, represented by Moses and Aaron. The pre-fight battle of words does not go well for the Israelites. Pharaoh decides that the reason Moses and Aaron have been able to rally the people around the LORD is because they have too much leisure time on their hands (5:8). So Pharaoh issues a command that a critical ingredient for brick-making, straw, will no longer be provided to the Israelite workers. They will have to go into the fields and get the straw themselves. But the quota of bricks for each day will not change; and when Israelite supervisors fail to meet their quota, they are beaten and asked why they failed to produce (5:14). It takes little time for the people to turn on Moses and Aaron: "Let the LORD see and judge what you've done! You've made us stink in the opinion of Pharaoh and his servants. You've given them a reason to kill us" (5:21). In turn, Moses turns on the LORD, "My Lord, why have you abused this people? Why did you send me for this? Ever since I first came to Pharaoh to speak in your name, he has abused this people. *And you've done absolutely nothing* to rescue your people" (5:22–23, emphasis mine).

The LORD patiently calms Moses and reiterates the key points of his mission (6:6–8):

- I am the LORD
- I will free Israel from the burdens of the Egyptians
- I will take you as my people, and I will be your God
- I will bring you into the land that I swore to give to Abraham, Isaac, and Jacob

Moses tells the people, but they won't listen "because of their discouragement and their cruel bondage" (6:9 NIV). The "exodus" of Israel from Egypt is going nowhere, fast. If the people are going anywhere, the LORD must step into the ring—*now*—and fight for them.

IV. The Purpose of Ten Plagues

The LORD knew, before he ever called Moses, that Pharaoh would never let the people go without a fight (4:21–23). Even so, the assortment of plagues the LORD is about to bring on Egypt raises questions about what the LORD is doing and why? Clues are scattered throughout the text, and even though we are jumping ahead in the story for a moment, consider the following statements:

- Spoken to Pharaoh:
  - After the frogs: "As you say! So that you may know that there is no one like the LORD our God." (8:10 NIV)
  - Before the flies: "But on that day I will deal differently with land of Goshen . . . no swarms of flies will be there, so that you will know that I, the LORD, am in this land." (8:22 NIV)
  - Before hail: " . . . or this time I will send the full force of my plagues against you and against your officials and your people, so you may know that there is no one like me in all the earth." (9:14 NIV, see also 9:29)

- Spoken about Egypt:
  - Before the plagues: "The Egyptians will come to know that I am the LORD, when I act against Egypt and bring the Israelites out from among them." (7:5)
  - Before the Red Sea: "I'll make Pharaoh stubborn, and he'll chase them. I'll gain honor at the expense of Pharaoh and all his army, and the Egyptians will know that I am the LORD." (14:4, see also 14:18)

- Spoken about Israel:
  - Before the locusts: "Go to Pharaoh; for I have hardened his heart . . . in order that I may show these signs of mine among them, and that you may tell your children and grandchildren how I have made fools of the Egyptians . . . so that you may know that I am the LORD." (10:1–2 NRSV)

- Spoken about the world
  - Before the hail: "By now I could have used my power to strike you and your people with a deadly disease so that you would have disappeared from the earth. But I've left you standing for this reason: in order to show you my power and in order to make my name known in the whole world." (9:15–16)

The LORD is not hitting Egypt with random plagues, but with blows that appear to be directed against the gods of Egypt, so that Pharaoh, Egypt, Israel, and the world will have the opportunity to come to know the LORD. In fact, prior to the final plague, the LORD explains, "I will pass through the land of Egypt that night, and I will strike down every oldest child in the land of Egypt . . . I'll impose judgments on *all the gods of Egypt*. I am the LORD" (12:12, emphasis mine). This final statement suggests that the LORD has been making calculated strikes against Egyptian gods all along. So, following this lead, a number of researchers have made suggestions as to what god of Egypt each plague may have been hitting (see Table 4.1 below and "For Further Reading").

PLAGUE	POSSIBLE GOD AGAINST WHOM THE PLAGUE WAS DIRECTED
1. Nile to Blood	*Hapi* (god of the Nile), *Isis* (goddess of the Nile and powerful magician)
2. Frogs	*Heqet* (frog-headed goddess of fruitfulness)
3. Gnats	Uncertain
4. Flies	Uncertain
5. Death of Livestock	*Hathor* (cow-headed goddess), *Apis* (bull sacred to Osiris, symbol of fertility), and others
6. Boils	*Sekhmet* (goddess with power over disease), and others
7. Hail	*Nut* (sky goddess), *Osiris* (god of crops)
8. Locusts	*Serapia* (protector from locusts)
9. Darkness	*Re* (sun god of Heliopolis), *Horus* (sun god)
10. Death of Firstborn	Pharaoh's firstborn son, considered a god, and others

Table 4.1. Plagues and the Gods of Egypt

V. The Fight with Pharaoh (Exodus 7–13)

With better awareness of why the LORD is hitting Egypt with these particular punches, we can go back to the pre-fight press conference. Aaron throws down the gauntlet, issuing a challenge with his Amazing Two-in-One "Snake-in-a-Stick," to show off just a little of the power and pizzazz they and the LORD will bring to the upcoming fight (7:10). The Egyptian magicians, however, are quick to match Aaron's move with their own (7:11), though they are bested when Aaron's snake swallows all of theirs and they are forced to leave the meeting disgraced and without their staffs.

Round One. The first round opens early in the morning at the Nile as Moses and Aaron wait to meet Pharaoh as he comes to the river. Moses makes the first move by speaking on behalf of the LORD, demanding that Pharaoh release the Hebrews; then, to show the LORD's power, he reaches out with the staff turned snake, turned back to a staff, and strikes the Nile, turning the water to blood (7:15–21). Then Aaron continues to jab away at Pharaoh, as he apparently goes around Egypt striking more and more water, turning it into blood. His blows, however, are soon countered by the Egyptian magicians as they use their secret arts to turn water to blood (7:22)—just what Egypt needs, less water and even more blood. Nonetheless, Round One must be scored as a draw; Pharaoh is unimpressed (7:23).

Round Two. The second round comes about a week later in Pharaoh's palace (7:25). Speaking for the LORD, Moses demands the immediate release of the LORD's people and warns that anything less will result in a flood of frogs every possible place you can imagine, and where you can't imagine (8:1–4). So, without further warning, Aaron summons the frogs from the waters of Egypt (8:6). And without hesitation, the Egyptian magicians do the same, bringing even more frogs (8:7). Pharaoh briefly shows signs of throwing in the towel; but no sooner does he promise to let the people go than he changes his mind. Round Two also ends in a draw.

Round Three. The third round begins without conversation, just action. Instructed by God through Moses, Aaron reaches out with his staff and strikes the dust, turning it into an invasion of gnats (8:16–17, or "lice," NJPS). And, for the first time, the Egyptian magicians are unable to match Aaron, incapable of producing their own gnats (8:18). Back in their corner, the magicians come to Pharaoh with their assessment: "This is the finger of God!" (8:19 NRSV). Round Three goes to Moses and the LORD, though like any good fighter, Pharaoh refuses to admit his loss (8:19b).

Round Four. In the fourth round, the magicians neither leave their corner nor enter the picture. The LORD sends Moses and Aaron to the river to meet Pharaoh and demand the release of the LORD's people, namely, to worship the God to whom they belong (9:20–21). If Pharaoh refuses, the LORD threatens to send a plague of flies upon Egypt, except for the land of Goshen where the LORD's people live, so that "you will know that I, the LORD, am in this land" (8:22b). So, the next morning, swarms of flies are everywhere in Egypt, but not in Goshen (8:24). Pharaoh has lost Round Four; all he can do is maneuver so that he can stay on his feet to come out fighting in the next round. He summons Moses and Aaron for peace terms—anything to get rid of all these flies. Moses works in good faith, assuring Pharaoh that the flies will fly away in return for Israel leaving to worship her God. Pharaoh agrees to the terms up until the last fly leaves and then changes his position; no one is going anywhere (8:28–32). Round Four may go to the LORD, but Pharaoh has shown that he has no intention of throwing in the towel.

Round Five. The fifth round begins with Moses and Aaron warning Pharaoh not to continue holding people who belong to a different God. If he does, there will be an outbreak of a deadly disease among Egyptian livestock, with Israel's livestock safely immune in Goshen. Pharaoh appears unconvinced until the next day when the Egyptian herds are decimated by disease, while not a single head of Israelite stock dies. Round Five clearly goes into the books as the LORD's; but with the damage already done, Pharaoh sees no reason to give up.

Round Six. Without warning, the LORD strikes first in the pivotal sixth round. With Pharaoh watching, Moses throws handfuls of soot into the air. The fine dust causes an eruption of festering boils on humans and animals alike—but only on Egyptians; Israel and her animals suffer no harm (9:8–10). The magicians who had begun the fight for Pharaoh, standing toe to toe with Moses for the first two rounds, reappear in Round Six. Or, to be more precise, they reappear because of their inability to stand before Moses due to the boils. In prize fight terms, *we have our first knockdown.* From the mat the magicians beg Pharaoh not to continue, but Pharaoh will not listen because what was once within his control is now out of his control. *God is now hardening Pharaoh's heart* (9:11–12). Previous texts have described Pharaoh's heart problem as either

"Pharaoh hardened his heart" (e.g., 8:32 NRSV), or "the heart of Pharaoh was hardened" (e.g., 9:7 NRSV). And, although the LORD predicted this moment would come before Moses left for Egypt (4:21), this is the first time the text states that the LORD has taken over. Hope for Pharaoh is lost; from this point forward, the LORD is in control of Pharaoh's heart. Consequently, this fight will not end with anything less than a complete knockout (see Appendix IV).

The final four rounds begin with a dire warning from the LORD that he could take Egypt down anytime he wanted (9:13–16, see above).

Round Seven. And so, in the seventh round, the LORD sends a hail storm unlike any Egypt has ever seen. The hail further destroys Egypt's agriculture and proves deadly for humans or animals caught out in the storm. Pharaoh buckles against the ropes, telling Moses he has had enough—take away the hail and Israel may leave. And despite the fact that Moses knows Pharaoh does not yet fear the LORD, he agrees to stop the hail (9:27–29).

Round Eight. Off the ropes in round seven, the LORD hardens Pharaoh's heart so that he immediately changes his mind once the hail stops. So the eighth round begins with another trip to see Pharaoh (10:1–2) and another warning—of locusts (10:3–6). Even Pharaoh's officials urge him to relent on the simple premise, "Do you not yet understand that Egypt is ruined?" (10:7b). So Pharaoh tries to negotiate. But when he sees, as he has suspected all along, that once Israel goes to worship her God she will never come back to serve him, he drives Moses and Aaron out of his presence. So locusts come on Egypt (10:12–15). Pharaoh begs for mercy (10:16–18), but as soon as the locusts are gone, the LORD hardens Pharaoh's heart again so that he does not let Israel go (10:19–20). God will not let Pharaoh stop; the fight will not end until the LORD is finished.

Round Nine. In the ninth round, Moses brings a dense darkness over the land of Egypt, so dark that for three days people could not see and could not move; yet, all the Israelites had light where they lived (10:21–23). Against the ropes, Pharaoh again buckles to his knees and tells Israel to leave without its herds. When Moses refuses the deal, the LORD hardens Pharaoh's heart so that he changes his mind, yet again, and will not let Israel leave (10:24–27).

Figure 4.2. The Sphinx and Pyramid. Photo by David Anderson.

Beaten up and bloody at the end of round nine, Pharaoh is furious with Moses and Aaron, threatening their lives if he should see them again. At this point, or perhaps later, Moses warns Pharaoh that the LORD will bring this fight to an end in the next round by putting to death the firstborn of every person and beast in Egypt—from Pharaoh to the slaves (11:4–7). Then, Moses says, your officials will beg for me and all Israel to leave, and we will. Then "Moses, furious, left Pharaoh" (11:8b).

Round Ten. The events of the tenth and final round are a bit harder to trace in Exodus 12–13. The text not only conveys the events in Egypt, but interweaves instructions for the annual celebration of these events in the Passover and the Feast of Unleavened Bread. The day of the final round, the Israelites are brought into the action. In preparation, they are to select an unblemished lamb or goat and hold it until the fourteenth day of the month. On that day, they are to (1) slaughter the animal at twilight; (2) use the blood as paint for their doorposts and top lintel; (3) roast and eat the lamb or goat with unleavened bread and bitter herbs; (4) burn any leftovers; (5) dress in traveling clothes, ready to leave Egypt at a moment's notice; and, finally, (6) not go outside their houses for any purpose that night, because the LORD and/or destroying angel will be going through the land killing the firstborn of anyone outside the protection of the blood (12:1–11). This day will become a day to remember, celebrate, and share with every subsequent generation who will not only remember, but relive the night of the Passover (12:14). They will obey the same instructions, participate in the same meal, and so become one with the generation that left Egypt—whether one year or a thousand years later (12:14–20).

This final punch of the tenth round brings with it the knockout blow—at midnight, all Egypt realizes they have lost their firstborn children, including Pharaoh. Without waiting until morning, Pharaoh summons Moses and Aaron and demands that Israel leave the land (12:31–32). The fight has come to a decisive conclusion, the final right hook executing judgment on all the gods of Egypt (12:12).

VI: Learning to Trust the LORD (EXODUS 14–18)

Up to this point in the story, the LORD has required little of Israel other than to follow the instructions given on the night of Passover to be ready to leave Egypt. More confidence in Moses and Aaron at the beginning would have been nice, but was not ultimately necessary. Once Israel leaves Goshen, however, far more is required. It is easy to stand back and let God (or Moses) punch his way to your salvation; it is far more difficult to trust this God who has saved you. Thus, the journey across the wilderness from Goshen to Mount Sinai becomes a school for learning to live with, and most of all trust, the God who has saved Israel from oppression. It is easy to be saved, but the six episodes recorded in Exodus 14–18 demonstrate the challenge of living by faith.

1. The Crisis at the Sea of Reeds. Once Pharaoh had some time to recover from the technical knockout in his fight with the LORD and has some time to think about what he has done in releasing Israel (14:5), God hardens his heart one last time (14:4). Pharaoh rallies his military to chase and bring Israel back to work. The LORD lures Pharaoh by leading Israel in such a way that it gives the impression they are lost and have no idea what they are doing, even to the point of allowing themselves to be trapped between the Sea of Reeds (Hebrews, "Red Sea" in the Old Greek translation) and the Egyptian army (14:1–9).

When the Israelites look back and see Pharaoh's army and their situation, they cry out to Moses with great fear—the first of many complaints to come:

> Was it because there were no graves in Egypt that you have taken us away to die
> in the wilderness? What have you done to us, bringing us out of Egypt? Is this not
> the very thing we told you in Egypt, "Let us alone and let us serve the Egyptians"?

For it would have been better for us to serve the Egyptians than to die in the wilderness. (14:11–12 NRSV)

Despite their ingratitude, Moses tries to help the people rely on the LORD:

Do not be afraid, stand firm, and see the deliverance that the LORD will accomplish for you today; for the Egyptians whom you see today you shall never see again. The LORD will fight for you, and *you have only to keep still.* (14:13–14 NRSV, emphasis mine)

Their task is to relax, stop panicking, and watch the LORD deal with the problem—to replace their fear with faith that the LORD can—and will—take care of them.

The angel in the cloud moves to a defensive position, keeping Pharaoh's troops from attacking the Israelites. Meanwhile, the LORD kicks up a strong east wind to push the sea back. By morning, the sea was far enough back and the seabed dry enough for Israel to have a clear path (14:23). The Egyptian army pursues but is soon thrown into a panic by the LORD. They realize they have

The Message of the Old Testament

Exodus 1–19 reinforces a number of insights we have been taking in about God—how God chooses to work in the world, God's ultimate hopes, and God's desire for those who live in relationship with him. As in Genesis, God continues to work in the world through people, selecting flawed individuals and families to do what needs to be done and promising his presence or full support (Exod 3:12). Also, just as in Genesis, God's hope remains with one family as a means of reaching the world, a family that has grown into thirteen tribal groups, known collectively as "the Israelites"—a family that God has now called to be priests who reach out to the world (Exod 19:6).

The most prominent feature of Exodus 5–12, the ten plagues, as strange as it sounds, continue to witness to God's hope for the world. In this narrative, we read over and again that the plagues come *so that Pharaoh, Egypt, Israel, and the world* will know that the LORD is God, not the gods of Egypt. In fact, after the sixth plague, the LORD tells Pharaoh that the only reason he has left him alive is to show him what a true God can do and so the whole world will hear about the LORD (9:16). The LORD still has confidence in his plan and is committed to the promises he made to Israel's ancestors long ago.

Finally, as with the family stories of Genesis, the narrative of Israel's journey from Egypt to Sinai demonstrates God's faithful care and tremendous patience. The LORD's desire is for his people to trust him, to know that he has their back no matter what happens. And even though the LORD's people most often respond with doubt and an occasional full-blown panic attack, the LORD is patient as he tries to teach his people—to reach his people with a faithful love that transcends any love they have ever known.

been drawn into a trap, the wheels of their heavy chariots clogging in the mud of the seabed (14:23–25). They abandon their chariots and begin a desperate run for the shoreline, but it is too late. On the other shore, the Lord instructs Moses to close the sea, and he does (14:26–27). Pharaoh's troops drown in the rushing water (14:28).

Most important, that day, "Israel saw the amazing power of the Lord against the Egyptians. The people were in awe of the Lord, and they believed in the Lord and in his servant Moses" (14:31). They realize, even if briefly, that they can entrust their lives to the Lord.

2. The Crisis at Marah. Traveling a few days into the wilderness, water supplies soon give out and the only water they find is bitter (Heb. *marah*)—undrinkable. So the people turn on Moses, asking, "What will we drink?" Moses turns to the Lord, who provides a strange solution: throw a tree branch into the water (15:25). The issue, however, is bigger than a drink of water. Israel must learn to obey and trust her God. Faith is the only way to avoid what happened to the Egyptians (15:26).

3. The Crisis in the Wilderness of Sin. As Israel moves even further into the wilderness, an inevitable food shortage develops. All Israel complains, "Oh, how we wish that the Lord had just put us to death while we were still in the land of Egypt. There we could sit by the pots cooking meat and eat our fill of bread. Instead, you've brought us out into this desert to starve this whole assembly to death." (16:3). Again, the real problem is a matter of faith or trust.

On this occasion the Lord provides a solution that not only teaches Israel to trust God today, but to trust God every day. The Lord begins to rain down a layer of heavy dew; when the dew lifted, it left behind a thin edible residue the people could collect and eat. The catch (or test), however, was in collecting just enough for one day and no more, relying on the Lord to make the manna (Heb. *man hu,* "What is it?") available every day, including special provisions for the Sabbath. In a unique way, the manna raises two questions—"What is it?" followed by "Who is it?"—through which Israel will make the decision to trust themselves, other gods, or the Lord.

4. The Crisis at Massah and Meribah. For the second time, the people complain about water—this time, the lack of water. And for the third time, the people accuse Moses: "But the people were very thirsty for water there, and they complained to Moses, 'Why did you bring us out of Egypt to kill us, our children, and our livestock with thirst?' So Moses cried out to the Lord, 'What should I do with this people? They are getting ready to stone me.'" (17:3–4). The Lord provides instructions for how to provide water by striking a rock, which erupts into a spring of water (17:5–6). But again, the real issue, the writer reminds us, is trust. Moses calls the place *Massah* (Heb. *testing*) and *Meribah* (Heb. *quarreling*) because the Israelites quarreled over the question, "Is the Lord among us or not?" (17:7).

5. The Crisis at Rephidim. Without apparent provocation, the Amalekites attack Israel, drawing an odd response from Moses. He appoints a young military commander to lead the army down into the valley, Joshua—our first introduction to Israel's future leader (17:8–10). Meanwhile, Moses treks up to the top of the hill where he does what looks like an early version of "the wave." Whenever he lifts his hands, Israel wins; whenever he lowers his hands, Amalek wins. Strange. How Moses' actions relate to the battle in the valley seems bizarre, at least until we explore possible meanings associated with the lifting of one's hands. The book of Psalms is most instructive:

> Listen to my request for mercy when I cry out to you,
>> when *I lift up my hands* to your holy inner sanctuary.
>>> (Ps 28:2, emphasis mine)

> So I will bless you as long as I'm alive;
>> *I will lift up my hands* in your name. (63:4, emphasis mine)

Moses's action on the hill most likely represents calling upon or praying to the LORD for help in the battle. Thus, whenever Moses lifts his hands in reliance on God for victory, Israel wins; but when he drops his hands, symbolizing a lack of trust or reliance, they lose. Once again, the issue for Israel (and the reader) is learning to trust the God who has saved them from Egyptian slavery.

6. Moses's Crisis at Sinai. The final crisis occurs at Israel's first destination on their journey: the mountain of God (18:5), Mount Sinai (or Mount Hor). Jethro, Moses's father-in-law, comes to meet Moses, bringing along his family that had been sent back home at some point, presumably for safety (18:2–5). The next day, Jethro observes Moses sitting as judge for the people from morning until evening, and he expresses grave concern over Moses's practice. When Jethro asks Moses why he is doing this, Moses replies innocently enough, but notice all the first person pronouns in his reply:

> Because the people come to *me* to inquire of God. When they have a dispute, they come to *me* and *I* decide between one person and another, and *I* make known to them the statutes and instructions of God. (18:15–16 NRSV, emphasis mine)

Jethro's diagnosis is on target: "What you are doing isn't good. You will end up totally wearing yourself out" (18:17–18a). The problem with Moses's practice, and his explanation, is his assumption that the only person capable of the work is himself; it's the philosophy *the only way to get something done right is to do it yourself.* And the philosophy comes from the same heart problem the people have struggled with since leaving Egypt: Moses is trusting himself, not the LORD. The more seductive issue for Moses (and many who have followed) is that Moses's work is religious; he is serving God, after all. Jethro advises Moses to teach and empower others, and by this action trust the LORD to work through others who will come alongside him (18:17–23).

Conclusion

The major movements in Exodus 1–18 take us from (1) the astronomical growth of God's chosen people in Egypt and the crisis this creates for them and for Egypt (Exod 1); (2) to the selection of a reluctant leader, who, despite his excuses, is obedient to God's call (Exod 2–4); (3) to the battle of the gods/God and their representatives through the ten plagues (Exod 5–13); to (4) Israel's journey across the wilderness to their arrival at Mt. Sinai, the mountain of God (Exod 14–18).

Through these chapters we have observed the LORD to be a God who (1) hears the cries of his people (2:23–25); (2) selects and works through humans (3:10); (3) fights for his people, whatever it takes to free them (Exod 5–12); and (4) patiently teaches his people that they must and can trust the LORD to provide for them (Exod 13–18). The LORD's life with his people has only just begun, but the primary themes they need to learn and remember are already becoming quite clear. The LORD is a merciful and compassionate God, who raises up leaders and fights for his people, only asking in return that his people trust him to be their God.

To Discuss

1. What do you think about the midwives' response to Pharaoh? Do you think their lie is acceptable or unethical given the circumstances? Can you think of similar circumstances in history that you would argue are ethical, despite breaking a commandment? How does God's response to the midwives influence your answer?

2. Consider again the story of Moses at the burning bush. How odd does it seem to Moses that a voice is coming out of a burning bush? That the God-in-a-bush knows his name? Analyze each of Moses's arguments. Which seem reasonable, which unreasonable? Why? What arguments does Moses fail to make (that you would have made)?

3. Read Appendix IV: The LORD and Pharaoh's Heart Disease. Establish the issue—what is the problem with Pharaoh's heart? Consider the data and common explanations. What other explanations should be considered? In view of the data available to you in the Appendix, what is the best explanation? Defend your response.

4. The author suggests that the ten plagues may have been strikes against the various gods in Egypt (see Table 4.1). Does the correlation between the plagues and Egyptian gods appear strong to you? What else can you think of that might explain the use of these specific plagues?

5. To what extent do you think the Israelites in Egypt knew the stories of Abraham and Sarah, Isaac and Rebekah, Jacob and his wives? How do you think the knowledge of these stories, or lack of knowledge, may have impacted their response to Moses? (What about Moses? Did he know the stories?)

6. Why do you think it was so difficult for the Israelites to trust the LORD in the wilderness, after the LORD had just rescued them from Egypt and performed so many miracles?

7. Do you agree or disagree with the author's analysis of the story from Exodus 18 (Jethro's advice to Moses)? Explain your position. Does Moses also struggle with trusting the LORD? If so, why?

8. How do you think the magicians were able to duplicate the staff-to-snake miracle, as well as the first two plagues?

To Know

1. The significance of the following in this chapter:

Aaron	Moses
Joshua	Mount Sinai
Jethro	Passover
LORD	YHWH
Manna	Zipporah
Miriam	

2. The changes for Israel since the end of Genesis, documented in the first chapter of Exodus. Israel's situation at the beginning of Exodus.

3. Pharaoh's three strategies to control Israel's growth and the outcome of each strategy.

4. Three stories the biblical writer tells about Moses to introduce him into the story (Exod 2). What these stories emphasize about Moses.

5. The five excuses Moses made at the burning bush and the LORD's response to each excuse. The key idea in the LORD's responses.

6. The ten plagues and the four purposes for the plagues.

7. Israel's six crises on the way from Egypt to Mount Sinai and the underlying theme.

8. The name of God given to Moses at the burning bush and why most English translations replace this name with "the LORD."

9. Locate the following on a map (see Figure 4.1): Egypt, Great Sea, Sinai (region), and the land of Midian.

To Dig Deeper: Research Topics

1. After Moses starts back for Egypt, one night in camp the LORD attacks Moses and tries to kill him (see Exod 4:24–26). Somehow Zipporah knows what to do and acts quickly to circumcise one of their sons and touch Moses' genitals ("feet") with the bloody skin. Then the LORD left him alone. Investigate common explanations. What conclusion(s) are you able to reach?

2. Scientists have often tried to explain how the ten plagues may have occurred. To the best of your ability, discuss whether the theory(s) seem logical or convincing? Does an explanation of the plagues as natural events change the way you read the plagues narrative and/or the claims made in the text for or about the LORD? Explain.

3. Investigate further the correlation between the gods of Egypt and the plagues. Is there a strong correlation?

4. Consider the ethical issues raised by the LORD hardening Pharaoh's heart. Begin with the data provided in Appendix IV: The LORD and Pharaoh's Heart Disease as a starting place for further research and for developing your own explanation.

5. Read Exodus 9:20–21 and 18:8–12, and Joshua 2:8–11. To what extent was the LORD's strategy for the plagues initially successful? What was necessary in order for the LORD's strategy to work (after Israel left Egypt)?

6. Many other potential topics or texts may raise your interest in Exodus 1–18. Select one of these areas of interest for a research paper or report to the class.

For Further Reading

Davis, John J. *Moses and the Gods of Egypt: Studies in Exodus.* 2d ed. Grand Rapids: Baker Book House 1986.

El Mahdy, Christine. *Mummies, Myth, and Magic in Ancient Egypt.* London: Thames & Hudson, 1989.

Hamilton, Victor P. *Handbook on the Pentateuch.* 2d ed. Grand Rapids: Baker, 2005.

Schnittjer, Gary Edward. *The Torah Story: An Apprenticeship on the Pentateuch.* Grand Rapids: Zondervan, 2006.

A **Wedding** Invitation
The Marriage of the LORD and Israel

O ne way to describe the relationship between Yahweh and Israel is to use the classic tale of the damsel in distress. In Egypt, the young woman (Israel) cried out for someone to rescue her. Yahweh came and swept Israel off her feet, flexing his muscles to impress her (and everyone else), and beating the gods of Egypt to a pulp. Israel was impressed enough to run away with Yahweh into the wilderness, escaping Pharaoh's slavery and seeing a new possibility for her future. So Israel and Yahweh traveled through the wilderness "dating" and getting to know each other as they neared Mount Sinai. Their relationship was rocky, to say the least. More than once, Israel asked herself why she ever left Egypt. While on the other side, all Yahweh wanted was for Israel to trust him—to fall in love with him; but, after all those years with Pharaoh and the gods of Egypt, trust did not come easily for Israel. Nonetheless, anyone could see that something special was happening between these two.

So perhaps it is no big surprise that, once Israel and Yahweh reach Mount Sinai, Yahweh pops The Question. In Yahweh's words:

> You have seen what I did to the Egyptians and how I bore you on eagles' wings and brought you to myself. Now therefore, if you will obey my voice and keep my covenant, *you shall be my treasured possession out of all the peoples.* Indeed, the whole earth is mine, but *you shall be for me a priestly kingdom and a holy nation.* (Exod 19:4–6a NRSV, emphasis mine)

READING ASSIGNMENTS
EXODUS 20

EXODUS 21–25
(SKIM 26–31), 40

KEY TERMS
Alien: a person living in a foreign country where they are not citizens

Apodictic Law: command law, absolute law without conditions: *you will,* or, *you must not*

Casuistic Law: case law, stated with conditions: *if . . . then . . .*

Law of Talion: punishment must fit the crime, e.g., *an eye for an eye* (Exod 21:23–25)

Ordeal: a physical challenge to demonstrate a person's guilt or innocence

Sabbath: the seventh day of the week, a day of rest for Israelites

Tabernacle: a portable tent with a surrounding compound formed by a curtain fence

Priest: an intermediary between the gods/God and people

Vestments: the robes or clothing a priest wears

Moses brings the LORD's offer down from the top of the mountain, and asks the people what they want to do. "The people all responded with one voice: 'Everything that the LORD has said we will do.'"(19:8a) In other words, Israel speaks a strong: Yes, we will marry you! We will enter into a covenant relationship.

The marriage or covenant ceremony between Yahweh and Israel is recorded a few chapters later in Exodus 24, and looks much like our own marriage ceremonies—well, at least a little bit. Just before the ceremony begins, Moses asks Israel one last time if she is certain that she really wants to go through with the covenant/wedding. Without hesitation Israel responds yes: "Everything that the LORD has said we will do" (24:3). So Moses writes out the scroll/book of the covenant, builds an altar, and offers sacrifices (24:4–6). He reads the scroll of the covenant (probably some form of Exodus 21–23) and asks the people if they accept the terms; they reply (again), "Everything that the LORD has said we will do, and we will obey" (24:7). At this point, Moses dashes blood from the sacrifices on the people, a bit different from our weddings, when the groom is told, "You may kiss the bride."

The final movement in the ceremony, however, is just like our weddings—Yahweh hosts a reception with food. So Moses and the leaders of Israel go up the mountain where they eat and drink in the LORD's presence (24:9–11). And, afterward, Moses heads further up the mountain where Yahweh will give him the tablets of stone with written instructions (24:12–14).

The chapters between the LORD's proposal (19:1–9) and wedding or covenant service (24:1–14) function somewhat like premarital counseling. Although Israel was impressed with what the LORD did for her in Egypt, and Israel and the LORD have been together for at least six months, Israel does not really know what it means to live in relationship with this God. Consequently, chapters twenty through twenty-three—containing the Ten Commandments (20:1–17) and the Covenant Code (21:1–23:32)—serve as an introduction to life with Yahweh, providing Israel with a basic sense of what she may expect from her God and what her God will expect from her.

Again, rather than a summary of all the chapters, we will limit our study to four key questions: (1) How are we to read the Ten Commandments? (2) What are the principles behind the Ten Commandments? (3) What is the Covenant Code and what is its purpose? (4) What is the significance of the tabernacle? With these questions, and at the appropriate time, we will take an excursion outside of Israel's texts to ask about ancient Near Eastern law codes.

I. Reading the Ten Commandments

The Ten Commandments may be the most recognized text from the Old Testament; so, it seems a bit odd to stop and ask how we should read these commandments—just read and obey, right? Yes and no. How these commandments function in Israel's society is actually a much more complicated issue. So, at the outset, we need to consider two radically different ways of understanding the Ten Commandments:

1. A Perimeter Ethic. On the one hand, we may read the commandments as something like setting posts that establish a fence line, inside which the LORD's people must stay. As long as they stay inside the boundaries, the relationship is fine; it does not matter how far they go, so long as they do not cross over the line. With this understanding of the commandments, the most important questions pertain to locating the fence posts with absolute precision and resolving the question, "How far can I go?"

For example, the seventh commandment prohibits adultery. Read as a part of a perimeter ethic, the most important questions are: What constitutes adultery? How far can a couple go before they have crossed the line? Where, exactly, is the fence post located (see Figure 5.1)? So we ask:

Figure 5.1. The Ten Commandments as a Perimeter Ethic

- Is an emotional romance okay, as long as no physical contact takes place?
- What about making out, as long as the couple doesn't go too far? (How far is too far?)
- Is an internet relationship okay?
- What about pornography?
- Is oral sex adultery? What about sexual foreplay—is it okay, as long as there is no penetration? Does adultery pertain only to those who are married—what about the unmarried?

In other words, precisely where is the fence post located? Because when read as a perimeter ethic, locating the fence line is the most critical thing interpreters can do—so we know what we can do, how far we can go, and still stay in relationship with the LORD.

2. Centering Principles. On the other hand, we may read the Ten Commandments as expressions of principles by which to center our lives. Now, instead of looking for a fence line not to cross, we are looking for the principles that stand behind a commandment. We understand these principles to express what the LORD is like and what the LORD would or would not do. So, as a people drawn into covenant with the LORD, Israel's ultimate desire is to live more and more closely to God's heart. So, if we look at Figure 5.2, we reverse the ultimate question from "How far can I go?" to "How close can I get to the heart of God?"

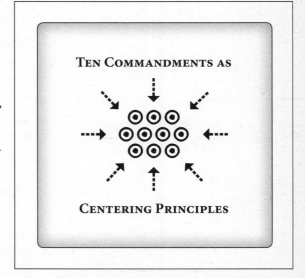

Figure 5.2. The Ten Commandments as Centering Principles

To take the same example as above, instead of defining adultery so that we know how far we can go without stepping over the line, we ask a different set of questions. Most important, we ask: What is the principle behind the commandment? Answer: The prohibition of adultery expresses the principle of faithfulness to my spouse and respect for the covenant relationships of others. So we then ask:

- How may we live more faithfully to our spouses?
- How may we best support the marriages of others around us?
- How may we encourage our community to be a place that keeps covenant agreements of all types?

The difference in understanding this commandment could not be greater. Now, we are no longer looking for the precise placement of a line we must not cross, but looking instead in the opposite direction—toward the center, and how to live closer and closer to the ideal; closer and closer to the Lord.

So then, despite their fame, it is not often that readers consider how they should understand the Ten Commandments. In what follows, it will be clear that I regard the Ten Commandments to be an expression of a centering ethic or principles for God's people.

II. The Principles within the Ten Commandments

Prologue: The Ten Commandments begin with a historical prologue that further defines how we understand the commandments: "I am the Lord *your God*, who brought you out of Egypt, out of the house of slavery" (20:2, emphasis mine). Surprisingly, before stating the covenant stipulations, and even before the formal covenant ceremony (24:1–18), the Lord claims to be in a relationship with the people; the Lord is already "your God." *It is not obedience to the commandments* that makes Israel the people of God; God made Israel his people when he claimed them and brought them out of the land of Egypt (or before, see Gen 12:1–9). Consequently, obedience is an expression of gratitude for what God has already done. Israel does not work to earn a relationship with God; that relationship is a gift.

Command One: *Do not have other gods before me*. The principle behind the first commandment is God's desire for an exclusive relationship with those who follow him. And at the same time, God accepts Israel's long-held beliefs in the existence of many gods. In time, the prophets will assert that there is only one God, but not here. Here, the Lord enters Israel's life where she is—with a worldview filled with Marduk, Tiamat, Baal, Re, Horus, and many other gods. For now, it will do to demand a position above all other gods in Israel's life. Deuteronomy will restate the commandments (Deut 5) and take up this idea with even greater force throughout the book as a single-minded allegiance to the Lord. And of all that follows in Israel's story, it is this commandment that stands out as most important. Israel may fail the Lord in many ways, violate other commandments, and frustrate the Lord by their actions, but when Israel accepts other gods alongside or in place of Yahweh, the Lord's reaction is entirely different (Deut 6:14–15). The first commandment comes from the most important principle of life with the Lord: more than anything else, the Lord wants a monogamous relationship and a single-minded allegiance from his people.

Command Two: *Do not make a divine image or representation of anything in the sky above or on the earth below or in the seas below the earth. Do not worship them or serve them because I am Yahweh your God—a jealous God.* The second commandment is a natural companion to the first. The Lord (1) demands a monogamous relationship, and (2) disallows the production of idols. This command, however, reaches for an even deeper principle. On the one hand, the Bible celebrates art and uses many images to help readers understand what the Lord is like: shepherd (Ps 23), king (Gen 1), even a thunderstorm (Ps 29). On the other hand, this command prohibits making an image of anything for the purpose of worship—even for worshipping the Lord. The question "why not?" leads us to the principle at stake. Anytime a person creates an image for worship, he or she restricts, reduces, or limits God to a single image (that we like) and worships the one image at the expense of the full mystery of God. So we might reword this commandment in other ways: "don't fence me in" or "don't put me in a box." Recognize and worship the Lord, who is above all and beyond any single image; do not limit God in any way—not by physical objects of worship or by word images that become exclusive ways of understanding God, addressing God in prayer, or speaking of God. The Lord cannot be captured by any image made by humans.

Command Three: *Do not misuse the name of Yahweh your God.* First, we recognize that the name to which this command refers is the name Israel's God gave to Moses at the burning bush: Yahweh (Exod 3:15). Second, misusing or "taking a name in vain" is not simply about how someone uses a word, but the respect given to the person whose name is spoken. Third, the command does not forbid someone from taking an oath in the Lord's name (e.g., as a person swears in court before giving testimony). In fact, Deuteronomy insists that God's people must take seriously any oath they make in the Lord's name (Deut 6:13, 10:20). Consequently, the principle at stake is treating the Lord with respect, which begins with reverence for the Lord's name.

As a side note: From early times, Jews who had hearts of respect for the Lord and did not want to break this command, refused to speak the name of God at all—a decision that caused difficulty when they read their Bible aloud in the synagogue, since the name of God (*yhwh*) occurs over 6,000 times in the Hebrew scriptures. The solution was to substitute a different word for the name of God, a word of honor and respect: Lord (as in master). Most English Bibles continue this tradition by substituting the word "Lord" and printing it in small capital letters (Lord) when the name *Yahweh* appears in the text (for an exception, see the Jerusalem Bible).

Command Four: *Remember the Sabbath day and keep it holy.* The fourth command is the final commandment that pertains explicitly and directly to a person's relationship with God; the final six commandments turn the reader's attention to relationships with other people, teaching us that a relationship with God includes how we live among and treat others (see Matt 22:34–40; Mark 12:28–34; 1 John 4:7–12). Despite common assumptions, I am unable to find any Old Testament text that connects the Sabbath with worship for a layperson. Instead, at its beginning, the command is for everyone in the household to stop for rest. At first glance, this command looks easy to do: everyone gets a day off! With a second look, however, I assume that human nature has not changed, so people resist a Sabbath rest (by any name, on any day of the week) because we think that we must keep working to pay our bills, to keep the company running, to catch up, to get ahead, or for a dozen other reasons. The principle of the Sabbath challenges us to stop and rest; a rest that is possible only if we trust completely in the Lord rather than relying on ourselves.

Command Five: *Honor your father and mother.* Stated in positive form, the principle behind the fifth command seems clear—until we ask who is addressed by these words. Just before, the fourth commandment prohibited work for "you (ms = masculine singular), your (ms) son or your (ms) daughter, your (ms) male or female slave, your (ms) livestock, or the **alien** resident in your (ms) towns" (20:10 NRSV). All of the pronouns speak to adult males in control of a household. Still ahead, the tenth commandment confirms the same audience: "You (ms) shall not covet your (ms) neighbor's house; you (ms) shall not covet your (ms) neighbor's wife . . ." (20:17 NRSV). In fact, all of the commandments speak first to adult males living in community, with secondary application for females and children. Consequently, while a fair application, the primary meaning of this text is not that children should honor and obey their parents. Rather, to honor one's parents in an ancient society meant to take responsibility for their wellbeing. Jesus supports this idea when he quotes this commandment, condemning those in his audience who acted religious and sacrificial for finding ways around supporting their parents (see Matt 15:4–9).

Command Six: *You shall not murder.* Due to traditional translations (e.g., "Thou shalt not kill" CEB, KJV, ASV), confusion has existed as to whether or not the sixth commandment prohibits capital punishment or killing in war. Newer translations clarify the meaning of the text, "do not murder" (e.g., NRSV, NIV, NLT, NJPS, MSG, ERV), as do references in chapters 21 and 22 that call for capital punishment (21:12,14–17, 22:18–20) and the LORD calling Israel into battle on more than one occasion (Exod 17:8–14, Josh 6–12). The principle behind this command calls for honoring human life—life created in the image of God (Gen 1:26–27, 9:5–6). Thus, honor for life not only refuses murder, but upholds life and provides for human life with dignity.

Command Seven: *Do not commit adultery.* Earlier, I mentioned the questions that a perimeter ethic raises about the seventh commandment. As a principle, however, this command leads us to faithfulness in our covenant relationships, and to respect those of others. Reasoning in terms of principles helps avoid a potential death trap in fence-line thinking. For example, since domestic abuse is not "sexual adultery," some claim that God demands an abused spouse (usually a woman) to stay with her husband. Our decision between a *perimeter ethic* and *centering principles* is no idle academic exercise! A principle is at stake, not simply stepping over a line. When a husband strikes his wife, his action breaks covenant. That does not mean she must leave him, but it also does not mean the LORD demands that she stay in a physically abusive relationship.

Command Eight: *You shall not steal.* A commandment against theft, like the other commandments, is essential for community life—especially for a nomadic group living together in close quarters. But then again, the commandment is no less relevant for an urban society in the twenty-first century, nor is the principle that undergirds the command. God's people are called to respect and value the work and possessions of others. Consequently, the interests of a God-follower change from what he or she can do without breaking the law, to how they may best honor another person's work and property. In this light, many typical fence line debates vanish: copying a friend's CD onto our playlist, passing off a used car as better than it is, or turning in a paper lifted from the internet. The covenant requires a shift in priorities from self (e.g., what I want, what I can get for me) to other people who work to make my life better, even the waiter or waitress serving a meal. It is a sad commentary on believers that the after-church Sunday lunch crowd notoriously gives the worst tips of the week to wait staff. The eighth commandment calls God's people to a higher principle.

Command Nine: *Do not give false testimony against your neighbor.* The command specifically envisions a judicial setting, in which we are called to give testimony for, or against, our neighbor. The supporting principle is perhaps the most obvious of all the commandments: God's people are to be people of truth, the whole truth, and nothing but the truth. And yet this principle is, in fact, a principle, not an absolute law; and principles are always guided by even higher values (e.g., love for God and love for others, Deut 6:5; 10:12, 19; Lev 19:18, 34; Matt 22:34–40; Mark 12:28–34). Consequently, freed from fence line religion, sometimes the most covenant-loyal action is to lie. The midwives in Egypt found themselves in this position and the LORD rewarded them (Exod 1:17–20); and soon in our story, Rahab will hide and lie about Israelite spies (Josh 2:2–7). In fact, such challenges continue to occur in modern history, e.g., in Nazi Germany where many Christians decided God's desire was for them to hide Jews and others at risk, lie to interrogators, and risk their lives for the lives of others—the supreme act of love (John 15:13).

Command Ten: *Do not crave your neighbor's house.* The final command is itself a statement of an attitude that, if left unchecked, will lead to all types of trouble. Like the sixth commandment, but more pervasive, the traditional translation of this command is problematic: "Do not covet" (KJV, NRSV, NIV) has little, if any meaning today (the CEB is not much better in its translation, "do not desire"). The Hebrew verb (*hmd*) reaches beyond the idea of *desire* or *wanting something* to the point of an *illicit desire that consumes a person* and *leads them to do anything* to get the object of their desire; hence, my translation "Do not crave." Contentment, satisfaction, and serenity are on the opposite pole of craving or coveting; not the lack of desire, but peace with what we have or what we must do to rightfully earn the object of our desire. That said, there is no greater disease that we in the United States struggle with than a raging materialistic consumerism that teaches and urges us to crave (covet) more and more: *What we need to be happy is always something more than we have, often something we cannot afford to purchase. But wait—fast credit is easy . . .* and we only discover when it's too late that we have bought into a lie that destroys us.

Conclusion: As our review of the ten basic principles comes to a close, one observation needs emphasis. Each of the Ten Commandments relates to life with Yahweh—the first four directly pertaining to God, and the last six to life with other people. As briefly mentioned above, the message is vital: how we deal with and interact with others is part of our relationship with God. My relationship with God includes Sabbath rest (Command Four) and honoring my parents (Command Five); life with God demands a single-minded allegiance to the LORD (Command One) and being truthful with others (Command Nine). The New Testament makes explicit what the Ten Commandments presume everyone knows: it is impossible to love God without loving other people (1 John 2:9–10, 4:20–21). Or, as Jesus replied when he was asked what is the most important command,

Text in Conversation

The book of Deuteronomy takes as its setting the end of Israel's time in the wilderness (just ahead in Chapter Six). Israel is ready to enter the promised land as Moses steps up to remind the people of the covenant that they have with the LORD (not just their parents, Deut 5:1–3). Moses will repeat many of the laws from Exodus 21–23 (and elsewhere), and he will develop several prominent themes unique to Deuteronomy. He also repeats the Ten Commandments (Deut 5:6–21) just as we find them in Exodus 20, with one noticeable and significant difference. In Exodus, Moses explains that Israel keeps the Sabbath because the LORD finished creation in six days and rested on the seventh: "That is why the LORD blessed the Sabbath day and made it holy" (Exod 20:11). In Deuteronomy, however, Moses appeals to Israel's experience in Egyptian slavery and the LORD's rescue as the foundational reason for the Sabbath. Israel should rest and allow every person in the household (male and female, slave or free) to rest because of their memory of what it is like to be a slave who is never allowed to rest (Deut 5:15). A rationale more fitting and compelling for people about to cross the Jordan and begin new lives in the land of their own.

This change allows us to see that, as circumstances change, so does the basis of appeal for allowing the LORD's instruction. But even more, as life for God's people changes, so too do some of the specific laws. For example, while the people were encamped around the tabernacle, all animals to be butchered for food must be presented as peace offerings at the tabernacle to prevent sacrifices to goat demons in the wilderness (Lev 17:5–7). But once the Israelites are in the land and it becomes unreasonable to travel to the tabernacle or temple, the law changes: a person may slaughter an animal in their home town, as long as they do not eat the blood (Deut 12:20–25). Thus, we learn important insights into the nature of the Law in the Old Testament. The law is not hard and inflexible, but elastic, so that it may change as circumstances change—as long as the principle remains intact.

> *You must love the Lord your God with all your heart, with all your being, and with all your mind.* This is the first and greatest commandment. And the second is like it: *You must love your neighbor as you love yourself.* All the Law and the Prophets depend on these two commands. (Matt 22:37–40)

In the same way, the Ten Commandments pertain to life with God, directly in the first four commands, and, just as important, indirectly in the last six commands.

III. The Covenant Code and Its Purpose

As part of the covenant/marriage service in Exodus 24, Moses "wrote down all the LORD's words" (24:4). Later in the service, "he took the covenant scroll" and read it to the people for their agreement. Most likely, this scroll consisted of an early form of Exodus 21–23, what scholars aptly call the "Covenant Code." This short book serves several purposes in the growing story of the LORD's relationship to Israel. First, the Covenant Code continues to clarify what a relationship with the LORD looks like. On the one hand, the Code does this by providing explanations for how the community may put the Ten Commandments into effect. It would be wonderful if Israel only had to articulate its guiding principles, speak the subsequent laws, and everyone would agree and obey. In real life, however, every nation must deal with what to do when its principles are broken. This is the first benefit of the Covenant Code.

For example, the sixth commandment said, "You shall not murder" (20:13, NRSV). But what is the community to do if there is a murder? The Covenant Code raises the key questions to be asked: Was the murder premeditated or accidental (21:12–14)? Had the ox that gored a person to death done so in the past? If so, was the owner warned to take precautions (21:28–32)? Or what if, despite the eighth command, a theft takes place? Again, what are the key questions for the community to process? The Covenant Code helps: when a thief is caught selling stolen goods, what should be the penalty (22:1, 4)? What if a thief is caught breaking into a home during the night and the homeowner kills the intruder—is the homeowner guilty of murder (22:2–3)? Or, what if the theft is an action some might not recognize as theft? What if I graze my herd on someone else's field (22:5, effectively stealing what their herds would have eaten), or if I set a fire that burns someone's grain (22:6, effectively stealing their grain)?

The many questions raised by the Covenant Code are a matter of dealing with **casuistic law** or "case law" (if—then) as compared to the all-encompassing statements of law in the Ten Commandments (**apodictic law**). With all its statements of casuistic law, the Covenant Code is attempting to establish *lex talionis*, the **law of talion**—in other words, the punishment must fit the crime.

> If there is further injury, then you will give a life for a life, an eye for an eye, a tooth for a tooth, a hand for a hand, a foot for a foot, a burn for a burn, a bruise for a bruise, a wound for a wound. (21:23–25)

The reader should be careful not to fall into either of two common misunderstandings of this statement of talion. First, *lex talionis* is a principle for communal or state law, not private vendettas (a point misunderstood by the time of Christ, Matt 5:38–42). In fact, most nations (including the United States) attempt to set up law systems on the basis of *lex talionis*—the punishment should fit the crime. Second, just because a law may permit a harsh penalty, does not mean that punishment is carried out to the full extent of the law. *Lex talionis* sets the upper limit of fair punishment; but in most cases, reduced sentences and what we would call "plea bargains" occur (see Exod 21:28–30).

The Covenant Code also continues to clarify life with the LORD by the statement of other apodictic laws. Some of these laws are understandable and leave us to again consider the principles behind the laws: Don't mistreat or oppress an immigrant, because you were once immigrants in the land of Egypt. Don't treat any widow or orphan badly (22:20–21). Other laws, however, undoubtedly made sense for ancient Israel, but challenge our imaginations as to their inner logic:

"Don't boil a young goat in its mother's milk" (23:19b, perhaps on the basis of compassion for the mother?). And then there are laws we would prefer not to imagine: "Anyone who has sexual relations with an animal should be put to death" (22:18; and unfortunately, laws tend to be written because people are doing what they should recognize as forbidden or wrong). In what follows, we briefly explore two groups of laws that further clarify life with God:

The Poor. The Ten Commandments say nothing about the poor. The Covenant Code, however, steps in with instruction for how God's people should treat the poor. The Code itself begins with instructions regarding debt slavery and fair treatment of those who have paid their debt or served a maximum of six years (21:2–11). In no particular order, the Code forbids partiality to the poor in a lawsuit (23:3), just as it condemns bribes and perverting justice away from the poor (23:6–8). The Code also dictates appropriate financial interactions with the poor; it assumes the LORD's people will help the poor with loans (for survival, not a new house). In such cases, (1) taking interest on a loan to a poor person is unthinkable; no one should take advantage of the poor in order to make money from their misfortune (22:25). (2) If a loan is made to the poor, it is appropriate to ask for collateral; but, if their only collateral is the cloak they sleep in, it must be returned each night—which will discourage taking such collateral at all (22:26–27).

The Alien and Enemy. Along with the widow and orphan, the Covenant Code forbids any practice that would "wrong or oppress" a resident alien, on the grounds that Israel should remember what it is like to be an alien mistreated in a foreign country (22:21; 23:9). As for an enemy, he or she is to receive treatment equal to that of a friend. If their donkey has fallen under a heavy load, a person in covenant relationship with the LORD will help free the donkey (23:5); and if their donkey is going astray, a person in covenant relationship with the LORD will catch it and bring it back to its master—the enemy (23:4).

An Excursus: Israel's Law Codes and Ancient Near Eastern Law Codes

The existence of ancient Near Eastern law codes from numerous sources should no longer come as a surprise to most students. Archaeologists have unearthed and advances in linguistics have translated law codes (most are fragmentary) from as long ago as the early third millennium BCE: the Code of Ur-Nammu (2050 BCE), the Code of Eshnunna (1980 BCE), the Code of Lipit-Ishtar (1930 BCE), and, most famous, the complete Code of Hammurabi (1792–1750 BCE). It should also come as no surprise that many biblical laws have counterparts in ancient Near Eastern legal codes that say essentially the same thing as the biblical text. In order for the student to get a feel for these law codes, both biblical and non-biblical, the following chart provides comparable laws from the Covenant Code in Exodus (NRSV) and the Code of Hammurabi (translated by Martha Roth):

Topic	Covenant Code (Exodus nrsv)	Code of Hammurabi
Debt Slavery	When you buy a male or female slave, he shall serve six years, but in the seventh he shall go out a free person, without debt. (21:2)	If . . . he sells or gives into debt service his wife, his son, or his daughter, they shall perform service in the house of their buyer or of the one who holds them in debt service for three years; their release shall be secured in the fourth year. (117)
Goring Ox	When an ox gores a man or a woman to death, the ox shall be stoned, and its flesh shall not be eaten; but the owner of the ox shall not be liable. If the ox has been accustomed to gore in the past, and its owner has been warned but has not restrained it, and it kills a man or a woman, the ox shall be stoned, and its owner also shall be put to death. If a ransom is imposed on the owner, then the owner shall pay whatever is imposed for the redemption of the victim's life. . . . If the ox gores a male or female slave, the owner shall pay to the slave owner thirty shekels of silver, and the ox shall be stoned (21:28–32)	If an ox gores to death a man while it is passing through the streets, that case has no basis for a claim. (250) If a man's ox is a known gorer, and the authorities . . . notify him that it is a known gorer, but he does not blunt its horns or control his ox, and that ox gores to death a member of the noble class, he shall give 30 shekels of silver. (251) If it is a man's slave, he shall give 20 shekels of silver . . . (252)
Miscarriage	When people who are fighting injure a pregnant woman so that there is a miscarriage, and yet no further harm follows, the one responsible shall be fined what the woman's husband demands, paying as much as the judges determine. If any harm follows, then you shall give life for life . . . (21:22–23)	If a noble strikes a woman of the noble class and thereby causes her to miscarry her fetus, he shall weigh and deliver 10 shekels of silver for her fetus. (209) If that woman should die, they shall kill his daughter. (210) If he should cause a woman of the commoner class to miscarry . . . [he shall pay] 5 shekels of silver. (211) If he strikes a noble's slave woman and [she miscarries] . . . [he shall pay] 2 shekels of silver. (213) If that slave woman die . . . [he shall pay] 20 shekels of silver. (214)
Violent Son or Daughter	Whoever strikes father or mother shall be put to death. (21:15) Whoever curses father or mother shall be put to death. (21:17)	If a child should strike his father, they shall cut off his hand. (195)
Kidnapping	Whoever kidnaps a person, whether that person has been sold or is still held in possession, shall be put to death. (21:16)	If a man should kidnap the child of another man, he shall be killed. (14)
Items for Safekeeping Go Missing	When someone delivers to a neighbor money or goods for safekeeping, and they were stolen from the neighbor's house, then the thief, if caught, shall pay double. If the thief is not caught, the owner of the house shall be brought before God, to determine whether or not the owner had laid hands on the neighbor's goods. (22:7–8)	If a man gives silver, gold, or anything else to another man for safekeeping and he denies it, they shall charge and convict that man, and he shall give twofold that which he denied. (124)

Table 5.1. The Covenant Code and the Code of Hammurabi (see "For Further Reading" for a full translation)

Comparable laws between the Covenant Code of Exodus and the Code of Hammurabi also include theft or loss of property (Exod 22:1–6; Ham. 9–13) and various injuries (Exod 21:24–27; Ham. 196–207). Parallels to almost, if not, every topic in Hammurabi occur in other Old Testament legal texts (e.g., The Covenant Code of Exodus 21–23, The Holiness Code of Leviticus 16–27, The Deuteronomic Code of Deuteronomy 12–26, and scattered texts in Numbers). For example, like Hammurabi (132), when a husband accuses his wife of adultery and the only evidence is that she is pregnant (and the husband does not believe he is the father), she is forced to go through an **ordeal** to prove her innocence. In Hammurabi, however, this ordeal is life-threatening. In Numbers, she is forced to go through an ordeal that will end her pregnancy if she is guilty, but not kill her as in Hammurabi (Num 5:11–31). And although frequent in Hammurabi (195–197, 200, 282), corporal punishment by cutting off some part of the body is assigned in only one biblical case (Deut 25:11–12).

I will suspend my analysis for that of the student and for class discussion, with one exception for the reader to consider. Some would like to claim that the biblical laws and punishments are consistently superior to their ancient Near Eastern counterparts. The evidence, however, simply will not hold the weight of the claim. Let's take two examples from chart above. First, take the case of an ox that gores a person to death and the owner has been warned before about the ox. In Hammurabi, the owner is fined (251–252); but, in the Bible, the ox and its owner are put to death unless the family of the deceased will accept a ransom (Exod 21:29–30). Second, in Exodus, should a person strike their father or mother, they are to be put to death (Exod 21:15); but, in Hammurabi, the person's hand is to be cut off (Ham. 195).

IV. The Significance of the Tabernacle

Marriage is for the purpose of living with the person you love and to whom you have pledged your life. God's "marriage" covenant with Israel was for the same purpose; God loves and wants to live with his people, restoring one piece of the perfection that was lost in Eden. Thus, after the covenant ceremony in Exodus 24, the LORD directs Moses to collect an offering (25:1–7) so Israel might "make me a sanctuary, so that I may dwell among them" (25:8 NRSV). Moses goes back up the mountain to receive the plans for a tabernacle— a tent that included a fenced-in compound (24:18)—plans laid out in Exodus 25–31.

On the one hand, these plans appear incredibly detailed. So much so that any two people should be able to follow the directions and recreate identical tabernacles. On the other hand, various recreations of the tabernacle turn out looking quite different. So, while the detail threatens to overwhelm the reader, the blueprints actually leave a good bit of freedom to the creative abilities of the craftsmen and women. In order for us to get to the purpose and significance of the Tabernacle, it will be necessary to provide a brief sketch of the blueprints and furnishings, with special attention given to the ark of the covenant.

1. A Survey of the Plans (25–27). First, the plans for the tabernacle (see Figures 5.3 and 5.4) begin with the furniture: (a) the ark of the covenant (25:10–22), (b) the table for bread (25:23–30), and (c) the lampstand (25:31–40). Second, the plans lay out the dimensions of the tabernacle and

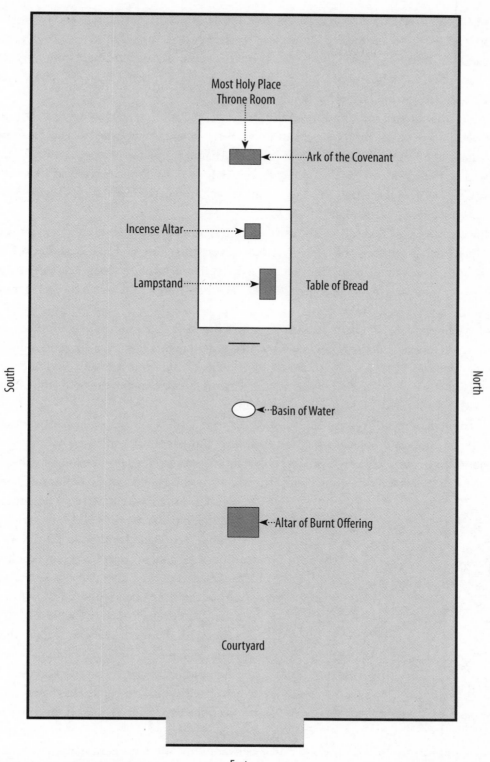

Figure 5.3. Diagram of the Tabernacle

give instructions on how to construct the tent so that it will be portable, yet sturdy and weatherproof (26:1–30). In addition, a screen or curtain separates the tent into two rooms: the holy place and the most holy place (26:31–37). Third, the plans describe the outer courtyard, created by a fence of curtains hung on another portable framework system (27:9–19). The centerpiece of the courtyard is the altar for burnt offerings (27:1–8).

2. Vestments and Ordination of the Priests (28–29). The second section of the plans describes the **vestments** for the **priests** who will work in and around the tabernacle—especially the ornate robe, ephod (long vest), breastplate, turban, and sash of the high priest (28:1–39)—followed by the vestments for the other priests (28:40–43). Next, the text describes procedures for the ordination of the priests (29:1–35), the consecration of the altar (29:36–37), and the daily offerings to be made at the altar (29:38–44).

3. Furniture and Taxes (30). The third section returns to descriptive plans: (a) for two additional pieces of furniture—the altar of incense (30:1–10)—and a large bronze basin for water (30:17–21), (b) an annual temple tax that will support the needs of the tabernacle (30:11–16), and (c) the recipes for making anointing oil (30:22–33) and incense (30:34–38) for use in anointing priests and objects in the tabernacle.

4. Workers (31). The final section identifies the lead craftsmen for the building project, Bezalel and Oholiab (31:1–11), and closes with a restatement and expansion of the Sabbath law from Exodus 20 (31:12–17). This reiteration of the Sabbath law stands as a reminder to those about to start work on God's tent: no matter what the work may be, the Sabbath rest must be observed, even if the work is making God's tent.

5. The Ark of the Covenant (25:10–22). The instructions for the tabernacle begin with the single most important object or piece of furniture. But why this is so and what the ark of the covenant is, is not immediately clear. The blueprints describe a small box, no longer than four feet, just over two feet wide, and two feet high. The box or chest is plated with gold, has gold trimming, feet at each corner, and rings of gold fastened to each foot so that the box may be lifted and carried by two long poles (also plated with gold). A lid or "mercy seat" made of gold fits over the top of the chest, and on either end of the lid sit cherubs—fierce angelic creatures that face one another, with wings spread out over the ark that touch in the middle.

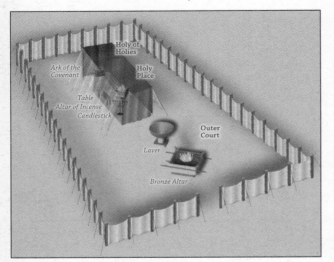

Figure 5.4. An Artist's Rendering of the Tabernacle

The instructions are clear enough. But the bigger question remains: What have we built? In Exodus 25, the Lord says, in reference to the ark, "There I will meet with you. From there above the cover, from between the two winged heavenly creatures that are on top of the chest containing the covenant, I will deliver to you all that I command you concerning the Israelites" (25:22). Two later texts help further identify the ark—and why it is so important. First, Leviticus 16 warns the high priest, Aaron, that "he cannot come whenever he wants into the holy area inside the inner curtain, to the front of the cover that is on the chest, or else he will die, because I am present in the cloud above the cover" (16:2). In some way, the LORD appears above the mercy seat—either above the lid or, more likely, above the wings of the cherubs. But again, why? The mystery continues for us until the book of First Samuel, when the Israelites urgently call for the priests to bring the ark to join them in battle:

897.—Ancient Egyptian Palanquin.

Figure 5.5. An Egyptian Palanquin

> So the people sent to Shiloh and brought from there the chest containing the covenant of the LORD of heavenly forces, *who sits enthroned* on the winged heavenly creatures. (1 Sam 4:4, emphasis mine)

Mystery solved. The ark of the covenant is a portable throne for Yahweh, to match the portable tabernacle. Once we recognize the ark, we recall that monarchs throughout the ancient Near East used palanquins similar to the ark for travel (see figure 5.5). More important, we recognize that the holy of holies, the Hebraic way of saying "the holiest place," is the LORD's throne room, where the LORD sits enthroned upon the wings of the cherubim.

6. Implementing the Plans: The final chapters of Exodus put the plans for the LORD's tabernacle into motion. After another brief reminder to keep the Sabbath (35:1–3), Moses asks for donations of the vast array of material needed for constructing the tabernacle (35:4–9) and calls for all those with skill to come forward to the work (35:10–19, 35:30–36:1). Moses gets both. Every morning the people continue to bring freewill offerings to the workers, until finally, the workers pass word to Moses that the people are bringing too much, far more than is needed to complete the work (36:5). So Moses gives an unusual command for a religious leader: stop giving. No one else was to bring any offering for the project (36:6–7).

Conclusion

The writer describes the creation of the tabernacle in mind-numbing detail (at least for Westerners), from the tabernacle itself (36:8–38), to the furniture to go inside (37:1–29), to the courtyard and its outdoor "furniture"—the water basin for washing and the Altar of Burnt Offering (38:1–20)—along with a summary of the craftsmen employed and materials used (38:21–31). Relentless, detailed descriptions of making the priests' vestments follow (39:1–31), until the work is declared finished: "The Israelites did *everything just exactly as the* LORD had commanded Moses" (39:32, emphasis mine). Now the unassembled parts are brought to Moses: hooks, frames, pillars, bars, animal hides, curtains, cords, pegs, and so much more (39:32–43). When Moses sees that "they in fact had done all the work *exactly as the* LORD had commanded, Moses blessed them" (39:43, emphasis mine).

Now, it is time for Moses (and those he directs) to erect the tabernacle and do everything "*exactly as the* LORD had commanded" (40:1–33; see vv. 16, 19b, 21b, 23b, 25b, 27b, 29b, 32b). And when the LORD moves into his palace: the glory of the LORD fills and consumes the tabernacle (40:34–35).

To Discuss

1. Read Exodus 19:4–6 carefully. For what purposes does the LORD "marry" Israel? In other words, what was Israel to be or become? How do you think Israel was to fulfill her purposes? How do the promises made to Abraham and Sarah relate to the purposes the LORD identifies for Israel in Exodus 19:4–6?

2. How do you read the Ten Commandments? As a perimeter ethic, centering principles, or in some other way? What are the strengths and weaknesses of each approach? (Read Matt 5:17–48; recognizing that "you have heard it said" refers to common teachings of their day, not necessarily what the OT teaches.) How do Jewish leaders during the life of Christ approach the commandments? How does Jesus read them?

3. The author makes a case for principles behind the Ten Commandments. Which commandment/principle do you think he has wrong or is his case weak? For which of the commandments would you argue a different principle? Go for it. If the class agrees and you believe your argument is sound, write to the author (see contact information through ACU Press).

4. The author claims that principles (e.g., truthfulness) are to be guided by a higher value (e.g., love). Do you agree or disagree with this claim? In what ways could this ethical system be misused? Can you think of any form of checks and balances to keep love from disregarding any or all of the commandments?

5. What is the principle of *lex talionis*? Is *lex talionis* a core principle of your nation's law code? Do you see places in your society where this principle breaks down (i.e., doesn't work so well)? What are common misunderstandings of *lex talionis*? How has your understanding of Exodus 21:23–25 and Matthew 5:38–42 changed as a result of this chapter? What new questions do you now have?

6. The chapter warns that it suspends its own analysis of the comparison between the Covenant Code (Exod 21–23) and the Code of Hammurabi for the sake of class discussion. So . . . what questions does the comparison of law codes raise for you? What do you take away from the comparison?

7. What is the crisis at the end of the book of Exodus? Does Israel understand the risk it is taking (depending on your previous answer)? So, what do you think of Israel now?

To Know

1. The significance of the following in this chapter:

Apodictic Law	*Lex talionis*
Ark of the Covenant	Oholiab
Bezalel	Perimeter ethic
Casuistic Law	Tabernacle
Centering principles	The LORD
Covenant Code	Yahweh

2. The prologue to the Ten Commandment and its significance.

3. Restate the Ten Commandments and articulate the principle behind each command.

4. What the tabernacle is and its purpose.

5. Be able to identify the objects and places in the tabernacle (see Figure 5.3).

6. Be able to identify three ways the Covenant Code clarifies what a relationship with the LORD looks like.

7. Identify two-to-three points of comparison between the Covenant Code and the Code of Hammurabi.

To Dig Deeper: Research Topics

1. From time to time, a public display of the Ten Commandments is debated in the news. Investigate a recent incident. What are the reasons for and against the display? If possible, your investigation should include believers on both sides of the question. How does your investigation change your opinion, if at all? What new questions does your research raise?

2. Continue researching into ancient Near Eastern law codes. Select a topic to study (with the help of your instructor) that runs through all or most of the law codes, including the Bible. Prepare an analysis of what you find. Formulate a sound hypothesis with support that might explain the similarities and differences.

3. Select one of the topics raised in Exodus 21–23 that you find to be especially interesting. Do some detective work. What do other biblical texts say about the topic? Continue your investigation with cross-analysis of the witnesses. Do the witnesses agree or disagree?

4. Bible majors: Take question 3 a little further. Interview others who have investigated the same topic (in research-level Bible dictionaries, encyclopedias, or journal articles). Prepare a report of your investigation. What are your conclusions? Include your own closing argument.

5. Artists: Read the description of the ark of the covenant carefully (as well as an entry in a research-quality Bible Dictionary, see Appendix V), and prepare your own drawing, painting, etc., based on your research. Write a paragraph that draws attention to and provides support for the decisions you have made.

6. Pre-Law and Political Science students: What piques your curiosity about ancient Near Eastern law (including biblical law)? Work with your instructor to identify a suitable project.

For Further Reading

Brueggemann, Walter. *Sabbath as Resistance: Saying No to the Culture of Now*. Louisville: Westminster John Knox, 2014.

Coogan, Michael D. *A Reader of Ancient Near Eastern Texts: Sources for the Study of the Old Testament*. New York: Oxford University Press, 2013. Translation of the Code of Hammurabi by Martha Roth. Note: Other law codes are also available in the resources for ancient Near Eastern materials (see chapter 3).

Friedman, Richard Elliot. "Tabernacle." Pages 292–300 in vol. 6 of *The Anchor Bible Dictionary*. Edited by David Noel Freedman. 6 vols. New York: Doubleday, 1992.

Miller, Patrick D. *The Way of the Lord: Essays on Old Testament Theology*. Grand Rapids: Eerdmans, 2007. Part One of this book includes many excellent studies on the Ten Commandments (pp. 3–163).

———. *The Ten Commandments*. Interpretation: Resources for the Use of Scripture in the Church. Louisville: Westminster John Knox Press, 2009.

Leaving **Sinai**
Round and Round We Go

6

READING ASSIGNMENTS
EXODUS 32–34
LEVITICUS 1–5, 16, 19, 25
NUMBERS 11–17, 20–25

KEY TERMS
Atonement: to make amends for a wrong or for causing ritual impurity; to cleanse what is polluted

Blood: a ritual detergent for making objects and people clean

Clean/Unclean: categories for objects and people; their ritual status

Ordain: to appoint to a religious office or role

Sanctify: to make an object or person especially holy, or set apart for God

Seer: a term for a prophet

Tribe: an extended family group of one of Jacob/Israel's sons

Transjordan: the land on the East side of the Jordan River

At the end of Exodus, all the fanfare associated with the LORD moving into the tabernacle masked serious problems—matters of life and death, or, if possible, even worse. Despite appearances, the marriage between Yahweh and Israel is on the rocks, about to break up after only a short time together. So we begin this new chapter with an attempt to understand the couple's problem(s), and to get to the bottom of the matter, we must return to Exodus 32–34. After getting a grip on the problem, we will then see how Yahweh resolves the crisis in Leviticus. Finally, fully prepared and organized in Numbers 1–10, we will leave Mount Sinai for the promised land, with yet more crises erupting on the journey, followed by God's intervention (Num 11–36). Our study, then, follows the contours of the text—crisis/resolution, crisis/resolution, crisis/resolution, on and on it goes—and the faith issues that emerge, trying to ask the right questions that will help us see and understand God better.

I. The Rebellion at Sinai (Exodus 32–34)

Shortly after the covenant/wedding service for Yahweh and Israel, Yahweh called Moses up the mountain with two stones for the Ten Commandments, and to give him the plans for the tabernacle (Exod 25–31). Whatever the cause, Yahweh kept Moses up on the mountain, away from the people, for an extended time (40 days, Exod 24:15–18)—too long for the nervous newlywed Israelites at the base of the mountain. They panic at the apparent loss of their leader and their God and come to Aaron in desperation, "Come on! Make us gods who can lead us. As for this man Moses who brought us up out of the land of Egypt, we don't have a clue what has happened to him" (32:1). Aaron shows no hesitation, and even seems to jump at the opportunity, "All right, take out the gold rings from the ears of your wives, your sons, and your daughters, and bring them to me" (32:2). They do, and Aaron casts a golden image of a young bull; he then proclaims, "These are your gods, Israel, who brought you up out of the land of Egypt!" (32:4). And, I have no idea what was going through Aaron's mind when he then built an altar in front of the calf and announced: "Tomorrow will be a festival to the LORD!" (32:5b). The LORD, *yhwh,* the one who just said . . . *what is the future high priest of Israel thinking?*

It is worth a moment of our time to pause and count the number of primary principles (Ten Commandments) that have been shattered here, within only weeks of the marriage ceremony. To say the very least, the heart of the covenant between Yahweh and Israel has been destroyed. And, as a result of Israel's actions, the LORD threatens two overwhelming and devastating consequences. First, the LORD returns to a well-known formula: kill all the people and start over with someone else—Moses (32:9–10).

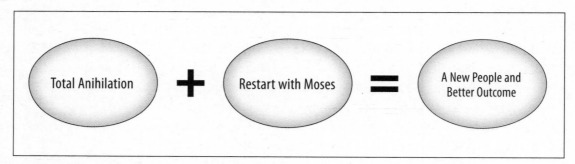

Figure 6.1. A Tried and Not-So-True Formula

We've seen this equation before with the generation of Noah (see Figure 6.1); and it appeared that the LORD had learned then that wiping out one group just to start over with another doesn't work (Gen 8:21). People have the same heart problem wherever you go. So, Moses, in direct defiance of the LORD's command ("Now leave me alone"), steps up and refuses to back down until the LORD hears him out. Moses gives three reasons the LORD must not do what he has threatened.

1. The LORD just told Moses, "Go down at once! *Your* people, whom *you* brought up out of the land of Egypt, are ruining everything" (32:7, emphasis mine). But Moses does not let God off the hook so easily. He responds, "O LORD, why does your fury burn against *your own* people, whom *you* brought out of the land of Egypt" (32:11, emphasis mine). It is like parents arguing over "whose child is this?" when Junior sneaks his pet hamster Buford into church and Buford escapes, running free in the sanctuary, igniting a spirit-filled revival. Moses refuses to let the LORD pass off the ownership of the people to him (Moses). Israel belongs to the LORD and they are the LORD's responsibility.

2. If the LORD wipes out Israel, Moses warns, the LORD will lose his reputation with the Egyptians (and other nations) who will think that the LORD only brought Israel out of Egypt to kill them (32:12).

3. Finally, Moses reminds the LORD of the promises he made to Abraham, Isaac, and Jacob, to make them into a nation and give them the land of promise (32:13).

These brief but strong arguments are enough to persuade the LORD to change his mind (32:14; see Table 6.1). The first crisis is prevented, but Israel is not yet out of danger.

HOLD THAT LINE! Did God *really* change his Mind?	
Your Answer	
If *no*, why does the text say, "the LORD changed his mind"?	If *yes*, why would God change his mind?
Your Answer	
So the best explanation of the text is to say that God was (e.g., kidding, teaching) . . .	
Your Answer	
What do you think Moses would say in response to God's actions (1) if he knew God never really intended to destroy Israel, (2) if he knew God really did intend to destroy them until Moses spoke?	
Your Answer	
Finally, what does your interpretation say about God?	
If God *did not really* change his mind, then God is . . .	If God *really did* change his mind, then God is . . .

Table 6.1. Hold That Line! An Exercise in Interpretation and Theology

The second consequence God threatens comes from love rather than anger. The LORD tells Moses to leave for the land,

> I'll send a messenger before you. I'll drive out the Canaanites. . . . Go to this land full of milk and honey. *But I won't go up with you* because I would end up destroying you along the way since you are a stubborn people. (33:2–3, emphasis mine)

And again:

> You are a stubborn people. If I were to go up with you even for a single moment, I would destroy you. So now take off your jewelry, while I figure out what to do with you. (33:5)

The LORD wants to live with his people, but he realizes there is no way to live with them without killing them. And to their credit, the people also recognize the danger but still want to live with the LORD (33:4, 6); without the LORD, they are nothing. The problem is complex with dire consequences at stake. The LORD loves his people and wants what existed in Eden—to live with them. He has plans for a place to live; *but how?* He is a holy God and they are unholy people; how can a holy God live with the people he loves, and who love him, without killing them?

Moses steps in again. He begins with the same argument he used in the first crisis—remember "this nation is *your people*" (33:13, emphasis mine)—and continues with an ultimatum—"If you won't go yourself, don't make us leave here" (33:15). In other words, if you (the LORD) will not go with us, then we are not going anywhere. Moses is so intense, however, that he fails to hear God speak. Between "this nation is your people" and *if you won't go we won't go*, the LORD agrees, "I'll go myself, and I'll help you" (33:14a).

Because of how important it is to Moses that the LORD goes with them, or perhaps because of his insecurity, Moses pushes for an opportunity to see God: a confirmation that the LORD is still with them (33:18). The LORD explains the danger in Moses's request: to see the LORD fully, face-to-face is deadly. Nonetheless, the LORD agrees to the request with strict conditions for protecting Moses (33:20–23). So Moses comes back up the mountain the next day with two new stone tablets to replace the earlier set Moses broke (see 32:15–20). Then, with Moses protected behind a rock, the LORD descends in a cloud, passes near Moses, and proclaims his name—who he is at his most basic, fundamental level—his nature:

> The LORD! The LORD!
> a God who is compassionate and merciful,
>> very patient,
>> full of great loyalty and faithfulness,
>> showing great loyalty to a thousand generations,
>> forgiving every kind of sin and rebellion,
>> yet by no means clearing the guilty,
>> punishing for their parents' sins

their children and their grandchildren,
    as well as the third and the fourth generation. (34:6–7)

Moses bows in worship in the presence of the LORD and asks one more time, "If you approve of me, my Lord, please go along with us. Although these are stubborn people, forgive our guilt and our sin and take us as your own possession" (34:9).

Both crises have come to a tentative resolution: God does not kill his people and start over with Moses (as the new "Abraham"), and the LORD agrees to go with Israel. Now, after a renewal of the wedding vows (34:10–28), work can begin on the tabernacle (Exod 35–40). Moses oversees putting the structure together for the first time (40:1–33), and the glory of the LORD fills the tabernacle (40:34–38). The LORD has come to live with his people.

What a wonderful, awesome, terrible, bad day! I hope you will reflect on what has happened at the end of Exodus and my claim. It is easy to see what is wonderful and awesome about the LORD moving into the tabernacle to take up residence among his people; one part of what was lost at Eden has been restored. So how could it be a terrible, bad day? The answer is back at Sinai—in the second crisis.

The LORD has moved into the tabernacle to live with his people, but the earlier issue has not yet been resolved: How can God live with the people he loves and not destroy them? How can the people live with the God they love and not die in the process? It is wonderful that God is now living with Israel, but nothing has been done that will enable the relationship to last beyond Israel's next failure. Something must be done to make this relationship possible, and that something—the resolution to the problem—is in the book of Leviticus.

II. The Resolution (Leviticus)

The book of Leviticus is the phone book of the Old Testament; who wants to read a phone book? Many resolutions to read through the Bible in a year have died a long, cruel death in the pages of Leviticus. Readers go in, but they never come out. The causes of death may be many, but ultimately, they don't come back because of the depth at which Leviticus is submerged in ancient Near Eastern culture and the reader's failure to recognize how Leviticus responds to the crisis at the end of Exodus. Without culture and context, readers don't stand a chance. Leviticus does not and will not make sense. If, however, we grant respect to cultural practices over two thousand years old and understand the issues to which Leviticus responds, then we have a better than average chance of survival and a good chance of understanding a difficult book with a tremendous message about God.

To begin, God takes over in Leviticus. Again and again the writer records the words, "The LORD said to Moses." The LORD takes responsibility for finding a way for this troubled relationship to not only have a chance of survival, but to thrive and grow.

1. Sacrifice (Lev 1–7). The sacrifices of Leviticus 1–7 are not all alike, and they are not all about sin. For example, the whole burnt offering (Lev 1) is primarily a voluntary act to express total surrender to the LORD (Lev 22:17–19); with overwhelming joy, a person gives the entire animal to

Figure 6.2. The Concept of Sin and Impurity in the Ancient Near East

the LORD (e.g., Ps 66:13–20). The peace offering (Lev 7:15–17, 32–24), on the other hand, returns part of the meat to the priest and the worshipper for the purpose of a feast or party with family, friends (Ps 54:6–7), and the LORD (Deut 27:6–7; 12:12–18)—a luxurious opportunity to eat meat in a society for which meat was an infrequent or rare treat. Sacrifices for the purpose of **atonement** of sin were also part of the system, though less frequent than most readers imagine. Behind these sacrifices are two critical cultural concepts: (a) sin and human impurity are like airborne pollution that pollutes holy objects such as the tabernacle (see Figure 6.2), and (b) **blood** is a ritual detergent that cleanses what has been polluted by sin or human impurity. So, for the primary atonement sacrifices (the sin offering and the guilt offering), the objective is not just to forgive the offender, but to purify the tabernacle by sprinkling or touching contaminated objects with blood.

Atonement sacrifice involved much more than just bringing an animal to be killed. Careful reading of Leviticus 4–6 reveals that before bringing a sacrifice, a person must realize their offense (4:13–14a), recognize and feel guilty for their wrong (4:13–14; 5:3–5; 6:4–5), confess their sin (5:4–6), and make restitution when appropriate (5:15–16; 6:5–6). Then—and only then—can an atonement sacrifice accomplish forgiveness and the cleansing of the tabernacle. In other words, a process that includes attitudes and actions must precede an atonement sacrifice, or the sacrifice itself is worthless and achieves nothing.

Even so, it is still valid to ask how such a system could ever work to achieve atonement and forgiveness. And Leviticus does claim that God forgives the people (4:20, 26, 31, 35). But how could the death of an animal and use of its blood repair the relationship between God and his people? The key comes later in Leviticus, in a prohibition against eating blood. Leviticus explains,

> A creature's life is in the blood. I have provided you the blood to make reconciliation for your lives on the altar, because the blood reconciles by means of the life. (17:11)

We need to unpack this verse and its cultural assumptions: (a) life is in the blood, (b) God owns all life/all blood (see also Gen 9:3–5), (c) God gives the lifeblood of animals for the purpose of atonement. In other words, the person bringing the sacrifice is not earning or doing anything to achieve forgiveness. Instead, it is God's gift—and only by God's gift of what God owns—that a person can be forgiven and the tabernacle kept clean. A good synopsis of the system in Leviticus comes from the New Testament: "You are saved by God's grace because of your faith. *This salvation is God's gift.* It's not something you possessed" (Eph 2:8, emphasis mine).

2. Priests (Lev 8–10). If the LORD is going to live with Israel, someone must attend to the LORD's home; a tabernacle requires priests. Consequently, Leviticus 8–10 describes how Moses, Aaron, and Aaron's sons followed the directions in Exodus 29 to **ordain** Aaron as high priest and his sons as priests. Their duties included offering various sacrifices, distinguishing "between the holy and the common, and between the **unclean** and the **clean**" (see below), and teaching Israel the word of the LORD (Lev 10:10–11). (On the actions of Nadab and Abihu, see "Dig Deeper" at the end of this chapter.)

Later, all of the men from the **tribe** of Levi will be ordained as aides to the priests at the tabernacle (Num 8). These "Levites" will have special duties to guard and transport the tabernacle, as well as put it up and taking it down (Num 3:4–4:49). One may fairly imagine that the Levites did much more to assist the priests, as long as they did not enter into the tabernacle (the tent) itself.

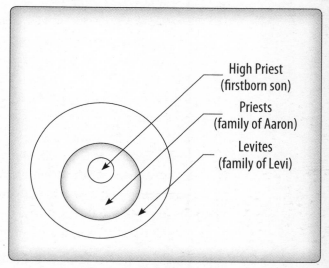

High Priest (firstborn son)

Priests (family of Aaron)

Levites (family of Levi)

Figure 6.3. Levites, Priests, and the High Priest

The relationship among the high priest, priests, and Levites often causes some confusion, which may be remedied with a simple chart (see Figure 6.3). All of these servants are members of the tribe of Levi, and thus, they are all Levites. But not all Levites are from the priestly family of Aaron, from which the firstborn son of the high priest becomes the next high priest.

3. The Purity Code (Lev 11–15). If we have been able to keep one foot in the twenty-first century as we have read Leviticus 1–10, chapters 11–15 demand that we jump into Israel's culture with both feet. However strange the contents of this text may seem, at the end of chapter 15, the writer reminds us what is at stake:

> You must separate the Israelites from their uncleanness so that they don't die on account of it, by making my dwelling unclean, which is in their midst. (15:31)

Every culturally embedded word is about keeping God's tent clean from Israel's impurities (not sin). Five clear sections unfold before us:

a. **Clean versus Unclean Animals (Lev 11).** Israel must discern between clean animals (that may be eaten) and unclean animals that will defile them; instead, Israel must be holy, like her God (11:44–45). Of course, from Israel's perspective, clean animals are those most like those they herd—with split hooves and who chew the cud (11:3): sheep, cows, and goats.

b. **Childbirth (Lev 12).** Uncleanness associated with childbirth must be contained or controlled so that the woman, while unclean from childbirth, does not come into the tabernacle and defile it (12:4).

c. **Leprosy (Lev 13).** Multiple concerns drive this chapter: (1) how to diagnose an infectious disease of the skin (13:59; not "leprosy" as we commonly understand the term), (2) how to recognize dangerous mold or mildew in cloth, leather, or building materials, and (3) the use of quarantine outside the camp to contain communicable diseases (13:45, 46).

d. **Purification Rituals (Lev 14).** The rituals in this chapter are not for the purpose of healing someone with leprosy, but for reincorporating them back into the community after they have become well.

e. **Bodily Discharges (Lev 15).** Once again, this chapter seeks to identify what makes a man or woman unclean—in this case, by bodily discharges (most are sexual in nature). Such discharges have nothing to do with sin. And yet, like other forms of uncleanness, these too threaten the cleanness or purity of the tabernacle (15:31), which, if defiled, leaves God with few options—none of them good.

What is going on with all of the instruction regarding Israel's culture and God's tent? (1) The LORD has fully entered into Israel's culture. So, instead of God saying Israel's way of thinking is backward or stupid, God works with it. (The mark of good cross-cultural communication and a point that should slow our criticism of Israel; no doubt, in a thousand years, people will look back at us and laugh at how backward we were.) (2) Most of what makes a person unclean are normal parts of human life that have nothing to do with sin: reproduction (sex), food (clean and unclean animals), and health. Consequently, for the Israelites, these purity laws may have served as a constant reminder of their humanity (they are not gods). (3) Based on the work of anthropologist Mary Douglas, the food laws may have also reminded Israel of her calling to be holy or pure, the ideal type of human in God's world.

4. The Day of Atonement (Lev 16). The most important place to keep clean is also the most dangerous to clean: God's throne room, the most holy place. Once a year, the LORD provides a way for the high priest to enter this most sacred space, purify it, and live to see another day.

In order for the Day of Atonement to succeed, both the high priest and the people of Israel must fully participate. The high priest must wash and put on the clothes of a common servant before offering the various sacrifices (16:4): first for his own family members and their sin (16:6, 11–14) and then for Israel (16:15–19). In the same way that the high priest humbles himself, the people must also observe the day with no work and fasting (16:29–32). The various rituals on the day, including confessing Israel's sin over a goat that is then led out into the wilderness to be set free, where it belongs among all the other forces in the wilderness that stand against God's good order of life—"demons," so to speak (16:20–22; see also 17:5–7); these rituals cleanse the tabernacle—along with everything and everyone associated with the tabernacle—so that the LORD may continue to live with the people he loves.

5. The Holiness Code (Lev 17–27). The final block in the LORD's plan to live with Israel is a code of conduct that explains to Israel what it means to be holy—to be like the LORD. Notice just a few important points established by these chapters. First, the Holiness Code covers all of life, not just when a person is at worship. Second, the Code emphasizes that because the LORD is the God of the Israelites, they must live by the LORD's standards and not the standards of the gods of Egypt or the gods of the people in the land of promise. The god of a people determines their ethics—how they will live (18:1–5; 26:1–2); so, because Israel's God is holy, Israel must be holy (19:2; 20:7, 26).

Third, the Holiness Code has to do with the presence of the LORD's tent *and the land* to which they are going. If they pollute the land by sin or impurity, the land will vomit them out, just as it is about to vomit out the current residents for their sin (18:24–28; 20:22–26). Or, if Israel pollutes God's tent by sins, such as child sacrifice, God will set his face against them (20:1–5). But if they make the LORD their God and follow the LORD's way of life, then the LORD promises,

> I will place my dwelling among you, and I will not despise you. I will walk around among you; I will be your God, and you will be my people. I am the LORD your God, who brought you out of Egypt's land—who brought you out from being Egypt's slaves. I broke your bonds and made you stand up straight. (26:11–13)

In terms reminiscent of the Garden of Eden, God will be restored to his people.

Fourth and finally, at first glance, God's plan has a flaw the size of the Grand Canyon—a problem the LORD seems to keep forgetting: humans are not and cannot be holy—just take a look back at Gen 8:21. Just when we thought there might be a way for people to walk with LORD, the whole system appears doomed; the Holiness Code will never work. But, if we don't give up and continue to read carefully, we discover another idea:

> You will keep my rules and do them; I am the LORD, *who makes you holy.* (20:8, emphasis mine)

Yes, the LORD wants obedience; but, at the end of the day, it is the LORD who makes people holy. Consider another text:

> You must keep my commands and do them; I am the LORD. You must not make my holy name impure so that I will be treated as holy by the Israelites. I am the LORD—*the one who makes you holy* and who is bringing you out of the land of Egypt to be your God; I am the LORD. (22:31–33, emphasis mine)

The LORD wants people to follow his ways and he understands that people cannot be or make themselves holy. Only God can make a person holy—like God; and that is what God determines to do. What appeared impossible at the end of Exodus is not just possible, but certain, because it depends on what God does in the lives of his followers.

III. The Journey to the Promised Land (The Book of Numbers)

The Israelites break camp almost a full year after arriving at Mount Sinai (compare Exod 19:1–2 and Num 10:11–13), but only after final instructions, a census for the purpose of forming an army, and preparations for the trip across the wilderness to the promised land (Num 1:1–10:10; see Appendix V). Over the past eleven months, they have learned much about the God of their ancestors, the God of Abraham and Sarah, the God who sent Moses, Aaron, and their sister, Miriam, to lead Israel out of Egypt (Mic 6:4). They have also entered into a covenant relationship with this God (Exod 24), learning more and more what the LORD is like and what they are called to become (Lev 17–26). But it is time to leave Sinai and test their young faith in Yahweh against the harsh realities of life in the wilderness. Now God's people must answer a simple and difficult question: Has Sinai changed you? Will you trust the God who not only saved you from Egypt, but who has committed himself to you in love? So, just as the Israelites were challenged to live by faith on their way from Egypt to Mount Sinai (Exod 12–19), now, as they leave Mount Sinai, they must decide what their experience with the LORD at Sinai will mean for life away from Sinai: Now will they trust the LORD?

In the heart of the book of Numbers (12–21), the writer relates seven stories in which everyone in Israel—from the leaders to the people—are challenged to live by faith. The first story sets the pattern for what is to come in subsequent stories: the people complain about their troubles (11:1a), the LORD hears and becomes angry (11:1b), and his anger turns to punishment. Here, the LORD's fire begins to consume outlying parts of the camp (11:1c). The people cry out to Moses (11:2a), he prays to the LORD (11:2b), and "the fire subsided" (11:2c). This basic pattern holds for all but one of the seven stories (the political challenge in 12:1–16; see Figure 6.4).

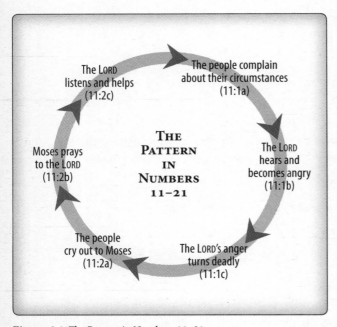

Figure 6.4. The Pattern in Numbers 11–21

Rather than rehearse each of the seven stories (see Figure 6.5), we focus on four key themes. First, the LORD has higher expectations for the people after Sinai than before. Prior to Sinai, the Israelites struggle with many of the same problems they face after Sinai: fear in the face of the Egyptian army (14:10–14), a lack of drinkable water (15:22–25), a lack of food (16:2–4), and no water at all (17:2–7). Before Sinai, in each crisis the LORD provides what the people need without any punishment for their lack of trust. After Sinai, however, when the people complain about these same issues, the Lord becomes angry and strikes out against his people before providing what they want or need: a fire burns in the camp for the vague complaint about their troubles (11:1–2), a plague comes after their craving for meat (11:33), fear of the armies in the promised land costs the adult generation their lives (14:33–34), Moses and Aaron's failure to trust the Lord also costs them entry into the land (20:10–12), and Israel's impatience brings poisonous snakes (21:4–6). What the Lord overlooks and takes in stride before Sinai is not excused after Sinai. After the people have accepted the covenant and been taught the Lord's ways, the Lord has higher expectations for his people than for those who do not know the Lord.

Second, the people continue a trend set before arriving at Sinai of complaining to Moses and the Lord. See if you can identify themes that emerge when we put their complaints together before and after Sinai. At the beginning, facing the Egyptian army, the people said to Moses,

> Weren't there enough graves in Egypt that you took us away to die in the desert? What have you done to us by bringing us out of Egypt like this? Didn't we tell you the same thing in Egypt? "Leave us alone! Let us work for the Egyptians!" It would have been better for us to work for the Egyptians than to die in the desert. (Exod 14:11–12)

When the food ran out, they said,

> Oh, how we wish that the Lord had just put us to death while we were still in the land of Egypt. There we could sit by the pots cooking meat and eat our fill of bread. Instead, you've brought us out into this desert to starve this whole assembly to death. (16:3)

And when the water ran out,

> Why did you bring us out of Egypt to kill us, our children, and our livestock with thirst? (17:3)

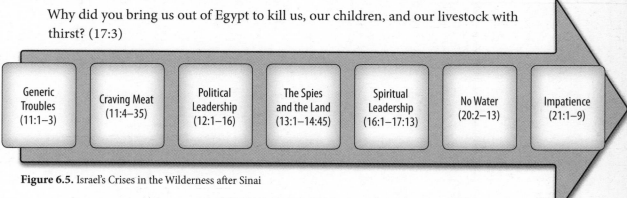

Figure 6.5. Israel's Crises in the Wilderness after Sinai

Then, after nearly a year at Sinai, they leave and their complaints resume. When they crave meat, they say,

> The riffraff among them had a strong craving. Even the Israelites cried again and said, "Who will give us meat to eat? We remember the fish we ate in Egypt for free, the cucumbers, the melons, the leeks, the onions, and the garlic." (Num 11:4–5)

After the spies return with their negative assessment of invading the land,

> All the Israelites criticized Moses and Aaron. The entire community said to them, "If only we had died in the land of Egypt or if only we had died in this desert! Why is the LORD bringing us to this land to fall by the sword? Our wives and our children will be taken by force. Wouldn't it be better for us to return to Egypt?" So they said to each other, "Let's pick a leader and let's go back to Egypt." (14:2–4)

When Korah and his group challenge Aaron's family over the priesthood, they begin with an accusation:

> You've gone too far, because the entire community is holy, every last one of them, and the LORD is with them. Why then do you exalt yourselves above the LORD's assembly? (16:3)

And responding to Moses's request to come to the tabernacle,

> We won't come up! Isn't it enough that *you've brought us up from a land full of milk and honey* to kill us in the desert so that you'd also dominate us? Moreover, you haven't brought us to a land full of milk and honey, nor given us the inheritance of field and vineyard. Would you also gouge out the eyes of these men? We won't come up! (16:12–14, emphasis mine)

Again, when the water runs out,

> If only we too had died when our brothers perished in the LORD's presence! Why have you brought the LORD's assembly into this desert to kill us and our animals here? Why have you led us up from Egypt to bring us to this evil place without grain, figs, vines, or pomegranates? And there's no water to drink! (20:3–5)

Finally, when they become impatient they again speak against the LORD and Moses,

> Why did you bring us up from Egypt to kill us in the desert, where there is no food or water. And we detest this miserable bread! (21:5)

I have listed and provided all these citations in order to identify common themes that emerge when we see all of these texts together. But instead of identifying the common themes that I see, let me provide some clues for what you might look for (please do not limit yourself to these clues):

1. What do they think about the past? How does their image of the past develop? Finally, what significant terminology do they use to describe their past life?
2. What do they wish for . . . over and over again? How do you read this wish, as literal or other?
3. Who do they complain against?
4. Why do they complain so often? And why with such strong language or dramatic flair?

The Message of the Old Testament

So many stories about so many people and so many events, sometimes it is not easy to see the big picture. So we pause to ask, "What's it all about?" or maybe, "What does it mean?" or even better, "Who is it all about?"

> *The LORD! The LORD! (Exod 34:6)*

The LORD is the star, the hero of Genesis through Deuteronomy, not Moses or any other human. And despite a delay, for reasons only briefly explained (Gen 15:16), the LORD is determined to rescue his people: to enter their world, punch out any god with a claim on them, and bring them out of slavery (Exod 1–12). The LORD is determined to prove his reliabilty as Moses leads them to Sinai, no matter the crisis, and to show his love and ability to take care of his people (Exod 13–19). The LORD wants nothing less than to live with his people in a covenant relationship (Exod 20–24), even when the people shatter the covenant by turning to other gods (Exod 32–34).

> *a God who is compassionate and merciful,*
>> *very patient, full of great loyalty and faithfulness,*
>> *showing great loyalty to a thousand generations,*
>> *forgiving every kind of sin and rebellion . . . (Exod 34:6–7)*

Still, the LORD is determined—too much is riding on the success of the LORD's plan (Gen 12:1–3; Exod 19:5–6). So the LORD forgives and pitches his own tent in the middle of the camp (Exod 40). That's not to say that the LORD just looks the other way when the people fail to live up to their promises—to be like their God.

> *yet by no means clearing the guilty,*
> *punishing for their parents' sins*
> *their children and their grandchildren,*
> *as well as the third and the fourth generations. (Exod 34:7)*

But even when there appears to be no way the relationship can last past Israel's next betrayal, the LORD makes a way (Lev 1–26). Disappointment after disappointment, the people struggle to trust, to understand that the LORD is not like all the other gods they've known (Num 10–36). But regardless, the LORD continues with them for the sake of his love, for the sake of the world.

Finally, not a common theme in the text, but a worthwhile consideration: Can you identify with the Israelites and their complaints? Can you understand where they are coming from and empathize with them?

The complaints witness to a claim the text makes about Moses: "The man Moses was very humble, more so than anyone on the face of the earth" (Num 12:3 NRSV). The strength to handle all of the accusations made against him comes from humility, an awareness of who he is in relationship to the Lord. Moses recognizes that as long as he is in a leadership position of the Lord's people, their complaints against him are really complaints against the Lord. For example, early in his experience, "The people argued with Moses and said, 'Give us water to drink.' Moses said to them, 'Why are you arguing with me? *Why are you testing the* Lord?'" (Exod 17:2, emphasis mine). This humility, a strength from knowing who he is in relationship to the Lord, is the only thing that can account for Moses continually fighting for these people—praying to the Lord on their behalf over and over (e.g., Num 11:2, 12:11, 21:7), and going to bat for them when the Lord is ready to kill them and start over with Moses (14:13–19, 16:10–22, 16:45–50). Moses is not perfect; he has his moments when he has had all he can take from Israel and moments he also fails to trust the Lord (e.g., Num 1:10–15, 16:13, 20:6–13), but he is also an exemplary leader. He knows that Israel belongs to the Lord (not to himself) and that he is a servant of the Lord (he is not God). So, he works tirelessly for the Lord on behalf of the people, even when—especially when—he knows that he will never enter the land to which he has been leading the people for all these years.

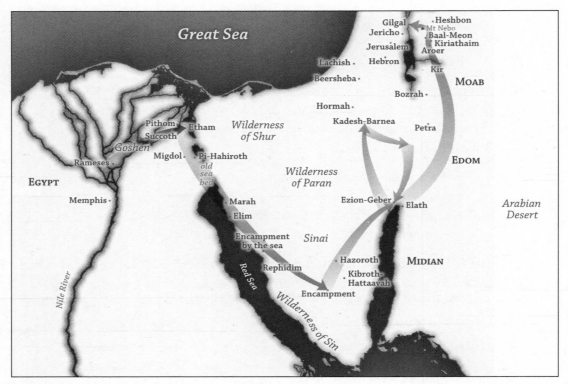

Figure 6.6. A Possible Route of the Wilderness Wandering

Conclusion

Four events at the end of Numbers position Israel for an invasion of the promised land. First, by the time Israel's complaints end, the nation has begun to move up into the **Transjordan** region, east of the Jordan, with the promised land on the other side of the river. Here, they begin to fight and take lands in which they settle: the conquest, for all practical purposes, has begun. Two kings are defeated, whose names become famous later in Israel's literature: King Sihon of the Amorites (Num 21:21–32) and King Og of Bashan (Num 21:33–35; see Ps 136:16–22). Another king is so alarmed by Israel's presence that he will do anything to save his kingdom. So Balak, the king of Moab, sends for a famous prophet to come curse Israel and stop them—Balaam, who lives at Pethor on the Euphrates River (22:1–7).

Balaam's story is filled with humor and irony (a talking donkey who can see better than the famous **Seer**, 22:22–35), mystery (why does God approve of Balaam's mission and then become angry with him for going? 22:20, 22–35), and frustration for King Balak who hired Balaam to curse Israel. Time after time, despite Balak's instructions, Balaam blesses Israel. Seven times he speaks a blessing: 23:7–10, 18–24; 24:3–9, 15–19, 20, 21–22, 23–24. Balak is infuriated by the prophet and revokes his "payment" for services (24:11), even though Balaam had warned him that he could only speak God's Word (see 22:38, cf. 22:20). For Balaam, however, there are other ways to curse Israel than by an oracle. So, at some point Balaam offers advice—the only way to curse Israel is to tempt the men to have sex with the women of Moab and worship Baal (25:1–3, see 31:16). This is exactly what they do, infuriating the LORD (25:3), hurting Israel, and later costing Balaam his life (31:8).

Second, a second census prepares the army, determines how much land each tribe will receive, and confirms that all of the prior adult generation has died in the wilderness (26:52–56, 63–65). Third, Joshua is appointed to be the next leader of Israel after Moses dies (27:18–23). And fourth, the tribes of Reuben, Gad, and half of Manasseh decide that the land east of the Jordan is perfect for their lifestyle and ask Moses for permission to settle here (32:1–5). After a serious misunderstanding on Moses's part (32:6–15), these tribes assure Moses they will help with the conquest of the remaining land (32:16–19), and Moses agrees to their plan (32:20–27). The Israelites are almost ready to begin taking the land promised to their ancestors hundreds of years ago. Almost—because Moses has some things to say before he dies.

To Discuss

1. What commandments did the Israelites break in the rebellion of Exodus 32?

2. Read Exodus 32:7–14 and complete Table 6.1. Did Moses change God's mind? What difference do your answers make to your understanding of God (or is your prior understanding driving how you answer the questions)? Two or more students might do additional research and conduct a debate in class.

3. Consider Aaron's role in the rebellion at Sinai. Why do you think he is so quick to do what the people ask? What does he mean when he says, "Tomorrow shall be a festival to the Lord" (32:5)? Who is the Lord they will celebrate?

4. What is Aaron's excuse for his behavior? How does he say the golden calf came to be? Put yourself in Moses's position. What is your first emotional response to Aaron's excuse? (Use your own words.) What other thoughts might Moses have about his brother?

5. Discuss the common themes in Israel's complaints. Consider the questions raised in the text:

   a. What do they think about the past? How does their image of the past develop? Finally, what significant terminology do they use to describe their past life?

   b. What do they wish for . . . over and over again? How do you read this wish, as being literal, metaphorical, or other?

   c. Who do they complain against?

   d. Why do they complain so often? And why with such strong language or dramatic flair?

6. What other common themes do you see in Israel's complaints?

7. Do you agree or disagree with the author's claim that after the events at Sinai, the Lord had higher expectations of his people? Explain your position. Does this principle have relevance for Christ-followers?

8. Why does Moses not get to enter the promised land? What did he do wrong? What was so bad about his actions? Do you think it is fair? Do you think God is fair?

To Know

1. The significance of the following in the assigned chapters:

Aaron	Holiness Code
Abiram	Joshua
Abihu	Jubilee Year
Atonement	Korah
Balaam	Law about Revenge
Balak	Law of Interest (on loans)
Bronze Serpent	Miriam
Caleb	Moses
Dathan	Nadab
Day of Atonement	Sabbatical Year

2. The three arguments Moses uses to persuade God not to destroy all the people at Sinai. The other arguments Moses uses later to persuade God not to kill all the people.

3. The two crises at Sinai (Exod 32–34) and the crisis at the end of Exodus.

4. How Israel distinguishes between clean and unclean animals (the primary guideline).

5. The five parts of Leviticus and how each contributes to God living with his people.

6. List and explain what happens in the seven crises in Numbers. Then identify the basic pattern in these events.

7. What Balaam must say to Israel when he speaks on behalf of the LORD. What Balaam advises as a way to "curse" Israel or bring Israel down.

8. Memorize God's self-revelation in Exodus 34:6–7. Identify the tension present in this description of God.

9. Locate the following on a map (see Figure 6.6): Great Sea, Red Sea, Egypt, Goshen, Sinai, Kadesh-Barnea, Edom, Moab, and Jericho.

To Dig Deeper: Research Topics

1. Exodus 34:6–7 is influential throughout the Old Testament. Identify three other places where part or all of this text is quoted or clearly in the background. How is the text used? What is the role of Exod 34:6–7 in its new context?

2. Many artists, including Michelangelo, have produced paintings and sculptures of Moses that include horns protruding from his head. The reason for depicting Moses with horns comes from Exodus 34:29–35. Investigate this topic: Why did artists portray Moses with horns? When did the practice begin? Create a video with voice-over or a PowerPoint presentation.

3. Investigate the proposed rationales for what makes animals clean or unclean. Explore at least three proposals, including the work of Mary Douglas. Make a compelling argument for one of these (or your own) rationale.

4. Investigate the death of Nadab and Abihu. Read evidence left by Leviticus 10:1–8 (9–20), and 16:1–2. What clues do these texts provide as to what Nadab and Abihu were doing or attempting to do? To what conclusion does the evidence lead? Should the LORD be charged with a crime? If so, what is the charge and why? If not, why not?

5. Compare the character of Moses, as developed in the biblical text, to an opera or musical in which Moses appears. What do you discover? What causes the musical or opera to develop Moses's character as it does?

For Further Reading

Douglas, Mary. *Purity and Danger: An Analysis of the Concepts of Pollution and Taboo*. London: Routledge, 1966.

Wright, David. "Unclean and Clean." Pages 729–741 in vol. 6 of *The Anchor Bible Dictionary*. Edited by David Noel Freedman. New York: Doubleday, 1992.

Finally Comes the **Land**
Conquest—Success or Failure?

7

The Book of Deuteronomy is a hinge point, marking the end of the Pentateuch and at the same time beginning the **Deuteronomistic History (DH)**. On the one side, the writer composes the book as Moses's final speeches to Israel before he dies—concluding the Pentateuch. On the other side, Deuteronomy begins the Deuteronomistic History—a unified composition of seven books: Deuteronomy, Joshua, Judges, 1–2 Samuel, and 1–2 Kings. These texts take the reader on a wild ride with Israel, from just before her entry into the promised land (Deuteronomy) to her loss of the northern territory to Assyria (2 Kgs 17) and then Judah to Babylon (2 Kgs 24–25).

The DH is not, however, history in the modern sense of the term: an objective reconstruction of events. The DH is theological history: a retelling of select events from a theological (faith) perspective in order to establish ideas about God and the life of faith. Whether visible or behind the scenes, the DH views all of the events in its history through the lens of faith. How this works and what the DH is trying to teach its reader is the challenge before us in this chapter, and many to come. In this chapter, we will identify three central themes introduced into the DH by Deuteronomy; we will then take quick snapshots of Joshua and Judges from twenty thousand feet above, before diving down for a close look at examples of their essential ideas.

READING ASSIGNMENTS
DEUTERONOMY 1–10
JOSHUA 1–8, 23–24
JUDGES 1–5, 13–16

KEY TERMS

Collateral: property or goods given or promised as security for a loan

Concubine: a secondary wife, usually due to her family's lower economic status

Deuteronomistic History (DH): the books of Deuteronomy through 2 Kings, excluding Ruth

Deuteronomistic Theology: the basic idea that God rewards those who do what is right, but punishes those who choose to do wrong (a theme nuanced in the DH and other books)

Deuteronomists (Dtr): the authors/editors of the Deuteronomistic History

Herem: the Hebrew term translated as "the ban" (CEB) and used to command total destruction in a battle

Tribute: a tax imposed on a smaller or conquered nation by a superior nation or empire

129

Deuteronomy

As the first book in the DH, Deuteronomy is the headwaters for central ideas that begin in these chapters and grow like a river, becoming wider and deeper as each theme moves through the books ahead. Here, we identify three themes that unite the books of the DH and use events from the history of Israel to teach and illustrate each message about God and the life of faith.

Theme 1: Love for God

The single most important theme in the DH and Deuteronomy is the appeal for a single-minded allegiance to the LORD. This idea is stated powerfully in many texts, perhaps none more powerful than the *Shema*, so called because its first word in Hebrew is *Shema* (an imperative meaning, "listen," or even "pay attention").

> Israel, listen! Our God is the LORD! Only the LORD!
>
> Love the LORD your God with all your heart, all your being, and all your strength. These words that I am commanding you today must always be on your minds. Recite them to your children. Talk about them when you are sitting around your house and when you are out and about, when you are lying down and when you are getting up. Tie them on your hand as a sign. They should be on your forehead as a symbol. Write them on your house's doorframes and on your city's gates. (6:4–9)

Love, as a commitment (not a mere emotion), is also the answer to the question, *What does God really want or expect from his people*?

> Now in light of all that, Israel, what does the LORD your God ask of you? Only this: to revere the LORD your God by walking in all his ways, by loving him, by serving the LORD your God with all your heart and being, and by keeping the LORD's commandments and his regulations that I'm commanding you right now. It's for your own good! (10:12–13)
>
> So circumcise your hearts and stop being so stubborn, because the LORD your God is the God of all gods and Lord of all lords, the great, mighty, and awesome God who doesn't play favorites and doesn't take bribes. He enacts justice for orphans and widows, and he loves immigrants, giving them food and clothing. That means you must also love immigrants because you were immigrants in Egypt. Revere the LORD your God, serve him, cling to him, swear by his name alone! (10:16–20)

And once again:

> It's true: if you carefully keep all this commandment that I'm giving you, by doing it, *by loving the LORD your God*, by walking in all his ways, and by clinging to him, then

the LORD will clear out all these nations before you. You will inherit what belonged to nations that are larger and stronger than you are. (11:22–23, emphasis mine)

Above all else, Deuteronomy calls for devotion to the LORD that comes from the heart, the very core of a person's being—a near infinite distance from the caricature of Old Testament religion as nothing more than actions divorced from attitudes. Instead, actions mean nothing to the LORD unless they are fueled by an inner commitment to him. The LORD's goal is a relationship with people that restores the intimacy lost in the Garden of Eden, an intimacy only possible by a single-minded allegiance to the LORD and the LORD alone.

The last citation from chapter 11 introduces a challenge for Israel and for the reader: the presence of other nations in the land and what to do about them. The first aspect of the challenge has been an obvious issue, since the LORD promised the land to Abraham. It is good land, so many people live there. The second aspect of the issue, however, makes me uncomfortable and leaves me with questions I cannot answer. To deal with the residents, the LORD orders *herem* ("the ban"), the destruction of every threat to Israel's well-being:

> Now once the LORD your God brings you into the land you are entering to take possession of, and he drives out numerous nations before you. . . seven nations that are larger and stronger than you—once the LORD your God lays them before you, you must strike them down, placing them under the ban. Don't make any covenants with them, and don't be merciful to them. (7:1–2)

The practice of *herem*—total destruction of every living being—is often a reason cited by those who reject the Old Testament or the Bible. How could a good God order such violence? How could God destroy innocent children? Deuteronomy, however, defends *herem* on the basis of two principles: First, it is because of the wickedness of the people in the land. Because of their wickedness, including the practice of child sacrifice, that the LORD is destroying or driving them off the land (9:5; 12:31; 18:9–12; see also Gen 15:16 and Lev 18:24–25). The second principle is the danger the native population poses to Israel. Should Israel adopt their practices and worship other gods (7:3–4; 12:2–4, 31–32), the LORD will destroy Israel (6:14–15; 7:4b). Thus, Israel faces the same destruction if she does not keep a single-minded allegiance to the LORD, turning to other gods (see 13:1–18; 17:2–7). The LORD is consistent in invoking *herem*—against Canaanites *and Israelites*. In fact, as we will see, the Lord will drive Israel off the land for her failure to keep the first commandment: love and serve no other God.

The situation, however, is far more complicated than an image of Israel entering the land and killing everything alive. God doesn't invoke *herem* all that often, nor does Israel always keep *herem*. In fact, in time to come, some marriages to those outside of Israel will be celebrated (see the books of Ruth and Esther). In simple terms, we do not know all the details that might help us further understand the rationale behind *herem* (please see the recommended books at the end of the chapter in "For Further Reading"). Because of this, in a sense, we are working in the dark and put in a position similar to Israel: Will we trust the LORD? Will we accept that the LORD knew what was best for Israel in her place and time? Or will we reject the LORD and take matters into our own hands? To some degree, the writer has set us up: now we must decide if we trust the LORD or not, and to some degree we feel the same struggle Israel lived with on a near-daily basis.

Theme 2: Love for Others

On the other side of the universe from the first theme Deuteronomy introduces, the second theme expresses concern for those who live on the margins of society (see also Exod 21–23 and Lev 19): love for the poor, widows, orphans, aliens, and Levites. Ideally, Israel was to practice a Sabbatical Year every seven years, in which all debts were forgiven (Deut 15:1–2) and debt slaves released with provisions for a fresh start that would keep families out of a continuous cycle of poverty (15:12–18); what meager evidence that exists, however, suggests that Israel rarely, if ever, kept the practice (see 2 Chr 36:21; Isa 58:13).

Deuteronomy urges those with wealth not to be tight-fisted, but to help those in need with loans (15:7–11), even if the Sabbatical Year is near and it is unlikely that the loan will be repaid before debts are cancelled. **Collateral** for loans was appropriate. However, those with wealth were not permitted to disgrace the poor by storming into their houses to collect the collateral (24:10–11), take a person's means of livelihood as collateral (24:6), or keep a person's only robe as collateral overnight (24:12–13). The wealthy should not refuse to pay workers at the end of the day (24:14–15), strip the harvest bare so that there is nothing for the poor to pick up or glean (24:19–22), or use their money to take justice away from the poor or aliens (24:17). In an ancient society, those with wealth could get away with all these things, pushing the poor around and becoming wealthier at the expense of the poor.

In the DH, how a society treats the poor and others on the margins of society is a reliable indicator as to how well a society loves their "neighbor" (anyone other than my family) and is faithful to the second half of the Ten Commandments (repeated in Deut 5:1–21, see esp. vv. 12–15).

Theme 3: The Deuteronomistic Theology

The third theme Deuteronomy introduces is what is frequently called the Deuteronomistic theology. In essence, this theology promises blessings from God for those who are obedient, and threatens curses for those who refuse to obey, especially those who turn to other gods. Toward the end of Deuteronomy, this theology is stated with force. Moses begins a speech:

> Now if you really obey the LORD your God's voice, by carefully keeping all his commandments that I am giving you right now, then the LORD your God will set you high above all nations on earth. All these blessings will come upon you and find you if you obey the LORD your God's voice: You will be blessed in the city and blessed in the field. (28:1–3)

He concludes this section:

> The LORD will make you the head of things, not the tail; you will be at the top of things, not the bottom, as long as you obey the LORD your God's commandments that I'm commanding you right now, by carefully doing them. Don't deviate even a bit from any of these words that I'm commanding you right now by following other gods and serving them. (28:13–14)

On the other hand, Moses warns the people:

> But if you don't obey the LORD your God's voice by carefully doing all his commandments and his regulations that I am commanding you right now, all these curses will come upon you and find you. You will be cursed in the city and cursed in the field. (28:15–16)

> That's how all these curses will come over you, pursuing you, reaching you until you are completely wiped out, because you didn't obey the LORD your God's voice by keeping his commandments and his regulations that he gave you. (28:45)

Even the promises to Abraham and Sarah will be suspended:

> Once as countless as the stars in the night sky, only a few of you will be left alive—all because you didn't obey the LORD your God's voice. And just as before, the LORD enjoyed doing good things for you and increasing your numbers, now the LORD will enjoy annihilating and destroying you. You will be torn off the very fertile land you are entering to possess. (28:62–63)

This theology is supported elsewhere in Deuteronomy (e.g., 27:1–26), and God assures the people that what he asks of them is not so difficult that they cannot obey (30:11–20). Other books in the DH also support this theology, as over and over again God blesses the nation when it is trying to be obedient, and brings trouble when Israel turns to other gods.

At the end of Deuteronomy, Moses makes the trek up Mount Nebo where the LORD shows him the good land Israel will enter. Although it seems harsh and maybe even unfair, Moses will not go with the people because of his own failure to trust the LORD at Meribah (Num 20: 9–11) and perhaps earlier (Num 11:11–15, 21–23); although, Moses later blames the people for what happened (see Deut 1:37–38, 3:26, and 4:21). He argues with the LORD. Moses begs to enjoy the destination to which he has been leading the people all these years. But the answer is no, and finally the LORD tells Moses to stop: "That's enough from you! Don't ever ask me about this again!" (Deut 3:26). The man who argued so effectively for Israel so many times cannot get God to change his mind about his destiny. So, Moses hikes up one more mountain, Mount Nebo, to the peak of the Pisgah slope where the LORD shows him the land—from the far north, where the tribe of Dan will ultimately settle, to Judah's land and the southern plain, even westward to the Mediterranean Sea (34:1–3). Here, on the mountain, Moses dies (see Figure 7.1).

Texts in Conversation

The book of Deuteronomy is strong in its assertion of the Deuteronomistic theology. Consequently, believers often hear the voice of Deuteronomy but do not hear other texts inside and outside of the DH. When this happens, it is easy for a reader to arrive at a gospel of health and wealth in which as long as a believer has enough faith, their lives will be filled with good things. They will be healthy, or overcome any serious illness; they will become wealthy, or lack any need. All because the LORD promises to bless them (28:13).

Other texts challenge such a one-sided view of life and faith, beginning with texts inside the DH. One of the best kings to follow David (the man who followed the Lord's heart, 1 Sam 13:4), was Josiah. He came to throne at an early age and soon after led a major religious reformation. The **Deuteronomists (Dtr)** write of Josiah, "There's never been a king like Josiah, whether before or after him, who turned to the LORD with all his heart, all his being, and all his strength, in agreement with everything in the Instructions from Moses" (2 Kgs 23:25). A prophet even declared that though the nation would suffer a terrible end, Josiah would go to his grave in peace (2 Kgs 22:20). But he doesn't. This great spiritual man went to face Egypt in war and suffered a violent death in battle (2 Kgs 23:29).

Texts outside of the DH especially challenge a one-sided idea of "do good, get good" or "do bad, get bad" theology. One of the best kings to follow David was Josiah. This writer has seen that doing the right thing does not guarantee a reward, just as Job discovered that his righteousness did not oblige God to do anything. Job, "a person of absolute integrity" (Job 1:1) this innocent man suffers tremendous pain and loses children he never recovers (1:13–19), not because he did anything wrong or needed to learn something; all such causes are dismissed in chapters 1–2. His friends will argue for the Deuteronomistic theology: because it is the wicked who suffer, Job must have done something wrong and needs to confess his sin and turn back to God (8:3–7, 11:5–6, 13–17, 22:4–11, 21–28). Job, however, refuses to confess what he has not done and tells his friends what he has seen: the wicked often prosper while the righteous suffer (21:7–21, 27–33). And at the end of the book, God will side with Job as he speaks to one of Job's friends: "I am angry at you and your two friends because you haven't spoken about me correctly as did my servant Job" (42:7).

All of these texts, and many others we could read, warn us against a simplistic, one-sided reading of Deuteronomy and the DH. Yes, God blesses the righteous, but not all the time. Yes, the wicked suffer, but so do the righteous. Does wisdom agree that living a good life is still to be preferred over a wicked life? Absolutely! We will do well as long as we hear this promise against the background of these voices from the Books of Job, Ecclesiastes, 1–2 Kings, along with many other voices in the Book of Psalms who cry out to God—though they have done nothing wrong (see Chapter Fifteen)—and warnings from the Book of Proverbs that oppression often trumps God's blessing of the righteous (e.g., see 13:23, 28:6).

The Book of Joshua

Since Genesis 12, we have been waiting for the moment when Israel will enter the land promised to Abraham and Sarah. The family has had to wait four hundred years and has been oppressed by Egyptian slavery, until the current residents deserved to lose their land (Gen 15:13). But finally, after all the hype, all the talk about going to the promised land, when Israel finally gets to the land and begins the conquest, the book of Joshua has little to say. It's all much to do about nothing. The book of Joshua is composed of three types of material that we will explore in order: a narrative of the conquest (1–12), the allotment of land to the tribes (13–22), and Joshua's final speeches (23–24).

Figure 7.1. The Memorial to Moses at the Top of Mount Nebo. Photo by David Anderson.

1. A Narrative of the Conquest (Josh 1–12).

In the conquest narrative, little is actually said about conquering the land. The first five chapters describe preparations for taking the land:

- God affirms Joshua as the new leader (1:1–18) and urges him "to be strong and courageous" (1:6, 7, 9, 18);
- Joshua sends spies to the first target, Jericho (2:1–24);
- Israel crosses the Jordan (3:1–4:24) just as their parents crossed the Sea of Reeds (14:21–25), bringing the era of wilderness wandering to an end;
- Joshua orders the circumcision of all the men in preparation for the Passover (5:1–9);
- the people celebrate their first Passover in the promised land (5:10–12);
- and finally, the commander of the LORD's heavenly forces arrives with instructions (5:13–6:5).

The conquest narrative recounts only three battles with any detail:

Battle One: The Battle of Jericho, which isn't much of a battle at all. While Jericho is under siege (6:1), the commander of the LORD's heavenly forces directs a ritual march around the city: circle the city once a day for six days (6:3) and then, on the seventh day, circle the city seven times; shout and watch the walls fall, then rush into the city. This is not military strategy, but what people in the ancient Near East might do on special worship occasions (see Neh 12:27–39).

And so, the writer's message: the LORD gives Jericho to Israel (Josh 6:2, 16). Everything in Jericho belongs to the LORD, who has invoked *herem* (6:17–19).

Battle Two: The Battle of Ai. This battle differs from the ritual strategy at Jericho. Here, sound military tactics come into play. The first attempt fails because of Achan's failure to respect *herem* at Jericho: taking a robe, silver, and gold for himself (7:20–21). Once he is found out, he and his whole family are put to death (7:22–26)—a concept of corporate identity and guilt that we find almost impossible to grasp in our world. On the second attempt, Israel sets an ambush for Ai (8:1–29), and in this battle, the people are allowed to keep the cattle and other goods (8:27). If only Achan could have waited.

Battle Three: The Battle for Gibeah. The Battle for Gibeah involves a tale of deception by the people living in Gibeah (9:3–13, 15), Israel's failure to inquire of the LORD (9:14), and a battle to protect Israel's new allies—the people of Gibeah—when they are attacked (10:1–7). In this battle, we find a mixture of Israel's soldiers engaged in fighting and the LORD actively helping Israel—throwing large stones from the sky (hail stones? 10:10–11) and in some way extending the day so Israel could complete the rout (10:12–14).

So we have three stories: one in which the LORD is solely responsible for the victory, another in which Israel uses sound military strategy, and a third in which the LORD and Israel work together. Nothing more needs to be said about the conquest. These three battles say it all—the conquest of the promised land takes place in these three ways. All that's left to do is list the victories: in the south (10:28–43), the north (11:1–15), east of the Jordan by Moses (12:1–6), and then a final list of kings defeated west of the Jordan (12:7–24).

By all appearances, the invasion has been a rapid, decisive conquest of the land:

> Joshua captured all these kings and their cities. He struck them down without mercy. He wiped them out as something reserved for God. This was exactly as Moses the LORD's servant had commanded. (11:12)

> So Joshua took this whole land: the highlands, the whole arid southern plain, the whole land of Goshen, the lowlands, the desert plain, and both the highlands and the lowlands of Israel. (11:16; see also 11:23 and 18:1)

Israel has completed a decisive, textbook invasion.

Or have they? Alongside the texts that proclaim a decisive conquest are other voices that express a different opinion: the invasion was not complete at all, but fragmentary, stalled, and incomplete.

> Now Joshua had reached old age. The LORD said to him, "You have reached old age, but *much of the land remains to be taken over*. (13:1, emphasis mine)

> But the Israelites didn't remove the Geshurites or the Maacathites. So Geshur and Maacath still live among Israel today. (13:13)

But the people of Judah couldn't remove the Jebusites who lived in Jerusalem. So today the Jebusites still live along with the people of Judah in Jerusalem. (15:63)

But they didn't remove the Canaanites who lived in Gezer. So today the Canaanites, who were used for forced labor, still live within Ephraim. (16:10; see also 17:12–13)

And when we turn a few pages over to the Book of Judges, news of the failed conquest overwhelms the first chapter (emphases in the following citations are mine).

Thus the LORD was with **the tribe of Judah**, and they took possession of the highlands. However, *they didn't drive out* those who lived in the plain because they had iron chariots. (Judg 1:19)

But **the people of Benjamin** *didn't drive out the Jebusites* who lived in Jerusalem. So the Jebusites still live with the people of Benjamin in Jerusalem today. (1:21; cf. Josh 15:63)

The tribe of Manasseh *didn't drive out* the people in Beth-shean, Taanach, Dor, Ibleam, Megiddo, or any of their villages. The Canaanites were determined to live in that land. When Israel became stronger they forced the Canaanites to work for them, but *they didn't completely drive them out.* (1:27–28)

The tribe of Ephraim *didn't drive out* the Canaanites living in Gezer, so the Canaanites kept on living there with them. (1:29; cf. Josh 16:10)

The tribe of Zebulun *didn't drive out* the people living in Kitron or Nahalol. These Canaanites lived with them but were forced to work for them. (1:30)

The tribe of Asher *didn't drive out* the people living in Acco, Sidon, Ahlab, Achzib, Helbah, Aphik, or Rehob. The people of Asher settled among the Canaanites in the land because *they couldn't drive them out.* (1:31–32)

The tribe of Naphtali *didn't drive out* the people living in Beth-shemesh or Beth-anath but settled among the Canaanites in the land. The people living in Beth-shemesh and Beth-anath were forced to work for them. (1:33)

The Amorites pushed **the people of Dan** back into the highlands because *they wouldn't allow them* to come down to the plain. (1:34)

The reader has good reason to be confused, even frustrated with the text. What's going on? Did Israel conquer the land or not? Some texts appear to say *yes, absolutely*, while others appear to say *absolutely not*. In some places Israel takes control, while in others the native residents remain in control; and, as for the tribe of Dan, it loses its allotted territory back to the Amorites (1:34). As a result of these texts and other evidence, some researchers propose different models for understanding Israel and her emergence in the land (see "For Further Reading").

To follow the information in Joshua and Judges, at the very least we need to revise our mental picture of what happened when Israel entered the land. On the one hand, the conquest was a much longer, drawn out affair than often assumed. Israel does fight key battles and take control of some areas (as claimed in the book of Joshua), but she has a long way to go in her claim upon all the land. Not until the time of King David (ca. 1000 BCE) does the nation finish dealing with non-Israelites in and around the promised land. Then, but only then, was the nation of Israel the largest and most powerful country it would ever be.

On the other hand, the book of Joshua assures the reader that God kept every promise ever made to the people:

> The LORD *gave to Israel all the land he had pledged* to give to their ancestors. They took it over and settled there. The LORD gave them rest from surrounding danger, *exactly as he had pledged* to their ancestors. Not one of all their enemies held out against them. *The* LORD *gave all* their enemies into their power. *Not one of all the good things that the* LORD *had promised to the house of Israel failed. Every promise was fulfilled.* (21:43–45, emphasis mine)

The writer emphasizes that any failure of the invasion is not the LORD's fault. The LORD kept every promise and gave all their enemies into their power. But Israel failed to keep her part. Joshua recognized what was happening and in frustration asked the Israelites, "How long will you avoid going to take over the land that the LORD, the God of your ancestors, has given you?" (18:3; see also 17:14–18). And near the end of his life he said, "Look. I'm now walking on the road to death that all the earth must take. You know with all your heart and being that *not a single one of all the good things that the* LORD *your God promised about you has failed. They were all fulfilled for you. Not a single one of them has failed*" (23:14, emphasis mine).

2. The Distribution of the Land (Josh 13–22).

Although Israel has yet to conquer all the land, the LORD instructs Joshua to allot the land to the various tribes and to urge them to finish the conquest of their land (13:1–7). So, Joshua describes the borders for the tribes east of the Jordan (13:8–33), and then casts lots for the large tribes within the promised land (14:1–5): Judah (15:1–63), Ephraim (16:1–10), and Manasseh (17:1–18). The tabernacle is set up at Shiloh (18:1), where Joshua authorizes a survey of the remaining land for allotment to the seven tribes still without land, and reprimands these tribes for being lethargic about taking their land (18:3). Then, the final tribes are allotted their land: Benjamin (18:11–28), Simeon (19:1–9), Zebulun (19:10–16), Issachar (19:17–23), Asher (19:24–31), Naphtali (19:32–39), and Dan (19:40–48; see Figure 7.2).

Along with the allotment of land, Joshua also designates six cities as "cities of refuge" (20:1–9), three on each side of the Jordan. These cities function as places of sanctuary or safety for anyone accused of murder: the accused could run here (literally) before the family of the deceased could catch them and put them to death for the crime. Israel, like other ancient societies, had no police system—only family justice. But at a city of refuge, the accused would be safe until a trial determined guilt or innocence. If guilty, the guilty person was handed over to the "blood avenger" from the family, who then put the murderer to death.

The cities of refuge were among the forty-eight cities given to the Levites, scattered among all of the tribes (21:1–42). These "Levitical cities" were needed so that all Israel had access to a Levite who could teach the law, as well as render decisions regarding what is holy or common and what is clean or unclean (Lev 10:10–11).

3. Joshua's Farewell Address (Josh 23–24).

From time to time, it becomes popular for couples to renew their wedding vows. Why? They are already married, sometimes for thirty, forty, or even fifty years. So what's the purpose of renewing vows already taken? I leave the question with you while we turn to the final scene in the book of Joshua: a

Figure 7.2. The Twelve Tribes

covenant-renewal ceremony. Joshua summons the leaders of Israel to meet at Shechem (24:1) where the ceremony begins with a reminder of what God has done for Israel, reaching back to Israel's origins with Abram and Sarai, and culminating with God's gift of the land (24:2–13). On the basis of what God has done for them, Joshua calls for the renewal of Israel's vows to serve the LORD—and only the LORD—tossing aside all the other gods they have collected through the years (24:14). *Choose today whom you will serve—the gods of Egypt, the gods in the promised land, or the gods of the ancestors—but make a choice.* Joshua says, "But my family and I will serve the LORD" (24:15). Decide. You need to make your decision *and stick with it*.

The people say they will serve the LORD and no other god. They even add more to the story of what the LORD has done for them (24:16–18), to which Joshua replies, "You can't serve the LORD" (24:19)—a baffling response for a covenant renewal ceremony. What did he want the people to say?! We will pick up this question again in the "To Discuss" questions at the end of the chapter.

The Book of Judges

Joshua is a remarkable man: his death is recorded at the end of the book of Joshua (24:29), his death is recorded again in Judges chapter 1 (1:1), and yet again in chapter 2 (2:8–9). What a man! Of course, he only dies once, but the multiple references emphasize that: First, Joshua dies at the end of the book of Joshua; second, the book of Judges continues Israel's story, slightly overlapping with the book of Joshua; and third, Judges begins with a double introduction (1:1–2:5; 2:6–23), each of which starts with the death of Joshua.

Baal's Country and Baal's Story

As Israel crosses the Jordan River, a large billboard on the side of the road announces the struggle the nation will have for the next five hundred years.

Welcome to Baal's Country   **Bienvenue au Country de Baal**

Willkommen in Baals Land   **Bienvenido a la tierra de Baal**

Our best source of knowledge about Baal comes from fragmentary tablets written in Ugaritic, dated to ca. 1400 BCE, some found between 1929–1939 and others after 1950 CE at Ras Shamra (the ancient city of Ugarit) on the Mediterranean Sea (about thirty miles south of Antioch). Because of their fragmentary nature, the order of the narrative is uncertain and varies in different translations. In general, the story unfolds along the following lines (and at points is quite funny to me):

A dispute breaks out between Baal (god of the thunderstorm, rain, fertility, and life) and Yam and Nahar (gods of the sea and river, respectively) whose floods destroy life. Baal is victorious and takes Yam and Nahar captive and puts them under his control. He is not happy, however, that he—the ruler of the divine assembly, king of the gods—still lives with his parents. Baal wants his own place, so he complains to his sister, Anat (a fierce god of war), and asks her to go talk to his dad, Father El, about getting his own house. His sister goes and, with a mixture of flattery and threats, persuades their father to order the construction of Baal's own palace. Soon, Baal is enthroned in his very own house.

Despite Baal's position of authority and his control over life-destroying rivers and seas, he must continually battle with Mot (god of death and infertility). Every year, Mot picks a fight with Baal. He stops the rain from coming and dries up all of Baal's moisture from the land. This action signifies Baal's death, his descent into Mot's huge mouth, and the end of the growing season. With Baal's death, the gods attempt to find someone who can sit on Baal's throne, but no god is equal to the task. One god who tries to sit on Baal's throne discovers that his feet are far from touching the floor. He is like a child sitting on Baal's throne. The god of life is dead and all hope is lost.

Anat, however, refuses to believe Baal is really dead. So she hunts down Mot, finds him, and demands that Mot raise Baal from the dead, but he refuses. Months pass until she comes back and slaughters Mot, chops him into pieces with her sword, and sows him like seed in the field. Father El then has a dream and realizes that Baal is still alive. He laughs and tells the people to sow their seed in the dry fields because he knows Baal is alive and rain is sure to come.

Indeed, after a world-wide search for Baal, he returns to his throne, bringing life-giving rains to the fields. Once again, death has been conquered by life and fertility.[1]

---

[1] Summary with citations from Michael Coogan, "Ugarit," pages 18–28 in *A Reader of Ancient Near Eastern Texts: Sources for the Study of the Old Testament* (New York: Oxford University Press, 2013); and Victor Hamilton and Don Benjamin, "Stories of Ba'al and Anat," pages 244–256 in *Old Testament Parallels: Laws and Stories from the Ancient Near East*, rev. and exp. 2d ed. (New York: Paulist Press, 1997).

The first introduction to Judges describes the geo-political situation in Israel that we began to see in the book of Joshua: First, the conquest is faltering, with control of the land an unsettled question. In some areas, at best, the Israelite tribes are firmly in control with the native population peacefully living among them (1:21, 29), or even forced to work for them (1:27–28, 30, 33). Elsewhere, however, the tribe of Asher was unable to exert their rule and had to "settle among the Canaanites" (1:31–32). And at worst, the tribe of Dan lost its allotted land back to the Amorites and had to find new land to settle (1:34; see the story in 18:1–31). Second, the tribes are not united, and there is certainly no nation of Israel. Tribal independence was partly by plan (see 13:1–7, 23:1–13), but also a failure to rally to one another when needed (Judg 5:15–18, 23). Unfortunately, they pay a high cost for their lack of unity, with larger and stronger groups such as the Philistines picking one Israelite village off at a time. But we are beginning to get ahead of the introduction now.

The second introduction describes a six stage spiritual pattern in which Israel is trapped (2:11–19): First, Israel abandons the LORD for the gods of the land; second, the LORD becomes angry and "hands them over" to others who will punish Israel; third, Israel will groan and cry out to the LORD; fourth, the LORD will send a judge, or military hero, to lead Israel to freedom; fifth, the land will enjoy a time of peace until the death of the leader; and then sixth, Israel will start the pattern all over again.

The stories in Judges 3–16 come from throughout the tribes allotted land, each using the same basic pattern in order to demonstrate the widespread nature of the problem and to show how the spiritual problems in Israel are getting worse (see Figure 7.4). Israel is caught on a runaway roller coaster, picking up more and more speed, and growing more and more out of control. It is only a matter of time before Israel jumps the tracks and crashes in a heap. To illustrate the problem, we will examine the first and last story about the judges: Ehud and Samson.

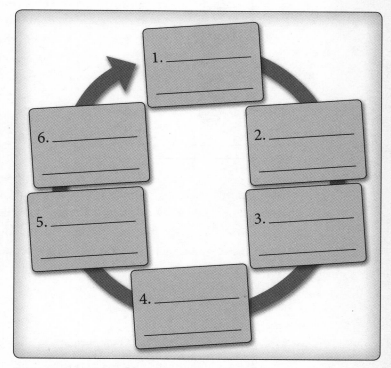

Table 7.1. The Recurring Pattern in the Book of Judges

Ehud

The first story is a raw comedy about a most unlikely hero: Ehud, a left-handed man from the tribe of Benjamin (which means 'son of my right hand'). Ehud is a literary misfit. Because Israel did what was evil in the LORD's sight, they had served Moab eighteen years (3:12–14). When

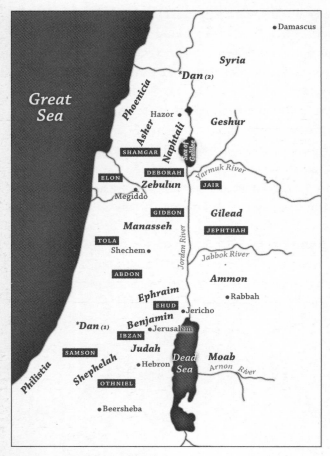

Figure 7.3. Map of the Judges in Israel

Israel cried out to the LORD, the LORD raised up Ehud (3:15). So one day, Ehud brought the tribute payment to Eglon, the king of Moab and a very fat man (in Hebrew his name is related to the word for "cow"). After giving the payment, Ehud told Eglon that he had a secret message. Kings love secrets, so everyone left the cool second story room (that doubled as the king's restroom). Ehud delivered the secret message—a double-edged sword into Eglon's belly, going in so far that the fat closed around it and caused Eglon's "guts to spill out" (CEB) or caused his bowels to release ("the dirt came out" NRSV). Ehud closed and locked the doors, and made his escape to rally Israel (3:20–23).

A bit later, outside the cool upper room, the king's servants didn't know what to do. With the doors locked, they assumed that the king must have been relieving himself; the smell may have aided their assumption. Finally, so much time passed they opened the doors to find their king dead (3:24–25). But by this time, Ehud had rallied Israel (i.e., Ephraim) into fighting the Moabites for their freedom (3:26–30).

While Israel (and the reader) may find humor in mocking Moab's king and how he died, Israel's constant turning away from the LORD to other gods is no laughing matter. The cost to Israel is enormous. God uses a wide variety of heroes to deliver his people: women (Deborah and Jael, chs. 4–5), a man afraid to move at first but then eager to set up his own monarchy (Gideon, chs. 6–9), a prostitute's son who bargains for power (Jephthah, chs. 11–12), and finally, Samson (chs. 13–16), a man born to be a lifelong Nazirite and to lead Israel against the Philistines. Samson, however, has other plans.

Samson

Instead of leading Israel against the Philistines, Samson wants to marry a Philistine (14:1–2). A constant theme in Samson's story is how God uses Samson despite Samson's refusal to keep his Nazirite vows or even follow the LORD. For example, he becomes so angry at his wedding that he goes on a rampage killing Philistine men (14:19–20). When he returns later for his "wife" and discovers that she was given to his best man (15:1–2), he lashes out in anger again (15:3–5). Then, when his "wife" is burned to death, Samson becomes so angry that he picks up an old jawbone of a donkey and uses it to hack and kill more Philistines (15:14–20).

Samson's weakness is women; and here, he is as weak as he is strong. He first wanted the Philistine woman of Timnah that caused so much trouble (14:1–2). He visits at least one prostitute (16:1–3). And finally, Samson (his name means 'Sun' or 'Sunny') falls for a woman named Delilah (her name means 'Night' or 'of the night'). Her nationality is unclear (Philistine or Israelite?), as is how she feels about Samson. Does she love him, or love the idea of hitting the Philistine jackpot? All Delilah has to do is discover the source of Samson's strength and hand him over to the Philistines. In the process, we discover that Samson not only has a weakness for women, but he is also dumb as dirt—or so in love that he can't see what Delilah is doing to him. In what may be some type of sexual play, Samson lets Delilah do all kinds of things to him and to his hair (16:6–14). Finally, he was exhausted by her tears and constant nagging, so he confesses the truth, and once he is asleep, she calls a man to shave his hair and the Philistines finally have their Israelite Rambo (16:15–21).

Just as other incidents in his life were used by God to lash out at the Philistines, so too is Samson's imprisonment used. His hair begins to regrow and the Philistines ignore it; they are not so bright or attentive, either. So when the Philistines bring him out as a blind fool to push around and laugh at, Samson, with his only recorded prayer, asks the LORD to help him by restoring his strength. So Samson brings down the house, ending the show and killing more Philistines in his death than he had in his life (16:23–30).

Conclusion

With the landed tribes of Israel falling to other gods over and over, the reader can only hope for better news from the one tribe without land, the Levites, who serve local communities as something like local pastors and health inspectors. Surely the Levites are not like the other tribes. In fact, they are nothing like the tribes with land. *They are far worse.* Just as the book of Judges began with a double introduction, it ends with a double conclusion: two stories about Levites. In the first, a Levite sells his services to the highest bidder; what god he serves makes no difference to him (Judg 17–18). In the second, a Levite treats his **concubine** horrifically—pushing her out to a gang of men so that he can get some sleep while they gang rape her. The next day, he speaks to her as if nothing had happened (19:28), puts her on a donkey, goes home, chops her into twelve pieces, and sends them like telegrams to the other tribes (19:29). His actions cause a civil war that almost wipes out the tribe of Benjamin and leads to even more violence against women: kidnapping four hundred young women so the male survivors of Benjamin can have wives (21:1–24).

In these final chapters, the writer makes an appeal for Israel's only hope:

> In those days there was no king in Israel; each person did what they thought to be right. (17:6)

> In those days there was no king in Israel. (18:1)

> In those days when there was no king in Israel. (19:1)

And the final sentence of the book reads:

> In those days there was no king in Israel; each person did what they thought to be right. (21:25)

These statements may mean several things: First, because Israel has no monarchy, no king, the people are going wild; second, what Israel needs is a king, a strong monarch to bring the people under control; or third, not even the LORD is king of Israel anymore—the people have rejected God to make their own decisions about what is right or wrong, to do whatever is in their own best interest without concern for others. Israel cannot continue on her current path; something must change. Israel needs both an earthly monarch and God as their king.

To Discuss

1. Do any of the major themes introduced by Deuteronomy surprise you? Did you expect these ideas in the Old Testament? Consider each theme in turn. What verses or ideas from your assigned reading contribute to each theme? On *herem* (see Question 2 below)?

2. What thoughts or concerns do you have regarding *herem* ("the ban")? Reread Deuteronomy 7:1–4 carefully. If God intended the Israelites to totally destroy the residents in the land, why do you think the text includes a restriction on marriage (7:3) and a ban on covenants (7:2b)? Does the command expect or require something other than total annihilation? How do your thoughts or concerns change after rereading this text? What new questions do you have?

3. The author claims, "In an ancient society, those with wealth could get away with all these things, pushing the poor around and becoming wealthier at the expense of the poor" (see page 132. Explain how this would be possible in an ancient society. In what ways has this practice changed? In what ways has this practice stayed the same? What safeguards are in place in your native society to prevent such mistreatment? How well do they work?

4. Explain the ideas of the Deuteronomistic theology. Considered on its own, without input from other voices in the Old Testament, where do these ideas lead? To what conclusions might we come? What counterbalance does the information in "Texts in Conversation" provide? What would you say is the validity of the Deuteronomistic theology? To what degree is it true? Defend your hypothesis.

5. Why does Moses not enter the promised land? What is the witness of the book of Numbers? What is the witness of the book of Deuteronomy? Explain and defend your conclusion. Do you think it is fair that Moses only gets to see the land?

6. Read Joshua 5:13–6:5 carefully (and Exod 3:1–10). Who is the commander of the LORD's heavenly force? What clues in the text help you identify the commander? What is the significance of the commander arriving at this point of the narrative?

7. Based on the evidence in the biblical text, to what degree is the conquest successful (assuming recognition of some degree of failure)? Why do you think the Israelites failed to complete the conquest during the era of Joshua? Put yourself in their place. Why might you stop short of the finish? The author places the blame on the people. Do you agree? In what way(s) do you think God might hold responsibility for the failure?

8. What happens in the covenant renewal ceremony at the end of Joshua? Why does Joshua answer their claim, "We too will serve the LORD," by saying, "You cannot" (24:18–19)?

Reread Exodus 32:17–19. How might this earlier event impact what Joshua says now? What other moments might be in Joshua's mind?

9. Identify the role of women and the role of men in the story of Deborah (Judg 4–5)? What is one or more major theme from Deborah's song (the poetic retelling of the event in Judg 5)? What surprises you? What is the same as always? What questions does the story raise for you?

To Know

1. The significance of the following in the assigned chapters:

Anat	Horeb
Baal	Jericho
Barak	Joshua
City of Refuge	Levitical City
Deborah	Mot
Delilah	Philistines
Deuteronomistic History	Sabbatical Year
Eglon	Samson
El	*Shema*
Ehud	Sisera
Gibeah	The Ban
Herem	Woman of Timnah

2. The three themes introduced by Deuteronomy. Be able to write a short paragraph on each.

3. On what basis Deuteronomy defends the practice of *Herem,* or "the ban".

4. The book of Joshua retells three battles from the conquest: What are these battles? (Be able to briefly retell the each story.)

5. (After class) Be able to write an essay on the success or lack of success of the invasion led by Joshua.

6. The six-part recurring pattern in the book of Judges.

7. The possible meanings of "In those days when there was no king in Israel."

8. The appeal the Book of Judges makes in its final chapters.

9. Locate the following on a map (see Figure 7.4): Ammon, Beersheba, Dan (2), Dead Sea, Great Sea, Jordan River, Moab, Philistia, Phoenicia, Sea of Galilee, and Syria.

To Dig Deeper: Research Topics

1. Research biblical and other arguments used to support the practice of *herem* or "the ban" in Joshua's conquest of the land. Use research quality materials in your study (see below, "For Further Reading"). Assess the arguments. Take a position and support your hypothesis with strong evidence and argumentation.

2. Research the practice of total destruction and burning of cities in ancient societies. Did this ever take place in an invasion or at some other time? When? Why? What do you learn? Does their practice have any relevance for Israel's practice of *herem*?

3. Select one of the judges for closer scrutiny. First, read the story of the judge in at least two different translations. Study your story in research quality journals, dictionaries, or commentaries. Write either an editorial column or news report for a major Philistine newspaper of the time.

4. Investigate the way in which other ancient societies wrote their histories. How are they similar to or different from the DH? What insights or questions do they raise for reading the theological history in the DH?

5. Prepare an obituary for Moses (if you are unfamiliar with the genre, find the website of a local funeral home and read the obituaries posted). You may use some literary freedom, but most of the obituary should come from the witness of the Pentateuch.

6. A number of texts include the phrase "to this day." Investigate the places in Joshua and Judges where this phrase occurs. What does this phrase say about the time or setting of the initial writer or speaker? How do you explain the inclusion of this phrase in Joshua and Judges?

For Further Reading

On *herem* ("the ban") and the violence of God in general

Copan, Paul and Matt Flannagan. *Did God Really Command Genocide? Coming to Terms with the Justice of God.* Grand Rapids: Baker, 2014.

Cowles, C. S. et al. *Show Them No Mercy: 4 Views on God and Canaanite Genocide.* Edited by Stanley Gundry. Grand Rapids: Zondervan, 2003.

Schlimm, Matthew Richard. *This Strange and Sacred Scripture: Wrestling with the Old Testament and Its Oddities.* Grand Rapids: Baker Academic, 2015.

Seibert, Eric A. *The Violence of Scripture: Overcoming the Old Testament's Troubling Legacy.* Minneapolis: Fortress Press, 2012.

On Baal

Day, John. "Baal." Pages 545–548 in vol. 1 of *The Anchor Bible Dictionary*. Edited by David Noel Freedman. 6 vols. New York: Doubleday, 1992.

Note: See also the recommend sources for ancient Near Eastern literature in prior chapters.

On the Origins of Israel in Canaan

Survey

Hess, Richard S. "Early Israel in Canaan, A Survey of Recent Evidence and Interpretations." Pages 492–518 in *Israel's Past in Present Research, Essays on Ancient Israelite Historiography*. Edited by V. Philips Long. Winona Lake, Indiana: Eisenbrauns, 1999. Originally published in *Palestinian Exploration Quarterly* 125 (1993): 125–42.

Note: Most critical introductions to the Old Testament will include a section or more on the origins of Israel in Canaan.

The Conquest Model (W. F. Albright, G. E. Wright):

Bright, John. *A History of Israel.* 3d ed. Philadelphia: Westminster, 1981.

Wright, G. E. "Epic of Conquest." *Biblical Archaeology Review* 3 (1940): 25–40.

Yadin, Y. "Is the Biblical Conquest of Canaan Historically Reliable?" *Biblical Archaeology Review* 8 (1982): 16–23.

The Peaceful Infiltration Model (Albrecht Alt, Martin Noth):

Weippert, Manfred. "The Period of the Conquest and the Judges as Seen by Earlier and Later Sources." *Vetus Testamentum* 17 (1967): 93–113.

———. *The Settlement of the Israelite Tribes in Palestine.* London: SCM, 1971.

Peasant Revolt or Social Revolution Model (George Mendenhall, Norman Gottwald):

Dever, William G. *Who Were the Early Israelites and Where Did They Come From?* Grand Rapids: Eerdmans, 2003.

Gottwald, Norman K. *The Tribes of Yahweh: A Sociology of the Religions of Liberated Israel, 1250–1050 B.C.* Maryknoll, NY: Orbis, 1979.

Mendenhall, George E. "The Hebrew Conquest of Palestine," *Biblical Archaeologist* 25 (1962): 66–87.

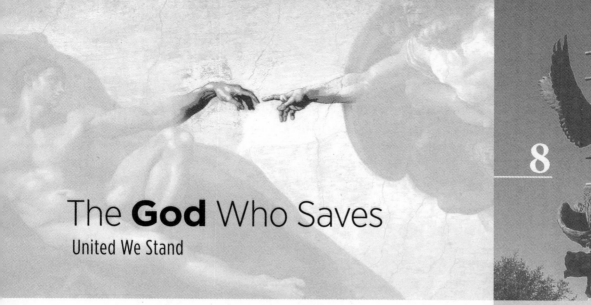

The **God** Who Saves
United We Stand

At the end of the Book of Judges, the nation of Israel is in crisis—again. At times it seems that Israel's story is little more than an escape from one crisis into another; or perhaps, since only the disasters make the headlines, our picture is somewhat distorted. At this point, however, it is arguable whether the *nation* of Israel really exists, or Israel is nothing more than a loose confederation of independent tribes living (with many other people) in the land once promised to their ancestors. They share a common history and an allegiance to a common God—at least in theory—and they share a common sanctuary at **Shiloh**, where the tabernacle has been set up (perhaps as a more permanent temple, see 1 Sam 1:3, 9). But whether a tribal confederacy or the nation of Israel, unless something drastic and far-reaching happens soon, they will not last for long. The tribes share pressures stacked against them, which threaten their existence in the land. Something must be done—fast, radical, and thorough enough to save the nation the LORD has chosen as his conduit of blessing to the rest of the world.

That radical move, described in the Books of 1 and 2 Samuel, is a united monarchy: a king who will unite the tribes, lead them in fighting their enemies, and return them to their God, the LORD. But such a sweeping change, we must keep in mind, is a major political change that does not come easy (as we should know from recent efforts to change systems of government in the Middle East), and it is this move that is at the heart of the events we will be looking at in this chapter. We will begin by identifying the forces or factors, external and internal,

8

READING ASSIGNMENTS

1 SAMUEL 1–8,
   DEUTERONOMY 17

1 SAMUEL 9–15

1 SAMUEL 16–17

KEY TERMS

Lyre: a small harp

Peace Offering: a type of sacrifice in which part of the meat is returned to the person who brought the sacrifice and to the priest

Pentapolis: five city-states bound together as one entity or group by way of a treaty

Prophet: often, a person who conveys messages from the LORD to select person(s)

Shiloh: the first centralized place for worship in ancient Israel, with the tabernacle and the ark of the covenant

Theocracy: government led by God or by divinely inspired kings or priests

bearing down on Israel and pushing her to adapt or perish. Next we will look backward to discover and examine the LORD's plan for Israel's king in the Book of Deuteronomy. Then, finally, we will observe Israel's initial efforts to establish a united monarchy with Saul and David, and try to understand why Saul failed while David became the great hero of the nation.

The Forces set against Israel

External Forces

The Philistines

The Philistines settled in Palestine around 1190 BCE, just after Israel's entry into the land (most likely around 1250 BCE). While the Philistines' origins are still uncertain, some came over land, destroying Hittites and the city of Ugarit in their path, and some came by ship via Crete ("Caphtor" in Jer 47:4). Amos, a **prophet** of the LORD, later tells Israel that the LORD brought the Philistines from Caphtor, just as he brought Israel out of Egypt (Amos 9:7). Their initial goal was to settle in Egypt, but in 1190 BCE, Rameses III defeated them and pushed them into the coastal towns of Gaza, Ashkelon, and Ashdod (see Deut 2:23). Within forty years, these towns overthrew their Egyptian overlords and formed the Philistine **Pentapolis** of Gaza, Ashkelon, and Ashdod with the two cities already settled by Philistines: Ekron and Gath (see Figure 8.1). Each Philistine city became a city-state, consisting of a "royal city" ruling over other regional villages, and in league with the other Philistine cities.

As was often true, the source of the Philistines' great power was their mastery of a new technology: the art of forging iron (1 Sam 13:19–21). Consequently, for the next 150 years, the Philistine Pentapolis was the most powerful force in this area of Palestine, ruling over an area that extended from Joppa in the north to Raphia in the south, and from the Mediterranean coast in the west into the hill country initially allotted to Israel, then pushing inland as far east as Bethlehem (2 Sam 23:13–17, see Figure 8.1). They even caused the tribe of Dan to seek new land in the far north of Israel (Judg 1:34; 18:1–31).

The Book of Judges attests to the constant threat of the Philistines against any Israelite tribe near them. All of Samson's life as a judge was spent in conflict with the Philistines (Judg 13–16). But his help was spotty at best, acting more like Rambo than as the leader of organized Israelite forces. Consequently, at the beginning of 1 Samuel, the Philistines are still a major threat to Israel. This eminent threat quickly

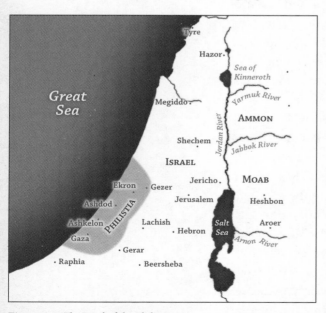

Figure 8.1. The Land of the Philistines

becomes the subject of the book as another conflict erupts between the two (1 Sam 4:1; see also later in the book: 13:2–15, 14:1–35, 14:47, 17:1–54, 23:1–5, 28:1–2, 29:1–11, 31:1–13). In the ensuing battle, the Philistines not only hand Israel a major setback at Aphek (a strategically important route from the coastal plain into the hill country) but they also do the unimaginable: they capture the ark of the covenant (1 Sam 4:11), and we learn from Jeremiah that the Philistines even destroy the sanctuary of the LORD at Shiloh (Jer 7:12). It is clear that if Israel is to have a future in the land God promised to their ancestors, something has to be done about the Philistines.

Other Nations

But the Philistines are only one part of the problem facing Israel. The Books of Judges and 1 Samuel also record pressure from the south (Moab: Judg 3:12–30 and 1 Sam 14:47; Edom: 1 Sam 14:47), the north (Hazor: Judg 4:1–4), the east (Ammon: Judg 10:17–18 and 1 Sam 14:47), and the northeast (Midian and Amalekites: Judg 6:1–3, 33, and 1 Sam 14:48, 15:1–9). In other words, the Israelites are engaged in battles on every front—in the north, east, south, and west (see Figure 8.2). Israel is caught inside a compacter with the switch turned on.

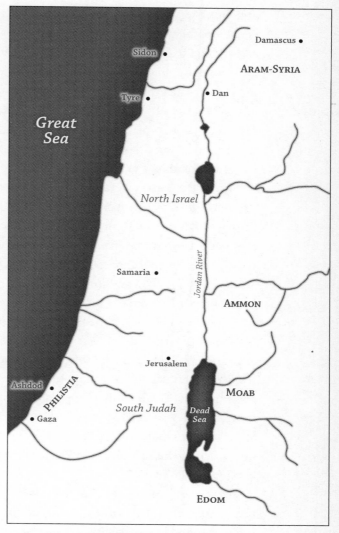

Figure 8.2. Nations Surrounding Israel and Judah

Internal Forces

The First Command and Consequences

As is often the case, even with all of the external pressures, Israel's greatest threat to her existence is from within: "We have met the enemy and he is us."[1] The Book of Judges establishes beyond any reasonable doubt that Israel refuses to keep the first and greatest commandment; instead, Israel chases after every god they find on a Facebook page for Canaanite gods. For example, prior to the rise of Jephthah, the writer observes: "They served the Baals and the Astartes, as well as the gods of Aram, Sidon, Moab, the Ammonites, and the Philistines. They went away from the LORD,

---

[1] Walt Kelly, originally published as a poster for Earth Day in 1970.

and didn't serve him" (Judg 10:6b; see also 2:11, 3:7, 6:25). If there is a god in the land that Israel is not worshipping, it is simply an oversight on Israel's part; they seem determined to worship every god, except for the LORD, who demands monogamy—a single-minded allegiance. In fact, as if there are not already enough gods to worship, some Israelites collect precious metals so they can create even more gods to worship (8:27, 17:3). And at least some Levites, who should be teaching Israel not to worship other gods, are eager to be priests for these new gods and their makers. They put their services on the market to the highest bidder. In one case, a Levite agrees to stay and be the priest for an idolatrous shrine (17:10–13) until he is given a better offer to be the priest for an entire tribe (18:18–20).

The god a person worships is not a neutral choice without consequences; a person becomes like the god he or she decides to serve. Consequently, as Israel worships and serves other gods throughout the era of the judges, the moral quality of the people goes into a steady decline—until they begin to do things they would have never imagined doing before. This moral decay is in the spotlight in the final chapters of Judges (chs. 17–21). Here we find God's people making shrines for new gods (17:3–6) and stealing gods, shrines, and priests from each other (18:18–20). Another Levite pushes his concubine out to a mob of men in Gibeah, to be raped throughout the night while he sleeps (19:22–26). The writer describes Gibeah, a city within the tribe of Benjamin, in the same terms as Sodom (Gen 19:1–11); Israel has deteriorated so much that it is difficult to tell any difference between who they have become and the awful city of Sodom.

The moral decline continues in 1 Samuel with the two sons of Eli, the high priest: Hophni and Phinehas. These brothers are best known for their corruption—stealing the best cuts of meat from sacrifices offered to the LORD (1 Sam 2:12–17) and having sex with the women who served at the tabernacle at Shiloh (2:22). Everyone can see what is going on, even their father. Eli warns his sons, but when Hophni and Phinehas refuse to listen, Eli chooses to turn a blind eye to what his sons are doing (2:22–25).

Israel's failure to keep the first commandment also leads to internal fighting and a threat from within that may cause them to destroy themselves. As early as the story of Deborah, the tribes are failing to work with one another (see Judg 5:9, 15b–17, 23), but she does not take action against those who failed to come when she called. Later, Gideon vows to return to two Israelite cities that refuse to give him aid in his chase and fight against two kings of Midian (8:4–9). When he finishes that battle, he returns with violent vengeance against Succoth and Penuel (8:13–21). Jephthah and his army went to battle against the tribe of Ephraim for their failure to come when he called them (12:1–5). As a result, "Forty-two thousand of the Ephraimites fell at that time" (12:6). Finally, at the end of the Book of Judges, the tribes attack the tribe of Benjamin because it would not give up the village of Gibeah for its crime against the Levite's concubine. By the time their bloodthirsty war comes to an end, only six hundred men from the tribe of Benjamin have escaped death (20:1–48). Now everyone suddenly becomes alarmed that they have almost destroyed an entire tribe. So naturally, the other tribes turn to even more violence to acquire wives for these men, so that the tribe of Benjamin will continue to live (21:1–24).

It is little wonder that by the end of the Book of Judges, the writer is naming the only possible solution for Israel: Israel must have a king. At that time, there is no king in Israel (Judg 17:6; 18:1; 19:1; 21:25); there is no human monarch to build a standing army to face all the external threats—and there is no human monarch to lead these people back to their one and only true King: the LORD.

The LORD's Plan for the Monarchy

Deuteronomy 17

The Book of Judges, however, is not the first to raise the issue of a monarchy in Israel. As early as Deuteronomy 17, both Moses and the LORD understood the need for the nation of Israel to eventually have a human king (a monarchy). There was simply no other form of government for nations in the ancient Near East other than a confederation of city-states (each of which had a king), or the occasional judge/military hero, which had proven to be a failure for what Israel needed to become the mighty nation God promised. Even in the promises to Abraham and Sarah, the LORD had not only stated their descendants would be a great nation (which requires some form of human government), but also said they would give birth to kings (Gen 17:6, 16).

The LORD's plan for Israel's monarchy, however, differs radically from the monarchies of all the nations around her. To begin, Israel's king was to come from among native-born Israelites; like American presidents, the king could not be foreign born (Deut 17:15). More important are the rules the LORD gives for the king and the nature of government and kingdom that would develop as a result of these rules:

Rule One: Limited Horses. First, the king must not have too many horses or send people back to Egypt to trade for horses (Deut 17:16)—a very odd restriction; *what does God have against horses?* As part of creation . . . nothing, but in view of their new purpose in ancient Near Eastern armies . . . everything. The principal use of the horse was for pulling chariots, and later, in the first millennium BCE, for mounted cavalry. In other words, the ban on "many horses" is a warning against militarism, setting a principle for Israel's king that the nation's strength must not be achieved through advanced military technology or a large standing army.

Rule Two: Limited Wives. Second, the "king must not take numerous wives" (Deut 17:17). An explicit rationale follows this command: these women will cause the king's heart to turn toward other gods—a violation of the first and greatest commandment. Another principle is also likely to be involved here: large numbers of wives do not come to a king because of romantic attraction or sexual desire. A king acquires wives as the result of political treaties made with other nations, sealed with the exchange of brides (see 1 Kgs 3:1). My country is less likely to attack your country if one of my daughters is among your wives. So once again, a principle emerges: Israel's kingdom was not to gain its strength or security through political maneuvers. Human alliances are notoriously unreliable; the LORD is the only reliable covenant partner.

Rule Three: Limited Wealth. Third, Deuteronomy forbids the king from acquiring "too much silver and gold" (17:17). The command is perfectly clear, but the principle at stake or reason for the law is not easy to discern. What could be wrong with a wealthy king or nation? It would seem to be a good thing to have great wealth. But in view of the other limitations set for Israel's king, we need to look again. These commandments prohibit gathering and stockpiling what most kings, governments, and their people trust for national security or their well-being: military weapons, treaties and alliances with other nations, *and wealth and a strong economy*. If Israel is to have a monarchy and a united kingdom, the instructions in Deuteronomy demand that the king and nation be like no other country—before or since.

Rule Four: Trust the Lord. Israel's king is to rely on the Lord and lead the nation in trusting God. For this reason, the king must write (or have written for him) "this instruction" on a scroll, keep it with him, and read it every day so that he learns to revere the Lord (17:18–19). Israel's king is not to fall to the common path of monarchs and political leaders and trust himself to build political power. Instead, by following these instructions, Israel's king will recognize the Lord as Israel's true King and not act as if he is more important than other people in the kingdom. If Israel's earthly monarch would only do these things, the Lord promises the king will have a lasting dynasty (17:20).

Samuel and the Monarchy

Despite these plans and instructions, early in 1 Samuel there is still considerable debate about the right course for Israel's future—debate that swirls around Samuel, the man for whom these books are named. Samuel emerges from the corruption at the Shiloh sanctuary as a man who not only keeps his mother's vows for his life (to be a Nazirite; see Hannah's story in 1 Sam 1:1–2:10), but who also becomes a strong leader who fills many different roles: a faithful priest (7:9), a spiritual judge who leads Israel toward God (7:3–6), possibly a judge/military hero who leads Israel in war (7:10–12), and a judge who holds court and gives fair decisions (7:15–17). He also holds the role of prophet, a person who tells others God's message (3:4–4:1). From every perspective, including Samuel's, it appears that he is destined to become Israel's first king. As he grows older, he appoints his own sons to be judges, establishing his own dynasty of judges/kings (8:1). Everything points toward Samuel—except for one small detail: the Lord has other plans.

The conflict between what the people want, what Samuel wants, and what God wants for Israel's future comes to a breaking point at a meeting held in Ramah (1 Sam 8). Samuel has grown old and appoints his sons to take positions in Beersheba. The elders of Israel, however, point out that his sons are not like him; they are only interested in the money they get through bribes and care nothing for justice (8:3). So the elders want Samuel to appoint "a king to judge us like all other nations have" (8:5). Their rationale may not be the highest or best reason for having a king, but, in their own way, the elders are keenly aware of what the writer observed at the end of the Book of Judges: without a king, Israel has no future. They need a king to unite and lead the nation in their battles—before the Philistines and other surrounding countries pick them off, one by one.

Samuel, however, is dead set against the idea. After a lifetime of dedicated service to the tribes, he feels the harsh sting of betrayal. The Lord tells him not to take the rejection so personally; the people are not rejecting Samuel but the Lord (8:7). Even so, when the Lord tells Samuel to warn the people about what a king will do, Samuel dumps a truckload of disappointment and anger

The Message of the Old Testament

What Deuteronomy and 1 Samuel say is wonderful on paper: discontinue military build-up, forget about political treaties and alliances, stop worrying about national wealth and the economy, and, instead, write out your own copy of the law to read (assuming each new king knows how to read and write, and if not, make the time to teach him) and just trust the LORD in all matters: military, political, and economic. Then how is the king to know exactly what the LORD wants him to do? (*Did the priests just put themselves in charge of the nation?*) Or is this the idealism of a new nation—like the idealism of youth? Many a nation has trusted in their god, or even God, only to be pulverized by an enemy with cutting edge military equipment and/or massive numbers of soldiers, paid for by money pouring in from savvy alliances and shrewd profit-driven economies.

Let's be clear up front: the *message* never intended for Israel to scrap the army, nor ever make a treaty or alliance with another nation, nor become irresponsible with the national treasury—*because after all, we read the law and trust in the* LORD. We also need to be careful of equating any contemporary nation with ancient Israel and the God-given laws for her type of government: a **theocracy** (a nation directly under God's rule). No matter how often we may say that we are "one nation, under God," we are not, and have never been, like Israel was. And finally, if we are to make sense of Israel's Scripture and its meaning or message for us, we must drop our presupposition that the Old Testament is a book of hard, inflexible laws, set up so we will fail. Yes, there are laws. But most either state a principle or are the application of a principle to Israel's cultural setting. Our failure to recognize how the Hebrew Bible is embedded within a culture, just as the New Testament is embedded in a specific time and place, will forever rob Christian ears of the testimony and *message* of the Old Testament.

So, have we managed to sweep away any significance of Deuteronomy 17 for anyone other than Israel three thousand years ago? Hardly. Now we can see that these laws carry principles valid for any person or nation at any time, principles that require wisdom to see and apply anew. Let me give a couple of examples to ignite your own insight or, perhaps, vigorous discussion.

- My trust in God must come above trust in myself: my wealth (whatever my *wealth* may be) or my strength (whatever I imagine to be my *strength*).
- New technology is a wonderful thing and our tendency is to believe, perhaps even trust, in the new to save us (just as war horses changed the ancient Near East). Do we misplace our confidence?

on the people (8:11–18); and when the LORD tells Samuel to appoint a king (8:7, 22), he tells all the people to go back home. It is difficult to tell if Samuel is being stubborn and disobedient or following further unwritten directions.

The people demand a king, Samuel hates the idea, and the Lord is somewhere between the two extremes. The Lord tells Samuel to cooperate with the people's request (8:7, 22) and explains that if anyone is being rejected as king, it is him (8:7–8). But this is nothing new; Israel has been rejecting their true King since the day God brought them out of Egypt (8:7–8). Political realities lead the Lord to agree with the people. It would be wonderful if Israel would be united in the service of the King who is enthroned on the cherubim of the ark of the covenant, but the Lord is in the business of working with realities, not unrealistic expectations about the human heart (once again, see Gen 8:21). Israel will never become the great nation God intends for her to become without some form of human government. The only questions now are who will be king and how well will Samuel work with what he hates.

The Beginning of Israel's Monarchy

Saul

The answer to our first question comes quickly in the next chapter of 1 Samuel: the first king will be Saul, the handsome son of a wealthy family from the tribe of Benjamin (9:1–2). As we have already observed, the process of changing the form of government from a loose confederation of twelve tribes to a united kingdom with a centralized monarchy is no easy move. Unless Israel's first king is a political genius, a man of great faith, and has strong support from Samuel, he is bound to fail. Unfortunately, Saul does not appear to be a genius or a man of great faith, and he certainly doesn't have Samuel's support. He does, however, take the first wobbly steps for a monarch in the new, united nation of Israel.

Three stories take Saul from being no one special to the throne of a united kingdom (9:1–11:15). As you read these stories and prepare to discuss them in class, you might fill in the following chart, which will help guide your reading.

Story	What Do We Learn about Saul's Character?	How Does Saul Seem to Feel about Becoming the King?
1. A Private Anointing (9:1–10:16)		
2. A Public Selection at Mizpah (10:17–27)		
3. Saul Leads the Army to Rescue Jabesh-Gilead (11:1–15)		

Table 8.1. Saul's Rise to the Throne

In addition to what you have learned about Saul's character and his attitude about becoming king in these stories, three further observations will be helpful for unpacking the contents of the text. First, at the end of the first story, only Samuel and Saul know about the private anointing to be king, and neither man is telling anyone anything. Saul is evasive, especially when his uncle asks him directly what Samuel said to him (10:15). I wonder if his uncle could tell something was on Saul's mind or if he had changed in some way since his talk with Samuel.

Second, in the next story, God's selection of a king comes through the process of casting the holy lots, probably the Urim and Thummim, to discover the LORD's choice. These "lots" were likely a set of two small flat stones with the same mark or paint on one side of each stone. Consequently, when shaken like dice or tossed in the air like coins, the two stones would either land with both marked sides up (the answer is yes), both unmarked sides up (the answer is no), or one marked side up and the other down (meaning no answer); in this way, a priest could ask a series of yes or no questions to discern God's will. We will see the use of these "lots" frequently in the texts ahead of us. Curiously, when Saul is selected by casting lots at Mizpah, he is hiding among the baggage.

STORY	INSTRUCTIONS (IF ANY) GIVEN TO SAUL	THE SITUATION AND SAUL'S ACTIONS	WHY DOES SAUL ACT AS HE DOES?	CONSEQUENCES TO HIS ACTIONS?
1. Saul's Sacrifice (13:1–15)	(see 10:8)			
2. Saul's Hasty* Decisions (14:1–46)				
3. Saul's Battle against the Amalekites (15:1–35)				
*"Hasty" means to do something rash or without really thinking about it—or, in Saul's case, doing things that were thoughtless and foolish.				

Table 8.2. Saul's Demise

Third, at the end of the public selection, Saul went back home to Gibeah with a few "courageous men whose hearts God had touched" (10:26). Again, the formation of a national government under the king's leadership is a slow process. In fact, as the third story begins, Saul is coming in from the field where he has been plowing—hardly the image of a strong ruler (11:5). Saul may have been anointed privately by the LORD's prophet and even selected in public by the holy lots, but the only way a new monarchy will ever gain traction in Israel is for the new king to lead his people to a military victory. Saul gets that opportunity in the third story when a crisis breaks out against Jabesh-Gilead (10:28–11:4). After he has proven himself in battle, some are ready to kill those who earlier doubted the selection of Saul (10:27), but he stops them, giving credit where it belongs, "Today the LORD has brought deliverance to Israel" (11:13). Samuel then leads the people to Gilgal to "renew the kingship"—and there "they made Saul king before the Lord in Gilgal" (11:12). Israel finally has her king.

Though Saul will remain king until his death at the end of 1 Samuel, the writer is anxious to tell us why Saul failed to establish his own dynasty, eventually losing that privilege to David. So, just as before, the writer uses three stories to document Saul's downfall. To guide your reading and facilitate class discussion, once again, fill out Table 8.2 as you read the three stories (13:1–15:35).

Two additional observations will help us put the whole picture together. First, the relationship between Saul and Samuel raises a number of questions about Samuel's behavior—especially in the first story. Saul waits seven days for Samuel, watching as his troops desert and his hopes for Israel disappear with them. Seven days and no Samuel. So Saul does what has to be done before any ancient army will go into battle: he offers the sacrifices (13:9)—and just as if Samuel has been watching from behind the bushes, no sooner does Saul offer the sacrifices than Samuel shows up and is furious at Saul for what he has done:

- Saul argues that Samuel was late; Samuel doesn't disagree.
- Saul says the Philistines could attack at any moment; Samuel has no response.
- Saul argues that the troops were deserting; Samuel doesn't seem to care.
- So Saul says he took control of the situation and offered the sacrifice; Samuel calls Saul "stupid" and says that his actions have cost him his dynasty (13:10–13).

Maybe Samuel is correct; maybe Saul panicked when he should have waited for the priest. But Samuel's actions raise equal, if not more serious, objections.

- Where has Samuel been for the past seven days?
- What has been so important that Samuel waits until the last second—or later—to come to Saul?
- Does Samuel not understand how serious the situation is for the new king—and for the entire nation?

Some will argue that Saul failed to trust the Lord and should have waited for Samuel, regardless of how late the prophet may be. Others will argue the whole thing was a trap—set and sprung by the prophet-judge-priest who hated the idea of the monarchy in the first place. And if it is a trap, it works. Samuel announces, ". . . but now your rule won't last. The Lord will search for a man following the Lord's own heart, and the Lord will commission him as leader over God's people, because you didn't keep the Lord's command" (13:14). Either way, the first story concludes with an announcement of a fast end to Saul's dynasty; Saul will continue to reign for many years—and many chapters in 1 Samuel, but his future has already been determined: Saul is a lame-duck king.

Second, viewing all three stories, we see the saga of a king who grows more and more self-confident—and trusts the Lord less and less. In the second story, Saul is out of control with his hasty decisions: (1) He stops the priest's inquiry of the Lord (14:16–19) and sends his troops into battle with his, but not God's, directions. (2) He puts a curse on anyone in the Israelite army who stops to eat anything "before evening when *I have taken revenge on my enemies*" (14:25, emphasis mine). Stupid—what else can we say? Jonathan, Saul's son, who knows nothing of the oath, stops later in the day to eat a little honey and regains strength for the fight (14:27). Matters turn worse that evening when troops ravaged by hunger begin slaughtering and eating animals, including the blood, a major infraction of the Lord's laws (see Gen 9:3–4 and Lev 17:10–12). Saul calls them all "traitors" and quickly builds an altar for the proper sacrifice and eating of meat (1 Sam 14:31–35); he then calls for a continuation of the battle through the night (14:36). The Philistines are on the run and Saul has a chance to score a major victory for Israel. The troops agree, but the priest Ahijah urges Saul to ask the Lord first; and when God refuses to answer (most likely one stone face-up and the other face-down) Saul realizes something has gone wrong and makes another terrible decision. He declares that whoever is to blame will be put to death—even if it is my son Jonathan. *It is Jonathan* who broke the oath and ate, and so Saul is ready to kill his own son until the troops put a stop to Saul's madness (14:38–45). (3) Finally, in the third story, Samuel orders Saul to attack the Amalekites and put them under "the ban" (*herem*, 15:1–4). So Saul summons the troops, goes to war, and acts as if he had not heard Samuel's instructions at all; Saul spares the king, along with all the best sheep, cattle, calves, lambs, and anything of value; the only things they completely destroy are things that are worthless (15:5–9).

That night, the Lord's word came to Samuel: "I regret making Saul king because he has turned away from following me and hasn't done what I said" (15:11). Samuel reacts in anger and cries out to the Lord all night (15:11b NRSV). It's not hard to imagine why he is angry and what he might have to say to the Lord that night. *I told you so* is probably near the top of the list. The next day Saul is at Carmel setting up *a monument to himself* (15:12)—not a good decision—when an angry Samuel finds him to tell him he is finished:

> So because you have rejected the command of the Lord,
> he has rejected you as king. (15:23 NLT)

Saul has changed from a man uncertain of himself and unsure that he even wants to be king, to a man who no longer trusts the Lord, but himself (Genesis 3 all over again). So, it's over. Saul will continue as king for years to come, but his reign is finished—he is on his way out.

David

Like Saul's rise to the throne, the writer brings David onto the stage of Israelite politics in three stories that are difficult to piece together (if we are even supposed to try; use Table 8.3 to make notes about David's rise and the difficulties you see).

Story one. The first story captures something of the political climate as the Lord commands a sulking Samuel to get up and go anoint a new king, a rather hazardous task since Saul still holds that position and most likely blames Samuel for at least some of his problems (16:1–2). So the Lord provides Samuel with a cover story about a **peace offering** and dinner party with part of the meat from the sacrifice. Nonetheless, when the city elders (leaders) spot Samuel coming, they go out to meet Samuel "shaking with fear" and ask if he comes in peace (16:4). The nation appears to be torn between Saul and Samuel—and supporting the wrong man might prove deadly. Samuel assures them of his peaceful intentions and invites them to the sacrifice dinner—the barbecue—later that evening; he also invites a man named Jesse and all his sons.

As guests arrive at the dinner that evening, Samuel watches the sons of Jesse to see who the Lord will point out as the next king. He sees the firstborn Eliab and thinks he must be the one, but the Lord speaks to Samuel:

> Have no regard for his appearance or stature, because I haven't selected him. God doesn't look at things like humans do. Humans see only what is visible to the eyes, but the Lord sees into the heart. (16:7)

So Jesse presents one son after another to Samuel, and one after the other is not selected (perhaps using the Urim and Thummim again). Finally, Jesse has presented all seven sons that have come with him, and the Lord has passed on all seven. So Samuel asks if there is not another son and discovers there is: the youngest son, whom Jesse considered unimportant and left behind to tend the sheep. Dinner is put on hold until this young man arrives (16:8–11), and when David does arrive, the Lord tells Samuel he is the one. Samuel takes the oil and anoints him, presumably in front of his brothers and the other dinner guests (16:13). But the writer doesn't tell us whether or not the brothers, other guests, or even David recognize the significance of the anointing. Maybe Samuel tells David secretly, as he did with Saul. But we are left with this and other questions about how David is to become king, as Samuel returns home to Ramah (16:13b). Ironically, however, despite what the Lord told Samuel about looking at the heart and not externals, David is good-looking, with a reddish-brown complexion and beautiful eyes.

Story	How David Rises to the Throne (or Rises in Saul's Court)	Point(s) of Tension within the Context or Other Stories
1. Anointed by Samuel (16:1–13)		
2. Entry into Saul's Court (16:14–23)		
3. Faces Goliath (17:1–58)		

Table 8.3. David's Rise

Story Two. Another feature of David's life brings him into Saul's presence in the second story: he wins "Israel's Got Talent!" by playing a small harp (a **lyre**). Before we get to this story, however, we need to deal with two technical issues that come into play. In the prior story, after David was anointed, "the LORD's spirit came over David" (16:13). Now we learn that "the LORD's spirit had departed from Saul" and instead, the LORD sent "an evil spirit" to torment him (16:14). Two issues are on the table:

1. Who or what is the Lord's spirit? Reading through Christian (or New Testament) glasses, it is easy to conclude the spirit is the Holy Spirit, the third member of the Trinity. The Common English Bible, however, is correct not to suggest such an idea by not capitalizing the word "spirit," because from the perspective of the writer and original audience, such a meaning would be a foreign idea. In the Book of Judges, the "LORD's spirit" came upon some of the judges and denoted the presence or power of the LORD working through the judge, perhaps inspiring courage or strength (see Judg 3:10; 4:12–16, 34; 11:29; 13:25). For example, in Judges 14, "the LORD's spirit rushed over" Samson and he was able to kill a lion with his bare hands (14:6). A similar episode occurs later in chapter 14 when the "LORD's spirit" rushes over Samson and he kills thirty Philistines in the town of Ashkelon (14:19). In 1 Samuel, the same concept continues when the LORD's spirit comes over Saul when he hears about the crisis in Jabesh-Gilead and "he burned with anger" (1 Sam 11:6–7). Consequently, the evidence from the surrounding context does not suggest that "spirit" denotes the Holy Spirit, but the special presence of the LORD that gives supernatural strength or courage.

2. What is the "evil spirit" the Lord sent? The "evil spirit from God" is not a demon, but the result of an unfortunate translation. The Hebrew term behind "evil" (*ra*) has a wide range of meaning, most often conveying such ideas as bad, degenerate, harmful, or even vicious. The term may denote moral evil, but more often lacks any moral sense or judgment. So, instead of God's spirit to help and encourage Saul, God sends "a spirit" that torments Saul; and whatever it is, David can play the lyre for Saul and "Saul would relax and feel better" so the harmful or painful spirit would "leave him alone" (16:23). If the "evil spirit" were a demon, it is unlikely that soothing music would be helpful; instead, the "punishing spirit" (my translation) causes physical pain, just as the "spirit of God" enables great strength.

Back to the second story. Once Saul begins to suffer from the "punishing spirit" he asks his men to find iTunes, Pandora, or Spotify and, since all are a few thousand years in the future, they find the next best thing: a young David, who plays the lyre. Oddly, however, Saul's men describe David as "a strong man and heroic, a warrior who speaks well and is good-looking too. The LORD is with him" (1 Sam 16:18). So, David enters Saul's service and Saul likes David; and in time, David becomes his armor bearer (1 Sam 16:21). Once again, how these stories fit together is not an easy puzzle to solve.

Story Three. The third story of David's rise is the best known and perhaps the least understood. Saul is with his troops at war against the Philistines, with the battle developing in ancient

Near Eastern style. Each day a hulk of a man named Goliath, somewhere over six feet tall[2] and as strong as any NFL lineman, would put on all his armor and step out into the valley to talk smack and challenge Israel to send out their own hulk for hand-to-hand combat. Goliath represents one of three types of military troops in ancient Near Eastern armies—(1) the heavily armored men prepared for hand-to-hand combat; (2) the troops of chariots and cavalry; and (3) the light infantry who were projectile warriors: archers, slingers, and javelin hurlers.[3]

It is at this point David enters the picture, having been sent from home to bring food to his brothers in the army and check on their condition (17:16–19). He arrives just in time to see the big daily show with Goliath (17:20–24) and to hear the rumor that the king has promised his daughter in marriage to any man who will face Goliath (17:25–27). A terrific prize, of course, provided the man escapes with his head still on his shoulders, instead of at the end of Goliath's spear. David, however, seems oblivious to the danger and keeps asking one man after another about the reward—and keeps asking why everyone is letting "that uncircumcised Philistine" insult the army of the living God? His presence and questions finally reach the ears of his older brother Eliab, who reacts in anger. He questions David's motives for coming to the front lines and charges him with arrogance (17:28). In Eliab's defense, we must admit that Jesse sent David to go find his brothers and deliver supplies, a task David seems to have forgotten about in all his excitement; but in David's defense, Eliab is his older brother, and we don't know what Eliab knows about the earlier anointing or how he feels about being passed over in favor of his little brother.

Eventually, David's questions also reach Saul, who sends for him (17:31). David confidently tells Saul he will go fight Goliath, to which Saul points out the obvious: David couldn't last a single round of hand-to-hand combat against the Philistine. He is just a boy and Goliath is a grown man. Goliath wears the armor of a Sherman tank; David can't even walk across the room with all of Saul's armor on (17:38–39). But Saul doesn't understand, nor do we—yet. David has no intentions of playing by the rules of the game—not now, not ever; he is not heavy infantry, but a sharp shooter. So, instead of coming out dressed in heavy armor to engage in hand-to-hand combat, David goes out as himself (with a loaded gun). He is Indiana Jones in *Raiders of the Lost Ark* when a large black-robed man appears with terrifying sword in hand, swinging it back and forth and shouting his battle cry. The people around step back in fear, while Indiana takes out his pistol and casually shoots the man dead.

For the Philistine Goliath, the fight was over before it ever began. First, as David points out in the pre-fight smack talk, the battle is not between two men—or even a man and a boy—but between Yahweh of the angelic armies and a man in Philistine battle armor who has insulted Yahweh (17:41–44). Now Yahweh has a point to prove about who holds power and who owns the war (17:45–47). Goliath is done. Second, while the Philistine is sneering at David and complaining about Israel sending out a boy to fight a man's battle (17:41–44), the sharp shooter is lining up

---

[2] Some texts put Goliath at over nine feet tall; but older, more reliable texts bring Goliath down to a more reasonable, though still formidable size, at just over six feet tall.

[3] See Baruch Halpern, *David's Secret Demons: Messiah, Murderer, Traitor, King* (Grand Rapids: Eerdmans, 2001), 11.

an easy kill shot. For an ace slinger, the shot is a no brainer—at least until the stone sunk into Goliath's skull (17:49). The hulk falls face first, and David uses Goliath's own sword to relieve him of his head (17:50–51). Goliath didn't count on a sharp shooter in what was supposed to be hand-to-hand combat. And so, all of our pep rally speeches about facing and defeating the mighty Goliath are forever ruined by a careful reading of the text in its ancient context. I would offer my apologies, but I would be insincere; this reading is a good example of what time travel into ancient Israel's world offers us.

Conclusion

As a result of David's heroic actions, strangely, he is introduced to Saul as if they have never met (17:55–58); and in what must be a summary of things to come, we learn that David becomes best friends with Saul's son Jonathan who, at some point in their friendship, recognizes that David will be the next king. He gives David the things that represent his own claim to the throne: armor, sword, bow, and belt (18:1–4). We also learn that at some future point Saul will put David in charge of his army (18:5). But for the present, back in the days following David's unconventional conquest of Goliath, a new song makes its way up the hit charts in the newly united Israel:

> Saul has killed his thousands,
> but David has killed his tens of thousands! (18:7)

The young women are singing, dancing, and crying out for their hero: David—not Saul. Kings never like being upstaged, or having someone's approval ratings higher than their own. The spirit of God may have left Saul, but it doesn't take a rocket scientist to understand what is happening between David and Saul. Saul knows exactly what all this means for his reign and his dynasty: David is the man who must be watched at all times, and if possible, be removed from the picture (18:8–9). For better or worse, David has soared into the public spotlight. His life will never be the same.

To Discuss

1. Consider Hannah's story. Why do her husband's words (1 Sam 1:8) fail to comfort her? Do you think she knew about the corruption at the Shiloh tabernacle when she left Samuel there? Do you believe awareness of their wickedness would have changed her actions?

2. Reconsider the commandments for Israel's king from Deuteronomy 17:16–17. Do you think these principles were realistic expectations for an ancient monarch? What about a contemporary nation? Divide into groups for and against and argue your position. Now have the groups switch and argue for the other side.

3. What principles derive from God's expectations of Israel and Israel's monarch? In other words, what principles stand behind and support the specific laws in Deuteronomy 17? How might the same principles be stated as laws today?

4. Travel back in time to when Samuel first approached Saul about being king. What do you notice about Saul's reaction? Do you think Saul wants to be king? How might his actions or attitude shape future events or how the nation responds to him?

5. What do you think about Samuel's relationship with Saul? What do you make of his arrival in the first story leading to Saul's demise (1 Sam 13)? Was Samuel late or on time? In view of the circumstances, why did Samuel wait so long to come? Did Saul act appropriately? Did Samuel speak for the LORD on this occasion (in 1 Sam 13:13–14)? How does their relationship affect Saul's reign?

6. What is the common element in the stories of Saul's fall or demise? What is the biblical writer trying to tell us about Saul through these stories? What picture do you develop of God in these stories?

7. Identify the ways in which the stories of David's rise do not seem to fit together. What are we to make of these conflicts? Do you see any way(s) to resolve these conflicts?

8. In at least two stories from our reading, God seems to work through chance (the Urim and Thummim). Is this a comforting thought for you, or a disturbing one? If God uses it, is it really chance? Would you be willing to approach God in a similar way?

9. New technology brings new power. Consequently, the Philistines had new power with their ability to forge iron. What new technologies have developed in the past fifty years? How are they creating new power? Consider your field of study: What knowledge or technology is new to your field? Does this new knowledge or technology create power; if so, how?

10. Brief discussion prompts:
    - Have you ever considered Samuel to be a bad guy? Is this troublesome to you?
    - Does the author ruin the story of David and Goliath? What new features emerge that might also be motivating?

To Know

1. The significance of the following in the assigned chapters:

   David   Jonathan
   Eli   Philistines
   Elkanah   Phinehas
   Goliath   Samuel
   Hannah   Saul
   Hophni

2. Hannah's story and her gift.

3. Samuel's call from the LORD and the various roles/tasks he takes in the assigned reading.

4. The saga of the LORD's ark among the Philistines.

5. The rules for Israel's king from Deuteronomy 17 and the principle(s) of these laws.

6. The position toward the monarchy and rationale for each (1 Sam 8): the people, Samuel, and God.

7. The three stories leading to Saul's rise to the monarchy and the three stories leading to the loss of his dynasty. Analyze each for common factors.

8. The three stories leading to David's rise in Saul's court.

9. Locate the following on a map (see Figure 8.1): Philistia, Edom, Moab, Ammon, Aram (Syria), the Dead Sea, and Jordan River.

To Dig Deeper: Research Topics

1. Political Science/History students: What research can you find about what commonly happens when a loose confederation of tribes/states decides to come into a unified nation? What insights does this research provide in understanding what happens in Israel?

2. Dig deeper into the relationship between Saul and Samuel. Read David Gunn's book *The Fate of King Saul* and find at least one essay (a journal article or book chapter) that responds to Gunn's work. What new data do you find? What conclusion(s) do you reach?

3. Conduct a literary analysis of the ark narrative (1 Sam 4:1–7:1). Consider one of the following studies: J. J. M. Roberts and Patrick Miller, *The Hand of the Lord: A Reassessment of the Ark Narrative of 1 Samuel* (Atlanta: Society of Biblical Literature, 2008); or Anthony Campbell, *The Ark Narrative (1 Sam 4–5; 2 Sam 6): A Form-Critical and Traditio-Historical Study*, SBLDS 16 (Atlanta: Society of Biblical Literature, 1975).

4. Further your consideration of the stories about David's entry and rise in Saul's court. Identify the difficulties present in the stories and find research quality discussions of those problem(s) in journals or commentaries. What options do you find? Establish your own thesis with supporting evidence and arguments.

5. Present an artistic interpretation of the rise of David (including all three stories) or the rise of Saul (including all three stories). Prior to beginning, be sure to read at least one research quality interpretation/analysis of the stories.

6. An Early Childhood Education student and an Art student: team up to rewrite a rough copy of the story of David and Goliath.

For Further Reading

Campbell, Anthony F.. *The Ark Narrative (1 Sam 4–5; 2 Sam 6): A Form-Critical and Traditio-Historical Study*. SBLDS 16. Atlanta: Society of Biblical Literature, 1975.

Gunn, David M. *The Fate of King Saul: An Interpretation of a Biblical Story*. JSOTSup 14. Sheffield: JSOT Press, 1980.

Halpern, Baruch. *David's Secret Demons: Messiah, Murderer, Traitor, King*. Grand Rapids: Eerdmans, 2001.

Katzenstein, H. J. "Philistines." Pages 326–328 in vol. 5 of *The Anchor Bible Dictionary*. Edited by David Noel Freedman. 6 vols. New York: Doubleday, 1992.

Robert, J. J. M., and Patrick Miller Jr. *The Hand of the Lord: A Reassessment of the Ark Narrative of 1 Samuel*. Atlanta: Society of Biblical Literature, 2008.

David, Solomon, and Rehoboam
War, Women, and a Lack of Wisdom

By every measurement, David is the most celebrated king in Israel. More text is devoted to David than any other person in the Old Testament. He comes onto the scene in 1 Samuel 16 and shares the spotlight with a fading King Saul until Saul's death in 1 Samuel 31 (sixteen chapters). David is the leading man in all of 2 Samuel (twenty-four chapters), and his final days and death are recorded in 1 Kings 1–2 (two chapters). In addition, just as the gospels in the New Testament retell the story of Jesus for their own purposes, 1 Chronicles retells the story of David for its own purposes (1 Chron 11–29, another nineteen chapters). Together, the **Deuteronomistic History (DH)** and Chronicles devote sixty-one chapters to David, 105 pages in my Bible, which is 6.7 percent of the Old Testament.

More significantly, David is celebrated by words of high praise. Before he is anointed to be king, Samuel says in reference to David, "The LORD will search for a man following the LORD's own heart, and the LORD will commission him as leader over God's people" (1 Sam 13:14). After his death, Solomon refers to David in positive terms as he prays to the LORD: "You showed so much kindness to your servant my father David when he walked before you in truth, righteousness, and with a heart true to you" (1 Kgs 3:6). And even God speaks highly of David as he tells Solomon, "As for you, if you walk before me just as your father David did, with complete dedication and honesty . . . then I will establish your royal throne over Israel forever, just as I promised your father David, 'You will never fail to have a successor on the throne of

READING ASSIGNMENTS
1 SAMUEL 18–31

2 SAMUEL 1–12, 22–24

1 KINGS 1–12

KEY TERMS
Census: either counting the number of people or determining the number of men available to fight

Chronicler's History (CH): the books of 1–2 Chronicles, Ezra, and Nehemiah

Dynasty: a succession of kings from a single family, from father to son or to the son's heir

Puppet King: a weak king from a dynasty set in place by a more powerful person who is not of the dynasty (not qualified to be king), but who controls the king

Succession Narrative: 2 Samuel 11:1–1 Kings 2:11, a story about who will become the next king in David's dynasty

Israel'" (1 Kgs 9:4–5). Finally, in the New Testament, Paul refers to David as he preaches, ". . . he raised up David to be their king. God testified concerning him, 'I have *found* David, Jesse's son, a *man who shares my desires*. Whatever my will is, he will do'" (Acts 13:22, emphasis in original).[1]

So it is little surprise that David becomes the example for the good kings who follow. Introductions to these kings sometimes include a reference to David.

> Asa became king of Judah. He ruled in Jerusalem for forty-one years. . . . Asa did the right things in the LORD's eyes, just like his father David. (1 Kgs 15:9–11, the term father often means "ancestor")

> Amaziah, the son of Judah's King Josiah, became king in the second year of Israel's King Joash. . . . He did what was right in the LORD's eyes, but not as well as his ancestor King David. He did everything his father Jehoash did. (2 Kgs 14:1, 3; see also 18:1–3 and 22:1–2)

Other kings might be described to be unlike David (the first example below); but more often, if they are wicked they are allied with a different, unrighteous king (see the second example).

> Abijam became king of Judah. . . . Abijam followed all the sinful ways of his father before him. He didn't follow the LORD his God with all his heart like his ancestor David. (1 Kgs 15:1, 3)

> Ahaziah, the son of Judah's King Jehoram, became king. . . . Ahaziah was 22 years old when he became king, and he ruled one year in Jerusalem. . . . He walked in the ways of Ahab's dynasty, doing what was evil in the LORD's eyes, just as Ahab's dynasty had done, because he had married into Ahab's family. (2 Kgs 8:25–27; see also 8:16–18, 13:10–12, 21:1–3, et al.)

Initial impressions, then, set us up to read about an incredibly righteous man who rarely, if ever, did anything wrong. But as we begin to read the stories about David, discarding the flannelgraph or VeggieTales™ movies and skits performed for us when we were children, we are likely to be shocked by what we see. If we are not startled at least a little, we are probably not reading as slowly and carefully as we should, or with adult glasses. Sharp-eyed reading again and again causes readers to wonder how anyone could declare David to be a faithful, righteous man. It's difficult to see how the claims in the text about David "following the LORD's own heart"—and the stories in the same text about David's enormous failures—could possibly be talking about the same man.

Nonetheless, David is "the man" in the Old Testament—with more high praise spoken about him and text devoted to him than any other figure, and his legacy serving as examples for every king in Judah. Consequently, much of this chapter will be devoted to unpacking David's life—the good and the bad—and trying to solve the mystery of David. In the last third of this chapter, we will

---

[1] A reference to 1 Samuel 13:14. Most translations are more like the NRSV: "I have found David, son of Jesse, to be a man after my own heart, who will carry out all my wishes."

move ahead to the succession of Solomon, David's son, to the throne—the Israelite king celebrated for his great wisdom. As with David, our challenge will be to read the narrative about Solomon with eyes wide open to see his wisdom and the great things he accomplishes, and to see the heavy debt he and the nation rack up for his accomplishments. Finally, we will watch as Rehoboam proves unable to negotiate the debts left by his father and grandfather, while his own folly pits Israel against itself.

1. David

A. The View from 25,000 Feet

In order to help guide your reading and set the context for whatever parts of the narrative you may read, we will first look at David's story from a distance that enables us to see the major parts or eras in his life and how they all fit together (see Figure 9.1). Even here, we should begin to exercise our critical thinking and evaluate what David is doing, whether his actions match what a person should do—if he is "following the LORD's own heart."

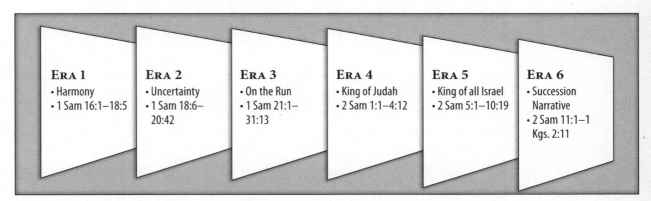

Figure 9.1. The Eras of David's Life

Era 1: Harmony with Saul 1 (Samuel 16:1–18:5)

As we have already seen, David enters the story in such a way that Saul has no reason to be suspicious of him (see Chapter Eight). He first comes to Saul playing music to soothe his suffering from God's punishing spirit. David also helps Saul out of a tough situation by not only facing, but killing the Philistine giant, Goliath. In our new reading, Saul's son Jonathan and David begin a lifelong, close friendship (18:1–4) and Saul promotes David to a position over the entire Israelite army (18:5). Had Saul known about David's private anointing to be king (16:1–13), or Jonathan giving up the emblems that signified who would be the next king (18:1–4), things would have been quite different. But since he didn't know, David was able to enjoy a time of favor with Saul.

Era 2: Uncertainty (1 Samuel 18:6–20:42)

The era of harmony did not last long. As David became more successful in war than Saul, women would come dancing, making music, and singing:

> Saul has killed his thousands,
> but David has killed his ten thousands! (18:7)

Upstaged and humiliated, Saul begins to keep his eye on David (18:9). Consequently, David can never be sure where he stands with Saul, whether it is safe to be with him or if David must be ready to jump away from a spear thrown at him while he plays music (18:10–16; 19:9–10), evade a trap set for him during the night (19:11–17), or overcome a plot Saul has planned to get David killed (18:17–30). Twice, Jonathan tries to reconcile his father with his best friend. The first time he succeeds (19:1–10), but only briefly; the second time Jonathan fails, so he and David know that it is no longer safe for David to be near Saul (20:1–42).

Era 3: On the Run (1 Samuel 21:1–31:13)

Once David recognizes the danger, he runs to Nob to see the priest, Ahimelech, where he takes a weapon (Goliath's sword) and food for his journey (21:1–9). He then seeks refuge in the Philistine city of Gath (21:10–15)—the hometown of Goliath. Soon he moves to the cave of Adullam where a large number of troubled and discontented people gather to him: a militia with a common bond against Saul (22:1–2). At this point, David seeks protection from the king of Moab for his parents (22:3–5). When David hears that the Philistines are attacking Keilah, an Israelite town, he consults God through a priest (now with him) and goes to their rescue (23:1–5). But, when the priest also tells him that Keilah is ready to betray David and hand him over to Saul (23:6–13), he's on the run again, into the wilderness where he and Saul play "ring around the mountain" (23:26). Just as Saul is about to catch David, a messenger informs Saul of a Philistine raid and he has to return home (23:26–29).

The game of chase continues with David having the opportunity to kill Saul twice but refusing to hurt the LORD's anointed king (24:1–22; 26:1–25). During this time he also has an encounter with a man by the name of Nabal ("Fool") and his wife Abigail ("Beautiful"); by the time the story concludes, Nabal is dead and David has a "Beautiful" new wife (25:1–42). Finally, David is worn down from the chase and thinks, "One day I will be destroyed by Saul's power" (27:1). So he moves into Ziklag, one of the villages associated with the Philistine king of Gath. David will live here with his army for almost a year and a half (27:1–12).

Era 4: David Becomes King of South Judah (2 Samuel 1:1–4:12)

At the end of David's time with the Philistines, Saul and Jonathan die in a war against the Philistines—a war in which David is nearly caught up on the Philistine side (1 Sam 28:1–2; 29:1–11). Instead, David is sent home, and after avoiding death at the hands of his own army (30:1–31), David learns of the death of Saul and Jonathan (2 Sam 1:1–27). Soon, the leaders of the southern tribes of Judah come to David and anoint him to be their king (2:1–4). In the north, however, the military leader, Abner, has set up one of Saul's sons, Ishbosheth[2] as a **puppet king**

---

[2]Ishbosheth is called "Esh-baal" in 1 Chronicles 8:33 and 9:39; "Esh-baal" means "Man of Baal" (most likely his original name), changed in 2 Samuel to "Ishbosheth," which means "Man of Shame" as a derogatory comment on his commitment to Baal.

(2:8–10). Soon a civil war breaks out between the north and south (2:12–32) with David slowly but steadily becoming more powerful (3:1). Eventually, through a series of events for which David denies any responsibility (3:22–4:12), he wins the war.

Era 5: David Rules all Israel (2 Samuel 5:1–10:19)

After the war, the northern tribes come to David and ask him to be their king (5:1–3). Finally, David reigns over a reunited Israel (5:4–5). He quickly takes steps to strengthen the unity and the nation as a whole: making Jerusalem the new capital city (5:6–12), attempting to relocate the ark of the covenant to Jerusalem (6:1–23), desiring to build a temple for the LORD in Jerusalem (7:1–17), reaching out in kindness to Saul's descendants (9:1–13), and defeating many longstanding enemies and establishing a state government (5:17–25; 8:1–18; 10:1–19).

Era 6: The Succession Narrative (2 Samuel 11:1–1 Kings 2:11)

The final era in the story of David's life is the **Succession Narrative**; or, more simply put, who will become king after David and how? The question is especially important because, despite common assumptions, Solomon is not the natural choice to be the next king. So, these chapters lead us through David's sin against Bathsheba, her pregnancy, and David's efforts to cover up his sin. The cover-up then leads to the murder of Bathsheba's husband Uriah, the birth of a child who dies, and finally, the birth of Solomon (11:1–12:24). David's family life is in shambles with one son, Amnon, raping his half sister, Tamar; and another son, Absalom, killing Amnon (13:39), for which Absalom is exiled from Jerusalem. After David restores Absalom back to the capital city (14:1–33), Absalom begins to plot an overthrow of David's government (15:1–12). His plan leads to another civil war that forces David to flee the capital city (15:13–17:29). The war finally ends with Absalom killed in battle—an incredible grief for David (18:1–19:8). David then returns to Jerusalem (19:9–43) to face another rebellion out of the north that is soon put down (20:1–22).

The book of 2 Samuel concludes with reports of wars (21:1–22), a thanksgiving psalm from David (22:1–51), final words from David (23:1–7), and a list of David's mighty warriors (23:8–39). David takes a **census** to which the LORD objects, leaving David to choose his punishment from a multiple choice quiz (24:1–25). First Kings opens with an old, feeble David and his oldest son, Adonijah, declaring himself king (1:1–10; and see 2 Sam 3:2–4). The prophet, Nathan, and Solomon's mother, Bathsheba, act quickly. They either remind David of an earlier promise he made to them (not in the text), or they devise a way to save their lives and put Solomon on the throne (1:11–31). Whatever the situation may have been, David declares Solomon to be the next king (1:32–52). Finally, after leaving last instructions for Solomon, David dies (2:1–11).

DAVID: THE MAN AFTER GOD'S OWN HEART		
Good or Admirable Actions (with text reference)	**Questionable or Other Activity** (with text reference)	**Bad Actions or Behavior** (with text reference)
		David lies to the fearful priest, Ahimelech (21:1–2)
		David tricks Ahimelech into providing food for his men (21:3–6)
	Doeg, one of Saul's servants, is present and sees everything that happens (21:7)	
		David tricks Ahimelech into providing a weapon—Goliath's sword (21:8–9)
	David runs away to the Philistine city of Gath (21:10; the home of Goliath, 17:4)	
	When King Achish is warned of David's presence and his position in Israel, David becomes afraid and acts like a madman (21:11–15)	
	David escapes to the cave of Adullam where his family joins him—as well as others who are in debt or unhappy with their lives; it seems David has attracted a small militia who dislike Saul (22:1–2)	
David asks the king of Moab to protect his parents (22:3–4)		
David listens to the prophet Gad and leaves the stronghold of Adullam (22:5)		
	As a result of David's lies to the priest at Nob, Doeg tells Saul that Ahimelech has given provisions and the sword of Goliath to David (22:6–10)	
	Saul accuses the priests of treason and massacres them and everyone in the village of Nob (22:11–19)	
	One priest, Abiathar, escapes the massacre. He flees to David and tells him what has happened (22:20–21)	
David confesses his responsibility for what happened to the priests at Nob (22:22)		
David offers Abiathar protection if he will stay with David (22:23)		

Table 9.1. David: The Man After God's Own Heart (Sample)

DAVID THE MAN AFTER GOD'S OWN HEART		
Good or Admirable Actions (with text reference)	**Questionable Actions or Other Activity** (with text reference)	**Bad Actions or Behavior** (with text reference)

Table 9.2. David: The Man After God's Own Heart (Blank)

B. The Man After God's Own Heart

The preceding survey has left the work of close reading and evaluation to the reader; again, I offer the survey so that whatever portion or portions of the David story you may read, you will be able to fit your text within its context. The challenge is for you to read critically—slowly and carefully—without blinders to the realities of David's actions. Use Table 9.2 below to assess his actions and record it in one of three categories: (1) a good or appropriate action; (2) a questionable, or vague event where you are unsure whether David should be involved (or the text shifts its focus to someone other than David); or (3) inappropriate or wrong—without question, David should not do this. As an example, my analysis of 1 Samuel 21–22:23 is provided in Table 9.1. Use the blank chart provided (make copies, or sketch three columns in your notes) to work through the texts you are assigned to read. Do not be alarmed at differences of opinion among your colleagues; different readers are likely to come to different conclusions about David's activities. As you read, you may also refer to Table 9.1, which provides a brief review of the eras of David's life.

Now that you have examined David's life more carefully, depending on which texts you read, you will have discovered a David who is very different from any childhood memories we may have. Instead, we see a deeply flawed man who lies (frequently), murders (frequently), rapes or commits adultery (depending on your view of the events in 2 Sam 11:1–4), marries many women (recall Deut 17), has a large idol at home (1 Sam 19:13), lives for a time as a common bandit (27:8–12), demands mafia-like protection money (25:1–11), and participates in many other activities that are, at a minimum, questionable. How can this man receive such high praise, including being called "a man following the Lord's own heart"? I hope you will pause long enough to wrestle with this question for yourself, and then write your own observations below (or in your own notes) before rushing on to my comments.

DAVID: THE MAN AFTER GOD'S OWN HEART WHAT CAN IT MEAN?
Observation #1:
Observation #2:
Observation #3:

Table 9.3. David: The Man After God's Own Heart: What Can It Mean?

How do we harmonize what we see in David's life with all the high praise given to him? As one who also wrestles with this question, I can only offer three observations. First, it is possible that our English translations have let us down. Kyle McCarter Jr. suggests that the Hebrew phrase may mean "a man of his [God's] own choosing." Rather than establishing Saul's **dynasty** by the natural selection of Saul's oldest son, God makes his own choice.[3] Even if correct, however, this change does not deal with all of the other accolades circling about David.

Second, we may confidently conclude that Solomon, God, and others knew the truth about David's life when they call him loyal, faithful, and righteous; a man with a true heart and complete dedication, who shares God's desires—with or without the phrase: a heart after God's own heart. The writers are not trying to do a snow job that covers over all David's flaws. David's character is painted by the text, warts and all. So we may conclude that to be or become all the things for which David is celebrated (e.g., righteous, loyal, faithful), does not require a person to be perfect—and that is good news for all of us. We too may be deeply flawed, wrestling with sin—just like David—and we can still be people who are righteous and faithful to God.

Third, but how? What is the secret or crucial element that is also present in David's life—that changes a sexually immoral man and murderer into a person of God? Let's identify and carefully read several texts.

1. When the priest, Abiathar, escapes the massacre at Nob (because of David's lies, see above) and comes to report the tragedy to David:

    > David told Abiathar, "That day, when Doeg the Edomite was there, I knew that he would tell Saul everything. *I am to blame for the deaths* in your father's family. Stay with me, and don't be afraid. The one who seeks my life now seeks yours too. But you will be safe with me." (1 Sam 22:22–23, emphasis mine)

    David not only accepts the blame for what has happened, he does his best to make things right by promising protection to Abiathar.

2. When David's small army is angry and ready to kill him for the loss of their families to bandits. (Ironically, this the same thing David and his men had been doing, except they killed everyone.) The writer describes David as follows:

    > David was in deep trouble because the troops were talking about stoning him. Each of the soldiers was deeply distressed about their sons and daughters. But *David found strength in the* Lord *his God.* (1 Sam 30:6, emphasis mine)

    After a time in his life when he lived as a bandit, ransacking villages and killing every witness, David turns back to the Lord for strength. He then calls upon the priest to ask directions from God, which he follows (30:7–8).

3. When David wants to build a "house" (temple) for the Lord, the Lord makes a covenant with David and his family. Instead of David building a "house" for God, the

---

[3]Kyle McCarter Jr., *The HarperCollins Study Bible*, fully rev. upd. ed. (New York: HarperOne, 2006), 407, note to 1 Sam 13:14.

LORD promises to build a "house" (dynasty) for David. In this covenant, the LORD promises that "I will never take my faithful love away from him like I took it away from Saul" (2 Sam 7:15). When David's sons do wrong, the LORD will punish them (7:14). But much like the covenant after the flood, after seeing Saul's failures, the LORD realizes that pledging his faithful love is the only way a dynasty can exist in Israel. Every king will fail to measure up to God's standards, so the LORD promises that, despite their failures, a descendant of David will always be on the throne of Israel.

4. The prophet, Nathan, comes to David after his sins against Bathsheba and Uriah; Nathan confronts David about his sin, and David responds:

> I've sinned against the LORD! (2 Sam 12:13)

The superscription (heading) to Psalm 51 suggests that David wrote the psalm as part of his confession and prayer for forgiveness after his sin against Bathsheba (it is difficult to know, however, whether the superscriptions are a reliable part of the text; see our final chapter on Psalms and the God Who Saves). Whether accurate or not, the psalm expresses deep grief for sin that fits this occasion in David's life.

5. David conducts a census of the nation, either as a matter of pride or to determine the strength of his army, or perhaps both (2 Sam 24:2). When all the numbers are reported, before any prophet comes to tell David he has done wrong, the text reports,

> But after this David felt terrible that he had counted the people. David said to the LORD, *"I have sinned greatly in what I have done.* Now, LORD, please take away the guilt of your servant because I have done something very foolish." (2 Sam 24:10, emphasis mine)

In your reading, you may have found other texts that give further understanding into David's heart or how such a sinful person could be given such high praise. To be honest, I still would not want David to be my roommate or my next-door neighbor, but these texts do provide important insights into David's inner life. He has a heart that can be broken by sin and experiences deep distress when he realizes he has done wrong, qualities that were absent from Saul's life.

In terms of gymnastics or karate, David knows how to take a fall. He might get caught up in his own ego, but when he comes to his senses, he knows how to humble himself before the LORD. He appears to take (at least some) responsibility for helping those he has harmed (e.g., the priest, Abiathar, is given protection; he leads his men to recover their families). Beyond these simple observations, however, it still remains a question for you (and me) to settle. Now, however, at least you have some, if not most of the textual evidence to work with.

Texts in Conversation

The **Chronicler's History (CH)**—consisting of 1–2 Chronicles, Ezra, and Nehemiah—stands in relationship to the Deuteronomistic History (DH) like the four Gospels of the New Testament. Just as the Gospels tell the story of Jesus from distinct perspectives for different purposes, so the CH tells the story of Israel from a distinct perspective and for a different audience than the DH. Some of these differences stand out in bold print:

- The CH begins with an extensive genealogy that ostensibly stretches from Adam, through the twelve tribes of Israel, and into the post-exilic period (1 Chr 1–9).
- The DH begins its narrative with Moses, his final speeches to the new generation of Israel (Deut), and the conquest (Josh). The CH explains why Saul and Jonathan died: "Saul died because he was unfaithful to the LORD and hadn't followed the LORD's word. He even consulted a medium for guidance. He didn't consult the LORD, so the LORD killed him and gave the kingdom to David, Jesse's son" (1 Chr 10:13–14). A story also reported in the DH, but with the slight difference that Saul went to the medium because the LORD would no longer answer him through any approved means of consultation (1 Sam 28:6).
- Unlike the narrative tennis match back and forth between the north and south in the DH, after a common report of the division (2 Chr 10:1–19; 1 Kgs 12:1–19), the CH tells only the story of South Judah, with mention of the north only when it is relevant to South Judah (2 Chr 11–36).
- The DH concludes with Judah's fall to Babylon, the beginning of captivity, and four verses that announce the release of King Jehoiachin from prison in his thirty-seventh year of captivity (560 BCE, 2 Kgs 25:27). In the CH, 2 Chronicles concludes with the decree of King Cyrus releasing the captives to go back to Jerusalem and rebuild the temple (26:22–23). In addition, if the CH includes Ezra and Nehemiah (at one time a consensus among scholars, much less so today), then its story continues late into the post-exilic history of Jerusalem.

Of much greater significance are the ways in which the CH differs in theology. I draw our attention to the portrait of David in 1 Chronicles 11:1–29:30. It is as if David's story from the DH has been taken to the cleaners and brought back clean, pressed, and folded in the CH. Not every questionable action is erased, but most is nowhere to be found. Uzzah's death for reaching out to steady the ark remains (1 Chr 13:1–14), but the problem is soon remedied so that the ark comes to Jerusalem with only one phrase to replace the intense argument with Michal ("she lost all respect for him" [1 Chr 15:29; 2 Sam 6:20–23]), and, most noticeable,

David's sin against Bathsheba and Uriah is missing from the CH (2 Sam 11:1–25). So what is there left to say? What takes the place of all the questionable or sinful actions we identified in our study of David?

In one word, *worship*. Though David was not allowed to build the LORD's temple because he was a man of too much bloodshed (1 Chr 22:8), David prepares everything for the day when his son will build the temple (1 Chr 16, 21:28–26:32, 28:1–29:19). Ironically, it is the DH that tells us about the "man after God's own heart" and then describes a sinful man, when we would expect the CH to make such a claim in the way the CH describes David.

SOLOMON: A LIFE AT THE EXTREMES (SAMPLE)		
Terrific, Wise, Faithful (with text reference)	**Uncertain** (with text reference)	**Terrible, Foolish, Faithless** (with text reference)
Solomon sets up officials of state far beyond anything before (4:1–6).		At the end of the list of offices is an official in charge of forced labor (4:6e).
Solomon continues to establish state operations with taxation districts to support the government (4:7–19).	He attempts to break up old tribal allegiances by redrawing boundaries for the taxation districts.	Look again: the taxation districts are almost, if not entirely in the north (see Figure 9.2 below).
Judah and Israel are as numerous as the sand by the sea—the promise to Abraham (4:20).		The nation is called "Judah and Israel." Is the kingdom already divided or is this a later vantage point (4:20, 25)?
The borders of the land are at their largest ever (4:21).		
The nation enjoys an era of peace and prosperity (4:22–25).		Solomon has an enormous number of stalls for horses, also fed by taxation districts (4:26–28).
The LORD gives Solomon enormous wisdom (knowledge) so that he is famous, a prolific composer of proverbs and songs, and people come from everywhere to hear him speak (4:29–34).		

Table 9.4. Solomon: Life at the Extremes (Sample)

2. Solomon

Charles Dickens described the reign of Solomon with uncanny insight in the opening words of the *Tale of Two Cities*:

> It was the best of times, it was the worst of times, it was the age of wisdom, it was the age of foolishness, it was the epoch of belief, it was the epoch of incredulity, it was the season of light, it was the season of darkness, it was the spring of hope, it was the winter of despair.[4]

As we read the ten chapters devoted to Solomon (1 Kgs 2–11), we are apt to feel that everything is either this or that: terrific or terrible, wise or foolish, faithful or faithless, hopeful or hopeless. Solomon and the nation live at the extremes. There is also little doubt that the writer(s) intends for the reader to take into account the LORD's rules for the king in Deuteronomy 17:14–20, which Solomon tears through like a child opening presents on Christmas morning: horses—the more the better; wives—try seven hundred princesses and another three hundred concubines; wealth—so much that silver is worthless (see full discussion of the laws in Chapter Eight).

Our first order of business, consequently, is similar to our mapping of David's reign, with a few adjustments unique to the text before us (1 Kgs 1:28–11:43). We still need to read the text critically, watching for every terrific, wise, and faithful moment; and on the other side of the ledger, allowing ourselves to see all of the terrible, foolish, and faithless elements in Solomon's reign (see Table 9.4). It's hard to imagine much could fall between the extremes for Solomon, but for the sake of good class arguments, we will leave space in the middle. Once again, to illustrate the task, I will work through 1 Kings 4.

As you can see from my analysis of 1 Kings 4, despite an initial image in which everything looks great, sometimes the reader must be alert to clues the writer leaves. Readers need to look twice or even three times to make sure they are not missing warning signs. So, with this example and these warnings, please take the time to work through your assigned text before returning to my analysis (again, use Table 9.5 below, make copies, or sketch the columns in your own notes).

Solomon's story presents many of the same issues we dealt with in David's life; the apple did not fall far from the tree. That is to say, Solomon is much like his father, David. We should note, however, two significant differences between the two. First, whether good or bad, Solomon's activities reach to the extreme. Second, as readers, we do not have to deal with everyone singing Solomon's praises; no one is calling Solomon righteous, faithful, or a man after God's own heart. Instead, as we will see, by the end of his reign the LORD announces severe punishment for Solomon's failures.

---

[4]Charles Dickens, *A Tale of Two Cities*. Edited with an Introduction and Notes by Andrew Sanders (New York: Oxford University Press, 1988; reprinted from the original, London: Chapman and Hall, 1859), 7.

SOLOMON: LIFE AT THE EXTREMES		
Terrific, Wise, Faithful (with text reference)	**Uncertain** (with text reference)	**Terrible, Foolish, Faithless** (with text reference)

Table 9.5. Solomon: Life at the Extremes (Blank)

So what are some of the great things Solomon did? Without claiming an exhaustive list, here are a few things the writer(s) considers to be among his greatest accomplishments (most likely looking back, reminiscing on a golden age of Israel):

- At the beginning of his reign, Solomon prays for wisdom to lead the nation (2 Kgs 3:4–9); his wisdom is immediately illustrated in the case of the two women and the baby (3:16–29). Later, he becomes world famous for his knowledge (4:29–34), prompting a visit from the Queen of Sheba (10:1–13).
- Solomon radically increases the size of the state, its officers, and new taxation districts (4:1–19).
- Solomon builds a temple for the Lord, completed in seven years (5:1–6:38, 7:13–51). In his prayer of dedication,
  - Solomon recognizes that the Lord cannot possibly be confined to the temple he has built; he asks that the Lord's name be present at the temple and that God be attentive to their prayers (8:27–28).
  - Solomon also understands the missionary purpose of the temple, drawing people from all over the world to pray here and to learn about the Lord (8:41–44).
  - Solomon asks that the Lord pay attention to prayers offered toward the temple—now, and in the future when the people are in exile because of their sin (8:31–40). Solomon's prayer looks ahead to the Babylonian captivity and hopes for the day the people will turn their hearts back to the Lord (8:46–47). He prays for this day to come, and that when it does, the Lord will hear the prayers the exiles offer toward the temple, forgive them, and "do what is right for them" (8:48–53).
  - Solomon takes on numerous building projects, including his own palace, which was finished in thirteen years (7:1–12). He also rebuilds old cities and new cities (9:15–24).
- Because David fought wars to establish the kingdom, Solomon is able to be a merchant king who becomes enormously wealthy (10:14–25).

On the other side of the ledger, instead of compiling a list of failures or behaviors shorter than we might hope for, here we focus on the seeds of revolution Solomon planted that will eventually sprout into rebellion and the division of the nation:

- Solomon's building projects come at a high cost. While the text claims that he used slave labor from the native population still in the land (9:15–23), he also forced conscripted labor from all Israel: ten thousand a month in three shifts (5:11–14). The text later argues that the Israelites were not slaves, but held various other positions (5:15–22). These workers joined 70,000 laborers and 80,000 stonecutters of unclear origins.
- Solomon makes an arrangement with King Hiram of Tyre, in which Hiram will supply timber in exchange for the provision of food for his royal household (5:7–11); food was supplied to Solomon by his taxation districts (4:22–28). In other words, Solomon's magnificent

buildings are paid for through the labor of his people and twelve taxation districts (located primarily among the northern tribes; see Figure 9.2).

- At the end of building the temple (seven years) and Solomon's palace (thirteen years), a payment dispute arises between Solomon and King Hiram of Tyre. Instead of payment in food, Solomon pays his bill by giving away twenty Israelite cities in the region of Galilee (another questionable loss to the north). When Hiram surveys the cities, however, he either rejects them or accepts them under the protest that they are not worth the sum owed (9:10–14). It appears that Solomon may have overspent or stretched his resources too thin.

- To point out the obvious: Solomon has decimated the LORD's commandments from Deuteronomy 17:14–20. (1) In response to the limitation on horses (Deut 17:16), Solomon amasses chariots and horses: 1,400 chariots and 12,000 horses. The text even lists the excellent cost at which Solomon's traders could buy this military equipment, and how he then exported them to other nations (1 Kgs 10:26, 28–29). We would describe such behavior today as brokering the sale of military weapons. (2) While the LORD did promise riches to Solomon—"There won't be a king like you as long as you live" (1 Kgs 3:13)—it is difficult to discern whether the extent of Solomon's wealth was what the LORD had in mind. In the middle of describing Solomon's business in military arms, the text includes an odd verse for the context: "In Jerusalem, the king made silver as common as stones and cedar as plentiful as sycamore trees that grow in the foothills" (1 Kgs 10:27). The placement of this verse with Solomon's direct violation of dealing in horses may suggest that the text is offering a critique of how far the wealth had gotten out of control. (3) After the report on military arms and the economy, we receive a staggering report on Solomon's efforts in diplomacy and sealing treaties by marrying women from royal families in other countries. Solomon has married seven hundred "royal wives" and three hundred "secondary wives" (concubines;

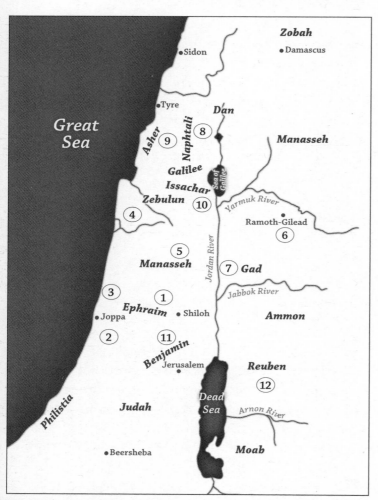

Figure 9.2. Solomon's Taxation Districts

11:1–3). These wives came with their gods, and just as warned, Solomon turned his worship to all of them (11:3–8).

We could point out other differences that are growing up between the north and south, including a more urban culture in the north, a different dialect of Hebrew (they speak "funny" Hebrew over there), different political ideologies (with the south much more committed to a single dynasty), and religious beliefs that already exist in the north (Baal worship) ready to step out into the mainstream.

As a result of Solomon's practices, in part begun by his father David, the LORD announces the end of the united monarchy (1 Kgs 11:11–13). In honor of David, however, the LORD does make two concessions: (1) the LORD determines to hold off the division until after Solomon dies, and (2) the LORD will allow David's family to keep one tribe, their own tribe of Judah—essentially, the southern half of the kingdom (1 Kgs 11:12–13).

3. Rehoboam

Because of his father and grandfather, Rehoboam inherits an explosive political situation after the death of his father. Unfortunately, he does not recognize the state of affairs for what they are; consequently, he is incapable of diffusing the bomb before it blows up in his face. He is no Abraham Lincoln. Rehoboam first misunderstands the nature of his meeting with "all Israel" (all of northern Israel's leaders) at Shechem, a frequent site for important national meetings far inside the borders of northern Israel. He thinks the meeting is a mere formality to anoint him king, just as his father, Solomon, and grandfather, David, had been. Rehoboam does not realize that these leaders have come to dictate non-negotiable terms. They are clear in their stipulations:

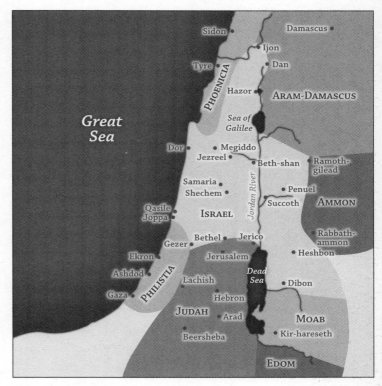

Figure 9.3. The Division of Judah and Israel

> Your father made our workload very hard for us. If you will lessen the demands your father made of us and lighten the heavy workload he demanded from us, then we will serve you. (1 Kgs 12:4)

When they put these conditions on the table, Rehoboam makes a second mistake of judgment: he believes he is in the position of power and need not *listen* (a key term in 1 Kgs 12) or *serve* (the other key term) the people he leads.

Rehoboam asks his father's (older) counselors what he should do. Their experience enables them to see the explosives just under the northern leaders' demands, so they advise him to be a servant to the people (12:7a), so they will be "your servants forever" (12:7b, emphasis mine)—an answer that requires Rehoboam to listen to the people and serve them rather than be served. But he has no desire or intention to listen to or serve anyone. For Rehoboam, the populace does the listening and serving—not the king. So Rehoboam turns to his friends for counsel more to his liking—young men who grew up with him "and now served him" (12:8b). They advise a bold power move: tell the people "my little finger is thicker than my father's entire waist!" (12:10b). Our English translations fail to capture the euphemism on a level equal to their crude, dismissive message. "My little finger" does not refer to Rehoboam's literal finger, but is a coarse reference to his penis. *That's how much more of a man I am than my father was!* If you think my father gave you a heavy work load and high taxes, "I'll make it heavier!" (12:11a). There'll be no more use of wimpy whips to punish you—as if whips are not harsh—I'll come at you with scorpions (12:11b). Northern Israel would just as well be back in Egypt, and that's the message Rehoboam chooses to send. He believes he can dictate the terms of this so-called negotiation.

"The king wouldn't listen" (1 Kgs 12:16), and when northern Israel saw that the king would not listen, they have their own message for Rehoboam:

> Why should we care about David?
> We have no stake in Jesse's son!
> Go back to your homes, Israel!
> You better look after your own house now, David! (12:16)

Or, in language a little closer to our own, they say:

> *Forget you!*
> We don't need you!
> So get out of here,
> and take your own problems with you!

And though the Israelites leave, Rehoboam still doesn't hear their message until he sends Adoram, his supervisor of forced labor, to the north and Israel stones him to death (12:18). *Now* Rehoboam understands, but it's too late. When Rehoboam comes back home ready to go to war against the north and bring them back in line, the LORD steps in and will not permit it (12:21–24).

Conclusion

The short time of the united kingdom is over. On one hand, given their differences and the weakness of the unity in the first place (recall that David fought three wars to keep the country together), we might be surprised that united Israel has lasted as long as it has. It's a wonder that the twelve northern taxation districts didn't rebel sooner. On the other hand, the nation of Israel was God's plan for reaching out to bless the rest of the world. God wanted the nation to be what it was called to be: "a kingdom of priests for me and a holy nation" (Exod 19:6). The LORD has tried to make this plan work. But the LORD will not stop the kingdom from collapsing under the combined weight of David, Solomon, and Rehoboam's failures—especially their failure to trust God: *now all the king's horses and all the king's men won't be able to put the kingdom together again.*

To Discuss

Note: *You must be prepared to discuss these topics beyond what is said in the chapter. In other words, read the assigned texts carefully.*

1. Are you startled by what you have learned about David from this chapter? How and in what ways? What new questions does this chapter raise for you? Which of the stories about David most alarms or concerns you?

2. Why do you think David refused to kill Saul, even when he had easy opportunities? In what way would this action have been a political disaster? At one point, David marched with Philistine armies against Saul, but was rejected by the Philistine leaders (1 Sam 29). Do you think David would have turned against the Philistines? How would his participation in this battle have been a political disaster?

3. The author identifies three distinct civil wars that David fights during his life: to gain control of the north when he is king of Judah, during Absalom's rebellion, and in Sheba's rebellion (2 Sam 20). How do you feel about David fighting these wars? What does this tell you about him?

4. From your study of David's life, what do you think it means to be a person following the LORD's own heart? Support your thesis with evidence and good argumentation. You may not simply overlook all the evidence against your thesis. How do you explain all of the questionable or wrong things David does and Scripture's high praise of David as righteous and faithful?

5. What is your assessment of Solomon's reign? In what ways does Solomon demonstrate great wisdom? In what ways does Solomon demonstrate foolishness? So, was Solomon a wise or a foolish king? Argue for your side. Now argue for the other side.

6. Do you think Rehoboam had any chance to salvage the political situation and keep the nation united? (What if the LORD had not decreed the division?) What would Rehoboam have had to do to keep the nation united?

7. Review 2 Samuel 7. Identify the elements of the LORD's covenant with David and his family. Once again, the text speaks of God changing his approach on the basis of experience (7:15). Why did God not start with this approach to Saul's dynasty?

8. List the women who are part of David's life. What experiences do they have with David? Which of them have tragic experiences? Explain. Does any woman who is close to David have a good life?

9. What do you make of the differences between the story of David in 1–2 Samuel and his story in Chronicles? Do the omissions trouble you? Why or why not? What questions does a comparative study raise for you?

10. Several of the "Dig Deeper" questions might also be productive discussion questions (see below).

11. Locate the following locations on a map (see Figures 9.2 and 9.3): North Israel, South Judah, Philistia, Edom, Moab, Ammon, Aram-Damascus, Phoenicia, and Jerusalem.

To Know

1. The significance of the following in the assigned chapters:

Abiathar	Michal
Abigail	Nabal
Absalom	Nathan
Ahimelech	Rehoboam
Bathsheba	Saul
David	Solomon
Doeg (the Edomite)	Song of the Women
God's Covenant with David	Taxation Districts
Jerusalem	The Queen of Sheba
Jonathan	Uriah
Keilah	Ziklag

2. The six eras of David's life.

3. Be able to list at least five good and bad things that David does (each event should be distinct, not different parts of the same story).

4. Be prepared to write on the topic, "David, a man following the LORD's own heart."

5. How Solomon deals with his political rivals.

6. Be able to list both wise and foolish things that Solomon does.

7. Be ready to write on the topic, "Solomon, wise man and fool."

8. The rules for the king from Deuteronomy 17 and how well David and Solomon obey these rules.

9. The consequences for Solomon's failures and the two concessions God makes for the sake of David.

To Dig Deeper: Research Topics

1. Study Solomon's prayer at the dedication of the temple (8:22–53). What is foreshadowed in his prayer? What does he say that resonates with earlier statements of Israel's purpose?

2. Further investigate the difficulties associated with the stories that introduce David. Identify the problematic features that arise when these stories are compared or read together (e.g., does Saul already know David when he kills Goliath?). State a hypothesis and establish it with evidence. Find articles in research journals and portions of commentaries that can act as helpful conversation partners in your work.

3. Early Childhood Education or Children's Ministry Students: Investigate how David (or Solomon) is represented in children's literature (at least three books). What do you discover? To what extent is this representation age-appropriate? How could the literature improve?

4. The book of 1 Chronicles presents its own distinctive perspective on David's life. Read 1 Chronicles 10–29. Identify three to four themes unique to Chronicles (from the DH) and establish each with evidence.

5. Economists, Political Scientists, and Business students: wrestle with the description of the economy during the reign of Solomon. What types of problems would you expect to develop when "even silver wasn't considered good enough in Solomon's time!" (1 Kgs 10:21; see 10:14–25). What additional issues are likely to develop as a result of the conscription of labor (5:13–18, 9:15–22)?

6. Several of the discussion questions could be turned into research topics. Discuss this possibility with your instructor.

For Further Reading

Moore, Michael S. *Faith Under Pressure: A Study of Biblical Leaders in Conflict.* Abilene, TX: Leafwood, 2003.

Thiele, Edwin R. *The Mysterious Numbers of the Hebrew Kings.* Rev. ed. Grand Rapids: Kregel, 1983.

On Saul

Gunn, David M. *The Fate of King Saul: An Interpretation of a Biblical Story.* JSOTSup 14. Sheffield: JSOT Press, 1980.

On David

Anderson, Lynn. *Finding the Heart to Go On.* San Bernardino: Here's Life Publishers, 1991.

Halpern, Baruch. *David's Secret Demons: Messiah, Murderer, Traitor, King.* Grand Rapids: Eerdmans, 2001.

For a side-by-side reading of the DH and the CH

Crockett, William D. *A Harmony of Samuel, Kings, and Chronicles.* Eugene: Wipf & Stock Publishers, 2006. (Original from 1800s now available from this publisher.)

Newsome, James D. *A Synoptic Harmony of Samuel, Kings, and Chronicles: With Related Passages from Psalms, Isaiah, Jeremiah, and Ezra.* Repr. Edited by James D. Newsome Jr. Eugene: Wipf & Stock, 2009.

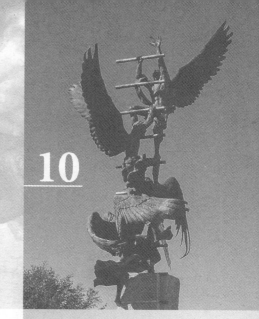

The Story of
Northern Israel
Kings, Prophets, and God's Mercy

10

n this chapter, we will walk alongside northern Israel from her beginning with Jeroboam to her final days when the nation is scattered throughout the Assyrian empire. To make this journey with northern Israel means spending time in court—the court where God is the judge, the prosecuting attorney who demands justice, and defense attorney who appeals for compassion and mercy. I admit it is an unusual court, with the LORD playing enough roles to turn any mortal god into a schizophrenic. And while we know that Israel will be found guilty of the charges—failure to keep covenant and breaking God's heart by giving themselves to other gods (breaking the first commandment)—we do not know how the trial will conclude. Will God's mercy prevail and God forgive, or will God's justice carry the day and demand a punishment that fits the crime? Israel lives with a God who is deeply conflicted between mercy and justice—like any parent who loves their children (see Exod 34:6–7). So, even if Israel is handed over for punishment, if we will stay to patiently watch, we will see an amazing obsession: time after time, the LORD is unable to endure seeing his people suffer. So the LORD will pardon their sin and reduce their sentence to time already served.

Hosea, a prophet we will hear from later in this chapter, provides a compelling picture of God's inner struggle between judgment and compassion:

> How can I give you up, Ephraim?
> How can I hand you over, Israel? . . .

READING ASSIGNMENTS

1 KINGS 12–14:20, 15:25–19:21, 21:1–29

2 KINGS 1:1–8:15, (9:1–10:36, 13:1–25), 15:8–31, 17:1–41

AMOS 1–9 AND/OR HOSEA 1–14

KEY TERMS

Asherah: the name of a goddess most often associated with Baal, represented by a wooden pole

Ephraim: a tribe that becomes so large its name is used as an alternate for Northern Israel

High Place: a place of worship in villages or in the country, most often for idols

Oracle: a short speech unit prophets use to convey the LORD's word to people

Samaria: the capital of northern Israel and an alternate name for the country

Synchronism: dating the beginning of one king's reign on the basis of another king's reign

Syncretism: merging the beliefs and worship practices of two or more gods

> My heart winces within me;
>> my compassion grows warm and tender.
>
> I won't act on the heat of my anger;
>> I won't return to destroy Ephraim;
> for I am God and not a human being,
>> the holy one in your midst;
> I won't come in harsh judgment. (Hos 11:8–9)

In a covenant lawsuit, God's final word is always grace.

So, this chapter will take the form of a trial or covenant lawsuit, like what we find in the prophetic literature (e.g., Isa 1; although I freely admit to taking great liberties with the form). We will begin with basic facts about the one charged (a mug shot, if you will), followed by the indictments (charges) and supporting evidence. At the end, I will ask you for your verdict and sentence.

Northern Israel: The Facts and Nothing but the Facts

Israel's case begins with basic data about the accused entered into the court's record: events, people, and dates. So far, we have not stressed or even mentioned more than one or two important dates. We will let these sail on by because, until David comes on the scene, we lack the evidence to be able to do little more than guess. Now, however, because of interaction with kings in Assyria, Babylon, and Egypt (who all kept good records), it becomes possible to assign dates to people and events in Israel with a fair degree of accuracy:

1. Most scholars in the field favor dating the exodus from Egypt in ca. 1290 BCE (1440 BCE is also considered; see "For Further Reading").

2. Most research also sets the division of the nation in ca. 922 BCE; thus, Jeroboam's reign and the independent nation of northern Israel begin at this time. Rehoboam most likely began his reign in Judah before 922 BCE. New kings often overlapped with the prior king while he is still alive—and both kings counted the same year(s) as part of their reign; one of many factors that make the precise chronology of Israel (and Judah) difficult to reconstructed (see "For Further Reading").

KEY DATES (BCE)	
The Exodus	1290
Saul	1040–1000
David	1000–960
Solomon	960–925
Division of the Nation	922
Assyrian conquest of Israel	722

Table 10.1. Key Dates for Northern Israel

3. Working backward from the division of the nation, we date Solomon's reign from ca. 960–925 BCE (1 Kgs 11:42), David from ca. 1000–960 BCE (1 Kgs 2:10), and Saul from ca. 1040–1000 BCE (1 Sam 13:1).

4. Researchers and biblical texts refer to the northern nation by a number of different names: northern Israel, Israel, **Ephraim** (because this tribe was the largest group in the nation), and **Samaria** (because Samaria becomes the capital city).

5. The Assyrians conquered northern Israel in 722 BCE and scattered much of the population into Assyrian captivity, marking the end of northern Israel after two hundred years as an independent nation.

From the time the nation divides until the end of northern Israel (1 Kgs 20–2 Kgs 17), reading the biblical text is like watching a tennis match, with stories alternating between northern Israel (or just "Israel") and southern Judah (or just "Judah"). Back and forth, forth and back (see Figure 10.1 below)—and so it goes, until the Assyrian Empire sweeps in and takes the game, set, match, and court from northern Israel.

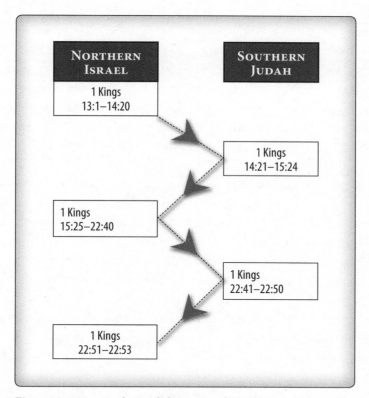

Figure 10.1. Mapping the Tangled Narrative of 1–2 Kings

But until this point, it can be difficult and frustrating for readers to keep up with the story line: what is happening, where is it happening, why is it happening, and especially, what does the writer(s) want us to notice? What is the point, the theological message or theme we are supposed to take in through all of the back and forth motion? To help with this problematic feature, here (and in Chapter Eleven) we will treat each nation individually, unraveling the strands of text that testify to events in each nation. I hope the literary purists will forgive me.

Indictment One: Political Turmoil Due To . . .

Israel is plagued by political turmoil, easily seen in the rapid rise and demise of one dynasty after another (with the exception of two dynasties, see Table 10.2). The charge is not the turmoil itself, but what causes the instability. Once we unravel the stories about Israel from those about Judah, the evidence reveals the problem behind the problem:

- Jeroboam establishes the nation and reigns for twenty-two years (1 Kgs 14:20); his son Nadab then reigns for only two years before he is assassinated by Baasha, who then attempts to set up his own dynasty (15:25–28).
- Baasha's dynasty fares no better than Jeroboam's. His son Elah reigns for two years before he is assassinated by Zimri (16:8–10).
- Zimri has a lengthy reign of seven whole days in Tirzah. In opposition to his self-declaration, the Israelite army made Omri king when they heard about the assassination of Elah (16:16). Then they came and laid siege to Tirzah, soon taking the city, prompting Zimri to commit suicide (16:8–10, 15–18).
- After Zimri's death, Omri must continue to fight and win a civil war to keep the crown (16:21–23). Once on the throne, however, Omri's dynasty becomes special on two counts: First, Omri builds and moves the capital city to Samaria (16:24). Second, Omri's dynasty lasts ca. forty-eight years (four generations) until Jehu, under God's direction, assassinates King Ahab and his family in a bloody massacre (2 Kgs 9–10), taking the throne (2 Kgs 9:6–7).
- After the purge of Ahab's family, the LORD rewards Jehu with a dynasty of four generations (after Jehu's reign). Thus, Jehu has the longest dynasty of any Israelite king (five total generations, ca. 102 years). Like others, however, his dynasty comes to an end with assassination (2 Kgs 15:8–10).
- Once Shallum assassinates Zechariah (the last king in Jehu's family), the nation becomes unstable again. Case in point, Shallum reigns for only one month before Menahem kills him (15:13–15).
- Menahem institutes a pro-Assyrian policy and pays off Tiglath-Pileser III in exchange for—well—not being destroyed (15:17–22). But when his son, Pekahiah, inherits the throne, he reigns only two years before Pekah (backed by an anti-Assyrian faction) assassinates him (15:23–26).
- Pekah stirs things up with Assyria, prompting the Assyrian King Tiglath-Pileser III to invade Israel and capture many towns. Before the Assyrian king gets to Samaria, Hoshea assassinates Pekah and becomes king (a move backed by a pro-Assyrian faction; 15:27–31).
- Hoshea comes to the throne in favor of paying off Assyria in order to save the nation; so, he pays tribute to Tiglath-Pileser III and the next Assyrian king, Shalmaneser V. But on the sly, Hoshea was working on a deal for Egyptian support in a rebellion against Assyria (2 Kgs 17:3–4).

THE MANY DYNASTIES OF NORTHERN ISRAEL				
Dynasty	**Text**	**Generations**	**Total Years***	**End of Dynasty**
Jeroboam (I)	1 Kgs. 15:25–29	Two	24 Years	Assassination
Baasha	1 Kgs. 16:8–9	Two	26 Years	Assassination
Zimri	1 Kgs. 16:15–16	One	7 Days	Suicide
Omri	2 Kgs. 9:21–24	Four	48 years	Assassination
Jehu	2 Kgs. 15:8–10	Five	102 years	Assassination
Shallum	2 Kgs. 15:13–14	One	1 Month	Assassination
Menahem	2 Kgs. 15:23–25	Two	12 Years	Assassination
Pekah	2 Kgs. 15:30–31	One	20 Years	Assassination
Hoshea	2 Kgs. 17:1–4	One	9 Years	Captivity
			241 Years	

Table 10.2. The Many Dynasties of Israel

*Often a father and son overlapped, claiming the same years. Thus, the total of 241 years, though the nation only lasted from 922–722 BCE.

Exactly what happened is unclear, but eventually Hoshea thumbs his nose at Assyria and stops paying tribute. While at first it looks like he has gotten away with his rebellion, in fact, the Assyrian king is preoccupied with other issues. Once he is free to come to Samaria, he comes in force, tired of all the trouble Samaria keeps causing. So when the city falls to the Assyrians siege (2 Kgs 17:1–6), they exile the people to places throughout the Assyrian kingdom and repopulate the north with people from other places Assyria has conquered (the beginning of what will become the Samaritans). *And so northern Israel exits the stage of the Old Testament story.*

The first indictment against Israel, which lies behind and causes the political instability, is a perpetual lack of trust in the LORD. As a result of this lack of faith, one king after another takes matters into his own hands. As material evidence, we introduce the initial words and events surrounding Jeroboam's rise to power.

Jeroboam began his career as a state official in Solomon's government, quickly climbing the ladder of success. As a "strong and honorable" young man, Jeroboam soon came to Solomon's personal attention, and was promoted to supervise "all the work gang of Joseph's house" (1 Kgs 11:28)—a good news/bad news scenario, given how those in the north feel about Solomon's forced labor. I can imagine his text exchange with friends back home: *I got a great promotion!* Wonderful! Congrats! What's the job? *I'm in charge of the forced labor from the north!* Traitor! Sell-out! @&$@! (and other words my editor would never permit).

Jeroboam might have been stoned to death alongside Adoram (12:18) if the direction of his life had not changed one day outside the city of Jerusalem, when he met the prophet Ahijah (11:29). Alone with Jeroboam, Ahijah took his own new robe, tore it into twelve pieces, and told

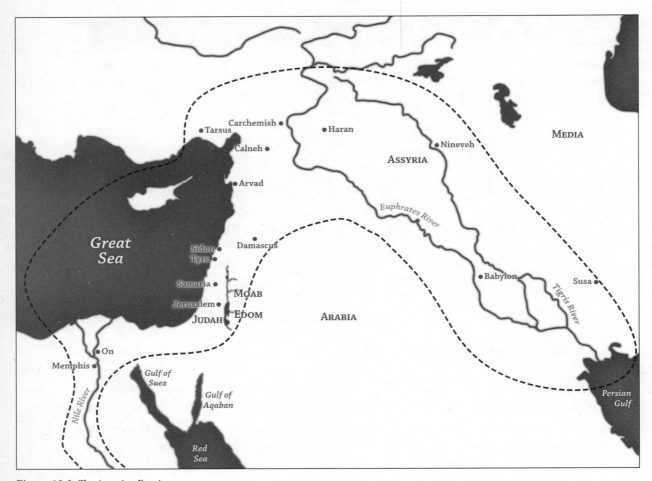

Figure 10.2. The Assyrian Empire

Jeroboam to take ten of the pieces (11:30–31a). Ahijah explained the object lesson: the LORD is taking the kingdom out of Solomon's hands and giving ten pieces to you—Jeroboam. David's family will keep only one tribe, because Solomon had turned the first commandment over and used it for scrap paper to take notes about new gods in the land to worship: Astarte (from Sidon), Chemosh (from Moab), and Milcom (from Ammon)—oddly, the most popular god, Baal, is left off the list (11:33). I suppose there is no use mentioning the obvious. The unused twelfth piece could represent Simeon, a tribe absorbed into Judah, or represent the Levites who lived in all the tribes without land of their own.

Ahijah tells Jeroboam: "You will be king of Israel" (11:37). The few conditions set on his reign and dynasty should come as no surprise (edited for emphasis):

> *IF*
>
>> you will listen to all I command
>> you will walk in my ways
>> you will do what is right in my eyes (like David)

THEN

> I will be with you
> I will build you a lasting dynasty (as I did for David)
> I will give you Israel

In other words, if Jeroboam will *trust the* LORD and the LORD alone, then the LORD will establish the nation of northern Israel and Jeroboam's dynasty (11:37–38; see again Deut 17:18–20). It is a strong promise with precise expectations; Jeroboam only needs to trust the LORD, instead of taking matters into his own hands (Genesis 3 all over again). If he will trust the LORD, the LORD will establish his kingdom and his dynasty.

But no sooner does Jeroboam become king than his fear overwhelms his trust in the LORD. He begins to think *the nation is in danger of going back to David's dynasty* (with Rehoboam), *especially if Jerusalem continues to be the religious center for his people* (12:26–27). To his credit, he realizes that religion is a powerful force, just as David recognized this power when he moved the tabernacle and the ark of the covenant to Jerusalem in order to help unify the nation (2 Sam 6). After all, *the family that worships together stays together*. So, Jeroboam's fear will lead him to do the unthinkable, to which we will return shortly. For now, we have established that Jeroboam, at least, introduced "fear over faith" and "taking matters into one's own hands" into the political world of northern Israel. Such fear and self-reliance will lead to one assassination after another.

This was the cause for Jeroboam's dynasty ending so quickly (see 1 Kgs 11:38, 14:7–10); his fear of the situation overwhelmed his trust in the LORD so that he did what he thought had to be done to save the nation and his life (1 Kgs 12:25–33). And so it was for each king and dynasty in northern Israel, one after the other; fear and human effort to save the kingdom replaced trust in the LORD.

Indictment Two: Corrupt Spiritual Leadership

Beginning with Jeroboam, northern Israel is plagued by corrupt spiritual leadership that leads the nation to violate the heart of the covenant. Jeroboam's fear—for his nation, for his throne, and for his life—leads him to take each fear into his own hands and wage a systematic attack on the first commandment (12:27–28).

1. Jeroboam has two golden calves made. If we listen with a little imagination, we can hear what Jeroboam might be thinking *or saying*: *All those new changes that have come with David's temple? No more! Give me that old-time religion—like what we had at Mount Sinai* (Exod 32:1–6). *Moses got it all wrong, he misunderstood; for Aaron, the calf was just like the ark of the covenant; Yahweh rides the calf. After all, once Aaron saw the calf, he built an altar and declared in front of the calf, "Tomorrow will be a festival to the* LORD!" (Exod 32:5, emphasis mine). *We are still serving Yahweh, just in a form that predates Sinai, the ark, and all these things Solomon and David have started in the Jerusalem temple. We are restoring true worship.* And it helps that what Jeroboam proposes fits with the other prominent god in his land: Baal.

Obviously, the biblical writer disagrees with Jeroboam's actions and sees them as nothing less than a flagrant violation of the first two commandments. But just in case we miss the author's position on what Jeroboam is doing, the writer finally comes out and says, "This act was sinful" (12:30). But for Jeroboam, we can be certain he was hard at work, persuading the people to accept his moves as he brought the two calves out for worship.

2. Jeroboam expresses great concern for the welfare of his people having to travel so far to worship—all the way to Jerusalem. We keep listening and reading with our imaginations open to what Jeroboam might have said: *Jerusalem is too far, so for your convenience and safety, one calf with its shrine will be in Dan (in the far north) and the other in Bethel (the far south).* Jeroboam has sanctuaries or shrines built in two locations—*to serve you.* (Without a doubt McDonald's and Starbucks got their idea for franchising and multiple locations from Jeroboam.)

3. Shrines require a staff—priests to attend to the people and their sacrifices and to serve other needs before God. But instead of the social stratification and hierarchy in the south (here goes the imagination again) where only Levites are allowed to be priests, here in the north, Jeroboam is an equal opportunity employer. *Anyone can be a priest who feels called to be a priest* (12:31). Perhaps a religion degree was required—more likely not. The less these priests know the better.

4. And finally, the calves, shrines, and priests mean nothing if the people keep going to Jerusalem for the big annual celebrations. *We need festivals, holy days that will rival anything happening in Jerusalem so our people will party here, worship here, spend their money here, and most of all, stay here instead of going there.* So Jeroboam establishes a festival that occurs about one month after the Feast of Tabernacles in the south (1 Kgs 8:2), perhaps delayed to fit a later harvest time in the north than the south. So he has another selling point—a more convenient worship time.

Without a doubt, Jeroboam's public relations spin machine went into overdrive to convince his people of the legitimacy of his actions; and given what we know of these people and human nature, it probably wasn't all that hard to win them over. Jeroboam succeeds. First, he leads the people to worship at Dan and Bethel, or one of the local "**high places**" where shrines were built for Baal (2 Kgs 17:9). Second, with all these efforts, Jeroboam also succeeds in becoming the king to which every subsequent king in northern Israel is compared. The only question is whether any king will be as bad as, or worse than Jeroboam. Thus, the typical introductory formula for Israelite kings includes:

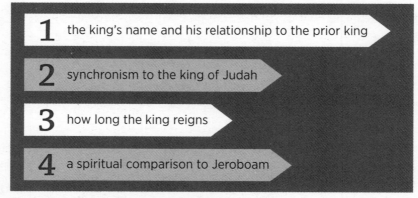

Figure 10.3. The Introductory Formula for Israelite Kings

The first three items in the introductory formula vary widely (item 1 will lack relationship to the former king in instances of assassination). But in every case, the spiritual comparison to Jeroboam centers on first commandment issues—the sin Jeroboam caused Israel to commit. Let's take Jeroboam's son as an example (1 Kgs 15:25–26):

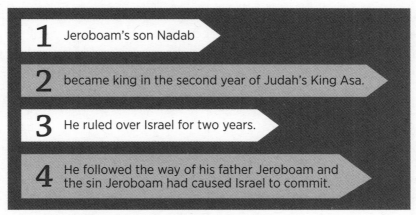

Figure 10.4. The Introductory Formula for King Nadab

Or, take another example from the next-to-last king of Israel, ca. two hundred years later (2 Kgs 15:27–28):

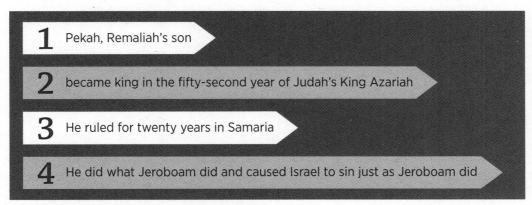

Figure 10.5. The Introductory Formula for King Pekah

And so the evaluations go, every king in Israel follows Jeroboam's spiritual lead and worships other gods. What happens among the people, however, is more difficult to uncover, simply because the DH keeps its focus on royal households and state history. So the best that we can do is look for glimpses among the people.

One such glimpse comes from the story of Elijah versus the prophets of Baal on Mount Carmel (1 Kgs 18–19). At least some, or perhaps many, Israelites are present that day because Elijah speaks to them.

> Elijah approached all the people and said, "How long will you hobble back and forth between two opinions? If the Lord is God, follow God. If Baal is God, follow Baal." The people gave no answer. (1 Kgs 18:21; see also 18:36–37)

Working backward from this circumstantial evidence, the people appear to have fallen to **syncretism**. They claim belief in the Lord as God, but they also believe in and worship Baal (among other gods). So Elijah asks the Lord to help the people to see that there is only one God for Israel and it is the Lord, not Baal. The people think the safe approach is to accept all the gods and their claims. But the Lord requires a single-minded allegiance—in marriage terms: monogamy. The Lord will not tolerate being one of many gods.

Additional evidence regarding the people comes from the writer's summary statement in 2 Kings 17 about why the Lord handed Israel over to the Assyrians (17:7–12, edited for emphasis):

- The Israelites sinned against the Lord their God.
- They worshipped other gods.
- They followed the practices of the nations.
- [They followed] the practices that the Israelite kings had done.
- The Israelites secretly did things against the Lord.
- They built shrines.
- They set up sacred pillars and sacred poles.
- At every shrine, they burned incense.
- They did evil things.
- They worshipped images.

What's in a Name?

Often, a name provides evidence regarding the god/God a person serves. For example, some names carry suffixes with special meaning, as in the suffixes "iah" or "jah"—a short form of God's name *Yahweh* (*Yah*). Thus, when suffixed to other words in names such as Ahijah, Elijah, Josiah, Hezekiah, Amaziah, Jeremiah, Isaiah, and others, these names stake a claim to some relationship with *Yahweh*. On the other hand, the suffixes "bal," "bel," or "baal" refer to Baal, as in the suffixes we see in the names Ishbaal, Ethbaal, and even Jezebel. Finally, sometimes a writer will communicate what they think by changing the suffix of a name. For example, Saul's son is named Ishbaal ("man of Baal" in 1 Chron 8:33, 9:39), but called Ishbosheth in the DH (2 Sam 2:8, 12; 3:6, 8, 11; the suffix "bosheth" means "shame"). Thus, the "man of Baal" is insulted as a "man of shame." In a creative move, the writer has just said what he thinks of Saul's son and Baal. The same change occurs with Jonathan's son Merib-baal (1 Chron 8:34), called Mephibosheth in the DH (2 Sam 4:4). Small features and slight changes will reward an attentive reader with insight otherwise passed over.

The evidence is overwhelming: the people not only follow their kings to worship Baal, but also follow the practices of the people left in the land. They demolish the heart of the covenant—their promise to worship and serve the LORD alone.

Indictment Three: Refusal to Listen to the LORD's Prophets

While northern Israel was racing to Sheol (the grave) faster than a Jaguar XJ220 V12 four-wheel drive production sports car can get you from your dorm room to the nearest library (okay, to your favorite pizza joint), the LORD did not just sit on the sidewalk hoping the people would learn from what was happening and turn it all around. Instead, the LORD sent one prophet after another in the hope that the people might listen and respond. They didn't. They wouldn't. God was proactive—he did all he could, while still respecting their dignity of free choice, but Israel refused to listen (2 Kgs 17:13–15).

To say the LORD sent prophets to northern Israel, however, is to tap into widespread misunderstandings in our own culture about what a biblical prophet was or did in ancient Israel and, to complicate the issue even more, not all prophets in Israel were alike. The Hebrew term *nabi*—"prophet"—is elastic, stretching in one direction to reach groups of people living together who are prone to ecstatic behavior. Saul experienced this form of "prophecy" on his way home from his first, private anointing with Samuel:

> When Saul and the boy got to Gibeah, there was a group of prophets coming to meet him. God's spirit came over Saul, and he was caught up in a prophetic frenzy right along with them. (1 Sam 10:10)

Saul has the same experience again in Ramah when he attempts to capture David (1 Sam 19:18–24). At the other end of the spectrum, the word "prophet" may refer to a man or woman who receives messages from God and conveys these messages to a particular person or group (see Exod 7:1–2). Some prophets are embedded in the king's court (e.g., Nathan, 2 Sam 12:1–15), while others work freely among the people. The first prophet we explore in northern Israel works with both the king and the people. He is a spokesperson for God and a prophet who can work miracles to support his message (another type of prophet on the spectrum).

Another common misunderstanding about prophets is that once they make a statement on behalf of God, Israel's fate is sealed (or whatever they have said is unchangeable). In fact, the prophetic word worked in the opposite way: to encourage a change before punishment comes or to encourage faithfulness so that God's Word develops as promised. The prophet Jeremiah put it this way:

> At any time I may announce that I will dig up, pull down, and destroy a nation or kingdom; but if that nation I warned turns from its evil, then I'll relent and not carry out the harm I intended for it. At the same time, I may announce that I will build and plant a nation or kingdom; but if that nation displeases me and disobeys me, then I'll relent and not carry out the good I intended for it. (Jer 18:7–10)

Prophetic **oracles** are not God's final word. God hopes that the threat of destruction will get a nation or person to listen and respond, just as God hopes the promise of blessing will motivate a nation or person to remain faithful. The LORD's promise through a prophet does not obligate the LORD to keep the promise if the people turn against him. So the LORD sent prophets to northern Israel with great hope that their work would bring Israel back to him.

First Prophet: Elijah

Elijah will enter the picture just as northern Israel and her king are falling head over heels for Baal. The new king, Ahab, promotes Baal more than any king before or after him. He marries Jezebel, daughter of Ethbaal (1 Kgs 16:31), builds a temple and new altar for Baal (16:32), and makes a sacred pole for **Asherah** (16:33). In fact, Ahab did more to infuriate the LORD, "*the God of Israel*, than any of Israel's kings who preceded him" (16:33, my emphasis). So, Elijah comes on stage just long enough to say that Israel's true God is going to turn off Israel's water supply for the next three years 17:1). The punch is directed straight to Baal's mouth. Baal can either put his

power where his mouth is and override the LORD's declaration, or be shown up as a second-rate nothing (see *Welcome to Baal's Country,* pp. 140).

Sure enough, Israel goes into a dangerous drought and, despite other stories within the story (17:2–18:4), our interests skip ahead to the conflict between Elijah, Ahab, and the question of who is God of northern Israel: Baal or the LORD (*Yahweh*)? For three years, the LORD's drought has been making a fool of Baal and anyone foolish enough to follow Baal (18:1–2). Now the time has come for Elijah to emerge from hiding and finish the fight.

Elijah proposes a contest to settle the matter: gather the people of Israel to Mount Carmel, deep within Baal's land (see Figure 10.6), along with the prophets of Baal and prophets of Asherah (18:19–20). When the people arrive, Elijah challenges them: "How long will you hobble back and forth between two opinions? If the LORD is God, follow God. If Baal is God, follow Baal" (18:21). The Israelites

Figure 10.6. Northern Israel

are trying to serve Baal and Yahweh, which Elijah says is not serving Yahweh at all. *Decide.* Follow one or the other, but quit pretending it is possible to serve both.

Elijah sets the rules of the contest to favor Baal: two bulls, each prepared as a sacrifice, but no fire: "The god who answers with fire—that's the real God!" (18:24). Deep inside Israelite territory, Elijah also gives the prophets of Baal home court advantage to go first. This, of course, should be an easy task for the god of thunderstorms and lightning. Baal's prophets accept the challenge, prepare their altar and sacrifice, and begin to call on Baal in the morning and continue into mid afternoon. They sing, shout, and dance around the altar, but "there was no sound or answer" (18:26).

Around noon, Elijah starts talking smack. He is confident that the LORD will win and Baal is no more than a make-believe friend. So Elijah starts providing excuses for why Baal is not doing anything:

> *Shout louder! Certainly he is a god!*
> *Perhaps he is lost in thought*
> *or wandering*
> *or traveling somewhere.*
> *Or maybe he is asleep and must wake up!* (18:27, my format and emphasis)

The translation glides over the sharp edge to Elijah's sarcastic tone. He is not trying to be nice, but derogatory. For example, the term "wandering" may be a euphemism for a bowel movement. In our time we might say, "Maybe Baal is on his throne—*doing his business*!"

Elijah's words only cause Baal's prophets to intensify their efforts; they shout with a louder voice and cut themselves so that blood is all over them (18:28). But "still there was no sound or answer, no response whatsoever" (18:29). Their hysteria is met by a profound silence.

Elijah decides it is his turn as he calls the people closer to watch; he prepares an altar of twelve stones, digs a trench around the altar, lays out the wood, butchers the bull, and puts the bull on the wood. He then instructs people to fill four jars with water and pour them all over the altar, the sacrifice, even the wood—*water? In a drought?* Elijah orders four more jars full of water, and then orders it one more time—three times, until everything is soaked and the trench is full of water. *This had better work; look at all that water wasted!* Elijah comes close so the people can hear, and then prays:

> LORD, the God of Abraham, Isaac, and Israel, let it be known today that you are God in Israel and that I am your servant. I have done all these things at your instructions. Answer me, LORD! Answer me *so that this people will know that you,* LORD, *are the real God* and that you can change their hearts. (18:36–37, emphasis mine)

Without another word—no shouting, no dancing, no cutting—"the LORD's fire fell; it consumed the sacrifice, the wood, the stones, and the dust. It even licked up the water in the trench!" (18:38). Lightning—not from Baal, from Yahweh—vaporized everything. And the people fell to the ground in worship, shouting, "The LORD is the real God! The LORD is the real God!" (18:39). Baal's prophets go down with their god, a bloody scene I could do without—but this is not my culture or place to judge (18:40).

Elijah's story is not over. As soon as matters are settled on Mount Carmel, he sees rain coming and urges Ahab to hurry back home before he is caught in the storm. The events at Mount Carmel have broken the drought (18:41–46). But the next day, Elijah must run for his life—away from an enraged Queen Jezebel (19:1–3). Oh how he runs—eventually, all the way to Mount Horeb—a weary, tired, burned out prophet who feels very much alone (19:4–10). As much as he and we might hope, Mount Carmel didn't change anything.

Second Prophet: Elisha

Elisha is the God-selected heir of Elijah's ministry to northern Israel (1 Kgs 19:16, see also 2 Kgs 2:1–12), and yet, Elisha is a very different type of prophet than his predecessor. Elisha rarely speaks on behalf of God; instead, he is a miracle worker. In the narrative about his ministry in 2 Kings 2:13–9:13, I count no less than twelve miraculous events (most of them in 2:3–7:20); not to mention the dead man who is tossed into Elisha's grave and immediately comes out alive (13:20–21). To help guide your reading and class discussion of 1 Kings 2–7, Table 10.3 below (copy or sketch in your own notes) allows you to compile your own record of Elisha's miracles, including any moral, message, or lesson you might discern from the story (or not).

Everyone will have his or her own favorite Elisha story. One story that most have or will put on their list is the story of Elisha, the young men, and "da Bears" (2 Kgs 2:23–24). The story is compact, only two verses, with every detail of significance. First, notice where the prophet of the LORD is going and what we know about this place. Bethel is not just any town, but the southern sanctuary for Baal worship in Israel. As we reflect on this information, there can be only one reason Elisha is going up to Bethel—and it is not to pay his respects to Baal and offer a sacrifice. Second, the ones who come out of the city to meet Elisha on the road are not "little kids" (MSG), nor are they young people (CEB), but most likely "a gang of young men" (LB) or a "group of boys" (NLB). Third, they ridicule the LORD's prophet by calling him "Baldy" and, more significant, tell him to go away: "Get going, Baldy! Get going, Baldy!" or "Go away, baldhead! Go away, baldhead!" (NRSV). These young men don't want the LORD's prophet in or anywhere near Bethel. The fourth detail, "they came out of the city," makes me wonder if someone has sent them to drive away the prophet.

Elisha's response is "to curse them in the LORD's name" (2:24a), then it is the LORD's decision to send two bears out of the woods to "mangle" forty-two of the youths—perhaps all, or perhaps only a few of a much larger group (2:24b). And yet, they accomplish their purpose. Instead of going into Bethel, Elisha goes to Mount Carmel (2:25).

ELISHA: THE MIGHTY MIRACLE WORKER		
Text	**Description of the Miracle**	**Purpose? Moral or Lesson?**
1.		
2.		
3.		
4.		
5.		
6.		
7.		
8.		
9.		
10.		
11.		
12.		

Table 10.3. Elisha: The Mighty Miracle Worker

The big issue for our reading about Elisha's ministry is the purpose of all his miracles. What were the people to learn as a result of Elisha's wild and crazy actions? What are we to learn as readers? Too often we think every story in the Bible must carry its own specific moral or lesson. But if we try this approach with Elisha, we end up with bizarre lessons: never make fun of bald men (2:23–25), men should never cook (4:38–41, *well—perhaps not a bad idea*), or we should never borrow a tool (6:1–7). Other Elisha miracle stories defy any lesson or moral to the story—a strong clue that we are reading in the wrong direction. The miracle stories do not fit into a lesson-for-the-day. So what is their purpose?

At Elijah's contest on Mount Carmel, Elijah prayed that God would make it known that the LORD is God in Israel "and that I am your servant" (1 Kgs 18:36). Here, the presence of the LORD's prophet equals or signifies the presence of the LORD in the land. This same idea is hinted at in the stories in 2 Kings 1:1–16 and 3:11–12, and made explicit in 2 Kings 5, the story of Naaman. To begin, Elisha hears that the Israelite king has torn his clothes in grief because the king of Aram has sent Naaman to Israel to be healed; the Israelite king thinks, "I am not a god" (meaning, I am unable to heal Naaman). This request may be a pretext for war because no one or god in Israel can heal Naaman (2 Kgs 5:6–7); but Elisha sends word to the king: "Why did you rip your clothes? Let the man come to me. Then he'll know that there's a prophet in Israel" (5:8). It is fascinating that Elisha says he will know there is "*a prophet in Israel*" instead of saying "*a God in Israel*," which I would expect. But for Elisha, *if there is a prophet who heals, then there must be a mighty God*. In fact, this is precisely what Naaman learns: "Now I know for certain that there's no God anywhere on earth except in Israel" (5:15). Elisha's miracles are not about a moral or lesson; instead, the miracles demonstrate the presence of a mighty God in Israel: the LORD. *As long as the LORD's prophet is in Israel—so is the LORD.* Elisha's ministry is testimony to the presence of the LORD. The LORD has not given up on Israel; he has not walked out. A powerful and faithful God is still in and with northern Israel—if only they will see.

A Brief Recess: In addition to the narrative records of Elijah and Elisha, we are ready to enter evidence from the prophetic books of Amos and Hosea. These short texts are part of the Book of the Twelve in the Hebrew Bible, and assigned to the Minor Prophets in Protestant Bibles. The prophetic books contain tricky testimony, however, because on cross-examination, it becomes relatively clear that while these prophets were active during the life of northern Israel, their oracles were not written down until some time later. When these oracles were formed into books, additional material (some about South Judah) was included. Of course, it is possible the prophet said these words too, but it is more likely that others added them (e.g., editors or the prophet's disciples). Nonetheless, with due care, it is possible to hear the messages God sent to northern Israel.

Third Prophet: Amos

Amos is an unusual prophet for at least two reasons: (1) Amos is not a professional, full-time prophet. Instead, he is a man of the land: he tends sheep and grows sycamore trees (Amos 7:14). (2) Amos is not from northern Israel, but South Judah—the village of Tekoa, south of Bethlehem. So when a priest of Bethel tells Amos he is not wanted there and should go back home (7:10–13), Amos tells him it was never his idea to come proclaim the LORD's word to the north in the first place. God took him from his day job and sent him north to preach (7:14–17).

Based on the opening words of the book (1:1), Amos comes to the north during a peaceful and prosperous time—at least for the few who are living at the expense of the many. Amos is overwhelmed by what he sees: the wealthy mistreating the poor to enrich themselves (2:6–8; 4:1; 5:11–12; 8:4, 6). It is difficult to imagine how anyone could justify getting rich at the expense and suffering of other people—unless they believe they are entitled to wealth because they are God's chosen people. And based on Amos's words, that's exactly what they think. *We are chosen and special; therefore, God will always bless us and never harm us.* Amos says they are dead wrong. Yes, God chose them (3:1), but that means higher expectations, not entitlements. Their chosen status also means "the day of the LORD" for which they long and hope, is not going to be a great day of even more blessing (as they think), but a day of judgment and punishment (5:18–20). The Israelites are confused, but they can't see it. God has tried so many times to get them to return to him, but they won't come back (4:6–11). Now, all Amos knows to say is, "Prepare to meet your God, Israel!" (4:12).

They love to go to Bethel and present their sacrifices, especially when their friends are there to see them (4:4–5). They love to go to their religious festivals and sing their praise songs (5:21–23). They love the life of ease, listening to music that their God has given them—because they are chosen, because they are so good, or just because (4:1, 6:3–6). But they can't see that God hates all of these things. Nor can they see what God wants.

> Seek me and live.
> But don't seek Bethel. . . .
> Seek the LORD and live. (5:4–6)

> Seek good and not evil,
>   that you may live;
> and so the LORD, the God of heavenly forces,
>   will be with you just as you have said.
> Hate evil, love good,
>   and establish justice in the city gate.
> Perhaps the LORD God of heavenly forces
>   will be gracious to what is left of Joseph. (5:14–15)

> But let justice roll down like waters,
>   and righteousness like an ever-flowing stream. (5:24)

They are blind and cannot see their own need to change; they cannot see any problems with their lives or their society. And because of this, they are destined for punishment: 2:13–16; 3:2, 11, 12–15; 4:2–3, 12; 5:1–3, 7–9, 16–20, 26–27; 6:3–7, 9–11, 14; 7:7–9, 16–17; 8:1–3, 7–14; 9:1–6, 8–10. So many words, so many warnings—and the tragedy is not that it will happen, but that it doesn't have to happen.

Fourth Prophet: Hosea

Hosea, unlike Amos, is from the north—so what is happening has to do with *his* people and *his* family and evokes deep passions within him. If he were called to testify against Israel, we should expect his testimony to be interrupted frequently by tears, times when he will need to compose himself before we can continue.

Hosea chapters 1–3 create widespread disagreement among interpreters as to how we are to understand what is happening (or not happening). Does Hosea go look for and marry a prostitute (Gomer)? Was Hosea married to Gomer and she became unfaithful? Or are these chapters just a parable, so the events did not really happen? (And how does chapter 3 relate to chapters 1–2?) However we answer these questions (I lean toward Hosea marrying a prostitute), these opening chapters establish the primary field of images for the book: marriage and family. In chapters 1–3, Hosea's marriage represents God's marriage to Israel. God is Israel's husband and

The Message of the Old Testament

Nine dynasties, nineteen kings, seven assassinations. Two hundred years. Prophets here and there, one from the south on a spring break campaign, another prophet running about doing incredible things as if auditioning for Ripley's *Believe it or Not*. What are we supposed to see in all this? What do we see?

Perspective. The LORD will turn Israel over to Assyria and her war machine and the devastation will be thorough and lasting. But too often, people of faith read Israel's story as if looking through a telescope. They see everything that happens all at once, including the LORD's punishment. So these readers make the assumption that all these events took place in a short period of time, and conclude that Israel never had a chance. From the start, Israel was up against an angry God with unreasonable demands, eager to whack his people should they break the least little law. A corrected perspective: the text covers two hundred years of prophets, hope, and disappointment.

Determination. The LORD refuses to give up on Israel, but is determined to do everything he can to bring them back into their covenant relationship. The LORD sends passionate prophets like Hosea and miracle-workers like Elisha to convince Israel that Baal is a fraud. The LORD is determined to save his people, but the people are more determined to reject the LORD in favor of other gods. And despite the heartbreak their action brings, the LORD refuses to revoke Israel's right to decide for herself.

One and Two. The more we read and reread Israel's story, the more we become aware that only one thing really matters. All of the laws, every one of them, come down to just one idea: love—love as a decision of singular commitment and faithfulness, love for the LORD. And within this decision is a second love—love for the other. These are the principles standing behind the first four commandments and the principles upholding the final six commandments, utterly impossible to separate from one another. From a Christian perspective, we affirm the answer Jesus gave to the question, "What is the most important commandment?" Love the LORD your God with all your heart (Deut 6:5), and the second is a vital part of the first: love your neighbor (and immigrant) as yourself (Lev 19:18, 34).

Simple. I suppose we tend to make things more complex than they are, and far more complicated than they need be. But for the DH and the prophets that connect into this history, once we get past the cultural boundaries and past the *long ago and far away* nature of the text, what we see is not all that complicated. Perhaps—just perhaps—what is most difficult for us is the simple. What do you see?

Israel's worship of other gods is like adultery or prostitution, which breaks God's heart. God is eager to take Israel back to the wilderness and relive their first romantic days when God had rescued her from Egypt (2:14–15), to renew their wedding vows (2:16–20), and change the names of their children (2:21–23). God is desperate to find and bring Israel back home, to the point that God will do anything to bring his wife back to him (3:1–5).

Without question, Hosea's greatest concern for Israel is her idolatry (5:11, 8:4, 13:1) and all the practices that go with the worship of other gods. Israel builds more and more altars to take away their sin, but these altars to idols only increase their sin (8:11, 10:1). Hosea refers to the golden calf at Bethel (8:5–6), but he prefers to call it the calf of Beth-aven (4:15; 5:8; 10:5, 8)—deftly changing Bethel ("house of god") into Beth-aven ("house of sin"). He also slips into sarcasm toward other practices: the people "take advice from a piece of wood" (4:12), and God's people are "kissing calves" (13:2). Israel is so caught up in the worship of other gods she cannot see her folly or remember that the Lord has always been her God (8:14, 13:4–6).

Breaking the first commandment means far more than just worshipping at a different place or just worshipping a different god. Who or what a person worships has real-life implications. For example, because Israel no longer relies on the Lord, the nation flies back and forth between alliances with Egypt and Assyria (5:13, 7:11–12, 8:9–10, 12:1). Their fickle foreign policy feeds the energy behind all the assassinations of one king and dynasty after another (7:7, 8:4). Without a steady, reliable, strong ally to depend on, the nation is a silly bird flying from one place to another (7:11–12).

Judgment is coming, another major theme in the book (5:8–11; 7:13; 9:5–7,10–17; 10:2–4, 8–10, 13–15; 11:6–7; 13:7–16). God will be a moth (5:12), a lion (5:14, 13:7), a leopard (13:7), a bear robbed of her cubs (13:8), and a hunter (7:12, 9:8), and Israel will be destroyed. Hosea, however, sees more. Israel will not only be decimated by invading armies, Israel will also return to Egypt (8:13, 9:3, 11:5, 12:9), a way of saying the nation will go into exile (9:3, 17; 10:6, 7; 11:5). And yet the Lord is deeply conflicted regarding what to about Israel. The Lord is Israel's husband, and no matter what she has done or does, he still loves her (chs. 1–3). Or to change the metaphor, God is Israel's mother:

> When Israel was a child, I loved him,
>> and out of Egypt I called my son.
> The more I called them,
>> the further they went from me;
>> they kept sacrificing to the Baals,
>> and they burned incense to idols.
> Yet it was I who taught Ephraim to walk;
>> I took them up in my arms,
>> but they did not know that I healed them.
> I led them
>> with bands of human kindness,
>> with cords of love.

> I treated them like those
>> who lift infants to their cheeks;
>> I bent down to them and fed them. (11:1–4)

So yes, they deserve punishment for breaking their vows and breaking the Lord's heart. But that's the troublesome thing; the Lord still loves the people.

> How can I give you up, Ephraim?
>> How can I hand you over, Israel?
> How can I make you like Admah?
>> How can I treat you like Zeboiim?
> My heart winces within me;
>> my compassion grows warm and tender. (11:8–9)

All God wants—for his people, his wife, his children—is for them to acknowledge that he alone is their God (6:1–3, 10:12, 12:6, 14:1–3). The Lord wants their love, and the intimate relationship of "knowing" a person.

> I desire faithful love and not sacrifice,
>> the knowledge of God instead of entirely burned offerings. (6:6)

At present, "My people are destroyed from a lack of knowledge" (4:6a). If only they will return, the Lord is waiting like a parent to "heal their faithlessness" and to love them freely (14:4).

Conclusion

The jury is out for your deliberation: if you were in ancient Israel, you would be in the city gate with other city leaders to debate and decide the fate of the accused. The Lord exercised patient love from the beginning of northern Israel. For the next two hundred years, while the nation continued to turn to more and more gods and built its society on the backs of the poor and helpless, the Lord continued to exercise patient love. After two hundred years, the nation was far from the heart of God. And yet, Hosea reports that the Lord is still deeply conflicted about what to do with them; despite what they have done to the Lord, they are God's wife, God's children, God's people—and so God's heart *winces* (11:8 CEB), *recoils* (RSV), or *is torn* (NLT) about what to do in response. Those who want to throw the case out because they think the God of the Old Testament is an angry tyrant who walks around killing anyone who crosses his path cannot possibly have read this material, which offers two hundred years of opposing evidence.

Nonetheless, the verdict is unavoidable: they are guilty. And this time, drastic punishment follows. The Assyrians conquer and then exile the Israelites, scattering them throughout the Assyrian empire (2 Kgs 17:18–23). Then Assyria resettles depleted northern Israel with people taken captive from other conquests (17:24–25). Some from the north will escape to the south, bringing their stories and experiences with them. And some from the north will intermarry with the people brought from distant lands—the beginnings of what will later be known as the Samaritans.

To Discuss

1. In practical terms, what did Jeroboam need to do in order to secure his kingdom, according the prophet Ahijah? Why was this so hard for him to do? How might you have handled the situation? Try to put yourself fully within his situation (it is easy to judge from the outside looking in). What are the stakes for Jeroboam?

2. What seems to be behind the rapid succession of dynasties in northern Israel? How would you feel about becoming king or queen of Israel during this time of rapid succession? Why? How would you feel if there was more stability? How would you create stability?

3. Compile your list of Elisha miracle stories. What is your favorite Elisha story? Be prepared to tell your story (have alternates ready in case someone gets your first selection). What would you say is the point to all these stories?

4. What do you make of Elijah's behavior after Mount Carmel? What's going on with him? Why? How does God respond to him?

5. As far as you can see from all the assigned readings, what is going on with the people in Israel? What are their religious beliefs and practices? How do these beliefs and practices affect their daily life? To what degree do the beliefs and actions of the king influence the people?

6. The author claims that the god a person worships has real-life implications (p. 213). What real-life implications can you see for Israel in the books of Amos and Hosea? Why? How does serving this god rather than that god change a person's life?

7. Compare and contrast the ministries of Amos and Hosea. What are their primary messages? In what ways are they similar? How do they differ? What accounts for the similarities and differences? Do these prophets give any hope for Israel?

8. Read Jeremiah 18:1–12 (study 18:7–10 carefully). What is the nature of the prophetic word? What does God hope will happen as a result of prophetic declarations? How does this compare to what your friends believe about biblical prophets?

To Know

1. The significance of the following in the assigned chapters:

Ahab	Hosea
Amos	Hoshea
Asherah	Jeroboam
Assyria	Jezebel
Baal	Mount Carmel
Bethel	Naaman
Dan	No compassion
Elijah	Not my people
Elisha	Oracle
Golden Calves	Prophet
Gomer	Samaria
High place	Syncretism

2. The dates for the following persons (their reigns) and events.
   a. The Exodus
   b. Saul
   c. David
   d. Solomon
   e. Division of the Kingdom
   f. Fall of Israel to Assyria

3. Jeroboam's actions to secure his throne and the nation.

4. The nature of the Prophetic word about the future.

5. The three indictments against Israel made by the author.

6. What happens at Mount Carmel and the significance of this event.

7. At least five of Elisha's miracles and their purposes.

8. Three major themes in the Book of Amos. Be able to write a short paragraph on Amos.

9. Two major themes in the Book of Hosea. Be able to write a short paragraph on Hosea.

10. Identify Hosea's actions in chapters 1–3 that have some special meaning. Explain the meanings behind each.

11. Locate the following on a map (see Figure 10.2): Assyria, Ninevah, Babylon, Tigris River, Euphrates River, Haran, Carchemish, Nile River, and Judah.

12. Locate the following on a map (see Figure 10.6): Sea of Galilee, Jordan River, Dead Sea, Mount Carmel, Dan, Bethel, Samaria, Jerusalem, North Israel, and Judah.

To Dig Deeper: Research Topics

1. Conduct your own trial of Israel in class. Assign roles to class members, in order of importance: Israel, Elijah, Elisha, Amos, Hosea, prophets of Baal, Jeroboam, Ahab, Jezebel, and others. You will also need a prosecuting attorney(s), defense attorney(s), judge, and a jury.

2. Provide a psychological analysis of Elijah, especially his behavior after Mount Carmel. Your analysis should draw from professional biblical research and professional psychological research. Your analysis should use professional, technical terminology from both fields.

3. Prepare a marketing campaign for the changes in religion that Jeroboam makes in northern Israel. Do not rely only on the information in this chapter; research the things that Jeroboam does, where he gets his ideas, and more.

4. Find pictures and images of calves recovered by archaeologists. Prepare drawings of what Jeroboam's calves might have looked like on the basis of your research.

For Further Reading

Brueggemann, Walter. *Finally Comes the Poet: Daring Speech for Proclamation.* Minneapolis: Fortress, 1989.

Hamilton, Victor P. *Handbook on the Historical Books.* 2d ed. Grand Rapids: Baker, 2001.

Moore, Michael S. *Faith Under Pressure: A Study of Biblical Leaders in Conflict.* Abilene: Leafwood, 2003.

Schmitt, John J. "Prophecy (Preexilic Hebrew)." Pages 482–489 in vol. 5 of *The Anchor Bible Dictionary.* Edited by David Noel Freedman. 6 vols. New York: Doubleday, 1992.

Thiele, Edwin R. *The Mysterious Numbers of the Hebrew Kings.* 3d ed. Grand Rapids: Kregel Academic, 1994.

The Story of
Southern Judah
Kings, Prophets, and God's Mercy

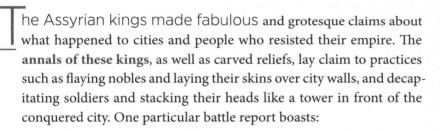

The Assyrian kings made fabulous and grotesque claims about what happened to cities and people who resisted their empire. The **annals of these kings**, as well as carved reliefs, lay claim to practices such as flaying nobles and laying their skins over city walls, and decapitating soldiers and stacking their heads like a tower in front of the conquered city. One particular battle report boasts:

> I captured many troops alive. I cut off of some their arms [and] hands; I cut off of others their noses, ears, [and] extremities. I gouged out the eyes of many troops. I made one pile of the living [and] one of heads. I hung their leaders on trees around the city.[1]

Sennacherib, an adversary with whom Judah will deal, surpasses his predecessors in the grisly detail of his conquests:

> I cut their throats like lambs. I cut off their precious lives [as one cuts] a string. Like the many waters of a storm, I made [the contents of] their gullets and entrails run down upon the wide earth. My prancing steeds harnessed for my riding, plunged into their blood as [into] a river. The wheels of my war chariot, which brings low the wicked and evil, were bespattered with blood and filth. With the bodies of their

---

[1] A. Kirk Grayson, trans., *Assyrian Royal Inscriptions, Part 2: From Tiglath-pileser I to Ashur-nasir II* (Wiesbaden, Germany: Otto Harrassowitz, 1976), 165.

READING ASSIGNMENTS
1 KINGS 15:9–24
2 KINGS 11–12
2 KINGS 18–23
ISAIAH 5, 7–8, 30–31
MICAH 1–7

KEY TERMS
Annals of the King: the written record of the king's accomplishments for each year of his reign

Exile: a forced migration away from a person's homeland and into a foreign country

Queen Mother: a powerful political position; often, but not always, held by the king's mother

Reformation: a religious movement to revive or restore the spiritual life of a group of people

219

Figure 11.1. "Two Assyrian Soldiers Attacking a City." Original photograph by Author from the Hermitage Museum, St. Petersburg, Russia

warriors I filled the plain, like grass. [Their] testicles I cut off, and tore out their privates like the seeds of cucumbers.[2]

These horrific claims, surely exaggerated at least a little, served to frighten cities and nations into submission, as well as to make any state in the empire think twice, or even three times, before considering rebellion. A miscalculation of one's power or the strength of an alliance made with other nations could prove to be much worse than fatal.

The Assyrian Empire and its claims interact with events in both northern Israel and southern Judah. In Chapter Ten, we studied the life and death of Israel by conducting a trial. We pressed charges of violating the covenant, especially the first two commandments, and then called witnesses from the Deuteronomistic History (DH), the prophets Elijah and Elisha, and the prophets Hosea and Amos. By the end of the trial, Israel's guilt was established beyond any reasonable doubt. The only remaining question was punishment—though not really a question; the LORD had been warning Israel for years what would come, if the nation did not turn back. The capital city, Samaria, was destroyed and the nation taken into **exile**—all at the hands of the Assyrian Empire.

Awareness of Assyrian propaganda about what they do to those who resist makes it much easier to appreciate the struggle to trust the LORD, and only the LORD, when a treaty with Egypt, or any nation, would bring much-needed military support. This awareness also helps us understand why the city of Samaria held out for three years under siege (2 Kgs 17:5). King Hoshea, the army, and the nobles of the city could only imagine what waited for them if the Assyrians took the city—and they did take it (in fact, two Assyrian kings both claim credit for the victory). We do not, however, have any records from Assyria or Scripture to tell us what happened when Samaria fell, other than that the people were exiled.

The Assyrian Empire that conquered Samaria in the late eighth century continued to expand under the direction of their kings, who set their sights on Palestine and Jerusalem. What happens with their invasion, however, is somewhat of a mystery. It is clear enough that the Egyptian army comes to the aid of the king of Judah (Hezekiah), but the Assyrians defeat

ASSYRIAN KINGS IN THE 8TH–7TH CENTURIES BCE

Tiglath-Pileser III	744–727
Shalmaneser V	726–722
Sargon II	721–705
Sennacherib	704–681
Esarhaddon	680–669
Ashurbanipal	668–612

Table 11.1. Assyrian Kings in the 8th–7th Centuries BCE

[2] Daniel Luckenbill, *Ancient Records of Assyria and Babylonia,* 2 vols. (Chicago: University of Chicago Press, 1926–1927), 2: sec 254.

Egypt—sending them running for home. It is also without debate that Hezekiah paid the Assyrian king (Sennacherib) rich tribute to leave Jerusalem (see Table 11.1). Even so, it is unclear to historians what causes the Assyrian army to ultimately leave Palestine. Just as an Ethiopian army enters the land to confront the Assyrians, on the night before their battle, something causes the Assyrian army to withdraw in confusion (see Hezekiah below). The next Assyrian king made the conquest of Egypt his military aim, which he achieved for a short time in 671 BCE.

Though outer appearances suggest the Assyrian Empire to be as strong or stronger than ever, the empire was, in fact, beginning to show signs of weakness by the mid-seventh century (650 BCE), just as the Babylonians began a rebellion that the Assyrians could not stop. The Babylonians won battle after battle, decimating Assyria and sending shock waves throughout the rest of the ancient Near East—including Egypt. As the Assyrian Empire began to sink, the mice jumped off the ship; in other words, large pieces of the Assyrian Empire broke off and made a run for their own independence—including Judah. Then, with Assyria on life-support, Egypt sent them military help (616 BCE). Why they

Figure 11.2. Map of Judah after the Fall of Northern Israel

did is anyone's guess. Even more inexplicable is Josiah's attempt to stop Egypt's effort to send more support to the Assyrian army, which led to his death in battle against Egypt (ca. 609 BCE). Whatever Egypt's motive may have been, their effort was too little and too late. The Babylonians kept pushing farther and farther north and west, taking Nineveh, Assyria's capital city, in 612 BCE.

Finally, at Carchemish (see Figure 10.2 on page 200), far north on the Euphrates River, Nebuchadnezzar led the Babylonian army in a surprise attack on the Egyptians and the remaining Assyrians. The Babylonian victory was decisive, driving the Egyptian army away and destroying what was left of Assyria. Consequently, the battle at Carchemish (605 BCE) marks a turning point in the history of the ancient Near East. With these obstacles out of the way, Nebuchadnezzar was ready to move on and claim all of Syria-Palestine for Babylon, but after the battle at Carchemish, he receives word that his father has died (King Nabopolasser). So, Nebuchadnezzar returns to Babylon to be crowned king.

After his coronation, Nebuchadnezzar leads a series of campaigns west and south of the Euphrates, including campaigns that reach into Judah. Some states accept Nebuchadnezzar's rule without a fight and begin to pay tribute to Babylon. Others resist, with the inevitable result of a siege that ultimately fell Babylon's way. The final years of Jerusalem/Judah will be spent in a tug-of-war between factions that support either siding with the Egyptians (still a western power) or accepting Babylonian rule. Eventually, Judah's poor choices will lead to a horrible three-year siege of Jerusalem and the fall to Babylon in 587 BCE.

⟶

Since we investigated Israel in Chapter Ten, it seems only fair that we also investigate southern Judah, if for no other reason than to answer a simple question: How does the south survive for so much longer than the north? Eighth century Judah was exposed to the same cultural forces (the worship of Baal and other gods) and external pressures (Egypt and the Assyrian Empire) that took Israel down, but Judah survives In fact, Judah lives on as an independent state for another 135 years—through the eighth (700s) and seventh centuries (600s), into the beginning of the sixth century (500s). Judah not only outlasted Israel, but Assyria, too. Was Judah's longer life just a matter of God's support? Or did the south keep the covenant better than the north? By the end of this chapter, we should be able to answer these questions. We will continue in Chapter Twelve with Judah's final years, as she dealt with the Babylonian Empire from the late seventh century (ca. 609 BCE), until Jerusalem's fall to Babylon in 587 BCE.

Earlier we charged and convicted northern Israel on three counts:

1. Failure to trust the LORD, which manifested itself in an unstable government;
2. Corrupt spiritual leadership that led the people to worship other gods; and
3. Failure to hear (and obey) the prophets.

In the interest of fairness, we will examine each of these three areas in Judah's life during the eighth through seventh centuries, to see if charges should be filed against Judah at that time. So, we proceed with our investigation of Judah, raising the same charges under which northern Israel was indicted and ultimately found guilty. Our task, however, is somewhat different. We now operate as a Grand Jury to determine if these charges (or others) should become indictments and the basis of a trial. As before, the witnesses we will interview include the testimony of the DH and two eighth century prophets: Micah and Isaiah (we will hold the seventh century prophets until we examine Judah's fall to Babylon in Chapter Twelve).

Charge One: Political Instability?

Rehoboam was slow to recognize that the north meant what it said about reducing their load, or else. Only after they kill Rehoboam's supervisor of forced labor does Rehoboam realize he has a serious problem. Then, he raced home to assemble an army and go back to attack the north with 185,000 select warriors (on the large number, see Appendix V)—at least until another prophet comes with word from God: "Don't make war against your relatives, the Israelites. Go home, every one of you, because this is my plan" (1 Kgs 12:24). So, they went home.

The writers are interested in only two aspects or events in Rehoboam's reign (after losing the northern kingdom). First, they convey the depth to which the nation plunges into worshipping other gods (to which we will return in a moment). You name it and they are into it: they build shrines and places to worship on the top of every high hill and under every green tree. They have "consecrated workers," or "male temple prostitutes" (14:24 NRSV), and are just like the people the LORD drove off the land. In one sentence: "The sins they committed made the LORD angrier than anything their ancestors had done" (14:22). As if no one could possibly be worse than Jeroboam and what he is doing in the north, the south is on a steep downward plunge.

Second, not long into Rehoboam's reign (five years), King Shishak of Egypt attacks Jerusalem. As the victor, Shishak takes the treasures of the temple (presumably the ark, unless it had been hidden), the king's palace, and Solomon's ornamental shields (14:25). Shishak is the first to plunder the temple for its treasure, but certainly not the last (e.g., 1 Kgs 15:18; 2 Kgs 12:18, 14:14, 16:8, 18:15–16, and 24:13).

Judah, however, experienced political stability as a result of national commitment to the LORD's selection of David's dynasty. With only two exceptions, every transition in the monarchy was a matter of identifying the king's heir and anointing him as king—even if the heir was still a child (e.g., Joash, seven years old in 2 Kgs 11:1–2; and Josiah, eight years old in 2 Kgs 22:1–2). In these cases, it is obvious that someone else ran the country until the child-king grew up (most likely the high priest).

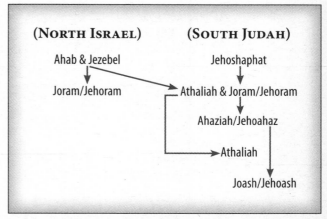

Figure 11.3. Kings of Judah and Israel: Athaliah and Joash/Jehoash

The exceptions to the normal father/son arrangement in David's dynasty occur at two points in the nation's history—both, times of political turmoil.

Exception one: The first exception requires a bit of backstory to understand. During Ahab and Jezebel's reign in the north, Judah's king (Joram or Jehoram) married their daughter Athaliah (2 Kgs 8:16–18), cementing a strong relationship between the two royal families. In time, Athaliah and Joram have a son (Ahaziah or Jehoahaz) who becomes king in Judah, with Athaliah serving as **queen mother** (8:25–26). By this time, Ahab and Jezebel's son (Athaliah's brother, *another* Joram or Jehoram) has become king in the north.

While Joram (king of the north) was recovering from battle wounds, Ahaziah (king of Judah) went to visit his uncle (8:29). During Ahaziah's time with his uncle, Jehu's rebellion and purge of the royal family in the north began, and Ahaziah was caught and killed, alongside his uncle (9:27–28).

Now the first exception in Judah occurs (you may follow the complicated relationships in Figure 11.3). When Athaliah, queen mother in Judah, learns of her son's death, she seizes the throne of Judah and begins her own massacre of the royal family in Judah, including the royal children (her children and grandchildren?). Only one child escaped: Jehoash, a son of the late king Ahaziah (11:1–3). So it happens that a person outside the Davidic dynasty reigns over Judah: Queen Athaliah (see Figure 11.3, Table 11.2, and 1 Kgs 11:3). The high priest, however, cut her reign short. After six years, the priest executed a successful coup that put Jehoash, the descendant of David, back on the throne of Judah and Queen Athaliah in the grave (11:4–20).

THE KINGS OF SOUTHERN JUDAH				
King (Relation to Previous King)	Queen Mother	Text	Years of Reign	End of Reign
Rehoboam (Son of Solomon)	Naamah	1 Kgs 14:21–31	17 Years	Natural Death
Abijam (Son of Rehoboam)	Maacah	1 Kgs 15:1–8	3 Years	Natural Death
Asa (Son of Abijam)	Maacah (Deposed)	1 Kgs 15:9–24	41 Years	Natural Death
Jehoshaphat (Son of Asa)	Azubah	1 Kgs 22:41–50	25 Years	Natural Death
Jehoram/Joram (Son of Jehoshaphat)	(unknown)	2 Kgs 8:16–24	8 Years	Natural Death
Ahaziah/Jehoahaz (Son of Jehoram)	Athaliah	2 Kgs 8:25–9:28	1 Year	Assassinated
Queen Athaliah (Mother of Ahaziah)	{None}	2 Kgs 11:1–3	6 Years	Assassinated
Joash/Jehoash (Son of Ahaziah)	Zibiah	2 Kgs 12:1–12:21	40 Years	Assassinated
Amaziah (Son of Joash)	Jehoaddan	2 Kgs 14:1–20	29 Years	Assassinated
Azariah/Uzziah (Son of Amaziah)	Jecoliah	2 Kgs 15:1–7	52 Years	Natural Death
Jotham (Son of Azariah)	Jerusha	2 Kgs 15:32–38	16 Years	Natural Death
Ahaz (Son of Jotham)	(unknown)	2 Kgs 16:1–20	16 Years	Natural Death
Hezekiah (Son of Ahaz)	Abi (or Abijah)	2 Kgs 18:1–20:21	29 Years	Natural Death
Manasseh (Son of Hezekiah)	Hephzibah	2 Kgs 21:1–18	55 Years	Natural Death
Amnon (Son of Manasseh)	Meshullemeth	2 Kgs 21:19–26	2 Years	Assassinated
Josiah (Son of Amnon)	Jedidah	2 Kgs 22:1–23:30	31 Years	Died in Battle
Jehoahaz (Son of Josiah)	Hamutal	2 Kgs 23:31–34	3 Months	Exiled to Egypt
Jehoiakim/Eliakim (Son of Josiah)	Zebidah	2 Kgs 23:34–24:6	11 Years	Natural Death or Assassinated
Jehoiachin (Son of Jehoiakim)	Nehushta	2 Kgs 24:8–12	3 Months	Exiled to Babylon
Zedekiah/Mattaniah (Son of Josiah)	Hamutal	2 Kgs 24:17–25:7	11 Years	Exiled to Babylon

Table 11.2. The Kings of Southern Judah

Exception Two: The second exception to the father-son succession of kings in southern Judah occurs in the final twenty-two years of the nation, when three of Josiah's sons become king. After Josiah's death on the battlefield against Egypt, the nation crowns Josiah's first son (Jehoahaz) king of Judah (23:31–34). Within three months, however, the Egyptian pharaoh (Neco) comes to Jerusalem and exiles Jehoahaz to Egypt (23:31–34). He then makes Josiah's second son, Eliakim, king, changing his name to Jehoiakim (2 Kgs 23:34). After the shift in power toward Babylon at Carchemish, Jehoiakim changed his loyalties to Babylon and paid tribute. Later, however, he rebelled against Babylon (24:1).

The record, however, is fuzzy about what happened next. Jehoiakim's rebellion was doomed for failure; and as his misjudgment became clear, he was most likely assassinated to save Judah from a horrible fate (recall from above how super-empires treat those in rebellion). So when Nebuchadnezzar finally gets to Jerusalem, Jehoiakim is dead and his son, Jehoiachin, who only has been on the throne for three months, quickly surrenders to the Babylonian king (2 Kgs 24:8–11). Nebuchadnezzar exiles Jehoiachin, his royal family, and many others to Babylon (24:12–16); he then takes Josiah's third son (Mattaniah) and installs him as king, changing his name to Zedekiah (24:17–19).

Be careful not to lose perspective with these two exceptions *and all these names*. We have just reviewed between twenty and thirty years (give or take five years) from a national history of 335 years. So, for three hundred years, the transition of authority was peaceful and without challenge—due to the nation's commitment to David's dynasty and the LORD's covenant with David. For only six years was there a non-Davidic ruler on the throne of Judah (Athaliah), and the priests and army rebelled as soon as it was reasonable to install the next king (when he had finally reached seven years of age). And even in the turmoil leading to the end of Judah, every king of Judah came from the family of David, even if three of the kings were all Josiah's sons.

Charge Two: Spiritual Leadership?

Southern Judah struggles with corrupt spiritual leadership that infects the population and leads them to violate both the first and second commandments. Much like Jeroboam in northern Israel, Rehoboam leads the south into all types of practices that break the very heart of the commandments. The DH writer summarizes:

> Judah did evil in the LORD's eyes. The sins they committed made the LORD angrier than anything their ancestors had done. They also built shrines, standing stones, and sacred poles on top of every high hill and under every green tree. Moreover, the consecrated workers in the land did detestable things, just like those nations that the LORD had removed among the Israelites. (1 Kgs 14:22–24)

Spiritually, Judah is off to little, if any better start than northern Israel. Judah is also worshipping all of the gods in the Canaanite Yellow Pages—worship that remakes them into the image of the new gods who do terrible things.

Other southern kings are described in various ways. Like the Israelite kings, the official introduction to each of the kings of Judah provides the same vital information, with one additional element: the name of the queen mother, a political position with significant power (see Figure 11.4).

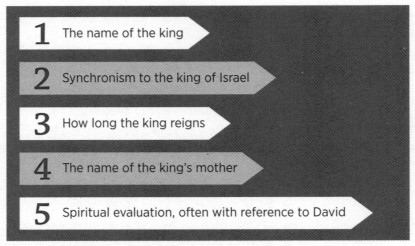

Figure 11.4. The Introductory Formula for Judean Kings

So for Rehoboam, the first king of southern Judah after northern Israel secedes, we read (1 Kgs 14:21–22; see Figure 11.5):

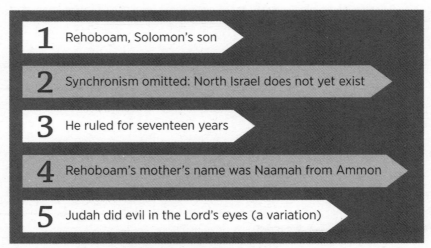

Figure 11.5. The Introductory Formula for Rehoboam

We take a final example three hundred years later for King Jehoiakim (2 Kgs 23:36–37) to demonstrate the resiliency of the formula (see Figure 11.6):

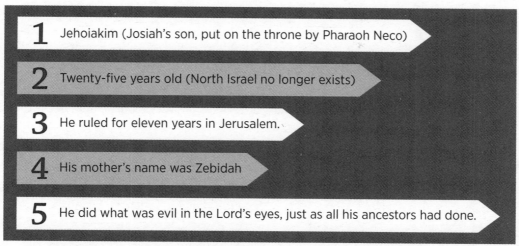

1 Jehoiakim (Josiah's son, put on the throne by Pharaoh Neco)

2 Twenty-five years old (North Israel no longer exists)

3 He ruled for eleven years in Jerusalem.

4 His mother's name was Zebidah

5 He did what was evil in the Lord's eyes, just as all his ancestors had done.

Figure 11.6. The Introductory Formula for Jehoiakim

And so the introductions go for every king in Judah, with the exception of Queen Athaliah, who took the throne by force (she had been queen mother; see 2 Kgs 11:1–3).

- If the new king's father and/or grandfather was evil, a king may be described as being *just like his father* or *just like his ancestors* (e.g., Abijam, Amnon, Jehoahaz, Jehoiakim, Jehoiachin, and Zedekiah).
- Some are described as being *like Ahab* or *like northern Israel* (e.g., Joram, Ahaziah, and Ahaz).
- Worst of all, two kings are described as *doing things the nations had done that the* Lord *had driven out before Israel*: Rehoboam (cited above) and Manasseh.

For Manasseh (ca. 687–642 BCE), the indictments are long, and, if they are proven, carry a death sentence (2 Kgs 21:2–8):

- setting up altars for Baal
- setting up a carved Asherah image in the temple
- worshipping the stars
- building altars for the stars in both courtyards of the Lord's temple
- consulting sign readers and fortune tellers
- using spirit mediums and diviners
- sacrificing his own son

The writer summarizes, "Manasseh led them (Judah) into doing more evil than the nations the Lord had wiped out before the Israelites" (21:9).

The evidence we need to defend Judah comes in four names: Asa, Jehoash, Hezekiah, and Josiah, four kings in the south who led vigorous **reformation** movements—efforts absent in the north. The DH writers describe three of the four as doing what was right in the LORD's eyes, *just like their ancestor David* (1 Kgs 15:11; 2 Kgs 18:3, 22:2); the fourth, Jehoash, did what was right because the priest Jehoiada taught him (2 Kgs 12:2). The difference these kings make to the spiritual and political history of southern Judah warrants close examination of their lives and efforts to bring Judah back to her God.

1. King Asa. We know the least about King Asa (ca. 913–873 BCE, 1 Kgs 15:9–24). What we know presents a man who is not perfect, but serious about serving his God. On the one side, Asa is eager to rid the land of idols and those who enable and encourage others to worship idols. He removes the "male temple prostitutes" (14:24 NRSV) from the land, and deposes the queen mother, Maacah, because she promoted the worship of Asherah.[3] He also takes away the idols his ancestors made and cuts down the image of Asherah and burns it (1 Kgs 15:12–13). Even more, Asa brings gifts back to the temple, gifts that his father and he had vowed to return (15:15). The writers summarizes, "The heart of Asa was true to the LORD all his days" (15:14b), a high compliment and strong evidence for Judah's defense.

On the other side, the writer does not hide Asa's failures. His reform does not reach to the high places in the land (15:14a). Asa also relies on a political alliance with Syria (Aram) to stop the construction of a northern Israelite fortress at Ramah, only five miles north of Jerusalem. The alliance comes at the cost of all the gold and silver left in the treasury of the king's house and the treasury of the temple (15:16–19). Syria accepts the money and attacks multiple sites in Israel to divert Israel's attention away from building the fortress at Ramah, giving Judah time to deconstruct the fortress (15:20–22). If the prosecuting attorney reads this text without knowledge of Deuteronomy, she or he is apt not to see the problem, but credit Asa for a clever political move. But for those aware of Deuteronomy's concern for the king's political alliances, Asa's actions are questionable (Deut 17:17, see the discussion in Chapter Eight, page 155).

2. King Jehoash. Jehoash (ca. 837–800 BCE) is the only son spared from his grandmother Athaliah's purge of the royal family when she seized power (2 Kgs 11:1–3, see above). Saved when he was no more than a year old, he comes to the throne at the ripe old age of seven. The text concedes what we suspect: in the king's early years, the high priest is in control (12:2). So it comes as no surprise that the young king gives an order to collect money for repairing the LORD's temple in Jerusalem. And yet, some years later, when money has been collected—but no repairs made—the king summons his mentor and other priests to ask why repairs are not being made and to make changes to the system to keep the priests' hands out of the collection box (12:4–7). Consequently, Jehoash makes his greatest contribution to the worship of the LORD by putting changes in place to ensure donated money passes directly to the craftsmen, so that the temple is kept in shape (12:8–16). Like Asa, however, Jehoash also uses holy objects dedicated to the

---

[3] Maacah also served as queen mother during the reign of Abijam (1 Kgs 15:2). She may or may not have been Asa's "grandmother" (CEB).

temple to pay Syria (Aram) not to destroy Jerusalem (12:17–18). Perhaps angry with Jehoash's foreign policy, a faction within his officials conspires and assassinates him—a faction that may be in support of the political ideas of Jehoash's son, Amaziah. If so, however, they misplayed their cards. Once Amaziah is in control of the nation, his first order of business is to have them killed (12:19–21).

3. King Hezekiah. Hezekiah (ca. 715–687 BCE) is on the throne of southern Judah when northern Israel falls to Assyria (2 Kgs 18:9–12). Like Asa, Hezekiah leads an aggressive campaign to rid the land of objects used in the worship of other gods: shrines, sacred pillars, Asherah's pole, and the bronze serpent Moses made in the wilderness to direct the people's trust to the LORD—now used as an idol (see Num 21:4–9). Hezekiah matches this negative campaign with the positive: he trusts the LORD and does his best to follow the commandments (2 Kgs 18:5–6).

The chronology of the stories about Hezekiah in 18:7–19:37 is notoriously difficult for interpreters. The text presents nine units:

- *Unit 1.* Assyria (Sennacherib) marches against Judah and Hezekiah pays tribute for Assyria to withdraw (18:13–16).
- *Unit 2.* Assyria sends representatives to Jerusalem, demanding surrender or destruction (18:17–37).
- *Unit 3.* Hezekiah tears his clothes (a sign of mourning) and sends messengers to the prophet Isaiah, informing him of the situation and asking for him to pray for the nation (19:1–4).
- *Unit 4.* Isaiah instructs the messengers to tell Hezekiah that the LORD says, "Don't be afraid of the words you heard. . . ." I'm about to send Assyria back home (19:5–7).
- *Unit 5.* The Assyrian representatives leave Jerusalem, to go back to their king (19:8).
- *Unit 6.* Assyria sends messengers to Hezekiah, warning him not to trust in his God and giving him letters from the Assyrian king (19:9–13).
- *Unit 7.* Hezekiah takes the letters and reads them. He then takes them to the temple, spreads them out before the LORD and prays (9:14–19).
- *Unit 8.* Isaiah sends word to Hezekiah, urging him to trust the LORD, who will protect the city: the Assyrians will not attack or set siege to the city (9:20–34).
- *Unit 9.* During the night, the LORD's messenger kills 185,000 Assyrian soldiers (or 185 troops, see Appendix V). When the others wake up and see all the dead, they withdraw from Jerusalem and return home (19:35–37).

The question for interpreters of Hezekiah's story is not only the order of events, but how many, if any, of the units are duplicates—retelling the same event? Is Unit 2 the same event as Unit 6? Is Unit 8 a duplicate of Unit 4? Is Unit 1 the result of Unit 2? Further evidence to consider comes from Sennacherib's own account of his invasion of Judah in 701 BCE:

> Because Hezekiah, king of Judah, would not submit to my yoke, I came up against him, and by force of arms and by the might of my power I took 46 of his strong

fenced cities; and of the smaller towns which were scattered about, I took and plundered a countless number . . . and Hezekiah himself I shut up in Jerusalem, his capital city, like a bird in a cage, building towers round the city to hem him in, and raising banks of earth against the gates, so as to prevent escape. . . . Then upon Hezekiah there fell the fear of the power of my arms, and he sent out to me the chiefs and the elders of Jerusalem with 30 talents of gold and 300 talents of silver, and diverse treasures, a rich and immense booty.[4]

Even though royal records tend to exaggerate the king's victories, here, Sennacherib admits setting siege to Jerusalem, but does not claim to have taken the city.

For our purposes, we continue to look for evidence of faith/trust in the LORD among the kings and people, versus the lack of faith. In other words, we want the theological meaning or assessment of the writers. So before you continue reading, I encourage you to stop for a moment, read 2 Kings 18–20, and reflect on which units and actions reflect trust, doubt, or some combination of the two.

An initial review of the evidence reveals a mixture of faith and doubt:

- *Unit 1.* Hezekiah follows Asa and Jehoash in using Temple resources to pay off a stronger nation (recall Deut 17). A lack of faith.
- *Unit 3.* Hezekiah asks the prophet to pray for the nation. A sign of trust.
- *Unit 4.* The prophet Isaiah replies with words of assurance that challenge Hezekiah to trust—the LORD will resolve the threat. A challenge to trust.
- *Unit 7.* In a remarkable scene of trust, Hezekiah has the threatening letters spread out before the LORD, so the LORD can see the threats and respond.
- *Unit 8.* Isaiah again sends word for Hezekiah to trust in the LORD's protection.

The text records one final story about Hezekiah: a story of illness, near death, healing, a miraculous sign, and an envoy from Babylon with a *"We are so glad you didn't die!"* gift (20:1–12).

Hezekiah plays the role of a proud host and shows the Babylonians everything—*everything* (20:13). When Isaiah hears about what has happened—*he goes ballistic!* He predicts a time when Babylon will be the one who takes everything, including the people, into captivity (20:14–19). But we are left, sitting in the bleachers, wondering what just happened on the field to make Isaiah call and assess such a drastic penalty. What is the problem? Look carefully at the list of items Hezekiah showed the envoy from Babylon:

Hezekiah granted them an audience and showed them everything in his treasury—the silver, the gold, the spices, and the fine oil. He also showed them *his stock of weaponry* and everything in his storehouses. (20:13, emphasis mine)

[4]James Pritchard, ed., *Ancient Near Eastern Texts,* 2nd ed. (Princeton, NJ: Princeton University Press, 1995), 287.

Now we see it—Hezekiah is not just being friendly, he is negotiating a treaty alliance with Babylon against Assyria; putting his trust in . . . ?

Isaiah urges Hezekiah over and over again not to be afraid of Assyrian conquest (19:5–7, 20–34), not to make military alliances with other nations—not with Egypt against Assyria (see Isaiah below), and not with Babylon against Assyria (20:12–18).

4. King Josiah. Josiah (ca. 640–609 BCE) begins his reign at the age of eight (22:1–2)—then the text goes silent for eighteen years, until Josiah is twenty-six years old and orders repairs on the temple (22:3–7). In the process, workers discover an "Instruction Scroll" (22:8). In a short time, the high priest and Josiah's secretary read the scroll and realize the king must be informed. So they bring and read the scroll to Josiah, who reacts with alarm (22:10–11): "The LORD must be furious with us" (22:13). Josiah has the authenticity of the scroll verified by a local prophet, Huldah, a female prophet living in Jerusalem. Many scholars today believe that what was found was an early version of the middle chapters of Deuteronomy. She tells Josiah that the LORD is indeed furious with Judah because "they've desecrated me and have burned incense to other gods, angering me by everything they have done" (22:17), and so "I am about to bring disaster on this place and its citizens" (22:16); but as for Josiah, because of his broken heart, he will go to his grave in peace (22:19–20).

Josiah, however, is not about to let things be and accept punishment as the LORD's final word for Judah; he knows the LORD too well to do that. Instead, he initiates one of the most aggressive and far-reaching reform movements in the Bible. Josiah knows that God's declaration of punishment can be changed—if the people will change (Jer 18:1–10, see discussion in Chapter Ten). So he begins with a public reading of the scroll and makes his own covenant with the LORD, vowing to obey all the commandments with all his heart; the people respond by also accepting the covenant (23:1–3). Then Josiah cleans house.

From the temple, he removes and burns

- all objects made for Baal, Asherah, and the stars (23:4)
- the Asherah image (23:6)
- the shrines for the male and female prostitutes (23:7)
- the altars Manasseh built in the courtyards (23:12)

Outside the temple, he defiles and/or burns:

- the shrines in all of Judah's cities (23:8)
- the shrines in Jerusalem's city gates (23:8)
- the place for people to burn their children alive to the god Molech (23:10)
- the chariots pulled by horses in honor of the sun (23:11)
- the altars on the palace roof, built by Ahaz (23:12)
- the shrines built by Solomon on the hill across from and facing Jerusalem (23:13)
- he also smashes sacred pillars and cuts down sacred poles (23:14)

Josiah even goes north into land that was once part of Israel:

- he tears down the shrine Jeroboam made (23:15)
- he burns the sacred pole for Asherah (23:15)
- he digs up bones and burns them on the altar in Bethel, desecrating it (23:16; see 1 Kgs 13:1–3)
- he tears down the altar in Bethel (23:15)
- he then destroys the shrines on the high hills throughout Samaria (23:19)

Along with all this physical destruction, Josiah also dealt with the people supporting these places:

- he got rid of the priests appointed to serve in Judean cities (23:15)
- he got rid of the male and female temple prostitutes (23:7)
- he killed the priests to the shrines at high places in Samaria (23:20)
- he killed and burned those who consulted the dead, as well as the spirit mediums for household gods (23:24)

Then, on the positive side, Josiah led a celebration of the Passover (23:21), which had either not been kept since the era of the judges or it had not been kept on such a wide and powerful scale since the judges (23:22). By the end of describing Josiah's efforts to turn the nation around, all the writer can say is,

> There's never been a king like Josiah, whether before or after him, who turned to the LORD with all his heart, all his being, and all his strength, in agreement with everything in the Instruction from Moses. (23:25)

It is difficult to imagine anything Josiah could have done that he did not do. But his efforts apparently still failed to reach the hearts of his people. The writer tells us,

> Even so, the LORD didn't turn away from the great rage that burned against Judah on account of all that Manasseh had done to make him angry. The LORD said, "I will remove Judah from my presence just as I removed Israel. I will reject this city, Jerusalem, which I chose, and this temple where I promised my name would reside." (23:26–27)

As soon as Josiah is gone, everything goes back to "normal"—just as it was before Josiah. The shrines are rebuilt and idols brought out from hiding, dusted off, and polished. And the people resume their steady transformation into becoming like these other gods, with their values in favor of riches and power over destitute, strong over weak, and oppressor over oppressed.

Charge Three: Judah's Response to the Prophets

The LORD also sent prophets to Judah. The narrative of 2 Kings has already introduced Isaiah, who supported King Hezekiah (2 Kgs 19:1–7, 19:20–31, 20:14–19), and Huldah, who supported

King Josiah (2 Kgs 22:14–20). Table 11.3 below provides a visual image of other prophets who lived and originally spoke to Judah. In the last part of this chapter, we keep our attention on the eighth century prophets of Judah: Micah and First Isaiah (see below). In Chapter Twelve, as we work through Judah's final years, we will supplement the DH with an examination of representative prophets from the seventh through sixth centuries.

THE PROPHETS LINKED TO JUDAH	
8th Century 800–700 BCE	Established by the book's introduction or contents
	First Isaiah (Isaiah 1–39)
	Micah
7th Century 700–587 BCE	Zephaniah
	Jeremiah
	Ezekiel
	Habakkuk
In the exile (Exilic; 586–536 BCE) or after the exile (Post-Exilic)	Second Isaiah (Isaiah 40–55)
	Haggai
	Zechariah
	Third Isaiah (Isaiah 56–66)
	Malachi
OTHER PROPHETIC BOOKS, IN THE TRADITIONAL ORDER OF PROTESTANT BIBLES	
	Daniel
	Joel
	Obadiah
	Jonah
	Nahum

Table 11.3. Prophets Linked to Judah

1. Isaiah was part of the royal establishment and a special encouragement to King Hezekiah when the Assyrians were threatening to take down Judah, along with northern Israel (2 Kgs 18–19). The book associated with Isaiah's name addresses this and other events from eighth century Judah (Isa 1–39). The book, however, also speaks about and to Judean exiles at the end of their captivity, encouraging exiled peoples to return home (Isa 40–55). Still not finished, the book also speaks to people living in Jerusalem during the Persian era (Isa 56–66). Consequently, the Book of Isaiah is frequently designated as First Isaiah (Isa 1–39), Second Isaiah (Isa 40–55), and Third Isaiah (Isa 56–66).

While interpreters widely agree on this division of the material, they do not agree on the composition history of the text. Some argue that the eighth century prophet Isaiah is responsible for all of the material, including chapters that address people and situations far in the future (Isa 40–66) through the gift of prophecy (as prediction). Others argue that prophets most often speak to people and their needs, much like pastors in our churches do. So, while not denying the possibility of prophetic prediction, these scholars think it is more likely that others who continued to speak in the tradition of Isaiah (perhaps even disciples of Isaiah) are responsible for Second and Third Isaiah.

Isaiah's testimony is substantial (thirty-nine chapters) and it is not possible here to summarize all he has to say. Instead, we will introduce key themes found in Isaiah 1–39 and provide references for those who want to prepare themselves to cross-examine all that he has to say about Judah.

A. Trust. We begin with the familiar. Just as in the DH, Isaiah emphasizes trusting the LORD over trusting in military alliances. During the Syro-Ephraimitic Crisis, Isaiah begs King Ahaz to trust the LORD, rather than sending for help from Assyria: "Be careful and stay calm. Don't fear, and don't lose heart over these two pieces of smoking torches [the kings of Israel and Syria]" (Isa 7:4; chs. 7–8). Despite Isaiah's efforts to persuade, Ahaz appeals to the Assyrian king, Tiglath-Pileser, for help—by sending gold and silver from his palace and the temple (2 Kgs 16:7). As a result, not only does the Assyrian king come with an army that conquers Damascus (capital of Syria/Aram) and sends its people into exile (16:9), but Assyria also influences (or perhaps *takes charge of*) the religious practices in Judah (16:10–18). Isaiah now warns Ahaz that, since he has rejected the LORD's peace, he will be overwhelmed by Assyria (Isa 8:5–8a). And yet, the LORD is still with Judah and will ultimately protect them from this new threat (8:8b).

> ### The Syro-Ephraimitic Crisis
> In ca. 733–732 BCE, Syria (Aram) and Ephraim (Israel) invaded Judah in an attempt to replace King Ahaz with a king who would join their military alliance in a rebellion against Assyria (2 Kgs 16:5–16:20).

Later, Isaiah speaks out in opposition of the decision to form a military alliance with Egypt against the Assyrians; most likely King Hezekiah's decision during an Assyrian invasion in 703–701 BCE (see 2 Kgs 18:13–19:37):

> Doom to you, rebellious children, says the LORD,
>> who make a plan, which is not mine;
>> who weave a plot, but not by my spirit, piling up sin on sin;
>> setting out to go down to Egypt without consulting me,
>> taking refuge in Pharaoh's refuge and hiding in Egypt's shadow.
> Pharaoh's refuge will become your shame,
>> hiding in Egypt's shadow your disgrace. (Isa 30:1–3)

And again, Isaiah passes the LORD's judgment on Jerusalem's short-sighted decision to trust Egypt:

> Doom to those going down to Egypt for help!
>> They rely on horses,
>> trust in chariots because they are many,
>> and on riders because they are very strong.
> But they don't look to the holy one of Israel;
>> they don't seek the LORD. . . .
> Egypt is human and not divine;
>> their horses are flesh and not spirit.
> The LORD will extend his hand;
>> the helper will stumble,
>> those helped will fall,
>> and they will all die together. (Isa 31:1, 3)

The LORD promises to be the one who will save Judah (35:3–4), but I suppose Isaiah's counsel is next to impossible to accept—even with the mysterious, wonderful victory over the Assyrians in 722 BCE when the army woke up one morning only to discover *they were all dead* (2 Kgs 19:35–37 and Isa 37:36–38; for further study of this theme see Isa 2:6–8; chs. 7–8; 28:14–18; 30:1–7; 31:1–9; and 35:3–4).

    B. Pride, Perversion of Justice, and Failure of Leaders. Isaiah's other concerns may be folded together because of the close relationship between the three: pride, the perversion of justice and righteousness, and the failure of the leaders. We take Isaiah 5 as a case study in the interrelationship of these themes. The LORD begins with the parable of the vineyard, in which he sings a love song for the vine he took from Egypt and transplanted as a master gardener (5:1–7). But instead of good grapes, the vine grew rotten grapes, even though God did everything he could for the vine. Now, all that is left to do is remove the protective hedge so that it is destroyed—all because "God expected justice, but there was bloodshed; righteousness, but there was a cry of distress" (5:7). Doom is coming to those who are rich, acquiring one house after another, one field after another, until they own everything (5:8–9). Doom is coming to those who do nothing more than drink and party with their music (5:11–12). They even think God will never do anything to them; so they taunt the prophet, telling him, *Bring it on!* (5:19). Doom is coming to those who deliberately confuse what is right and what is wrong, who think they are so clever (5:20–21). Doom is coming to those who are utterly corrupt, who don't care about justice at all—only the bribes they can get (5:22–23). These people care only for themselves, every thought is about themselves (pride); they don't care about the outcome of trials, other than their profit in bribes (injustice); and they lead only to expand their own wealth. Little wonder the LORD is furious and bringing a nation from far away to exact punishment (5:25–30; on pride, cf.: 2:9–18, 22; 3:16–26; 5:8, 15; 32:9–13; on injustice: 1:21–28; 3:5; 10:1–4; 29:18–21; 32:1; 32:16–20; on leaders: 9:16; 10:7; 32:1–8). But it will not be the Assyrians who finally destroy southern Judah, but the Babylonians, on whom the kings of Judah begin to depend for help against Assyria. The Babylonians will take the people of Judah into exile, leaving only a few in the land (Isa 39:1–7; 2 Kgs 20:12–18).

C. Hope. Isaiah 1–39 is filled with oracles of hope set side-by-side with judgment oracles— far too many texts to list here or put in a footnote. The message, however, comes through with great strength: there is hope for God's people, but only through the cleansing power of judgment: an unpopular message in an era of the rich getting richer and the poor getting nothing—then, and now.

2. Micah, our final witness to interrogate, is from the country (1:1), not a city man with royal connections, like Isaiah. Consequently, the country preacher sent to the city has a different perspective about what's wrong with Judah—and what's wrong starts at the top: the upper class, the rich and powerful, along with God's designated leaders for Judah (e.g., priests, prophets, judges). These are the people with money and power who are on the lookout for more of both, and regard the poor, the widows, and resident aliens as easy targets. Micah portrays the rich as people who fall asleep while dreaming of how to get more, and then wake up to execute their plans; they are oppressing the family farmer, until they drive him away and get his ancestor's land (2:1–2). Meanwhile, those who should enforce justice are in on the take; they don't care about the oppressed, just what they will get in the bribe (3:1–2, 11; 7:3). Micah describes them as cannibals, who feed on the flesh of the people they should be helping (3:3, 9–10). The religious leaders (priests and prophets) are no better; they teach only for the money they get (3:11) and they certainly don't want any of what Micah has to say (2:6). So Micah takes a verbal stab at the power-hungry and their religious leaders by suggesting that the best preacher for these people would be someone who talks about wine and liquor (2:11). These are the topics these people are most interested in—the practices they want to improve. The leaders—all of them—have failed the people, the nation, and God.

Terrible punishment is coming because of their sins (3:12, 4:9–10, 5:10–15, 6:9–16, 7:4–6); and yet, Micah provides some of the most memorable images of hope in the Bible— hope that may or may not escape punishment, but will come after God's people turn back:

> God will judge between the nations
>> and settle disputes of mighty nations,
>>> which are far away.
> They will beat their swords into iron plows
>> and their spears into pruning tools.
> Nation will not take up sword against nation;
>> they will no longer learn how to make war. (Mic 4:3)

> Who is a God like you, pardoning iniquity,
>> overlooking the sin of the few remaining for his inheritance?
> He doesn't hold on to his anger forever;
>> he delights in faithful love.
> He will once again have compassion on us;

> he will tread down our iniquities.
> You will hurl all our sins into the depths of the sea. (Mic 7:18–19)

Micah speaks of a Judge who is willing to take cases proven to be true beyond a shadow of a doubt and hurl them into the sea or crush the clay tablets holding our charges until there is nothing left of them. This is the Judge in whose court we come to argue Judah's case.

Conclusion

So, despite all of the evidence and the witnesses, hope remains for God's people. The only question is how or when hope will come to life. If Judah will decide that the LORD is her God, confess that they have messed up in the past by chasing every popular god that came along, and acknowledge that they have not loved other people the way God does and the way God teaches in his most basic commandments—if only—then Judah's hope may be realized now, before the necessity of conquest and exile. Again, as strange as it may seem and as marvelous as it really is, Micah testifies before a God who is not only Judah's Judge, but also Judah's defense attorney. So, while they may be as guilty (and foolish) as two criminals who post their self-recorded crime video on the web, the LORD can still get the charges dismissed, pardoned, and thrown into the sea.

But time is running out and their window of opportunity is closing fast. The good news, we learn later in the book of Jeremiah, is that Hezekiah does respond to Micah's message and the LORD does suspend judgment (Jer 26:17–19). The other good news is that Hezekiah will not let the people kill Micah because of his preaching. The not so good news is that a hundred years later, when Jeremiah's defenders appeal to Micah's case to keep him from being killed and convince the nation to listen to Jeremiah, they will save Jeremiah, but national matters will not turn out so well. To this era we turn in Chapter Twelve.

To Discuss

1. Why do you think Egypt races to Assyria's aid? What benefit would come to Egypt from keeping Assyria alive? Why do you think Josiah tries to stop the Egyptians?

2. When Huldah verifies the Instruction Scroll found in the temple, she promises that Josiah will go to his grave in peace because of his response to the scroll (2 Kgs 22:19–20). How then do you explain Josiah's death in battle against the Egyptians (23:29–30)?

3. Jehoash has to institute regulations to keep priests from taking money from the repair fund for the temple. Why do you think so many priests and/or clergy (today) seem to struggle with taking funds donated for religious purposes?

4. The bronze serpent Moses made in the wilderness (Num 21:4–9) has become an idol by the days of Hezekiah ("Nehushtan," 2 Kgs 18:4). Why would the bronze serpent have become an object of worship? What process do you imagine taking place? Can you explain how an object made to encourage trust becomes an object of trust itself? Reflect for a few minutes on how God-given objects or God-given practices in the Christian tradition might (or have) become idols? Identify the objects in your own Christian tradition that might be at risk.

5. Does it surprise you to learn that Judah once had a queen (even if for only six years)? Prior to this class, for those who attended Bible class as a child or teen, had you ever heard of Athaliah? If not, why do you think you had not heard of her reign?

6. Compare and contrast the four reformation movements in Judah. Identify the similarities and the differences of these movements. How do you explain these similarities and differences? What stands behind each movement, i.e., what motivates the king to try to reform the nation and what each king did?

7. Compare and contrast the ministries of Isaiah and Micah. What different perspectives do these prophets bring to the troubles in Jerusalem? How do their perspectives shape their messages?

8. If you were on the grand jury considering evidence against Judah for her life in the eighth through seventh centuries, how would you vote on each potential charge? Explain your vote and try to persuade those with differing views.

9. Locate the following on a map (from Figure 10.2 in Chapter Ten): Assyria, Ninevah, Babylon (city), Samaria (city), Jerusalem, Judah, Carchemish, Persian Gulf, Euphrates River, and Tigris River.

To Know

1. The significance of the following in the assigned chapters:

   Asa   Josiah
   Assyria/Assyrian Empire   Micah
   Athaliah   Manasseh
   Babylon/Babylonian Empire   Nebuchadnezzar
   Hezekiah   Nehushtan
   Huldah   Rehoboam
   Isaiah   Sennacherib
   Joash (Jehoash)   The Instruction Scroll

2. The date and significance of the Battle at Carchemish.

3. The propaganda for the Assyrian war machine (in general, not specific terms).

4. The findings of our investigation of southern Judah regarding the stability of the government, the spiritual leadership of Judah's kings, and Judah's response to her prophets.

5. The four kings of Judah who led reformation movements.

6. The concept of First, Second, and Third Isaiah and why interpreters give these designations to the Book of Isaiah.

7. Three concerns expressed by Isaiah. Be prepared to write a short paragraph on Isaiah's message as a whole.

8. What Micah thinks the problem is with Judah. Be prepared to write a short paragraph on Micah's message as a whole.

To Dig Deeper: Research Topics

1. Conduct a study that compares the events of Josiah's reformation and the middle chapters of Deuteronomy. Do you see any correspondence that would suggest that the Instruction Scroll was an early form of these chapters? Does your study conclude that the Instruction Scroll is unlikely to be an early form of Deuteronomy? Give specific evidence to support your findings.

2. As with Chapter Ten, conduct a trial of southern Judah in the eighth through seventh centuries. Assign roles to class members, in order of importance: Isaiah, Hezekiah, Micah, Josiah, Jehoash, and others. You will also need a prosecuting attorney(s), defense attorney(s), a judge, and a jury.

3. Investigate additional meanings for the term "prophet" in the Old Testament (see the resource by Petersen below). How is the term used today (perhaps conduct a survey)? Explore the interconnections of meanings.

4. One common element in Judah's reformation movements is the repair of the temple. What is so important about sacred space? Is sacred space important for people in the twenty-first century?

5. In this chapter, we have discovered powerful women (e.g., the Queen Mother, Athaliah, and Huldah). Conduct further research into one or more of these women and other similar roles in the ancient Near East. What surprises you? What questions does your research raise?

For Further Reading

Bleibtreu, Erika. "Grisly Assyrian Record of Torture and Death." *Biblical Archaeology Review* 17 (1991): 52–61, 75.

Grayson, A. Kirk. "Mesopotamia, History of (Assyria)." Pages 732–755 in vol. 4 of *The Anchor Bible Dictionary*. Edited by David Noel Freedman. 6 vols. New York: Doubleday, 1992.

———. "Mesopotamia, History of (Babylonia)." Pages 755–777 in vol. 4 of *The Anchor Bible Dictionary*. Edited by David Noel Freedman. 6 vols. New York: Doubleday, 1992.

Peterson, David L. *The Prophetic Literature: An Introduction.* Louisville: Westminster John Knox, 2002.

12

The **Fall** of Southern Judah
All the LORD's Prophets and All the LORD's Men

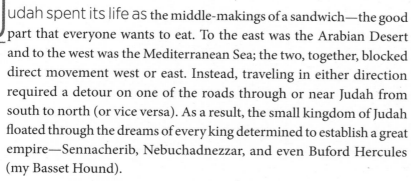

Judah spent its life as the middle-makings of a sandwich—the good part that everyone wants to eat. To the east was the Arabian Desert and to the west was the Mediterranean Sea; the two, together, blocked direct movement west or east. Instead, traveling in either direction required a detour on one of the roads through or near Judah from south to north (or vice versa). As a result, the small kingdom of Judah floated through the dreams of every king determined to establish a great empire—Sennacherib, Nebuchadnezzar, and even Buford Hercules (my Basset Hound).

In terms of the first three rules of real estate—(1) location, (2) location, (3) location—Judah could not possibly have been better situated. The problem, however, was that it was too good. Every empire wanted their land. So, with due respect, we have to wonder about God's real estate broker. Wouldn't other places with less risk have been better? Given forty years wandering in the wilderness, something else must have become available in the area.

The Fall of Judah

In our last episode of "Who controls Judah?" the Assyrian Empire was going down in flames to the Babylonian Empire—the next big thing in the ancient Near East. Babylon, however, was no new kid on the block. The Babylonian civilization began a little before 2000 BCE, with the world-famous King Hammurabi and his law code (ca. 1792–1750 BCE). In his time, Hammurabi was famous for conquering surrounding

READING ASSIGNMENTS
2 KINGS 25
JEREMIAH 1, 7:1–8:3, 26:1–24
EZEKIEL 1–3, 37
JEREMIAH 39–44

KEY TERMS
Lament: a form of prayer (or psalm) in which the person appeals to God regarding their troubles and asks for God's help

Speech-act: a message (from God) presented through some physical action (e.g., dressing like a person going into captivity to warn that captivity is coming)

Yoke: a wooden harness for joining animals (e.g., oxen) to plow the ground

city-states, so that a unified political entity of Babylon could emerge. After Hammurabi, Babylon went into a slow decline. . . .

> Due to space constraints and not wishing to bore the reader into a coma, we rejoin our story just over 1,000 years later.

. . . The Neo-Babylonian Empire (626–539 BCE) has Assyria on the run, conquering one city after another, including the capital of Assyria, Ninevah, in 612 BCE. Assyria continues to fall back and try to regroup; Egypt even races to their side—a strange move; but more mysterious, Josiah, king of Judah, tries to stop the Egyptians, and loses his life in the process (ca. 609 BCE). His servants return his body to Jerusalem for burial and make one of Josiah's sons king (Jehoahaz; 2 Kgs 23:30). Pharaoh, however, punishes Judah for Josiah's actions. He demands a high annual tribute and imprisons the new king (23:31–33). The Pharaoh then places another of Josiah's sons, Eliakim, on the throne and changes his name to Jehoiakim (23:34).

A few years later, Babylon ends the confusion over who is the next superpower at the Battle of Carchemish, far north on the Euphrates River. Babylon wins a decisive victory that kicks Egypt back to the Nile River and finishes off what little is left of Assyria (605 BCE).

The ancient Near East now lays wide open before Nebuchadnezzar (see Figure 12.1). After the battle, however, news reaches him that his father has died. So Nebuchadnezzar hurries home to be made king of Babylon. Then, like an eager pit bull, he runs back to Syria-Palestine to establish Babylonian rule, including the submission of King Jehoiakim of Judah, who pays tribute to Babylon for three years (2 Kgs 24:1b). Fiercely confident, King Nebuchadnezzar decides to invade Egypt—his first major tactical blunder. The Egyptian army fights the Babylonians to a draw; Nebuchadnezzar cannot overcome the Egyptians. So finally, his brain cells take control of his testosterone—he cuts his losses and returns home (601 BCE).

The Babylonian "loss" to Egypt has a profound effect on the western states in the empire who had seen the hope of a successful rebellion against Babylon, especially if Egypt promised their support. King Jehoiakim, along with Judah's pro-Egyptian faction, became part of the frenzy, eager to tell Babylon, "*If you want my tribute, just come try and get it*"—or something like that (24:1). A little later in the chapter, the prophet Jeremiah condemns this rebellion and tries to get the king and nation to stop before it is too late. But Jeremiah does just as well to argue with one of Jehoiakim's donkeys, for all the good he accomplishes.

It takes Nebuchadnezzar time to rebuild his army; nonetheless, by ca. 598 BCE, he is back to conquer Jerusalem. But by the time he arrives, his work has been done for him. Though the text is silent, it is not hard to imagine with some confidence that the anti-Babylon faction in Jerusalem had seen the trouble that King Jehoiakim brought on the nation and city of Jerusalem;

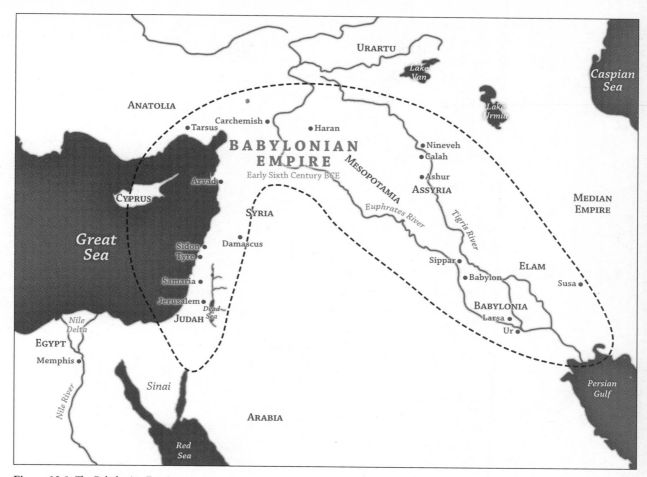

Figure 12.1. The Babylonian Empire

so, they assassinate him and place his son Jehoiachin on the throne, in hopes of sparing their city and their lives. This is the best hypothesis for what Nebuchadnezzar finds once he arrives at Jerusalem. The new king (of only three months) and all his servants come out to surrender to the Babylonian king (24:1–12); and the plan works.

Nebuchadnezzar spares the city, but he takes the king and his royal household, his servants, and many city leaders as captives back to Babylon (597 BCE). Among these leaders is the prophet Ezekiel. Nebuchadnezzar takes all of the political officials and all the military leaders, including skilled metalworkers. He also clears out anything of value from the LORD's temple and the king's palace. Then he installs Josiah's third son as king (Mattaniah)—of course, changing his name to Zedekiah (24:17)—a king who no doubt promises to support Babylonian rule.

Promises, promises, promises. In time, Zedekiah is persuaded by those who trust Egypt's power and reliability to help fight against Babylon; so he rebels against Babylon—*again*. And Nebuchadnezzar comes, *again*, capturing town after town, and treating the citizens with mercy (perhaps to encourage Jerusalem to surrender instead of fight). Left with no options, the Babylonian army sets siege to Jerusalem, with the prophet Jeremiah inside urging surrender. Egypt does come to help, but Babylon easily turns them back (Jer 37:5). Jerusalem is in trouble. *Big trouble.*

The siege of Jerusalem continues for three years and conditions inside turn savage. Finally, when Babylon breaks through the city wall, the king makes a run for safety through a secret gate, but he is caught and brought to Nebuchadnezzar. Judah's king, Zedekiah, is forced to watch as his sons are murdered, and then he is blinded; *the last thing he ever sees is the death of his children* (25:4–7).

Meanwhile, back in Jerusalem, Nebuchadnezzar's right-hand man goes about important tasks:

- destroying and burning the temple and other important structures (25:9);
- tearing down the wall that surrounds and protects the city (25:10); and
- exiling even more people, leaving only the poorest of the poor to tend the land (24:14, 25:12).

Now Nebuchadnezzar appoints a governor in charge over the land: Gedaliah (25:22–24). *Judah now has a governor, no longer a king, not even a **puppet king.*** Judah is no longer an independent state, just a province in the Babylonian Empire.

The Prophets

The Lord refused to let Judah go quietly into the night, not without a fight for Judah's life. Like North Israel, the Lord sent prophets to Judah and Jerusalem (for more on Isaiah and Micah, see Chapter Eleven, pages 232–236). The most significant of these prophets during Jerusalem's final years was Jeremiah (in Jerusalem) and Ezekiel (among the exiles). Both men come to have lengthy books associated with their ministries: the Book of Jeremiah (fifty-two chapters), and the Book of Ezekiel (forty-eight chapters). Consequently, we are in no position to survey all the contents or themes in either book (a good Bible dictionary or commentary can help you with that task). Instead, our aim is more modest: a brief portrait of each man and close look at one or two oracles from their work. In this way, we hope to provide background material for reading more texts from these books with confidence.

Jeremiah

The man

Jeremiah lived in Anathoth a few miles north of Jerusalem, and was a priest—but from the ousted line of Eli and Abiathar, who were no longer in charge at the temple (see Jer 1:1 and 1 Kgs 2:26–27). Even so, the Lord called Jeremiah into service at a young age (Jer 1:5–7)—young enough that Jeremiah

- complains he is too young for what the Lord is asking him to do (1:3–8).
- is not yet married and the Lord tells him "not to marry or have children" because of the sorrows coming on Judah and Jerusalem, especially for those with spouses and children to worry about (16:1–6).

- has a ministry that spans over five decades: from Josiah's thirteenth year (ca. 627; Jer 1:2), until well after the fall of Jerusalem (ca. 587; Jer 41–44).

When God calls Jeremiah into service, the LORD shoots straight about the essence of the message Jeremiah will proclaim—"to dig up and pull down, to destroy and demolish, to build and plant" (1:10; 66 percent destruction, 33 percent hope). God also explains to Jeremiah why he is to proclaim judgment on the people: ". . . for abandoning me, worshipping other gods, and trusting in the work of their hands" (1:16). So Jeremiah had best prepare himself for a fight (1:17) and for the punches to be thrown at him (1:19). His life will not be easy or his "best life now." No, his work will be hard and ultimately unsuccessful. The people will not listen and Jerusalem will fall to Babylon. Jeremiah's faithfulness will be measured by the truth of his message, not the number of people who follow him or the amount of money given to his ministry.

All that God promises to give is his presence (1:19b; an echo of God's call of Moses in Exod 3–4), to make Jeremiah strong (1:18), and to rescue him (1:8)—which implies Jeremiah will need to be rescued more than once. At times, Jeremiah seems to enjoy the task God gave him, such as when he says,

> When your words turned up, I feasted on them; and they became my joy, the delight of my heart, because I belong to you, LORD God of heavenly forces. (15:16)

He also has some optimism at first that his work might make a difference. The LORD sends him to find a single person in Jerusalem who "acts justly and seeks truth that I may pardon her [Jerusalem]" (5:1). How hard can that be? Jeremiah begins his search among the common and poor people, and fails to find a single person who lives with justice and seeks truth. Jeremiah reflects and decides it must be because they do not know better (5:2–4). So he turns to the rich and powerful who have access to teachers and time to know the LORD's teaching (5:5), only to be disappointed (5:6). Not a single person acts with justice or even tries to seek the truth. Jerusalem has become just as bad, maybe even worse than Sodom.

As Jeremiah's ministry progresses, few believe his warnings (25:3, 44:16). Instead, people refuse to listen (6:10), curse him (15:10), and harass him (17:15). Jeremiah becomes the butt of jokes in Jerusalem (20:7): *Knock, knock! Who's there? Jeremiah! Jeremiah who? Jere-my-ya own business!* Far more serious, his calls to surrender to Babylon led people to brand Jeremiah a traitor (37:13). So it's no surprise that the response to Jeremiah also went far beyond words. Jeremiah was barred from going into the temple (36:5) and forced into hiding for his life (36:19). He was beaten and arrested (37:14–15),

THE BOOK OF JEREMIAH
Chapters 1–25 "Baruch's Scroll" Oracles and Sign-Acts of Judgment
Chapters 26–29 Jeremiah's Life: Biographical Narratives
Chapters 30–33 The Book of Comfort
Chapters 34–45 Narrative of Jerusalem's Fall and Biographical Narratives
Chapters 46–51 Oracles for the Nations
Chapter 52 Epilogue: The Fall of Jerusalem

Table 12.1. The Book of Jeremiah

put in a "dry" cistern where he sank into the mud (38:6), and faced the possibility of execution more than once (26:8–9, 38:4, 15–16).

We have special insight into Jeremiah's inner life (far more than any other prophet) through the presence of six prayers of **lament** or complaint included in the book, some to which God responds, but most meet divine silence. For example, in the first prayer, Jeremiah expresses gratitude for the LORD making him aware of plots on his life from people in his own hometown of Anathoth; Jeremiah asks for the LORD's vengeance on them (11:18–20). On this occasion, the LORD assures Jeremiah that he will punish them for trying to stop Jeremiah's proclamation of the Word (11:21–23). In his second complaint, however, when Jeremiah charges the LORD with plotting and giving success to the wicked (while affirming his love for his God, 12:1–4), the LORD responds and challenges Jeremiah—his life is going to become much more difficult; in fact, it is already more dangerous than he was aware of because members of his own family are trying to trap him (12:5–6). So, like the coach who cares deeply for his players, the LORD challenges Jeremiah to "suck it up." This is only the beginning of what Jeremiah has to do for the LORD; he has not seen anything yet, considering what is to come.

Finally, in Jeremiah's last complaint, he accuses God of forcing him into a task he didn't want (20:7), giving him messages to which people respond with violence (20:8), and not letting Jeremiah stop (20:9). Meanwhile, people are watching and waiting for a chance to kill Jeremiah (20:10). In this case Jeremiah responds to himself; on the one hand, somehow he knows the LORD is with him and that the LORD will repay these people (20:11–13); but, on the other hand, at times, Jeremiah is not so optimistic and wishes he had never been born (20:14–18).

Sometimes ministry is lived out with great confidence in the LORD, and at other times, we wish we had nothing to do with the work. Contemporary pastors may find a friend who understands them by reading Jeremiah's laments. In addition to 11:18–20, 12:1–6, and 20:7–18, see:

- 15:15–21: Jeremiah asks the LORD to remember him and act on his behalf against those who torment him; he also complains that while he has been faithful to the harsh ministry God has demanded of him, the LORD has been unreliable. (God tells Jeremiah to return to him for strength.)
- 17:14–18: Jeremiah begs the LORD to save him, his only source of help against those who harass and threaten him.
- 18:18–23: Jeremiah asks the LORD to hear the threats being made against his life—by the very people Jeremiah begged the LORD not to punish. But now, Jeremiah prays, don't hold back your judgment or overlook any of the things they have done wrong.

The Message

It is already obvious that we cannot clearly distinguish a person from their message. Who a person is and what a person says are not distinct from each other, nor are they only loosely related. The message and the messenger are like the combination of hydrogen and oxygen to form water; they are one, a whole. We see this dynamic in one of Jeremiah's most famous oracles when the LORD sends Jeremiah to preach to the people as they enter the temple (most likely during some special festival). The LORD's hope is that the people will hear and change; but, if not, they will bear the responsibility for what happens (26:1–6). The narrative of events surrounding this sermon is in Jeremiah 26, but the content of the sermon is in Jeremiah 7:

> Improve your conduct and your actions, and I will dwell with you in this place. Don't trust in lies: "This is the LORD's temple! The LORD's temple! The LORD's temple!" No, if you truly reform your ways and your actions; if you treat each other justly; if you stop taking advantage of the immigrant, orphan, or widow; if you don't shed the blood of the innocent in this place, or go after other gods to your own ruin, only then will I dwell with you in this place, in the land that I gave long ago to your ancestors for all time.
>
> And yet you trust in lies that will only hurt you. Will you steal and murder, commit adultery and perjury, sacrifice to Baal and go after other gods that you don't know, and then come and stand before me in this temple that bears my name, and say, "We are safe," only to keep on doing all these detestable things? Do you regard this temple, which bears my name, as a hiding place for criminals? I can see what's going on here, declares the LORD. (7:3b–15)

Based on Jeremiah's words, we may safely assume that the people were convinced God would never allow anything to happen to his temple, his own house (7:4, 9–10). Consequently, it did not matter what they did—they were safe as long as the temple stood with them. We are far from the day when Solomon dedicated the temple with a prayer that recognized God cannot possibly be contained in the highest heaven, much less the temple (1 Kgs 8:27).

Jeremiah corrects their assumptions and beliefs on several levels. First, in Israel's history, God has destroyed his own dwelling place because of the sinfulness of his people—at **Shiloh** where Eli and his corrupt sons lived (7:12, see 1 Sam 2:12–4:18). So their assumption is wrong; God can do just fine without a temple. Second, Jeremiah insists that the LORD wants people who act with justice, instead of people who oppress the vulnerable (7:5–7). But they are smashing the covenant into little pieces—in the way they treat other people and by following other gods (7:9). Third, and consequently, because they will not listen, the LORD is about to "do a Shiloh"—destroy his own house, and send the people into exile (7:13–15).

The content of Jeremiah's "Temple Sermon" is not likely to win many friends. Back in Jeremiah 26, we learn that the religious leaders and people seize Jeremiah and threaten him, saying, "You must die," because he spoke against the temple (26:8–9). A trial immediately convenes: on one side are the priests and prophets who claim, "This man deserves to die for prophesying against this city as you all have heard first hand" (26:11). On the other side, Jeremiah speaks in his own defense, repeating parts of his earlier message and warning that his message is from the LORD. He says they can kill him if they want, but they will be guilty of killing an innocent man, sent by God (26:12–15).

The officials hearing the case recognize Jeremiah doesn't deserve to die (26:16); some speak in Jeremiah's defense, using Micah as a legal precedent—who also said Jerusalem (and the temple) would become a pile of rubble (Mic 3:12). But King Hezekiah did not execute Micah; instead he pled for the LORD's mercy (Jer 26:17–19). This argument and powerful officials with connections in the government save Jeremiah (26:24); but another short story included by the writer demonstrates that during this era, the LORD's prophets are being killed in Judah (26:20–23).

So the saga of the Temple Sermon comes to a close. On the one side, Jeremiah has offended, infuriated, and enraged the religious establishment in Jerusalem. And while Jeremiah may walk away today—courtesy of friends who happened to be at the right place at the right time—Jeremiah will not always be so lucky. Given another chance, the officials will take care of Jeremiah and his mouth. On the other side, God has promised to protect Jeremiah—though he came close to losing his life today. Nowadays, all those people who walk around searching for God's call on their life should take note: when God calls a person into special service, it most often stakes a claim on their whole life—like Jeremiah or the prophet Uriah. (Don't remember him? Look again in 26:20–23). So be careful what you wish for.

Ezekiel

The Man

Ezekiel was also a priest (Ezek 1:3); but, unlike Jeremiah, he was married—though his wife dies in captivity (24:15–27). He demonstrates both the education one would expect of a priest (e.g., ch. 28) and his identification with the upper crust in Jerusalem by his exile into captivity with King Jehoiachin in 598 BCE. Five years later, God calls him to the task of a prophet, most likely at the age of thirty (593 BCE, 1:1–3; see Table 12:2). It would seem most likely that Ezekiel would have children, given his age and marital status; but, if so, we are never told anything about them.

Ezekiel is an odd man, to say the least. Somehow, whether by messenger or God's Spirit, he keeps up with affairs back in Jerusalem (e.g., 17:15). He sees bizarre things in visions, and he does strange things. For example, he builds a model of Jerusalem and then lies on his left side for 390 days for the guilt of Israel, and then 40 days on his right side for the guilt of Judah. Meanwhile, he also prepares and eats a small portion of food to represent the famine in Jerusalem (4:1–17). But this is only one of many unusual actions: eating a scroll (2:9–3:3); becoming mute, except for when God speaks to him (3:26–27); shaving his hair and beard and doing odd things with measured portions of his hair (5:1–4); carrying his baggage, as if going into exile (12:1–16); and eating and drinking with fear and shaking (12:17–30). (Jeremiah also did his own share of such **speech-acts**: hiding/burying a used undergarment and retrieving it later [13:1–11], breaking pots [19:1–15], and wearing a **yoke** [27:1–22], just to mention a few.)

THE BOOK OF EZEKIEL
Chapters 1–24 Oracles, Visions, and Sign-Acts Leading to the fall of Jerusalem
Chapters 25–32 Oracles to the Nations
Chapters 33–48 Oracles of Hope and Restoration: A New Temple for a New Land

Table 12.2. The Book of Ezekiel

These object lessons were most likely performed as street theatre—performing an object lesson in one place, explaining its meaning, and then moving on to another place in town for a repeat performance. It is unlikely that Ezekiel does one or another of these actions constantly—24/7 and only in one place.

Ezekiel's visions are bizarre by any measure: he travels from place to place by the wind lifting him up and carrying him (e.g., 3:12, 11:1, 24), or being picked up by his hair (e.g., 8:3). Nonetheless, his visions are not terribly difficult to unlock if we keep reading. For example, one of Ezekiel's strangest visions comes at the beginning of the book when he sees creatures with wings and an object with a wheel within a wheel (i.e., one wheel facing north to south, the other wheel facing east to west). Interpretations of this object have ranged from a spacecraft to Ezekiel smoking a little too much weed in the desert. A better answer is in the text (and our memory of the ark of the covenant, equivalent to God's throne, from Exod 24). At the end of the vision, Ezekiel sees a throne (1:26) and the one on or above the throne looks a bit human—but is not human; instead, on the throne was "the form of the LORD's glory" (1:28)—in other words, it is the LORD enthroned. Now, working backwards, the throne is carried by winged creatures (1:4–14, 22–25; recall the winged creatures on the ark of the covenant), and alongside these creatures, moving up and down, are wheels that can go in any direction. In essence, Ezekiel sees the LORD enthroned—but this throne is completely free to move at anytime and go anywhere the LORD decides.

Throughout his report of this vision, Ezekiel struggles to find the right words—and can't. More than once he says "it looked something like" (1:4, 26, 27; see also 1:13, 22, 24), not just "like"—because Ezekiel finds it impossible to describe with words what he sees. The image is too elusive, too much of the other world. Artists may be the best interpreters of the text as they turn to postmodern forms and images, without trying to capture an exact photograph of Ezekiel's vision. Ezekiel's words communicate that no human photograph can capture what he saw, because, ultimately, he cannot even describe what he saw.

A little later, the LORD shows Ezekiel the same object again, but it is now in the temple—in the throne room (8:1–4)—where the LORD's throne should be. But other objects for the worship of other gods are also in the room, defiling God's throne (8:5–6). After other visions of sinful practices in the temple (8:7–18), Ezekiel sees the LORD's throne rise up and move toward the door of the temple (9:3). More thick description follows, again suggesting that it is impossible for Ezekiel to describe what he sees. But he does see and understand that God's portable throne continues to move up and outward (10:18–19), until finally:

> Then the winged creatures raised their wings. The wheels were next to them, and
> the glory of Israel's God was above them. The LORD's glory ascended from the
> middle of the city, and it stopped at the mountain east of the city. (11:22–23)

The LORD has left the temple—and the city—which cannot be good news for anyone still in Jerusalem, but it is good news for those in exile—to know that your God is with you, no matter where you go.

The Message

While Ezekiel also condemns the worship of other gods and how this worship is leading Judah to oppress the vulnerable (chs. 4–24), once a survivor from Jerusalem comes with the news, "The city has fallen!" (33:21), Ezekiel's message changes (for the most part) to what the people need now: *words of hope*. So we turn to two examples in Ezekiel 37.

Text One. Ezekiel 37:1–14. The first half of Ezekiel 37 is a vision report from a valley of dry bones—in other words, bones that are totally dead with not a single sign of life. The LORD asks Ezekiel a question, "Mortal, can these bones live?" (37:3 NRSV; the literal translation "son of man" simply means "mortal" or "human"). To which Ezekiel has the perfect reply, "LORD God, only you know" (37:3). So the LORD instructs Ezekiel to prophesy—to speak to these dead bones: "I am about to put breath in you, and you will live again. I will put sinews on you, place flesh on you, and cover you with skin. When I put breath in you, and you come to life, you will know that I am the LORD" (37:4–6). So Ezekiel begins to speak and the noise is faint, but he continues talking to the bones. He keeps repeating the LORD's words and the noise starts to get louder and louder. Then he looked to see what was causing the noise—and he saw it:

> Toe bone connected to the foot bone
> Foot bone connected to the heel bone
> Heel bone connected to the ankle bone
> Ankle bone connected to the shin bone
> Shin bone connected to the knee bone
> Knee bone connected to the thigh bone
> Thigh bone connected to the hip bone
> Hip bone connected to the back bone
> Back bone connected to the shoulder bone
> Shoulder bone connected to the neck bone
> Neck bone connected to the head bone
> Now hear the word of the LORD.
>
> Dem bones, dem bones gonna walk around.
> Dem bones, dem bones gonna walk around.
> Dem bones, dem bones gonna walk around.
> Now hear the word of the LORD.[1]

Bones, clattering and connecting—finding their match—the noise of thousands of bones. Bodies literally reforming, as far as the eye could see.

Now the LORD said, "Prophesy to the breath; prophesy, human one! Say to the breath, 'The LORD God proclaims: Come from the four winds, breath! Breathe into these dead bodies and let

---

[1] From the spiritual song "Dem Bones," lyrics by James Weldon Johnson, 1871–1938. Public domain. Musical arrangements and recordings are available on YouTube by the Delta Rhythm Boys: http://www.youtube.com/watch?v=pYb8Wm6 -QfA, and the Cathedrals Quartet: http://www.youtube.com/watch?v=sLg-v4CS4nQ.

them live" (37:9). Divinely mandated CPR. Blow into their lungs, fill them up and restart their lives. So Ezekiel spoke, the winds blew, and the valley came to life (37:10).

What does the vision mean? Sorry, but it's not about a literal resurrection of dead bodies; we are in a vision. The Lord explains: the story is about Israel—all of Israel, not just Judah—all who believe they are dead, their bones dried up, without hope (37:11). *No. No! Judgment is not God's final word!* Listen to what Ezekiel is saying (prophesying): I'm bringing Israel back from the grave, gathering the nation scattered all over the world, and bringing the nation back to life (37:12–14). The time for death is over—and "you will know I am the Lord" (37:14).

Text Two. Ezekiel 37:15–28. The second message in Ezekiel 37 is an object lesson that looks something like a magic trick—okay, a cheap magic trick:

> See, I hold in my hands two sticks (show the audience). On one stick I am writing: The Stick of Judah (show the audience). On the other stick I am writing: The Stick of Ephraim, Joseph, and all Israel (show the audience, and now move the sticks so that you hold them together in one hand and they look like one stick). Presto! (Now say:) "The Lord God proclaims: 'I'm taking Joseph's stick, which has been in Ephraim's hand, and the tribes of Israel associated with him, and I'm putting it with Judah's stick, and I'm making them into a single stick so that they will be one stick in my hand." (37:19)

The object lesson is easy—any four-year-old can do the trick. Even the idea is simple: the Lord will reunite the two nations into one nation. The difficulty is in the doing. How will the Lord combine two nations—that no longer exist, people scattered throughout the Near East—into one nation—that no longer has a place to be a nation?

Ezekiel explains in staccato sound bytes (with secondary explanation). Almost every phrase beginning with "I will"—the Lord says:

- I will take the Israelites from among the nations (37:21)
- I will gather them (37:21)
- I will bring them to their fertile land (37:21, 25)
- I will make them into a single nation (37:22)
- My servant David will be king over them (37:24, 25, 22)
- I will deliver them from all the places where they sinned (37:23)
- I will cleanse them (37:23)
- I will make a covenant of peace for them (37:26)
- I will set my sanctuary among them forever (37:26)
- I will be their God, and they will be my people (37:27, 23)
- Nations will know that I, the Lord, make Israel holy (37:28)

What the Lord promises to do is not hard to understand; the sentences are short and clear statements of action. In sum, the Lord plans to start all over with his people—bring them back to the land, unite them, make a covenant with them, set a king over them, make his dwelling place with them, live with them, and be their God—everything God has ever hoped for in this relationship.

Conclusion

We have finally reached the low point for the story of God and God's people in the Old Testament. Exile: loss of home, loss of land, loss of life—what feels like a loss of God. What Moses warned Israel about before she entered the land. He told Israel that the reason God was driving other nations off the promised land and giving it to her was because these nations had become incredibly wicked (see Gen 15:12–16, Lev 18:24–25, Deut 18:9–12). And Moses cautioned the Israelites that if they do what these nations have done—reject the LORD, follow other gods, and become like those nations and their gods: self-centered, violent, corrupt—and even sacrificing their children to the gods. The true God will drive Israel off the land and into captivity (Deut 28:45–68, 29:22–28). Now it has happened. God has evicted the people from the land. It is not what God wanted to do; after every effort to get the people to follow God's ways, and doing everything possible for them, yet still respecting their freedom, they still refused to listen. So, with God's people in Babylon, the LORD weeps for his people.

But judgment is never the LORD's final word; not even in the prophetic books that warned Judah and announced justice. God is not ready to give up on his people, or the world, or God's intentions to bring the world back to his original plan: for humans and animals, humans and the ecosystem, male and female (or human relationships), and humans and God (see Gen 2). Judgment has come, but grace will follow. A new day and a new opportunity.

I wonder if those in Babylon are able to hear Ezekiel's words? Second Isaiah will struggle with getting the people to believe the LORD still cares about them and is really going to take them back home (Isa 40:27; 49:14, 24–25). Ezekiel's words sound wonderful, and we might be ready to shake our heads at Israel again: will these people ever trust God? But before we do, let's reflect on our own experiences in life. Good news can be more difficult to believe than bad news; falling into captivity is a much easier story to live into than living into a narrative of life with the God who made us and loves us. For now, however, we leave these challenges and questions for the voices yet to come in Chapter Thirteen.

To Discuss

1. Given the geographical location of Judah (and Israel) why do you think God chose this land for the nation? What difficulties does this location carry? What possibilities does it provide?

2. Given their success rate, why do Judean kings keep rebelling against Assyria or Babylon? Would you have been pro- or anti-Babylon between the years 605–587 BCE? Explain and support your position. What would faith in the LORD lead you to do?

3. Have you ever been eager to find God's calling on your life? Are you still as eager after reading this chapter? Can you think of anyone in the Old Testament for whom a special calling ended well? How does this shape your response?

4. What hardships or difficulties did Jeremiah experience? What benefits did Jeremiah receive as a result of God's call? Did the LORD keep the promises he made to Jeremiah?

5. Discuss Jeremiah's Temple Sermon. What were the circumstances when Jeremiah spoke these words? What were the essential points of the sermon? How did people respond? What happened to Jeremiah? Now turn the sermon to a contemporary audience. In what do people around you trust? What would a temple sermon sound like to them? How do you think they will respond?

6. How do you imagine Jeremiah and Ezekiel? What present-day actors would be the best fit each role in a movie? What topics of conversation would come up if Jeremiah and Ezekiel were to meet (in their time)?

7. What did Ezekiel see at the beginning of his ministry? What does this object eventually do? What is the significance of this vision for Ezekiel's ministry? For his own life? For those in Jerusalem? For those in exile?

8. Revisit the two messages of hope from Ezekiel 37. Retell each message in your own words. How do the messages differ? Which of these do you think is the more powerful message? Explain. Do you agree that it is often more difficult to believe good news than accept bad news?

To Know

1. The significance of the following in this chapter:

Babylon	Shiloh
Carchemish	The Temple Sermon
Ezekiel	The Two Sticks
Jeremiah	Valley of Dry Bones
Josiah	Zedekiah
Nebuchadnezzar	

2. The geographical location of Judah/Israel and the significance of this location.

3. Those who went into exile in 597 BCE, both in general, and the specific king and prophet named in this chapter.

4. Jeremiah's counsel to the king and people living in Jerusalem when they are besieged by Babylon, and the response of the people to his advice.

5. The three things that happen to Jerusalem in the conquest of Babylon in 587 BCE.

6. Be prepared to write a paragraph on Jeremiah's Temple Sermon—its message and aftermath.

7. Ezekiel's vision at the beginning of the Book of Ezekiel. Ezekiel's description (in general), what the object is, and it's significance.

8. Be prepared to write a paragraph on Ezekiel's words of hope in Ezekiel 37.

9. Locate the following on a map (see Figure 12.1): Egypt, Judah, Jerusalem, Red Sea, Carchemish, Nineveh, Babylon (city), Persian Gulf, Tigris River, and Euphrates River.

To Dig Deeper: Research Topics

1. Like Ezekiel, prepare street theatre that you act out over the course of a few days (for one person or a group). You must decide what significant message your actions will deliver, who needs to hear this message, where you will perform, and what dramatic actions will best communicate your message. Will you explain your actions at some point? If not, why not? If so, when? How?

2. Dig deeper into Jeremiah's laments: 11:18–12:6, 15:10–21, 17:14–18, 18:18–23, 20:7–18. Read these texts in different translations. What do you learn about Jeremiah from these prayers? What do you learn about God? Write a paper on your findings. Secondary Challenges:

   a. Write your own lament that would fit with Jeremiah's.

   b. Use standard research journals and research-based commentaries to develop a paper on one of the laments.

3. For Artists: Create a painting, drawing, or sculpture based on Ezekiel's vision in chapter 1 (and the same object elsewhere in the book). Consult standard research resources as needed to understand the text. Write a paragraph that explains what you have done in your work (with a bibliography of resources used).

4. Rewrite a text from Ezekiel or Jeremiah as slam poetry or oral rap. Be sure to do your own due diligence to understand the text yourself, before you attempt to rewrite it.

For Further Reading

Ackroyd, Peter R. *Exile and Restoration: A Study of Hebrew Thought of the Sixth Century BC.* Old Testament Library. London: SCM Press; Philadelphia: Westminster, 1968.

Brueggemann, Walter. *Finally Comes the Poet: Daring Speech for Proclamation.* Minneapolis: Fortress, 1989.

Grayson, A. Kirk. "Mesopotamia, History of (Babylonia)." Pages 755–777 in vol. 4 of *The Anchor Bible Dictionary.* Edited by David Noel Freedman. 6 vols. New York: Doubleday, 1992.

Oded, Bustenay. "Judah and the Exile." Pages 435–488 in *Israelite & Judean History.* Edited by John H. Hayes and J. Maxwell Miller. Philadelphia: Westminster, 1977.

Thompson, J. A. *The Book of Jeremiah.* New International Commentary on the Old Testament. Grand Rapids: Eerdmans, 1980.

Reconstructing **Life** after Captivity
Temple, Walls, and God's People

13

READING ASSIGNMENTS
EZRA 1:1–2:2, 2:68–6:22
NEHEMIAH 1:1–2:20, 4:1–6:19
NEHEMIAH 8:1–9:38
HAGGAI 1–2
ZECHARIAH 1
(RUTH AND ESTHER)

KEY TERMS

Anachronistic: a chronological inconsistency, such as including an object in a story that did not exist until after the historical setting of the story

Diaspora: the scattering of a population outside its homeland

Festival of Booths (also known as *Sukkoth* or Tabernacles): a celebration of the last harvest of the year (grapes, olives, and nuts), a time to remember and relive life in the wilderness by living in huts or booths

Law of Moses: most likely the Pentateuch or some early form of the Pentateuch

Post-Exilic: refers to the time period after the exile of 587–536 BCE

Second Isaiah: Isaiah 40–55, chapters that address the end of the exile

Second Temple: the temple built by those who returned with Zerubbabel; also, the name given to an era or time period after the construction of this temple

Sin: the name of the Babylonian moon god

Province of Yehud: Persian province, roughly equivalent to the land of the nation of Judah

---

It is far too easy for us to say the words "Babylonian exile" and "captivity" without emotional response—without our stomachs twisting in knots, or without our hearts leaping into our throats. But exile, captivity, and forced migration by any name are hardly emotionally neutral events. While it is true that Babylon allowed exiled peoples to live together and establish their own communities (though not true for Assyrian captives, who were scattered throughout the empire), conquest still meant the loss of home and all that was familiar, loss of livelihood, and the likely death of family and friends during the siege or the forced march to Babylon. Regardless of how benevolent the conqueror may be or what term we use to name forced relocation, it still meant a faraway place with a strange language, strange customs, and—most of all—a place that is not home.

During the early days in Babylon, many of Jerusalem's exiles have strong hope that captivity would be brief; the LORD had taught them a lesson, so now they would go home. Some prophets reinforce this false hope by assuring the people to wait just a little while longer and God would act in a mighty way to reverse their captivity (see Jer 28:1–17 and 29:8–32). Jeremiah, however, intervenes with the hard truth from the LORD that exile would last a lifetime or "seventy years" (29:10; seventy years equaled human life expectancy in Ps 90:10). So he writes in a letter to those in Babylon: "Build houses and settle down; cultivate gardens and eat what they produce. Get married and have children . . ." (Jer 29:5–6). Perhaps most difficult, Jeremiah tells those in exile, "Promote the welfare of the city where I have sent you into exile. Pray to the LORD for it, because your future depends on its welfare" (29:7). This was a bitter pill to swallow—pray for the Babylonians, who took you away from your home and life in Jerusalem, and forced you to this place. Instead of defiance or even terrorist actions, Jeremiah and others encourage the captives to accept, support, and, when possible, become part of the government (see the lessons from Dan 1–3).

The End of Exile and the Rise of the Persian Empire

Empires come and empires go; no human empire lasts forever. Back in Mesopotamia, the Babylonian Empire stops expanding after the reign of Nebuchadnezzar (604–562 BCE), and within thirty years, the empire is gone with the wind. The last king of Babylon was Nabonidus (556–539 BCE), a rather odd man and downright strange king. On the one hand, Nabonidus promotes the worship of the moon-god, **Sin**, and cares little for Marduk, the traditional Babylonian god with traditional Babylonian priests. So let's just say that the priests of Marduk are not big fans of the new king. On the other hand, Nabonidus spends most of his reign in a mysterious ten-year self-imposed exile in the desert—and no one really knows why. Maybe he is trying to regain his health, or maybe he is out in the desert spending private time with the moon-god. Whatever his reasoning, someone has to actually be king while he is gone—and that task falls to his son, Belshazzar.

Farther to the East, Cyrus the Great begins his own dramatic rise and the world-changing growth of the Persian Empire. Coming to the throne at the age of thirty, Cyrus leads the Persian tribes to a successful revolution against their overlords, the Medes. He spends a few years consolidating his control of this territory before bypassing a fight with Babylon by circling around them to the north and moving west—going as far west as fighting against the Lydians at Sardis—and continuing west until, through war and diplomacy, he controls most of Ionia (modern-day Turkey). Now that the Persians have surrounded Babylon, Cyrus returns for a direct assault against Nabonidus in 539 BCE at Opis (near modern Baghdad), where he defeats the Babylonian troops. The city of Babylon then falls to Cyrus, with little or no fight, in October of 539 BCE; Cyrus then flips the entire Babylonian Empire into the Persian Empire—with extensive additions (see Figure 13.1).

Cyrus was a brilliant politician and statesman, as demonstrated by his treatment of all those people-groups Nebuchadnezzar and other Babylonian kings had exiled to Babylon. Cyrus fosters good will with all these people and their provinces, sending them home with encouragement to rebuild the temples for their gods that had

THE PERSIAN EMPIRE (BCE)	
Cyrus	550–530
Cambyses	530–522
Bardiya	522–522
Darius	522–486
Xerxes	486–465
Artaxerxes	465–425
Xerxes II	425–424
Darius II	424–404
Artaxerxes II	404–358
Artaxerxes III	358–338
Artaxerxes IV	338–336
Darius III	336–330
Artaxerxes V	330–329
ALEXANDER THE GREAT 330–323	

Table 13.1. Kings of the Persian Empire

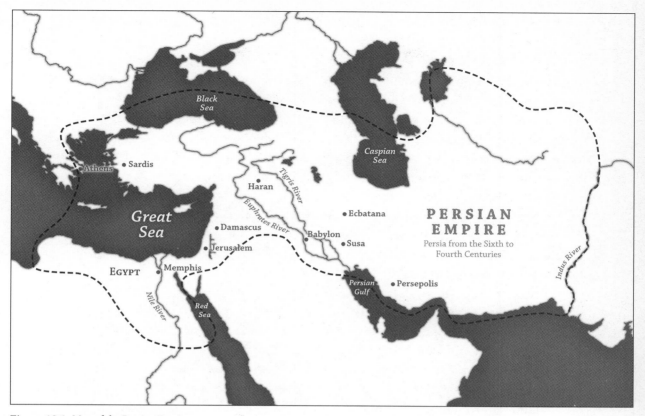

Figure 13.1. Map of the Persian Empire

been destroyed by Babylon. Even more, Cyrus is willing for the Persian Empire to pay the bill for necessary materials. One such decree (or edict), releasing the people of Judah and sending them home to Jerusalem to rebuild their temple, is recorded at the beginning of the Book of Ezra:

> Persia's King Cyrus says: The LORD, the God of heaven, has given me all the kingdoms of the earth. He has commanded me to build him a house at Jerusalem in Judah. If there are any of you who are from his people, may their God be with them! They may go up to Jerusalem in Judah and build the house of the LORD, the God of Israel—he is the God who is in Jerusalem. And as for all those who remain in the various places where they are living, let the people of those places supply them with silver and gold, and with goods and livestock, together with spontaneous gifts for God's house in Jerusalem. (Ezra 1:2–4)

To court more favor, Cyrus has the treasure troves of Babylon searched so that items belonging to the Jerusalem temple would also be returned (1:7–11).

The End of Exile

Returning Home?

For those living in Babylonian exile, they could not hope or ask for more: freedom to go home, imperial financial support, and the restoration of sacred objects. Cyrus gave them everything they could hope for, except for one thing: the desire to uproot their families (*again*) from what has become a settled life over the past fifty (from 587 BCE) or sixty years (from 598 BCE). Jeremiah said to build a life in captivity, and so they did—many built a good life, with a solid business or a productive farm with ample water to irrigate from the many rivers of Babylon. So now, it was a hard sell to get people to leave what they have built in order to "return" to a place they may have never seen, other than through the eyes of their parents or grandparents. And frankly, what they describe doesn't sound all that great: an arid land, dependent on rains that sometimes don't come. Why exchange what has become a good life in Babylon for a difficult life back in Jerusalem and the **province of Yehud**?

Much of **Second Isaiah** is spent in an effort to convince those in exile that the LORD's faithful love is at work in current events. For example, the LORD calls Cyrus his "shepherd" and his "anointed one" (44:28, 45:1; both royal terms) who has the LORD's support to conquer nations and set captives free, including Babylon and captives from Jerusalem (45:13; see also 41:1–2), even if Cyrus doesn't know the LORD or recognize what the LORD is doing (45:6). Consequently, the prophet must persuade the people that their God still loves them and that the time has come to go home. His task, however, is not easy. We hear the doubts of those in exile expressed through the words of the prophet:

> Why do you say, Jacob,
>   and declare, Israel,
>   "My way is hidden from the LORD
> my God ignores my predicament"? (40:27)

> But Zion says, "The LORD has abandoned me;
>   my Lord has forgotten me." (49:14)

Their concerns seem legitimate to me: after all these years in exile, why would they believe God loves them? And why should they get their hopes up that God has decided to do something now to send them home, when God hasn't done anything for fifty years or more? I think God understands too, because the response to these tough questions from the people is gentle, patient, and also firm.

> Don't you know? Haven't you heard?
>   The LORD is the everlasting God,
>   the creator of the ends of the earth.
>   He doesn't grow tired or weary.

> His understanding is beyond human reach,
>> giving power to the tired
>> and reviving the exhausted.
> Youths will become tired and weary,
>> young men will certainly stumble;
>> but those who hope in the Lord
>> will renew their strength;
>> they will fly up on wings like eagles;
>> they will run and not be tired;
>> they will walk and not be weary. (40:28–31)

And in response to their concern that the Lord has forgotten them:

> Can a woman forget her nursing child,
>> fail to pity the child of her womb?
>>> Even these may forget,
>>> but I won't forget you.
> Look, on my palms I've inscribed you;
>> your walls are before me continually.
> Your builders come quickly;
>> those who destroy and demolish you will depart from you.
> Look up all around and see:
>> they are all gathered;
>> they come to you.
> As surely as I live, says the Lord,
>> you will put them all on like ornaments,
>> bind them on like a bride. (49:15–18)

God has never stopped loving her people, and cannot forget them any more than a nursing mother can forget her baby (yes, it takes more than male imagery to describe Israel's God, see Num 11:12, Hos 11:1–4). And the Lord will never get tired, but will provide strength for the journey home (see also 44:8–16 and 51:12–16).

Convincing the people of the Lord's faithful love is the foundational message in Second Isaiah; everything else depends on their knowing God still cares about them. Then, to convince the people the time has come to go home, the prophet describes what the Lord is doing all over the ancient Near East:

> I am the Lord you God,
>> the holy one of Israel, your savior.
> I have given Egypt as your ransom,
>> Cush and Seba in your place.

Because you are precious in my eyes,
>you are honored, and I love you.
>I give people in your place,
>>and nations in exchange for your life.

Don't fear,
>I am with you.

From the east I'll bring your children;
>from the west I'll gather you.

I'll say to the north, "Give them back!"
>and to the south, "Don't detain them."

Bring my sons from far away,
>and my daughters from the end of the earth,
>everyone who is called by my name
>and whom I created for my glory,
>whom I have formed and made. (43:3–7)

The Lord God says:
Look, I will raise my hand to the nations,
>and to the peoples I will lift up my signal.

They will bring your sons in their arms,
>and will carry your daughters on their shoulders.

Kings will be your attendants,
>and their queens your nursemaids.

With faces to the ground they will bow down to you;
>they will lick the dust from your feet.

You will know that I am the Lord;
>the one who hopes in me won't be ashamed.

Can loot be taken from warriors?
>*Can a tyrant's captives escape?*

The Lord says:
Even the captives of warriors will be taken,
>and the tyrant's loot will escape.

I myself will oppose those who oppose you,
>and I myself will save your children.
>>(49:22–25, emphasis mine; these are the words of the captives)

The Lord is paying the ransom for his people and gathering them from wherever they may have been taken (see also 43:14–21). The Lord is also returning to Jerusalem (40:1–11), a city that will be resettled (44:23–28), and where he will reign (52:7–10). Another contributing factor in the people's struggle to believe the Lord will do what he claims is easy for us to overlook: Israel and other nations in the ancient Near East believed that nations at war engaged not only in human battle, but in conflict between their gods. So, when Babylon came and defeated Israel, the greater defeat was that of Marduk (god of Babylon) over Yahweh (God of Israel). Marduk even came onto Yahweh's turf and took Yahweh down on his home court. So, in view of that big-time loss at home, how are the people to believe that Yahweh will be able to come onto Marduk's turf and defeat him? This concern is behind the words cited above, "Can loot be taken from warriors? Can a tyrant's captives escape?" (49:24), to which the prophet said, *Yes, it will happen and it will be done.* Yahweh is able to do what he claims.

So, in view of these affirmations and what the LORD will do, the LORD calls his people to come home:

> Go out from Babylon;
> > flee from the Chaldeans!
> Report this with a loud shout, proclaim it;
> > broadcast it out to the end of the earth.
> > Say, "The LORD has redeemed his servant Jacob!" (48:20)

> Depart! Depart! Go out from there!
> > Unclean! Don't touch!
> > Get out of that place; purify yourselves,
> > carriers of the LORD's equipment!
> You won't go out in a rush,
> > nor will you run away,
> > because the one going before you is the LORD;
> > Your rear guard is the God of Israel. (52:11–12; see also 43:1–7)

You may already have noticed that the prophet reframes their return in terms of a second exodus, repeating the journey to the land their ancestors made centuries before. Now, the prophet stresses new and stronger faithfulness among the people (see 51:10–11).

Despite the efforts of Second Isaiah (and others), and while a fair number of people are ready to go home, not everyone is eager to sign up for tickets. Truth be told, the conditions back in the old homeland are tough—perhaps not exactly as advertised in the travel brochure. To start, Jerusalem is not the capital of anything, for the simple reason that the city is mostly ruins—the temple, the king's palace, and especially the protective wall around the city; these ruins await reconstruction by those who return. So, instead of Jerusalem, the Persians choose Mizpah, a city seven miles north of Jerusalem, as the capital city for the province of Yehud. The fact that the people are not going back to the kingdom of Judah is another big change for those returning. The nation no longer exists, nor does a king for the nation. So, whatever their hopes may have been for a future nation and a restored king from the line of David may have been (like their leader, Zerubbabel, from the line of David), the people who take a ticket go back to the province of Yehud—not the nation of Judah. And as they come back, they not only face rebuilding their homes, farms, and/or businesses, they also face major reconstruction projects for the city and Yahweh.

Project I: Rebuilding the Temple

The first wave of captives return to Jerusalem under the leadership of Zerubbabel (appointed governor after Sheshbazzar, see Ezra 1:8, 11; 5:14–16; Hag 1:1), and Jeshua (or Joshua, the high priest, see Hag 1:1), and others—all for the explicit purpose of rebuilding the temple of the LORD (Ezra 1:2–5). And they begin this work soon after their arrival by setting up the LORD's altar (3:2–3) in time for the **Festival of Booths** (3:4). A few months later, the builders lay the foundation (3:8) in a ceremony that brings together the priests, the Levites, and many of the people who have returned.

Naturally, when the builders lay the foundation, there is great joy and shouts of praise, singing with a responsive line: "He is good, his graciousness for Israel lasts forever" (3:11; compare to Ps 136). But at the same time, those "old priests and Levites and heads of families, who had seen the first house, wept aloud when they saw the foundation of this house" (3:12). The people expressed praise and profound sorrow all at the same time, so much and so loud that the writer adds, "No one could distinguish the sound of the joyful shout from the sound of the people's weeping" (3:13). What would prompt the old-timers to weep so loudly while the younger generation could only celebrate?

Soon after the foundation is laid, Zerubbabel, Jeshua, and the heads of the families are faced with a critical issue, set within an offer from those people living in what was once northern Israel: let us help with the building of the temple. The rationale of the locals is easy to follow: we have been worshipping the LORD since the Assyrians relocated us to this land (4:1–2). At issue, however, is a far greater matter: the identity of the LORD's people. Now that the LORD's people are spread throughout the world (the **Diaspora**), how are they to be identified or distinguished from others? The answer, which will be up in the air for some time, begins here: those who stayed in the north and intermarried with non-Israelites are not accepted as part of the LORD's people. So the answer to their offer to help is a firm and sharp *no*: "You'll have no part with us in building a house for our God. We alone will build because the LORD, the God of Israel, and Persia's King Cyrus commanded us" (4:3). And it's no surprise that their offer to help turns into active opposition—and that successful opposition shuts down work on the temple for sixteen years (4:24).[1]

For sixteen years, the people, who came back for a single purpose, did everything except what they came back to do. They tend to their own estates, build or rebuild their own homes, and start businesses or re-cultivate fields that were left vacant for years; there is plenty of work to be done. But they are already falling into the same pattern of life, or set of priorities, that led to the fall of the nation and captivity. And this is the message the prophet Haggai brings to the people, to startle them back to their senses.

---

[1] The chronology of the letters in Ezra 4:6–23 is notoriously difficult for interpreters. Ezra 4:8–6:18 is in Aramaic rather than Hebrew.

Project I and the Prophets

The Book of Haggai presents itself as a record of four oracles Haggai brought to the people in the province of Judah, during the second year of King Darius (ca. 520 BCE):

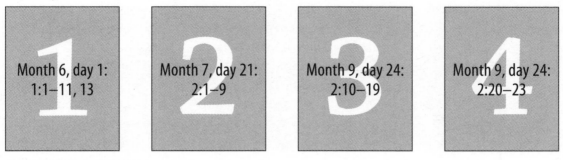

Figure 13.2. Haggai's Oracles

The first of the oracles challenges the attitudes just mentioned above. The people could always find a reason to say "The time hasn't come" to work on the temple (1:2). Perhaps one primary reason was the harsh economic conditions (1:6, 9), including, or perhaps stemming from, a drought (1:10, 11). Haggai explains that the cause of the drought and bad economy is the attitude of the people, putting their own interests above the LORD's interest (rebuilding the temple).

Haggai is one of only a few Hebrew prophets that may be regarded as "successful" in the sense that the people listen and respond (1:12–15), kick-starting the temple project that had been dormant for sixteen years. The prophet Zechariah also works during this era to encourage the rebuilding of the temple. He initially warns the people that they are moving back in the direction of their ancestors (Zech 1:1–6). Except for a passionate oracle in 8:1–23, the Book of Zechariah is a tough nut to crack: eight vision reports in 1:7–6:8, another difficult text in 6:9–15, and then chapters 9–14 appear to address a different time period and different interests.

The prophets, however, succeeds in getting the people back to work on the temple, and keeping them on the job when they become discouraged (see Haggai 2:1–9). Consequently, after a sixteen-year layoff, once back on the job, the people complete the work in the sixth year of Darius (Ezra 6:15), four years after Haggai first spoke on behalf of the LORD (Haggai 1:1). The new temple, what scholars and interpreters refer to as the "**Second Temple**," is dedicated with a joy-filled celebration (Ezra 6:16–18). One crucial element to life back in Jerusalem has been restored. Nehemiah will tackle the second.

Project II : The Walls of Jerusalem

Nehemiah was one of many exiles whose family had chosen not to return to Jerusalem with any of the early waves. Instead, Nehemiah had worked his way to an important position in the Persian government: cupbearer to the king (Neh 2:1). His story begins at the winter palace of Susa in the twentieth year of Artaxerxes (ca. 445 BCE), approximately seventy years after the temple was rebuilt, and one hundred and forty years since Nebuchadnezzar's conquest of Jerusalem (586 BCE).[2]

Nehemiah's story is plain enough that it requires no rehearsal in this chapter. Instead, we will focus our attention on key features in the narrative. For example, when Nehemiah hears the news about the condition of Jerusalem, especially its walls and gates, he breaks into tears as if he never knew about the conquest (but he had to have known)—weeping, mourning, and praying for days (1:4). In response to the news, he confesses the sins of the people of the LORD—his people, and so his sin too: sins "which we have committed against you. Both I and my family have sinned. We have wronged you greatly" (1:6–7). Then, Nehemiah takes his life in his own hands by allowing himself to appear sad in the presence of the king; *it is a dangerous thing to rain on the king's parade—he could lose his head over this*, a risk he recognizes when he prays to the LORD for success "in the presence of this man" (1:11). No one in Jerusalem or in the province of Judah, or anyone else in the Diaspora, has the level of concern for Jerusalem, its walls, and its people as does Nehemiah—a man who is a thousand miles away and 140 years after the event. How are we to account for this feature of the story?

Second, prayer plays an important role in Nehemiah's story—not just the presence of prayer, but its variety:

- Long prayers that speak of Israel's history: 1:5–11, 9:5–37
- An unspoken prayer of the heart, content not reported: 2:4 (in the presence of the king)
- A report of prayer in a certain circumstance, but without reporting the content: 4:9 (regarding the threat of opponents)
- Words directed to God in the narrative, but not identified as prayer: 4:4–5 (about enemies); 6:9 (for strength against opposition); 6:14 (about enemies); 5:19, 13:14, 22, 29, 31 ("Remember what I have . . .")

It is easy to conclude that prayer was an important part of Nehemiah's life and the story of rebuilding the walls. We also see that prayer takes more than one form: sometimes spoken words, sometimes silent prayers of the heart, and sometimes just a sentence or two tossed toward heaven. To push a little further into these prayers, Nehemiah prays most often (in one form or another) when he faces some form of opposition (2:4, 4:4–5, 4:9, 6:9, 6:14); and in this situation, he often prays that the LORD will remember his efforts to do the right thing when it was not easy (5:19; 13:14, 22, 29, 31). The longest prayer is ultimately a prayer of confession, retelling Israel's story as a means of acknowledging "our" consistent failures to be what the LORD called "us" to be.

A third motif, primarily present in the chapters that recount building the wall, is opposition and how Nehemiah deals with potential or real threats (outlined in Table 13:2, below). It begins in Susa with Nehemiah's concern for the reaction of the king: he prays and he has already thought

---

[2] Difficult chronological problems exist in the order and dating of Nehemiah (rebuilding walls) and Zerubbabel (rebuilding the temple). I take a common viewpoint here, but recognize that other strong options exist. See "For Further Reading" at the end of this chapter.

through a possible plan for the project so that he is ready when the king asks, "What is it you need?" (2:4). In the same way, when Nehemiah arrives at Jerusalem, he takes three nights to study the problem alone, before he begins calling people to the work (2:11–18).

Prayer and strategic planning are also Nehemiah's responses to the direct threats to stop the construction by attacks on the workers: "So we prayed to our God and set a guard as protection against them day and night" (4:8). And as the threats against the people intensify (4:10–12), so does the strategic planning (4:13–23). The same is true when the threats are against Nehemiah. When enemies try to draw Nehemiah away from the work to kill him (6:1–5), or try to discredit him by false accusations (6:6–7), Nehemiah exercises discernment: he refuses to be lured into the trap or react to their slander, and he prays for God's strength (6:8–9). Even when the threat comes from within, when a person who should be supportive of the work tries to trap Nehemiah in a compromising situation (taking refuge inside the temple, 6:10), Nehemiah sees through the trap (6:11–13) and prays (6:14).

Prayer is obviously important to Nehemiah, but prayer alone is not enough. Nehemiah prays *and* he does his own work of strategic planning, making himself fully aware of all the facts before he acts. He does not pray and leave everything up to God—he prepares himself and he goes to work. Nor does Nehemiah try to do anything without prayer. Too often believers do one or the other, but not both. Prayer without our best efforts is unlikely to succeed, just as our best efforts without prayer are apt to fail.

OPPOSITION TO THE WALLS

1. Verbal assaults (2:19, 4:1–3)
2. Threat of physical attack (4:7–8, 11–12)
3. Take out the leader:
   - ☑ Attempted assassination (6:1–4)
   - ☑ Attempted false accusations (6:5–9)
   - ☑ Attempted character assassination (6:10–14)

Table 13.2. Opposition to Building the Walls

Finally, Nehemiah also faces internal opposition: first, not everyone is willing to help work (3:5); second, financial pressures and oppressive practices by the rich against the poor threaten to shut the project down (ch. 5); and third, some insiders are connected to the external opponents by marriage and give the opponents inside information about Nehemiah's actions and plans (6:17–18). And yet, despite the opposition, both internal and external, Nehemiah keeps the work moving ahead. He ignores those who will not help, fights against—and resolves—oppressive financial practices, recognizes who he cannot trust, and ignores threatening letters. Nehemiah is a man who knows the task that God has given him to do, so he will not allow anything or anyone to stop him. He has a rare trait that we call *conviction*.

And so the wall is finished—in *fifty-two days* (6:15), after waiting for 140 years. *Amazing and sad*. Amazing that the people came together and did the work in only fifty-two days; sad because Jerusalem's walls have been in a state of disrepair for all these years without anyone stepping out to do something. Nonetheless, two of the three things destroyed in the conquest have now been rebuilt: the temple and the city walls. The third—the last, most difficult, and most important—is *the people*.

Texts in Conversation

After the revival of Nehemiah 8–10, we come upon a story that takes us back to the "ban" of the DH. This time, however, the key point is not total annihilation, but the prohibition of marriage to anyone outside the lines of Israel (Deut 7:3; Josh 23:12–13). Of course, just who constitutes the people of God is a hot-button topic for Ezra, Nehemiah, and the community returned from exile. In Joshua's time, identity was fairly easy: an Israelite was a hereditary descendant of one of the tribes. Now, in the **post-exilic** community, identity begins to be determined by Torah obedience, not ethnicity (or so I thought).

Nehemiah 13 reports a time when Nehemiah becomes aware of Jews in the province of Judah marrying foreigners: Ashdod, Ammon, and Moab (13:23). And Nehemiah goes a bit, well, you decide . . . "So I scolded them and cursed them, and beat some of them, and pulled out their hair" (13:25). He reminds them that this practice led Solomon into sin and Israel to go down a long slippery slope that led to the exile. So he makes them swear that they will not obtain wives for their sons or give their daughters to anyone who is a foreigner.

The same issue comes up in Ezra 9–10 and, though hard to believe, makes Nehemiah's response look like a slap on the wrist. Upon Ezra's arrival to Jerusalem, the leaders report to Ezra the problem of marriage with Canaanites, Hittites, Perizzites, Jebusites, Ammonites, Moabites, Egyptians, and Amorites (9:1–2). Ezra tears his robe, pulls his hair, and sits down "in shock" (9:3–4). He prays that evening, ashamed that the LORD has given them another chance and they are already doing what started the whole problem before (9:5–15). During his prayer, a large crowd gathers and an idea is hatched to deal with the problem: all the men would "send away" (divorce) their foreign wives, sending them and any children they may have away with them (10:2–3). Ezra seizes the moment and makes the men swear to the deal (10:5). To make a longer story come to an end: they do it. Ezra leads a task-force to enforce the policy: men divorce their wives and send them away, including their children (10:7–14).

We need to be careful not to read twenty-first century family values and practices into what is happening in these books. Even so, it will be difficult for anyone who has been touched by divorce not to react in horror. We could stop here and begin asking our questions, not the least being, *Is this the right thing to do? Does God approve? Do two wrongs make a right?* But before we begin a vigorous discussion, we need to include other voices from Scripture. So, to begin, read the short book of Ruth—a story about a family who escapes famine in Bethlehem by moving to Moab, where both sons marry Moabite women. After the father and both sons die, Naomi and her Moabite daughter-in-law, Ruth, return to Bethlehem. You can read the rest of the story and be ready for discussion. You also need to read the story of Esther, a voice from the exile—a Jewish woman who does what she must in order to save all Jewish people, including marry the Persian king (not an Israelite), and having a relative who says, "Maybe it was for a moment like this that you came to be part of the royal family" (Esther 4:14). Once you have read these stories, return to the following "starter" discussion questions:

1. What attitudes do each of the texts have toward marriage to non-Jews?
2. Does God approve of the decision made in Ezra?
3. Do you give stronger weight to any one, or perhaps more, of the texts? If so, why?
4. If you do not give stronger weight to any of the texts, how do you resolve the different voices?

Now, continue the discussion: What questions do these texts raise for you?

Project III: Rebuilding Life in Jerusalem

During the conquest of 586 BCE, Babylon killed high-ranking political officials, religious leaders (e.g., the high priest), and military commanders (2 Kgs 25:18–21). They exiled others left in the city (25:11) and left only the poorest of the poor to tend the land (25:12). Rebuilding life in Jerusalem is a far more complex issue than rebuilding the temple or city walls, if, for no other reason, than not everyone has the same experience during, or after, the conquest. Consequently, in this section, our analysis is forced into generalities rather than specifics.

Restoring or rebuilding life in Jerusalem begins with the physical return of the former Judeans to Jerusalem. The first wave of residents return with Zerubbabel (Ezra 2) and others come with Ezra (7:1–10 and 7:11–8:36). And although not documented in the biblical text, we can be certain that other waves of people continue to come at other times and from other places (e.g., Neh 2:7–11). During this time, as more and more people come back, an issue concerning leadership in the land develops. As we recall, Babylon exiled the leaders—the upper crust of Israelite society—and they left the poor behind to tend the land. Of course, those left behind did not wait fifty years for new leadership; they developed and recognized their own leaders. But when those exiled return, well—they are used to being the leaders and assume they will be leaders in the old homeland, an assumption not shared by those who have become leaders in their absence. But as we read Ezra and Nehemiah, we can see that those who return are the ones winning this debate and taking key leadership positions. By the time the walls are finished, however, few of those who return live in the city of Jerusalem (Neh 7:4). Most live in their own towns and villages outside of Jerusalem (7:6).

So a second step in restoring life in Jerusalem, beyond bringing people back to the land, was a lottery to select one out of every ten in the province who will move into Jerusalem (see 11:1–12:26). But even when Jerusalem is repopulated, there is still more to be done—a third step of restoring life at a deeper and more significant level. Rebuilding life with God—a *revival*. This is the story of Nehemiah 8–10.

What creates new life with God? It is possible that if we asked ten different people to provide an answer, we would receive ten different answers. In our own era, based on what most churches emphasize in their Sunday assemblies, our answer to what creates new life with God would most likely include dynamic worship with good music, a young "with-it" or stylish pastor/preacher who communicates with an interesting conversational style, and other common practices such as discipleship/small groups, serious Bible study, and prayer.

In the revival of Ezra/Nehemiah, the renewal of life with God begins with the Word of God. As the people gather in Jerusalem, Ezra brings out "the Instruction scroll from Moses" (8:1; "the book of the **Law of Moses**" NRSV, the first time this phrase is used in Scripture). When Ezra opens the scroll, all the people stand up (8:5) and he reads "to men and women and anyone who could understand what they heard" (8:2). He also reads for a long time—from early morning to mid-day with everyone listening attentively (8:3). Levites mix in with the crowd so that if someone has trouble understanding what Ezra reads, the Levites can help explain what the text means (8:7–8). While Ezra continues to read from the scroll every day for seven days (8:18), on the second day, Ezra also appears to give a more in-depth study of Scripture to leaders of families, priests, and Levites. As they study, they learn about the Festival of Booths, which was to be observed during the seventh month—and it was the seventh month (7:73b–8:2). So they immediately spread the word for what the people should do to observe the Festival (8:13–17).

Reconstructing the lives of the people toward life with God begins with hearing the Word of God. And although sorrow is a natural reaction when a person first learns God's way for his or her life, especially when that person has not been obedient (8:9–11), the spiritual leaders—Nehemiah, Ezra, and the Levites—encourage the people not to weep or be sad when they hear God's Word (8:9), but to celebrate with good food and drink, sharing with those who do not have anything ready or with them (8:10). The occasion of hearing and understanding the Word of God with the intent to obey is reason for a party—a celebration (8:11–12).

Just as the LORD's instruction called for celebration (8:10), on the twenty-fourth day of the same seventh month, it also called for a day self-denial, confession, worship, and hearing the Word of the LORD (9:1–3). On this day, Ezra[3] offers the longest recorded prayer in the Bible (outside the Book of Psalms), which is outlined below in Table 13:3. The first major section of his prayer is a rehearsal of the LORD's faithfulness to Israel, and Israel's unfaithfulness to the LORD (9:9–31). The second section then appeals for mercy (9:32–37). At this point, the formal prayer turns into a covenant renewal ceremony, with family leaders signing a document that pledges their allegiance to the LORD (9:38–10:39).

---

[3] The Hebrew text lacks the phrase "And Ezra said" at the beginning of 9:6; the Greek text, however, includes these words.

EZRA'S PRAYER	
What *The Lord* has done or does:	***Israel's* response:**
You delivered Israel from Egypt (9:9–11)	
You guided Israel through the wilderness (9:12)	
You made a covenant with us at Sinai (9:13–14)	
You fed us manna and provided water from the rock (9:15)	
	We did not obey, did not remember the Lord's miracles, wanted to return to Egypt (9:16–17)
You are a God ready to forgive, gracious and merciful, slow to anger and abounding in love (9:17)	
	We cast an image of a calf to worship (9:18)
You did not forsake them, but led them, fed them, and gave them water for forty years (9:19–21)	
The conquest of a good land and descendants like the stars of heaven (9:23–25)	
	Disobedient: we killed your prophets (9:26)
You handed them over to their enemies, but when they cried out you rescued them—over and over again (9:27–28)	
You warned them in order to turn them back (9:29)	
	But we did not obey but were stubborn and turned away from you (9:29)
You were patient with them many years: you warned them through your prophets, in your mercy you would not destroy them (9:30)	
	We would not listen (9:30)
An appeal to God for mercy:	
You, Lord—please do not overlook all the hardship that has come upon us since the time of Assyria until today (9:31–32)	
You have been just (9:33)	
	We have not kept the covenant (9:33–34)
Even with all the good things you gave (9:35)	
	We did not serve you (9:35)
	So now—we are slaves in the land you gave our ancestors; the rich yield of the land goes to the kings you set over us because of our sins (9:36–37)
	We are in great distress (9:37)

Table 13.3. Ezra's Prayer

Conclusion

While many biblical books from the Old Testament have not yet been set in the final form that we see in our Bibles, the storyline cast by the Old Testament is very near its end. The prophet Malachi will address a post-exilic audience during the Persian era, but its specific date is difficult to determine. Two other books, Esther and Daniel, meet fiercely divided opinions over the date of their authorship and historicity. Many scholars regard the stories in the Book of Daniel and Esther as fictitious legends, not historical events. Some identify the date of composition for Daniel 7–12 as happening during the era of the persecution of Jews during the reign of Antiochus IV Epiphanes (168–164 BCE), with chapters 1–6 possibly coming from an earlier time during the post-exilic Persian era. Some suggest that Esther originates in the very late Persian era or early Hellenistic period. Others, however, not only date each book according to the events described in the texts, but accept each as reporting factual history: Daniel (as a whole) during the lifetime of its namesake in the Babylonian exile, and Esther earlier in the Persian era (Ahasuerus = either Xerxes I or Artaxerxes I or II; between 486–358 BCE).

We want to close this chapter with an issue we raised earlier: how to identify the LORD's people, without the benefit of dedicated lands or national allegiance. The course of decisions in the post-exilic era came to recognize who belonged and who did not based on their obedience to Torah. So, no matter where a person might live, in the Diaspora or back in the land, Torah obedience determined their true identity. Later, as they develop their unique shape and then encounter and fight against Hellenism, this religious group will be called *Judaism* and individual members called *Jews*. Consequently, to speak of Jews prior to the exile is **anachronistic**; before the exile, those who followed the LORD and Torah were Israelites. While a study of Judaism is an excellent topic, it moves far beyond the historical confines of this introduction.

To Discuss

1. Why was it difficult to get people to want to go back to Jerusalem? What factors contributed to their desire to stay where they were? Would you want to stay or go? In what ways does Second Isaiah encourage the people to return home? Would this prophet convince you to return?

2. When the foundation of the temple was laid, the writer says that the younger generation celebrated while many of the older generation wept. What would prompt the older generation to weep so loudly, while the younger generation could only celebrate? Have you ever experienced an event that had such a sharp division in responses? Does Nehemiah's experience help you understand what caused such diversity?

3. When the people from what was once northern Israel offer to help with the building of the temple, Zerubbabel and other leaders said no (which prompted fierce opposition from these people). What is at stake in their answer? How would you have answered their offer? Why?

4. The writer says, "No one in Jerusalem or in the province of Judah, or anyone else in the Diaspora, has the level of concern for Jerusalem, its walls, and its people as does Nehemiah—a man who is a thousand miles away and 140 years after the event." Does his reaction surprise you? How do you account for Nehemiah's reaction? Do you accept what the author says about ways in which God may call people to special work?

5. Identify the types of opposition Nehemiah faced. How does he deal with opposition? What principles can you identify below the surface of his responses?

6. What do you believe creates new life with God? How do Nehemiah and Ezra foster a revival among the people? Do you think what creates new life with God might change over the years and in different cultures?

7. How does the post-exilic community decide the issue of identity? How do they determine who belongs to the LORD and who doesn't? How does this change affect those descended from Israel? What difficulties does this decision cause?

8. We have come many years since the LORD called Abraham and Sarah and made promises to them. Reflect on these promises for a moment. What is the status of each of the promises at the end of Nehemiah? What hope does there seem to be for God still working through these promises?

To Know

1. The significance of the following in the assigned chapters:

Babylon	Judaism
Cyrus	Nehemiah
Diaspora	Persia
Ezra	Province of Yehud
Haggai	Second Isaiah
Jerusalem	Zechariah
Jew	Zerubbabel

2. Cyrus's policy regarding former Babylonian captives.

3. Conditions in post-exilic Jerusalem.

4. The three rebuilding projects for those who return to the land.

5. The different reactions to the laying of the temple foundation and the factors behind each reaction.

6. The offer of the people already in the land, why it is rejected, and the consequences.

7. The prophets who get the temple project moving again.

8. Nehemiah's reaction to the news about Jerusalem's walls.

9. Be prepared to write a paragraph on the role of prayer in Nehemiah's life.

10. Identify the opposition Nehemiah faces in rebuilding the walls.

11. Be prepared to write on how the issue of identity is resolved in the post-exilic community.

12. Locate the following on a map (see Figure 13.1): Sardis, Babylon (city), Susa, Nile River, Euphrates River, Tigris River, Indus River, Red Sea, Persian Gulf, Caspian Sea, Black Sea, and the Great Sea.

To Dig Deeper: Research Topics

1. Research the conditions surrounding the return to Jerusalem and create a brochure that advertises a trip back home (and deals with the reasons not to go).

2. Research what happens in forced migrations (past and present) and design an exercise that helps your class feel the trauma or other emotions associated with exile.

3. How does the revival of Ezra–Nehemiah compare to one of the great revivals in Christian history? Select and research a revival for comparison, and complete further research on Ezra and Nehemiah's revival.

4. Go deeper into the "Texts in Conversation." Establish your own hypothesis for resolving the issue and prepare your case. If others are involved, conduct a debate with two or more persons on each side (assuming only two sides).

For Further Reading

On the History of the Post-Exilic Period

Grayson, A. Kirk. "Mesopotamia, History of (Babylonia)." Pages 755–777 in vol. 4 of *The Anchor Bible Dictionary*. Edited by David Noel Freedman. 6 vols. New York: Doubleday, 1992.

Widengren, Geo. "The Persian Period." Pages 489–538 in *Israelite and Judean History*. Edited by John H. Hayes and J. Maxwell Miller. Philadelphia: Trinity Press, 1977.

Young Jr, T. Cuyler. "Cyrus." Pages 1231–1232 in vol. 1 of *The Anchor Bible Dictionary*. Edited by David Noel Freedman. 6 vols. New York: Doubleday, 1992.

On the Chronology of Ezra and Nehemiah

Demsky, Aaron. "Who Returned First—Ezra or Nehemiah?" *Bible Review* 12 (1996): 28–33, 46, 48.

McFall, Leslie. "Was Nehemiah Contemporary with Ezra in 458 BC?" *Westminster Theological Journal* 53 (1991): 263–293.

Shaver, Judson R. "Ezra and Nehemiah: On the Theological Significance of Making Them Contemporaries." Pages 76–86 in *Essays on the Formation and Heritage of Second Temple Judaism in Honor of Joseph Blenkinsopp*. JSOTSup 149. Sheffield: JSOT Press, 1992.

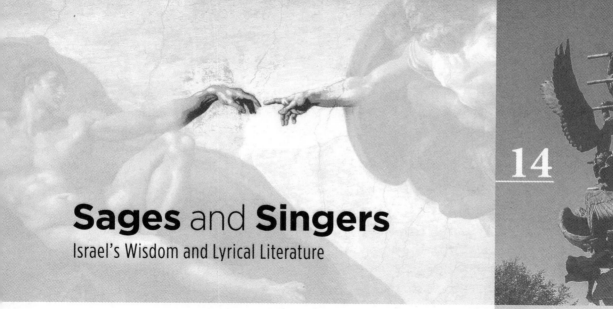

Sages and Singers
Israel's Wisdom and Lyrical Literature

14

We have reached the narrative end of the Old Testament, as told by the Books of Genesis through Ezra, into which we may fit the origins of the prophetic texts of Isaiah through Malachi. Now, the only genres we have yet to explore are the **lyrical** books (Psalms, Song of Songs, and Lamentations) and the various voices of the **sages** (Proverbs, Ecclesiastes, and Job). Most of the songs in Psalms and Song of Songs are ahistorical—lacking any tether to Israel's history (other than their superscriptions, e.g., Ps 13, 88, 139)—while several notable exceptions interlock the Book of Psalms within Israel's walk with God (e.g., 2, 89, 136). Here we will momentarily set the psalms aside for full treatment in our next and final chapter.

The Wisdom Books

The wisdom books break all ties to Israel's story—with the lone exception of two or three verses out of the whole—and take on a universal perspective and flavor. These books are tangible proof that more than one way of understanding life with God existed in Israel. In fact, we overhear a conversation in the Book of Jeremiah that affirms the existence of at least three perspectives or orthodoxies: the priests, the prophets, and the sages (18:18). A brief reconsideration of the priests and prophets will be a helpful starting point for introducing the sages.

Priests, along with Levites, were the keepers of **Torah** and the temple. Their perspective on life with God valued worship, sacrifice, purity, and a life of holiness. For direction in all these matters, they

READING ASSIGNMENTS:
PROVERBS 1–9
JOB 1–2, 3–5, 38–42
ECCLESIASTES 1–3, 11–12
SONG OF SONGS 1–8
 (OR 1–2, 4–5, 8)
LAMENTATIONS 1–5 (OR 3)

KEY TERMS

Acrostic: a Hebrew poem that begins each line with the next letter of the alphabet, from the first letter (*aleph*) to the last (*tav*)

Book of the Twelve: the books of the Hebrew Bible, elsewhere recognized as the minor prophets

Former Prophets: the Books of Joshua through 2 Kings, equivalent to the DH

Holiness Code: instruction for living in God's presence, found in Leviticus 16–26

Latter Prophets: the Books of Isaiah, Jeremiah, Ezekiel, Daniel, and the Book of the Twelve

Lyrical: song or songlike poetry

Sage: a wise person

Orthodoxy/Orthodoxies: adherence to accepted religious norms, holding a correct view of life with God

Torah: the Books of Genesis through Deuteronomy

Wasf: a love poem that describes the lover's body from head to feet or feet to head, sometimes concluding on an object of great interest

had the Torah to guide them. So the priests were not only intermediaries between the people and God, they taught what the Torah had to say about living a holy life in relationship to a holy God (Lev 10:10–11; see the "**Holiness Code**" in Lev 17–26).

Prophets had a different perspective on life with God. The prophets (the **Former Prophets** and **Latter Prophets** of the Hebrew Bible: Isaiah, Jeremiah, Ezekiel, Daniel, and the **Book of the Twelve** for Christian Bibles) prized the covenant relationship God established with his people and covenant values, such as a single-minded devotion to the LORD—and only the LORD—and social justice that comes from a love of others. Prophets are sometimes regarded as covenant lawyers for the LORD, pressing charges against the LORD's people when they fail to uphold their promises. Unlike priests, the prophet's source of information was not Torah, but direct revelation via dreams, visions, or some other means by which God would communicate a message. Consequently, a prophet would stand and say, "The LORD says," "The LORD has spoken," or "Hear the LORD's word" (e.g., see the various forms in Isa 1:2, 1:10, 3:16, 7:3, 8:1, 8:11).

Sages bring a third perspective to what it means to live with the LORD, a viewpoint that prizes wisdom. In the Hebrew Bible, the term *hokmah*, most often translated as "wise" or "wisdom," is used in two ways—the first is helpful for understanding the second. First, writers use the term *hokmah* to describe people who are highly skilled at some task. As an example, Ezekiel describes the city-state of Tyre as a magnificent ship (Ezek 27:4–8), with nobles of other cities rowing the boat and Sidon's own "skilled men" (NIV, NRSV) serving as the helmsmen (CEB) or pilots (KJV). Behind the key term "skilled" stands *hokmah*, shown here by two translations of verse 8 that use the word "wise": "Thy wise [*hokmah*] men, O Tyrus, that were in thee, were thy pilots" (KJV) and "Your own wise [*hokmah*] men were in you as your helmsmen" (CEB). So we see that *hokmah* may denote the idea of a high degree of skill or ability at a particular task. We find the same use of *hokmah* in Jeremiah 9 as the LORD weeps for Israel and issues a proclamation: "Summon the women who mourn, let them come; send for the best trained, let them come" (9:17). What the LORD wants are those who are good at crying and singing sad songs—those who are so exceptional they have turned professional and are paid to cry and sing at a funerals. Our key word stands behind the last phrase that describes these women: "best trained." In other translations, this phrase is translated as "the most skillful of them" (NIV) and "the skilled women" (RSV, NRSV). Literally, however, the text reads "send for the wise [*hokmah*] women, let them come." Again, this use of *hokmah* denotes a group of people who are especially good and/or well trained at a specific task.

This use and meaning of the term *hokmah* is helpful for understanding its abstract use in wisdom literature. If *hokmah* means special skill or expertise at one task, then *hokmah* for sages means skill and expertise for all of life—for living well. So, the one to whom the LORD provides wisdom will learn to live life at its best:

> Then you will understand righteousness and justice,
> as well as integrity, every good course.
> Wisdom will enter your mind,
> and knowledge will fill you with delight.

Discretion will guard you;
>understanding will protect you.
Wisdom will rescue you from the evil path,
>from people who twist their words. (Prov 2:9–12)

Or, picturing wisdom as a woman (a feature to which we will return), Proverbs describes the great gain to be had in finding this wisdom/woman:

Her profit is better than silver,
>and her gain better than gold.
Her value exceeds pearls;
>all you desire can't compare with her.
In her right hand is a long life;
>in her left are wealth and honor.
Her ways are pleasant;
>all her paths are peaceful.
She is a tree of life to those who embrace her;
>those who hold her tight are happy. (3:14–18)

For the sages, wisdom is nothing less than a recovery of the tree of life (Prov 3:18), lost in Genesis 3. Not so that sages will live forever, but so they know how to live life to its fullest potential—to genuinely live in all they do, day after day.

Priests find their perspective on life from the Torah, prophets look to the covenants and direct revelation from God, and sages learn wisdom from different resources. First, notice the shared element in the following verses from the Book of Ecclesiastes (NRSV). What practice or source brings this writer wisdom?

There is nothing better for mortals than to eat and drink, and find enjoyment in their toil. This also, I saw, is from the hand of God. (2:24)

I have seen the business that God has given to everyone to be busy with. (3:10)

Moreover I saw under the sun that in the place of justice, wickedness was there, and in the place of righteousness, wickedness was there as well. (3:16)

Again I saw all the oppressions that are practiced under the sun. Look, the tears of the oppressed—with no one to comfort them! On the side of their oppressors there was power—with no one to comfort them. (4:1)

Then I saw that all toil and all skill in work come from one person's envy of another. This also is vanity and a chasing after wind. (4:4)

Again, I saw vanity under the sun . . . (4:7)

> I saw all the living who, moving about under the sun, follow that youth who replaced the king . . . (4:15)

> There is a grievous ill that I have seen under the sun: riches were kept by their owners to their hurt . . . (5:13)

> This is what I have seen to be good: it is fitting to eat and drink and find enjoyment in all the toil with which one toils under the sun the few days of the life God gives us; for this is our lot. (5:18; see also 6:1, 7:15)

I expect that you can *see* how this writer gains knowledge: the first source of wisdom for sages is what they see in life (or what they experience) and their reflection on what they see, so that they understand or learn from it. In this way, the sages build a body of information about what is advisable or best to do in the most practical of circumstances. Thus, the older sages become, the more they know about how to live life to its fullest.

A second source of wisdom is the collected observations and teachings about life accumulated by previous sages, now handed down from one generation to the next. The Book of Proverbs is a compilation of such wisdom, collected and now made available to others so they can read, study, and gain from what past generations of sages have seen and learned about how life works. So it comes as no surprise when we read the Book of Job, we find Job's friends supporting their claims by appealing first to what they have seen and second to the traditional knowledge of the sages (e.g., 8:8–10, 15:9–10, 15:17–19). Consequently, Eliphaz (one of the friends) tells Job,

Appeal based on Source One:
> As I have seen, those who plow iniquity
>   and sow trouble reap the same. (4:8 NRSV)

Appeal based on Source Two:
> What do you know that we do not know?
>   What do you understand that is not clear to us?
> The gray-haired and the aged are on our side,
>   those older than your father. (15:9–10 NRSV)

And a little later, Eliphaz appeals to both sources of wisdom together:

> I will show you; listen to me;
>   what I have seen I will declare—
> what sages have told,
>   and their ancestors have not hidden, (15:17–18 NRSV)

Thus, wisdom comes from our own careful observations (investigation, research) and from the accumulated wisdom of previous generations.

The significance of recognizing these two sources of wisdom is tremendous. By its nature, wisdom is both intergenerational and international in scope. Anyone, at any time and any place on earth, can develop wisdom. And, in fact, civilizations from the ancient Far East to those of the New West, and all points between, have developed their own unique wisdom traditions flavored with the exotic or homespun nature of their roots. God's wisdom for learning how to live day-to-day life well and how to live life to its fullest is not the property of Israel alone. It is available to anyone and everyone who is willing to open their eyes to see, and open their minds to reflect on what they see and learn from it (similar to claims made in the New Testament; see Rom 1:19–25).

So, we find wisdom in ancient Chinese proverbs:

> ⌒ A book holds a house of gold.
> ⌒ To know the road ahead, ask those coming back.

Proverbs attributed to Confucius:

> ⌒ By three methods we may learn wisdom: First, by reflection, which is noblest;
> Second, by imitation, which is easiest; and third by experience, which is
> the bitterest.

> ⌒ If you think in terms of a year, plant a seed;
> if in terms of ten years, plant trees;
> if in terms of 100 years, teach the people.

Figure 14.1. Bronze Figure of Confucius

Or wisdom from the insights of Ben Franklin in *Poor Richard's Almanack* (see Figure 14.2):

> ⌒ Diligence is the mother of good luck.

> ⌒ Wish not so much to live long, as live well.

> ⌒ If you would not be forgotten as soon as you are dead and rotten, either write things worth reading or do things worth writing.

> ⌒ Up, sluggard, and waste not life; in the grave will be sleep enough.

> ⌒ Beware of little expenses, a small leak will sink a great ship.

> ⌒ One today is worth two tomorrows.

> ⌒ Fish and visitors stink after three days.

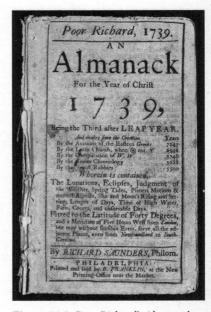

Figure 14.2. *Poor Richard's Almanack*

Thus, from Israel to Egypt, the ancient Near East to the Far East, and Confucius to Ben Franklin, by its nature, wisdom is an international enterprise.

The universal character of wisdom raises important questions: So, what is the difference between *Poor Richard's Almanack* or ancient Chinese proverbs and what we find in the wisdom literature of the Hebrew Bible? How does Israelite wisdom differ from other wisdom traditions? Or, to restate the question one more time: How does Old Testament wisdom literature differ from what we can buy at any bookstore today that claims to teach us how to live a better life?

For Proverbs, the answer, in a single word, is *Yahweh*—the LORD. Biblical wisdom texts stress that the beginning of wisdom—perhaps also claiming the very heart of wisdom—is a proper relationship with the LORD. The Book of Proverbs begins with these words:

> Wisdom begins with the fear of the LORD,
>> but fools despise wisdom and instruction. (1:7)

The conclusion of chapters 1–9 restates the claim:

> The beginning of wisdom is fear of the LORD;
>> the knowledge of the holy one is understanding. (9:10)

Unfortunately, the phrase "fear of the LORD" invites serious misunderstanding, as if wisdom begins with being afraid of God. In fact, the phrase does suggest fear as in proper respect for God, but it does not mean terror or being afraid. For the sages, "fear of the LORD" denotes the right type of relationship with the LORD, defined by the second half of 9:10 as "knowing" the Holy One—an expression of close intimacy.

So, for Israel's wisdom tradition, wisdom begins with, and has at its very core, a proper relationship with God, a relationship of respect and close intimacy: "the fear of the LORD." And for Israel's sages, this changes everything. Now, their observations are not theologically neutral, but theologically charged as investigations of life and the world as created and ordered by God, all so that we learn how life works best (see Prov 8:22–36). Therefore, instruction in wisdom is essentially and ultimately about our relationship with God. The study of how we may best live—in the day-to-day, ordinary events of life—is really a study of how a person lives with God in God's world. This is a perspective quite different from the priest's Torah, the prophet's direct revelation, and other wisdom traditions around the world, past or present.

We have already mentioned the primary wisdom texts: Proverbs, Job, and Ecclesiastes. In addition to these, scholars detect strong wisdom influence in other texts—such as the Joseph story (Gen 37–48), some psalms (see Ps 19, 119). We take this as a prompt to explain that priests, prophets, and sages were not opponents in determining *the correct* approach to life with God. Instead, they understood and accepted the need for more than one way to think about faith. In fact, some prophets (e.g., Jeremiah, Ezekiel) were also priests. So, rather than rivals, these three different ways of understanding life with God are mutually supportive of one another, because all three are needed for a full-bodied understanding of how to live today and tomorrow (and the next day) with the LORD. Priests lead us through holiness to close proximity and worship of the LORD, prophets refuse to let us live entitled lives without concern for the un-entitled throughout the world, and the sages teach us how to live our everyday lives with wisdom.

Proverbs

The Book of Proverbs is the foundational wisdom text to which Job and Ecclesiastes respond. Excluding its introduction (1:1–7) and conclusion (31:10–31), Proverbs develops the idea of wisdom in its two parts: chapters 1–9 and 10–31. Chapters 1–9 present three intertwined themes: the importance of wisdom (it is life!), wisdom as a path that one walks (not a destination to which one arrives and stops), and the necessity to choose wisdom (not to make a clear choice is to choose folly). With this appeal for wisdom finished and the reader led to choose the more difficult path of a wise life, Proverbs 10–31 then present the content of wisdom—what wisdom looks like in the details of life.

The forms or genres of these two halves also differ. In Proverbs 1–9, the writer or editor makes use of longer genres: ten father–son speeches (e.g., 1:8–19, 2:1–22); and four interludes, presenting the speech of wisdom personified as a woman (1:20–33, 8:1–36, 9:1–6) or giving a tribute to this woman (3:13–20). These different genres work together to develop the three themes mentioned above, ultimately convincing the young man (the primary intended audience of the book; see 1:4) to choose wisdom as a way of life. One other feature, difficult to miss in chapters 1–9, is the presence of many different women in relationship to the young man: his mother (1:8, 6:20), his wife (present or future, 5:15–19), any woman other than his wife (2:16–19; 5:3–14, 20; 6:24–35; 7:5–23), folly personified as a woman (9:13–18), and woman wisdom (1:20–33, 3:13–20, 8:1–36, 9:1–6). Why so many women? It seems that the writer recognizes what is on the mind of his intended audience more than anything else: young men think about women! So these women vie for the young man's attention in something of a soap opera within Proverbs 1–9. His mother (and father) with woman wisdom urge the son to listen to them rather than to the sly, provocative words of the "other" woman who wants him (sexually), but who will destroy him. Instead, he should find his sexual fulfillment in his wife. In fact, these chapters ultimately urge the young man to marry woman wisdom (see 3:13–18, and 7:14 with its language of marriage, e.g., "sister," meaning wife). Once understood—choosing the path of wisdom via marrying the personification of wisdom—the conclusion of the book makes better sense: the ode to the wife and mother in the **acrostic** of Proverbs 31:10–31 is an ode to woman wisdom. Within a book that nowhere else specifically addresses women, it seems odd to conclude the book with a speech that is aimed at women. Instead, read with Proverbs 1–9, we see that these verses present a final reminder to the young man of the blessings to be found in making woman wisdom his wife—a superwoman who never sleeps and will never stop blessing his life (see 31:15, 18, 27).

The second half of the book, Proverbs 10–31, uses, almost exclusively, the genre of the proverb—typically a two-line saying in which we find the meaning or primary idea in the relationship of the two lines. For example, Proverbs 10:2 reads:

> The treasure of the wicked won't profit them,
> but righteousness rescues people from death.

The idea, then, unexpressed but present in the relationship of the lines, is that righteousness does profit—and the wise person will acquire righteousness. Beyond this instruction in reading proverbs, two other features of the genre require our attention.

First, by nature, a proverb is an expression of general truth—not an absolute guarantee. In other words, a proverb is true only in certain circumstances, not all circumstances. The easiest proof of this claim is found in Proverbs 26:4–5. The first proverb instructs us:

> Don't answer fools according to their folly,
> or you will become like them yourself.

The idea is clear enough: if you talk like a fool or engage a fool on his or her level, you will become just like a fool. The second proverb also instructs us:

> Answer fools according to their folly,
> or they will deem themselves wise.

So what are we supposed to do? Now we are told that we should answer a fool according to his or her folly. Which proverb is true? Both—wisdom does not lay in memorizing and quoting each proverb, but knowing when each is true and appropriate to use. Any fool can spout proverbs (and many do), but when and how they use proverbs may be useless. As Proverbs 26:7 says, "As legs dangle from a disabled person, so does a proverb in the mouth of fools." Or worse, fools may cause damage with their advice: "Like a thorny bush in the hand of a drunk, so is a proverb in the mouth of fools" (26:9). Not only will fools hurt themselves, they may also hurt other people with their misapplication of a proverb. These short sayings are not one size fits all, but require a context in which they are true; outside of that context, they may not be true at all. For example, Proverbs 22:6 reads, "Train children in the way they should go; when they grow old, they won't depart from it." Great harm has been caused by the misuse of this simple proverb, causing good parents to feel guilty for the bad choices made by their children. Yes, it is generally true that good training will result in a good outcome, but not always. Children, especially grown children, are free to make their own choices—and sometimes, no amount of good training will prevent a child going their own way. Proverbs 22:6, like all other proverbs, makes no guarantee. We need wisdom to know when this proverb should be spoken and when it should not be mentioned.

A second feature of proverbs, crucial for our reading, is recognition that some proverbs give instruction about how things should be ("do this" or "don't do that," *a prescriptive proverb*), and other proverbs do nothing more than describe the world as it is ("so deal with it," *a descriptive proverb*). For example, Proverbs 17:8 describes rather than prescribes: "A bribe seems magical in the eyes of those who give it, granting success to all who use it" (see also 17:23, 21:14). It is a fact of life that bribes work, but this proverb does not suggest we should offer bribes. Rather, this is the way the world works—so deal with it. On the other hand, Proverbs 15:27 gives us instruction:

"Those who acquire things unjustly gain trouble for their house, but those who hate bribes will live." Here we learn that bribes cause trouble, so the wise person will refuse to take a bribe so that they may live fully or genuinely (as opposed to choosing a living death).

Of course, this second feature of proverbs raises a further need for wisdom—to know when a proverb merely describes reality and when a proverb prescribes what a wise person should do. Sometimes it is easy to know that a proverb describes the world: "People plan their path, but the LORD secures their steps" (16:9). So we should—and do—make plans, but we should also know that we cannot be certain of success, because God may or may not support and secure the plans we make. Then again, maybe this proverb does give us direction: make our plans, but rely on the LORD. Deciding between descriptive and prescriptive readings is not so easy; we really do need wisdom as we read.

We have already mentioned the international nature of wisdom, so it should be no surprise that ancient Near Eastern civilizations had sages and wisdom literature similar to what we find in Proverbs. Lessons from a teacher to a student (similar to Prov 1–9) are present in the instruction texts from Phahhotep, Merikare, Amenemhet, Ani, and Amenemope—each of which contains instructions from a teacher, high official, or even a Pharaoh to a student. Many of these and other wisdom texts include proverbs similar to the contents of Proverbs 10–31. Most important for the study of Proverbs is the "Instruction of Amenemope." Close similarities between this Egyptian text and Proverbs 22:17–24:22 have been recognized since the discovery and translation of "Amenemope" in the early twentieth century, raising questions about whether the much older Egyptian text had any direct influence on Proverbs. Recently, Michael Fox presented an elaborate and intricate study that demonstrates the writer of Proverbs 22:17–24:22 used "Amenemope" (some parallels identified in Fox's work are presented below; all translations by Fox):[1]

Fox demonstrates that the commonality between the texts is uncanny and can only be explained by the writer of Proverbs having the text of "Amenemope" before him as he wrote. As a closing note to Proverbs, other Egyptian and Mesopotamian texts similar to Job and Ecclesiastes also exist: "Dialogue of a Man with His Soul" and "Song of the Harper" (both from Egypt); and "Proverbs," "The Babylonian Theodicy," and "A Dialogue of Pessimism" (all Mesopotamian). Unlike "Amenemope," however, none of these texts appear to have any direct influence on Israelite wisdom literature.

Job

Proverbs attempts to build a wise life, and, in the process, makes many promises or assurances that a wise life is the best life. The other two biblical wisdom books offer a challenge and critique of Proverbs' claims, refining the observations of the sages. In fact, we could label each of these books as "texts in conversation" with one another.

---

[1] Michael Fox, *Proverbs 10–31*, in *Anchor Yale Bible Commentaries* 18B (New York: Doubleday, 2009), 757–760.

CITATIONS FROM THE "INSTRUCTION OF AMENEMOPE"	CITATIONS FROM PROVERBS 22:17–24:22
Give you ears, that you may hear the things that are said;	Incline your ear and hear my words, (22:17b)
apply your heart to interpret them.	and direct your heart to my knowledge (22:17c)
They will be a mooring post for your tongue	that they may all be secure on your lips. (22:18b)
Look to these thirty chapters:	Have I not written for you [thirty] (22:20a)
to return an (oral) response to one who says it, to bring back a (written) message to the one who sends it.	to teach you the truest of words, to give answer to those who send you. (22:21)
Beware of robbing the lowly,	Do not rob a lowly man because he is lowly, (22:22a)
of oppressing the weak	and do not oppress the poor man at the gate. (22:22b)
but the Moon declares his crime.	For Yahweh will strive on their behalf, and will steal away the life of those who steal from them. (22:23)
Do not join quarrel with the hot mouthed man, or assail him by words.	Do not consort with an ill-tempered man, lest you learn his ways and get yourself snared. (22:24–25)
Do not consort with the heated man, or approach him for conversation,	
Do not share a portion with the heated man or consort with a contentious man.	
Do not displace the stone on the boundary of the fields.	Do not encroach on the ancient boundary, which your ancestors made. (22:28)
Beware of encroaching on the boundaries of the fields,	
As for the scribe skilled in his office, he will be found worthy to be a courtier.	Have you seen a man adept in his work? He will stand before kings. He will not stand before the lowly. (22:29bc)
Do not eat food before an official,	When you sit to dine with an official, (23:1a)
Look at the bowl that is before you,	look carefully at what is before you, (23:1b)
If you become sated by that which is chewed deceitfully (?)	Do no desire his delicacies, for they are deceitful bread. (23:3)

Table 14.1. "Amenemope" and Proverbs 22:17–24:22

In the Book of Job, we meet a man who is the ultimate sage, Mr. Wisdom. Job is a man of honesty and absolute integrity, with a character defined by his fear of God and avoidance of evil; and, just as Proverbs assures us, Job's life prospers as befits a man of wisdom (Job 1:1–5). At least, until the day the LORD and the satan (a member of the LORD's royal court, not the "devil" or "Satan" we find in the New Testament)[2] make two wagers: the first wager is about how Job will

---

[2] A common error for Christians reading the Old Testament is to assume a word used in the Old Testament has the same definition as the same word found in the New Testament. To be specific, we assume "the satan" in Job 1–2 is the same "Satan" (devil) we find in the in the New Testament. Words, however, change meaning over time, which is precisely what has happened

respond if all his goods—both possessions and children—are taken away (1:6–22); the second wager, a continuation of the first—taking away Job's health (2:1–10). What will Job do if there is no reward for a wise life? In other words, is it possible for a person to "fear God" (live in proper relationship) if there is no reward? Will a person serve God for nothing—no blessing, no reward . . . nothing? The Lord says *yes, Job will still serve me*; the satan says *no, no one will serve you under those conditions*. This is the wager and *the question* that has been set up by the writer.

The issue of the book is not the cause of suffering. We already know the answer to why Job suffers from chapter 1 and 2: God causes it (see God's admission in Job 2:3). In addition, everyone in the book believes God is responsible for Job's suffering. No one argues otherwise. Of course, Job and his friends know nothing of the heavenly wager, so they spend much of their time arguing over who suffers and why. The friends, in an effort to help Job, persistently make three points: first, the wicked suffer to the degree that they are wicked (e.g., 4:7–9, 15:20–35, 18:5–21, 20:4–29), second you (Job) are suffering intensely, therefore you must be terribly wicked (e.g., 8:3–4, 11:5–6, 22:4–11; see also 5:17–26), and third, confess your sin to God and God will forgive you and restore all your blessings (e.g., 8:5–7, 11:13–17, 22:21–28).

Job, however, knows that their initial claim is false; he has observed the wicked prospering and the righteous suffering on many occasions (e.g., 21:7–21). Job also knows that he has not committed any sin so terrible that he deserves such horrible suffering (9:21–22, 10:2–7, 16:15–17, 23:11–12, 31:5–34). So he refuses to compromise his integrity and do what the friends suggest, just so he can get his stuff back (27:1–6). He is confused, however, by God's actions and God's failure to uphold what Proverbs taught about the system of merit: do good, get good; or do bad, get bad. Job believes the same principles of wisdom that his friends spout, but he sees that God is not upholding the system the way he believes it should work. Consequently, Job calls for a trial, a court case in which God is the defendant for what has happened to Job (e.g., 9:14–20, 32–35; 13:3, 18–22; 16:18–22; 19:23–27), even though Job knows that any trial against God is futile and he will be crushed by God's words (e.g., 9:14–22).

Eventually, God does show up and speak to Job, overwhelming him, just as Job had predicted. The LORD challenges Job in two speeches. The first asks over and over what Job knows and what Job can do, with the conclusion that Job doesn't know much about the world and he can do even less (38:1–40:2). In the second speech (40:4–41:34), the LORD challenges Job to try being God and see how well he can handle the work, especially how well he would deal with the strongest of mortal beasts—the behemoth (possibly a hippopotamus)—and the fearsome fire-breathing and fire-spouting dragon that represents the many chaotic forces constantly at odds with the LORD's good creation (see Isa 27:1, 51:9; Ps 74:13–14, 104:26). Since Job cannot handle either

---

with the term "the satan." Read the following Old Testament texts in a good study Bible and you will discover that the term "satan" is used to describe an angel sent by God to delay Balaam (Num 22:22, 32), a human sent by God to punish Solomon (1 Kgs 11:14, 23), and, apparently, another angel working in God's employ, so that the term "satan" and "God" become interchangable (1 Chron 21:1 and 2 Sam 24:1). Thus, it seems much more likely that "the satan" that comes into God's presence is not the New Testament devil, but a servant of God responsible for watching the world and bringing charges against those who rebel.

beast, his charges against the LORD—and his innuendo that he could do a better job than the LORD—are all set aside. The world may not work as Job would like, the promises of Proverbs (and Deuteronomy) may not be as absolute as he wants, but he cannot change the limits of what wisdom will bring to a person's life.

The epilogue of the book finds the LORD correcting Job's friends and sending them to Job for sacrifice and prayer (42:7–9). Then the LORD restores Job's fortunes—twice as much as he had before (42:10, 12), including ten more children—not his first children, *and children are hardly replaceable parts* (42:13–15). The original question of the book has been answered: yes, it is possible for a person to serve God, even when they are not blessed at all. However, what such a life looks like is far different than our Sunday school image of a saint who serves God. And though the book presents something of a happily-ever-after conclusion, the reader may wonder if that is possible for Job now, knowing that he could lose it all again for no particular reason.

Ecclesiastes

Ecclesiastes also challenges the world constructed by the Book of Proverbs with its own claim that all human work and effort is nothing more than chasing the wind; no human effort gains any lasting benefit, because, sooner or later, we all die. Many readings of Ecclesiastes, however, are far more pessimistic than the book itself—perhaps because they do not get past the first two chapters of the book. Here, Qoheleth (the name the writer gives himself in 1:1, 2, 12; 7:27; 12:8, 9, 10) conducts the "Royal Experiment" by testing the things that humans often chase in an effort to give meaning to their lives. Over and over again, Qoheleth concludes that these things do not work because they do not last: acquiring knowledge (1:16–17), pleasure (2:1–3), great building projects (2:4–7), money (2:8), sex (2:8b), the limited benefit of wisdom (2:12–17), and working to leave something to the next generation (2:18–23). All of these—and more—are just chasing the wind, and Qoheleth is right! Look through the list; then and now, these are the things humans try to get (or do) in order to give life meaning. But they don't work. No wonder people regard Qoheleth as a pessimist—he tells the truth. Just take his challenge and hold whatever you may be chasing up to the sun and ask, "Does this last? Does it really give life lasting value or meaning?"

After the Royal Experiment, Qoheleth does begin to rebuild, but only after scraping away all the pretenders. He begins with a new view of time (Eccl 3): all time belongs to God and is equally beautiful. And throughout the book, beginning in the Royal Experiment, Qoheleth returns over and over again to the same basic ideas: "There's nothing better for human beings than to eat, drink, and experience pleasure in their hard work. I also saw that this is from God's hand . . ." (2:24; see also 2:10, 3:12–13, 3:22, 5:18–20, 8:15, and 9:7–10). The first step to meaningful life (not the only or last step), where we must begin, is to learn how to enjoy the simple things we do every day: enjoy our food, our drink, and our work. The enjoyment of these things is God's gift to us. Qoheleth urges us to quit deferring happiness until a later point in life ("I'll be happy when_____;" *you fill in the blank*). If we put it off, we will never be happy. And we also need to stop looking back to the good old days, back when we remember we were happy, but probably weren't any happier then than we are now (7:10). We either learn to be happy now with God's simple gifts, or we will never learn to be happy.

To seize the moment, "decide to be happy now" is the only commandment issued in the Book of Ecclesiastes:

> Go, eat your bread with enjoyment, and drink your wine with a merry heart; for God has long ago approved what you do. . . . Enjoy life with the wife whom you love, all the days of your vain life that are given you under the sun, because that is your portion in life and in your toil at which you toil under the sun. (9:7, 9 NRSV)

And the book concludes, "So this is the end of the matter, all has been heard. Fear God and keep his commandments because this is what everyone must do" (12:13). Perhaps we should recall that the only commandment the book gives is to be happy with God's smallest gifts. So, if we refuse the happiness God gives us here and now, God will judge us for our refusal (12:14).

The Lyrical Literature

The Song of Songs and Lamentations

Every culture has its songs—whether deep in the Amazon, in the cotton fields of the old South, the streets of Detroit, or among the people of ancient Israel. Music provides a unique medium for us to express our greatest joys and our deepest sorrows, but also to convey our values. We speak what we believe to be true and provide encouragement for members of the community, and nothing speaks to the heart like a song. So it should not surprise us when we find various collections of songs in the Old Testament. We find a collection of love songs, the Song of Songs, though we may be startled by the inclusion of such songs in the Bible. On the other end of the spectrum, we discover a book of lament, or profound grief, that follows after Babylon's destruction of Jerusalem—the Book of Lamentations. In our final chapter, we will also see what we expect in a Bible, the Book of Psalms—a collection of religious songs that mirrors (somewhat) what we find in our church hymnal: hymns of praise to God, songs that teach lessons, and songs of trust and confidence in God's provision and presence. With this map of the landscape of Israel's music, we set out on our final trek into the Old Testament. As we visit each of these texts, each section of this chapter will function as a travel guide that provides some basic information, a list of things to watch for as you read, and tips to enrich your personal exploration.

The Song of Songs

Despite an apparent connection to Solomon, the Song of Songs (which means, "Greatest Song") is not likely to have come from this king. Late in the book, the writer or editor sharply criticizes Solomon as a man who knows nothing about true love between one man and one woman (8:11–12; recall Solomon's many political marriages, 1 Kgs 11:1–4). Consequently, the initial reference may be irony, a dedication to Solomon—or any number of different possibilities. Later references to his name in the book may be a way of talking about "Prince Charming"—a king who sweeps a woman off her feet.

Though many attempt to read the Greatest Song as something of a narrative that begins with courtship or dating and concludes with marriage and the consummation of the marriage, the book refuses to be so easily tamed. Love-making is part of, or alluded to, in many of the songs—including the opening lines, "Oh, your loving is sweeter than wine" (1:2) and "My king has brought me into his chambers" (1:4). The book reads better as a simple collection of love songs, songs that celebrate every aspect of intimacy.

Several themes recur in the songs, themes that are common to love songs in many different cultures. Consider the following themes from the Greatest Song and compare them to your own favorite love songs.[3] First, is aesthetic appreciation—a phrase that denotes physical compliments and flirting based on physical characteristics. We should take note here: while physical attraction has existed since the first man and woman saw each other (Gen 2:23) and attraction exists in every culture, the language of attraction differs from one culture to another and from one century to another.

The opening song features a duet between a man and a woman, a woman who is self-conscious about the way she looks (1:5–7; unlike today, a dark complexion was a sign of lower working-class at that time, not upper-class who were protected from the sun), and a man who believes she is beautiful (1:8–11; though we might not compare our date to a horse). Elsewhere, we find a unique form of love poetry all about physical attraction: the **wasf**, in which a person describes their love from head to toe or toe to head—or more often, from one part of the body to another part which is of greatest interest. In 4:1–8, a man describes a woman, concluding with her breasts; other wasfs of a woman occur in 6:4–10 and 7:1–5. A woman also describes her man in 5:9–6:3, with her greatest interest falling on his smell (5:13), his strength (5:14–15), and last of all, his sweet words (5:16). Physical attraction and compliments are a part of most, if not every culture. But step back a moment and ask yourself what these people looked like. Superstars? The person from the cover of the latest fashion magazine? Perhaps, but it is much more likely that they looked like you and me. What we hear in these poems/songs is the language of love, and when a person is falling or has fallen in love with someone, they tend to see that person like no one else does. They don't understand why others don't see the same qualities.

A second theme in the love songs of the Greatest Song is the intense desire to be together—alone—and the anguish of separation, along with anxiety over all the things that just keep getting in the lovers' way when all they want is to be together. We see her concern early in the book. She worries about how she will be able to find him (1:7–8) and about the little foxes (whatever they may be) that keep ruining things (2:8–17). We hear about the frustration of not finding one's lover (3:1–4) and the desire to be able to act on impulses in public spaces (8:1–4).

Third, affective depiction moves well beyond physical compliments. Compliments are innocent enough to give and rejection is easy to take. Affective depiction, however, describes what

---

[3] See Carey Ellen Walsh, *Exquisite Desire: Religion, the Erotic, and the Song of Songs* (Minneapolis: Fortress, 2000), 47–132.

the other person is doing to the first: "You have captured my heart, my sister, my bride! You have captured my heart with one glance of your eyes, with one strand from your necklace" (4:9; see also 4:10–5:1). Now the man has put himself at risk; if she should dismiss his words, the pain will be much greater than the dismissal of a physical compliment (e.g., "you look nice today"). But if a relationship is to grow greater in intimacy, one or both parties will have to risk themselves at some point (see also 5:1–8, 2:37, and 6:5).

Finally, a fourth theme in the Greatest Song is the power of love:

> Set me as a seal over your heart,
>> as a seal upon your arm,
> for love is as strong as death,
>> passionate love unrelenting as the grave.
> Its darts are darts of fire—
>> divine flame!
> Rushing waters can't quench love;
>> rivers can't wash it away.
> If someone gave
>> all his estate in exchange for love,
>> he would be laughed at to utter shame. (8:6–7; see also 2:7, 3:5, 5:8, 8:4)

Love is inescapable when it comes, so strong a person cannot get away, and nothing can put out the flames of love. These four themes—innocent flirtation, the desire to be alone, the description of what a person's lover is doing to her or him, and the power of love—are not all that the Greatest Song has to say, but they are a place to start when reading this beautiful book.

Lamentations

The Book of Lamentations follows after the Babylonian destruction of Jerusalem and is a collection of five songs that lament or grieve the situation in the city. The most significant literary feature of these songs is the use of an acrostic pattern. For example, each verse in chapter 1 begins with the next consecutive letter in the Hebrew alphabet—twenty-two verses for the twenty-two letters of the alphabet (e.g., in English, verse 1 would begin with an A, verse 2 with B, verse three with C, and so forth). Chapter 2 repeats this pattern, while chapter 3 intensifies the acrostic with three lines for each letter. Chapter 4 uses the earlier pattern from chapters 1 and 2, and chapter 5 has the same number of lines (twenty-two), but does not follow the alphabet. The purpose of the acrostic pattern in Lamentations is not entirely clear, especially since an acrostic is only visible to a reader, not so much one who only listens. Perhaps the idea is to express full and complete grief—from A to Z, or maybe the pattern is an aid for memorization (in addition to other possible purposes).

Another feature of Lamentations to watch for is the various voices that speak in the book. In chapter 1, an outside observer (1:1–9, 10–11, 17) and Jerusalem, personified as a woman, speak (1:9e, 11e–16, 18–22); in chapter 2, the only speaker is an observer, who weeps at what he sees in Jerusalem (2:1–22). Jerusalem and/or the nation personified speak in chapter 3 (in the singular,

3:1–36; in the plural, 3:37–45). An inside observer and participant during the fall of Jerusalem speaks in chapter 4 (in third person, 4:1–16; in first person, 4:17–20; and either third person or first person in 4:21–22). Finally, in chapter 5, an observer comes years after the fall, describes what he sees, and begs for the LORD's return (5:1–22, see especially 5:20).

Those who speak understand that the LORD has brought destruction and exile (1:5, 14; 2:1–9; 4:11, 16) because of the sins of the city/nation (1:5, 18–19; 2:14; 5:7). They say that what has happened is just or fair, but it is enough. The speakers urge the LORD to bring an end to the suffering (3:22–33, 40–66; 4:6–9; 5:1–18, 19–22) and to restore the city and people. But there is little hope in the songs. The only complete statement of hope comes in the middle of the book, a passage that has become somewhat famous:

> Certainly the faithfulness of the LORD hasn't ended;
>> certainly God's compassion isn't through!
> They are renewed every morning. Great is your faithfulness.
> I think: The LORD is my portion! Therefore, I'll wait for him.
>
> The LORD is good to those who hope in him, to the person who seeks him.
> It's good to wait in silence for the LORD's deliverance. (3:22–26)

And yet, everything that surrounds these verses drowns out and drains these words of life. So much so that, at the end of the book, the writer is still waiting and wondering if God will ever return to help:

> Why do you forget us continually;
>> why do you abandon us for such a long time?
> Return us, LORD, to yourself. Please let us return!
>> Give us new days, like those ago—
> unless you have completely rejected us,
>> or have become too angry with us. (5:20–22)

The poet believes that the LORD reigns, now and forever (5:19), but he does not know if the King will ever bring his people back—not to Jerusalem, but to himself.

Conclusions

This has been a chapter of extremes: from the assured claims of Proverbs to the challenge of Ecclesiastes and Job, and from the beautiful lyrics of love poetry in Song of Songs to the heartbroken cries of lament over death and destruction in Lamentations. The Book of Job reminds us that not everything works out as simply as it may seem in Proverbs (though, to be fair, Proverbs would remind us that the nature of a proverb is general truth, not an absolute guarantee). Nonetheless, real life begins as simply as Qoheleth claims, learning to enjoy the little things of life—here and now—not there and later. With the interaction and conversation of these three books, wisdom continues to learn and grow as it observes, tests, modifies, and then tries again.

The lyrical literature of the Song of Songs and Lamentations brings God into our greatest joys and deepest moments of grief. Or maybe it's not that we move God into these times of life, but that we bring our lives fully into God's presence—including our greatest joys and our deepest sorrows. Oddly enough, through these books and the Wisdom Literature, we recognize that life with God is not only what we do at church or at worship; life with God means *all of our life* with God: in day-to-day life and worship, joy and sorrow, good times and bad times. This is the level of intimacy God wants, the same intimacy God enjoyed with creation before things went so terribly wrong (Gen 1–2).

To Discuss

1. To whom would you compare priests, prophets, and sages in contemporary faith communities? How are they similar to or different from these roles in ancient Israel? From what resource(s) do they get their information about the life of faith?

2. What are the two key sources of knowledge for the sages? Does your faith community listen to or dismiss these sources of wisdom when making important decisions or discussing life with the Lord?

3. Do you think Proverbs 31:10–31 refers to a real woman or to Woman Wisdom? What links do you find between 31:10–31 and the references to or speeches by Woman Wisdom in chapters 1–9?

4. Why do we need wisdom to use proverbs? What do we need to understand before we quote a proverb to someone (as instruction or advice)? Why? How does your answer relate to the two basic attributes of a proverb? What other factors might be important for the interpretation of a proverb?

5. What is the question or challenge between the satan and God in the prologue to the Book of Job (chs. 1–2)? How is this question answered in the book? What new questions do you have now?

6. Why are the friends wrong in their argument with Job? What disables them from being able to accept Job's claims? What about Job—is he wrong, too?

7. Did you expect God to respond to Job? Did God respond as you anticipated? What do you wish God had said that he didn't?

8. What questions does the Book of Job resolve? What questions does it raise, but not resolve? How well do you think you would have responded to the challenges Job faced at the beginning of the book? What about the challenges at the end of the book?

9. What is the Royal Experiment in Ecclesiastes? How might it challenge us? What would the writer of Ecclesiastes have to say about our insatiable thirst for technology?

10. How does the Book of Ecclesiastes rebuild life after the Royal Experiment? Where do we start? Why?

11. What are the recurring themes in the Greatest Song (Song of Songs)? Do you find the same themes in love songs today? Give comparative examples from the Song of Songs and contemporary songs.

12. To what event does Lamentations respond? Does the book find or not find hope for the future?

To Know

1. The significance of the following in the assigned reading:

Bildad	Qoheleth
Elihu	The Women of Proverbs 1–9
Eliphaz	Wasf
Hokmah	Wisdom (2 meanings)
Job	Woman Wisdom
Lament	Zophar

2. The three major themes in Proverbs 1–9.

3. The soap opera-like narrative in Proverbs 1–9.

4. The two key features of a proverb and how these affect interpretation.

5. The question or challenge in Job 1–2 and its answer in the book.

6. The three points consistently made by Job's friends.

7. The challenges God makes in his two speeches to Job.

8. The Royal Experiment and its conclusion in Ecclesiastes.

9. The basic idea(s) about happiness Qoheleth returns to over and over again in Ecclesiastes.

10. Themes common to love songs in the Greatest Song.

11. The issue or event to which Lamentations responds.

To Dig Deeper: Research Topics

1. Read the ten father–son speeches in Proverbs 1–8. Study these speeches carefully and then compose a speech from a mother to a daughter that includes and reshapes the topics and concerns from the father–son speeches.

2. Study the Royal Experiment in Ecclesiastes 1–2 and then conduct your own experiment. What are people pursuing today for happiness? Conduct a poll. Examine the most common answers: Do they work? Do the people polled think what they are pursuing works or will work for them?

3. Replace the speech of Elihu with your own (better) speech. To accomplish this task, you must read and understand all that precedes in the book. Write a paragraph or two that describes how your speech differs from Elihu's speech and why.

4. Research the most common themes in contemporary love songs or love poetry. What similarities or differences do you find? What accounts for those differences?

5. Musicians: Take on a major challenge and compose music for one of the love poems in the Song of Songs. It may be necessary to change some words, but try not to change too many.

6. Artists: Let the beauty of one or more love songs in the Song of Songs inspire a fresh interpretation in your favorite medium. Or, let the darkness of one of the acrostics from Lamentations be your inspiration.

7. Scientists (Social Scientists too): Write a position paper in which you describe how the practice of your chosen discipline is an exercise of biblical wisdom. In other words, in view of biblical wisdom, how do you integrate faith into your work? In what ways do scientific and biblical disciplines (especially wisdom) compliment, and even complete each other?

8. Select a topic to study in Proverbs 10–31 (e.g., speech, listening, poverty, wealth, or other instructor-approved topic). Read Proverbs 10–31 (more than once would be greatly beneficial; use a different translation for each reading) and make careful notes each time your topic appears. Develop your own outline that organizes what the Book of Proverbs teaches on your selected topic.

For Further Reading

Clifford, Richard J. *The Wisdom Literature*. Nashville: Abingdon, 1998.

Fox, Michael V. *Proverbs 1–9*. Anchor Bible 18A. New York: Doubleday, 2000.

———. *Proverbs 10–31*. Anchor Bible 18B. New York: Doubleday, 2009.

Murphy, Roland. *The Book of Job: A Short Reading*. New York: Paulist Press, 1999.

———. "Wisdom in the OT," Pages 920–931 in vol. 6 of *The Anchor Bible Dictionary*. Edited by David Noel Freedman. 6 vols. New York: Doubleday, 1992.

Pemberton, Glenn. "Hebrew Wisdom and Lyrical Literature: A Brief Field Report for the Early Twenty-First Century." *Restoration Quarterly* 55 (2013): 129–138.

For Wisdom Literature in the Ancient Near East

Coogan, Michael D. *A Reader of Ancient Near Eastern Texts: Sources for the Study of the Old Testament*. New York: Oxford University Press, 2013.

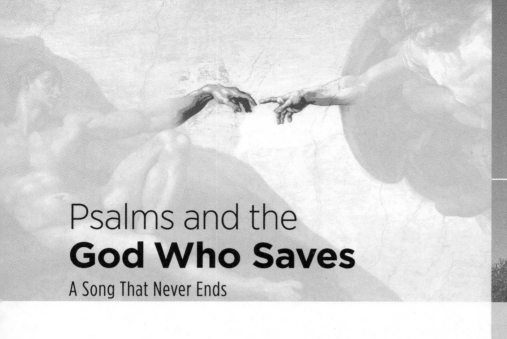

Psalms and the
God Who Saves
A Song That Never Ends

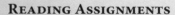

15

Songs are a powerful medium, windows into our lives and artists that shapes our souls. With a poet's words the music chisels our hearts, forming us according to the values of what we sing. Consider songs that you have not sung or heard for years; if you allow yourself, you would likely remember and begin singing the words. The union of music and words has a way of getting inside us, whether under our skin—those songs we cannot stand or get out of our mind—or deep inside our heart, where they not only have the staying power of a lifetime but slowly mold us into who we are or will become.[1]

Little wonder that the Bible makes full use of this tool, not only to provide the songs or prayers we will need during the course of our lives, but to transform us into people of faith, people who walk with the LORD. In the previous chapter, we saw two extremes—the poetic language of passionate human love (Song of Songs) and the cry of profound grief over Babylon's destruction of Jerusalem (Lamentations). In this chapter, we turn to the longest book in the English Bible, in terms of both chapters and pages: the Book of Psalms. This book also includes extremes—the extreme of passionate praise for God (e.g., Pss 92–99) and unflinching protest over God's failure, not only to stop the Babylonians from destroying Jerusalem (e.g., Ps 89), but to sustain individuals in the presence of chaos (e.g., Pss 42–43, 88). This book includes hymns that invite us into the presence of God (e.g., Pss 1,

---

[1] The title of this chapter plays upon Norman Martin's song written for children, "This Is the Song That Never Ends" (1988).

READING ASSIGNMENTS
PSALMS 117, 30, 13
PSALMS 136, 78, 104–105, 29, 150

KEY TERMS
Antiphonal: a song sung with call and response or back and forth between one person or group and another person or group
Doxology: praise of God, typically a short exclamation in praise of God's greatness
Karst Topography: landscape formed by the dissolving of rocks such as limestone, creating underground streams and caverns
Parallelism: a term that helps to describe the relationship of one line of Hebrew poetry to the next, e.g., synonymous parallelism (the second line repeats the idea of the first to emphasize or nuance the first line)
Psalmist: the writer of a psalm
Psalter: a book that contains psalms, often used as an alternate term for the Book of Psalms
Ugarit: an ancient kingdom on the Mediterranean coast (ca. 1400 BCE, now Ras Shamra)
Ugaritic: the language of Ugarit; a large number of Ugaritic texts have been recovered, giving insight to ancient Palestine and Baal worship.

121–131) and songs that send us out in praise of the God who saves (e.g., Pss 146–150). And while we're not looking, the Book of Psalms transforms us with its words and images, chipping away doubt and trust in ourselves, and remaking us into the image of God.

In this chapter, we introduce several entry points to the study of Psalms:

- basic information about the book itself, helpful for getting started
- a quick guide to the different forms or types of psalms we find in the book
- a primer on Hebrew poetry and what is oddly called "**parallelism**"
- an overview of what happens when we read the Book of Psalms *as a book* and discover a message that surpasses the sum of its individual parts
- and finally, brief consideration of Egyptian and Canaanite hymns written to Aten (the Sun Disk) and Baal, and what role these hymns might play in reading Psalms.

We have, then, taken on a challenging final chapter. But I am confident that if you have come with me this far, you can go a bit further.

1. The Book of Psalms

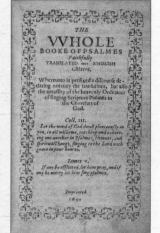

Figure 15.1. The Bay Psalm Book. (Printed in the Massachusetts Bay Colony, 1640. The first book printed in North America.)

The Hebrew title of the book of Psalms is *Sepher Tehillim,* the "Book of Praises," a fitting title for a book that proclaims the LORD is "enthroned on the praises of Israel" (Ps 22:3) and invites all Israel and all the world to join together in praise of the God who saves (147:12, 148:1–14, 149:1–9, 150:6). The book of Psalms consists of five books (most likely to model the Torah) concluded by brief **doxologies**, such as at the end of Book I, "Bless the LORD, the God of Israel, from forever to forever! Amen and Amen!" (41:13). The first two psalms function as a prologue to the book, introducing key themes that will wind their way throughout the **Psalter**: Psalm 1 contains blessings for those who walk on the path of the righteous versus the failure and loss of the wicked, and Psalm 2, the victory of the LORD and his anointed one (the king) over every enemy that dares to stand against them. These themes—the righteous and the wicked, blessing and loss, the LORD's king and his enemies, victory and defeat—run through the book of Psalms like a river. They are sometimes deep and slow, but, at other times, like mountain rapids speeding over the top of all obstacles, and at other times, a waterfall in which all assured results are up in the air and uncertain. The final five poems, in a similar way, lead the reader/singer out of the book on a trajectory of continued praise to a God determined to set or reset the world to the way it ought to be (Pss 145–150). The last of these psalms is a massive summons to praise the LORD with every instrument and every ounce of energy we may have.

2. Forms or Types of Psalms

Reading Psalms can be challenging because of the length of the book and because, after a short time of reading, the psalms begin to sound alike, as if we have already read the same psalm before—a dozen times. Most helpful to this sense of repetition is the recognition of forms or types of psalms that follow specific patterns. In other words, our sense of repetition is well-founded; the poets use and reuse the same templates over and over again, but as artists who reuse forms in imaginative, creative ways. For example, the basic pattern for a hymn of praise consists of the following:

THE HYMN OF PRAISE	
Pattern	*Example: Psalm 117*
A summons to praise (that identifies who should praise)	¹Praise the LORD, all you nations! Worship him, all you peoples!
Reasons to praise (articulate why those summoned should offer praise)	²Because God's faithful love toward us is strong, the LORD's faithfulness lasts forever!
Repetition of the summons to praise	Praise the LORD!

Table 15.1. The Hymn of Praise

The same pattern (with variation) recurs frequently in the Book of Psalms, especially in Books IV and V (see Pss 113, 135, 146–150).

Another common type of psalm is the thanksgiving song—a psalm sung when the LORD has answered a prayer and changed the **psalmist**'s life or the nation's life. This song likely originated as part of a thanksgiving sacrifice:

THE SONG OF THANKSGIVING	
Pattern	*Example: Psalm 30*
An immediate, explosive expression of thanks	¹I exalt you, LORD, because you pulled me up; you didn't let my enemies celebrate over me. ² LORD, my God, I cried to you for help, and you healed me. ³ LORD, you brought me up from the grave, brought me back to life from among those going down to the pit.
An invitation to others to join the song—to give thanks with the psalmist	⁴You who are faithful to the LORD, sing praises to him; give thanks to his name! ⁵His anger lasts for only a second, but his favor lasts a lifetime.

THE SONG OF THANKSGIVING	

Retelling the story of what happened, especially what God did to save (or help) the speaker	⁶When I was comfortable, I said,
	  "I will never stumble."
	⁷Because it pleased you, LORD,
	  you made me a strong mountain.
	But then you hid your presence.
	  I was terrified.
	⁸I cried out to you, LORD.
	  I begged my LORD for mercy:
	⁹"What is to be gained by my spilled blood,
	  by my going down into the pit?
	Does dust thank you?
	  Does it proclaim your faithfulness?
	¹⁰LORD, listen and have mercy on me!
	  LORD, be my helper!"
	¹¹You changed my mourning into dancing.
	  You took off my funeral clothes
	    and dressed me up in joy

Other expressions of thanks throughout the psalm	*See vv. 5, 11*
Consequence: Now I will/we will . . .	¹²so that my whole being might sing praises to you and never stop. LORD, my God, I will give thanks to you forever.

Table 15.2. The Song of Thanksgiving

As with a hymn of praise, the basic elements of a thanksgiving song may appear in a different order as the poet uses and reuses the basic building blocks in new, imaginative ways. For other examples of thanksgiving songs see Psalms 91, 107, 124, 136, and 138.

The most popular form in the Book of Psalms is the lament—an odd, but nonetheless true fact about what we consider to be the Book of Praises, a form that appears sixty times in the 150 chapters. The lament is a prayer of need, an objection to what God is doing or not doing, sometimes a confession of wrongdoing (but not often), and almost always a passionate appeal to God for help:

THE PSALM OF LAMENT	
Pattern	*Example: Psalm 13*
Address to the LORD God	¹How long will you forget me, LORD? Forever?
Description of trouble or need — Self or personal trouble — What others are doing to me — What God is or is not doing	How long will you hide your face from me? ²How long will I be left to my own wits, agony filling my heart? Daily? How long will my enemy keep defeating me?

Request for the LORD to act in specific ways (not just to help); addresses each aspect of the trouble or need (above)	³Look at me! Answer me, LORD my God! Restore sight to my eyes!

Attempts to motivate the LORD into action	Otherwise, I'll sleep the sleep of death,
	    ⁴and my enemy will say, "I won!"
	    My foes will rejoice over my downfall.
	⁵But I have trusted in your faithful love.

Statement of confidence or praise of the LORD	My heart will rejoice in your salvation. ⁶Yes, I will sing to the LORD because he has been good to me.

Table 15.3. The Psalm of Lament (Sample)

Again, these basic building blocks will appear in various orders—and yet, each element is almost always present in a lament. If an element is missing, its absence is likely an important key to understanding the lament. For example, Psalm 88 lacks the final element of confidence or praise; it also lacks almost any sign of hope in God. This absence suggests a psalmist who is desperate—in great need—a poet without the confidence that the LORD will act on his or her behalf and only enough faith to remember whom to pray to for help.

Because of the large number of laments in Psalms (see Table 15.4), it is appropriate to study a second example of the form: Psalm 38. We begin with my own translation of the text, followed by a blank chart to help you identify the various elements of a lament psalm:[2]

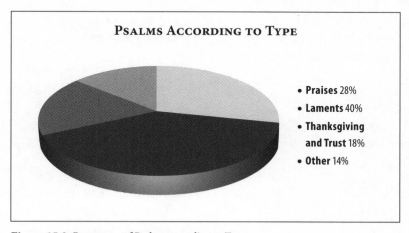

Figure 15.2. Percentage of Psalms according to Type

---

[2] Adapted from Glenn Pemberton, "Psalm 38," in *Timeless: Ancient Psalms for the Church Today, Vol. 1, In the Day of Distress,* ed., Mark Shipp (Abilene, TX: ACU Press, 2011), 273–275.

Psalm 38

A Song for David, for the memorial offering.

[1] O Lord,

not in your anger—rebuke me;

not in your wrath—correct me.

[2] Ah,[3]

your arrows have pierced me;

your hand has come down hard on me.

[3] My flesh has no health

because of your indignation;

my bones have no wholeness

because of my sin.

[4] Ah,

my iniquities have piled up over my head,

a burden too heavy for me.

[5] My wounds fester and stink

because of my follies.

[6] I am bent, stooped so low;

all day long—darkness—I walk.[4]

[7] Ah,

my loins are filled with burning pain;

my flesh has no health.

[8] I am numb, completely crushed;

I cry from the groaning within my heart.

[9] O Master,

all my desire is known to you;

my sighing is not hidden from you.

[10] My heart stutters;

my strength abandons me;

my sight even fails me.

[11] My friends and my companions

stand away from my affliction;

those close to me stand far away.

[12] Those seeking my life lay their traps,

those wanting to hurt me discuss destruction;

they plan deception all day long.

[13] But I am like the deaf—who cannot hear,

like the mute—who cannot speak.

[14] Indeed, I am like a person

who cannot hear;

and who has no response in my mouth.

[15] Ah,

It is for you, O Lord, I wait;

It is you who will answer, O Master, my God.

[16] Ah,

I said, "Only do not let them rejoice over me,

or when my feet stumble they will boast

against me."

[17] Ah,

I go on limping and limping,

my pain always the next step before me.

[18] Ah,

I confess my iniquity,

I am troubled by my sin.

[19] I have so many foes without cause;

so many who hate me for no reason.

[20] They repay evil for good;

they are my adversaries[5]

though I pursue what is good.

[21] O Lord, do not abandon me!

O my God, do not be so far from me!

[22] Hurry to my aid,

O Master, my Savior.

---

[3] Literally "for or because" (Heb. *ki*); the term, however, functions as a deep moan or cry throughout the psalm.

[4] Or, "I walk in darkness all day long."

[5] Or, "They accuse me."

Now use Table 15:4 below (you might copy or sketch the columns in your notes) to identify the basic elements used to create a lament psalm, as they are scattered throughout the psalm. (You may use this same form to analyze other psalms for discussion in class). Be sure to include the verse numbers for quick reference in class discussion:

A PSALM OF LAMENT	
Address:	
Complaint: Self:	
Others:	
God:	
Request: Self:	
Others:	
God:	

Motivation:		
Confidence or Praise		

Table 15.4. A Psalm of Lament (Blank)

As you look over your work on Psalm 38, several questions are likely to arise. Be sure to include the following questions with your notes:

1. The psalmist has many complaints about his or her health. Is this language literal (he or she has these physical problems) or it this language metaphorical to describe how bad or difficult life has become? Which do you think it is? Why?
2. Who or what is the primary cause underlying the psalmist's trouble?
3. According to the psalmist, what is the solution to the problem(s)? What needs to happen?

Don't stop here. What other questions do you have from your study of Psalm 38?

3. Hebrew Poetry: The Wonder of Parallelism

A feature of the Psalms and Hebrew poetry that can improve the reading and understanding of these texts is called *parallelism* (perhaps the most boring name we could come up with). So all I can ask, as Stephen King writes in "Rita Hayworth and Shawshank Redemption,"—"If you've followed along this far, you might be willing to come a little further,"[6] so maybe you can make it a few more pages. Parallelism is nothing more than the question of how lines of poetry relate to one another; and, of course, there are several types of parallelism, or ways in which lines may relate to each other. For example, in Psalm 117 (above), the first two lines feature *synonymous parallelism*—where two lines say the same thing with different words. So while "all you nations" and "all you peoples" may draw attention to slightly different ideas, the basic meaning is the same: "everyone." Awareness of this structure may help us understand some difficult texts. For example, Psalm 51:11 reads,

> Please don't throw me out of your presence;
>> please don't take your holy spirit away from me.

This is another case of synonymous parallelism. The idea of "your presence" is roughly the same as "your holy spirit." In other words, this verse does not refer to the Holy Spirit of the New Testament, but simply to the presence of the LORD. See other examples of synonymous parallelism in Psalms 29:3, 33:9, 35:1, and 148:1.

---

[6]Stephen King, "Rita Hayworth and Shawshank Redemption" in *Different Seasons* (New York: Viking Press, 1982), 99.

The Message of the Old Testament

Psalm 136

As you read Psalm 136, two very obvious literary features stand out. First, the repetition of the phrase "God's faithful love lasts forever." This is strong evidence as to how this psalm was most likely performed: one group or person would read the first line of each verse and another group would answer, "God's faithful love lasts forever." In other words, it would be **antiphonal**—a call and response performance. Second, based on the first feature, the theme of Psalm 136 is also very obvious: "God's faithful love lasts forever." After three opening verses that call people to give thanks to the *greatest God* (the meaning of "the God of all gods") and to *the greatest* LORD (the meaning of "Lord of all lords"), the poet sets the psalm's direction: "Give thanks to the only one who makes great wonders" (136:4a). The remainder of the psalm works out or identifies these great wonders that deserve our gratitude:

- Creation (136:5–9)
- Rescue from Egypt (136:10–15)
- Guidance through the wilderness and conquest of the Transjordan (136:16–22)
- Rescue from enemies (136:23–24)
- Provision of food (136:25)

Two additional features of the psalm merit special attention. First, note the shift that occurs between verse 22 and verse 23. Prior to verse 23, the writer speaks about Israel in the third person: what God has done for *them*. But beginning in verse 23, the writer changes to first person plural. Now, the poem is about what God has done for *us* by rescuing us from a recent humiliation (136:23–24). Second, the psalm tells a story, beginning with creation, followed by the rescue from slavery in Egypt, and then the conquest of the Transjordan—a massive sweep of events, all to conclude with a single line that gives thanks for food. As a result, it seems possible, even likely, that many Israelites would recite this psalm as a table prayer—a prayer we say before eating. But it is a table prayer that is remarkable in its recital of God's saving acts in the past and the present—now updated to give thanks for what God does *for us*.

Obviously, lines are not always synonymous; they can work together in other ways. Sometimes the first line will state an idea and the second line will advance the thought in some way: synthetic parallelism (and no, I did not make up these names). Of course, there are many different ways one line might build on the previous line. Sometimes one or more lines will make the prior idea more specific. In the case of Psalm 136, verses 8–9 advance the idea of verse 7 by making "great lights" more specific:

> [7]Give thanks to the one who made the great lights. . . .
> [8]The sun to rule the day. . . .
> [9]The moon and stars to rule the night. . . .

Verses 17–18 return to synonymous parallelism ("great kings" and "powerful kings"), and then use synthetic parallelism in verses 19–20 to make the identity of these kings more specific.

> [17]Give thanks to the one who struck down great kings. . . .
> [18]And killed powerful kings. . . .
> [19]Sihon, the Amorite king. . . .
> [20]Og, King of Bashan. . . .

In other cases of synthetic parallelism, lines may build meaning like stacking bricks, one idea on top of another. For example, in Psalm 117:2, the poet calls all people to praise the LORD (line a) because God's faithful love is strong, and (line b) because the LORD's faithfulness lasts forever. Synthetic parallelism is the most common relationship of lines in Hebrew poetry, present in every psalm we might explore.

Finally, a third way lines might relate to one another is by opposition: *antithetic parallelism*. So, in Psalm 30:7, the poet writes (line a), "LORD, you made me a strong mountain," and (line b), "But then you hid your presence"; or Psalm 71:1 (line a), "I've taken refuge in you, Lord," and (line b), "Don't let me ever be put to shame." Antithesis may also involve more than two lines, as in Psalm 35:12, "They pay me back evil for good, leaving me stricken with grief," followed by verse 13, "But when they were sick, I wore clothes for grieving, and I kept a strict fast."

You may want to explore other types of parallelism that scholars have identified (e.g., introverted or chiastic), but we must stop here for now. Awareness of these three specific types, and sensitivity to other ways in which one line relates to another, will reward anyone who reads the Psalms.

4. Reading the Psalms as a Book

In the early 1970s, Gerald Wilson began the argument that the Book of Psalms is not just a miscellaneous collection of individual psalms and groups of psalms, but is a carefully crafted collection that presents its own message, beyond that of the individual psalms (see "For Further Reading"). Scholars immediately began to put Wilson's hypothesis to the test—and now, the general consensus (with a few holdouts) is that Wilson is right. In essence, the Book of Psalms leads its reader on a journey from lament to praise, so the Book has its own message.[7]

Now we take up an abbreviated tour of the highlights.

We have already seen that the Book of Psalms consists of five sub-books, preceded by an introduction (Pss 1–2) that sets out Psalm's principle themes: the path of the righteous and the wicked— and their fates—and the bad blood between the nations and the LORD's anointed king in Zion. From this point forward, a story emerges by reading the psalms in order, especially noticing the *seams* at the end and beginning of each of five books. In Book I, the LORD's anointed one is under pressure due to enemies (see Pss 3–7). In fact, of the thirty-nine chapters in Book I (excluding chapters 1 and

---

[7]This section is adapted from Glenn Pemberton, *Learning to Lament: Psalms for Learning to Trust Again* (Abilene, TX: Abilene Christian University Press, 2014), 126–129.

The Message of the Old Testament

Psalm 78

Like Psalm 136 (see above), Psalm 78 retells the broad sweep of Israel's story from the Exodus and their travel through the wilderness (78:12–16, 23–29, 52–54) and the plagues in Egypt (78:43–51), to conquest (78:55) and rescue after the loss of the ark of the covenant to the Philistines (78:65-66), and then to the selection of a king from Judah (78:67–72). Unlike Psalm 136, however, Psalm 78 recalls the trouble that plagued Israel throughout her history: forgetfulness. The tribe of Ephraim forgot what God had done in the Exodus (78:11–16). Israel forgot about Moses striking the rock so that water gushed out (78:20). All too often, the people would "remember" God was their "rock"—but not sincerely; they only pretended to remember (78:35). And as difficult as it seems, the LORD's people didn't remember what God did in Egypt (78:42). So while the LORD worked among and for his chosen people, they couldn't or wouldn't remember all that the LORD did for them.

The result of forgetfulness is a lack of trust or faith. When the warriors of Ephraim forget all that God did in Egypt, they become cowards in battle and refuse to keep the LORD's covenant (78:9–11). Because Israel sees miracle after miracle but does not keep in mind the LORD's power, they test God over and over again, rebelling and provoking God to anger (78:40–42). The natural result of forgetting what God has done in the past is the failure to remember what God can do in the present. Consequently, Israel does not put their trust in the God who sent the plagues, delivered them from Egypt, took them into the promised land, and put the Philistines to rout. The lack of faith or trust comes from the loss of memory.

This archetype or model of the relationship between memory and trust is the reason Psalm 78 opens with an appeal to tell and retell the "wondrous works God has done" to new generations (78:4). This appeal is a commandment (78:5; cf., Deut 6:4–8), but God does not give commandments just for the sake of making people do something. The reason each generation must tell the stories to the next generation is so that they will have reason to put their hope and trust in God, and not be like their ancestors who forgot and failed to trust (78:5–8). How else will they come to have faith in the LORD?

Psalm 78 reminds us of another aspect of the LORD's character: a lover's passion that evokes the LORD's anger when his people will not remember and trust him. The LORD's steadfast love lasts forever (Ps 136), and a heart that loves forever is impassioned when his people turn away from him to trust others (or themselves). As a result, Israel's failure to remember, which leads to a lack of faith, also leads to a strong reaction from the LORD, who punishes Israel (78:30–33,58–64) until they come to their senses (78:34) or until the LORD cannot bear to see them suffer anymore (78:37–39,65–66).

The formula is all too simple: God acts on behalf of his people, God's people are rescued from slavery (whatever type of slavery it may be), and, in time, they forget who saved them. That forgetfulness causes them to have no basis on which to believe or trust in the LORD in the present, so they trust themselves or another god, and the LORD cannot bear the rejection. This is the other side of Psalm 136, the other side of a faithful love that lasts forever.

2) eighteen are laments. Book I ends with a psalm of trust (Ps 41) and words that express confidence in the LORD, despite all of the threats and troubles that have materialized against God's king:

> By this I know that you are pleased with me;
>> because my enemy has not triumphed over me.
> But you have upheld me because of my integrity,
>> and set me in your presence forever. (Ps 41:11–12 NRSV)

Book II begins with lament for some separation or exile from the presence of God (Ps 42–43); and lament continues in Book II even more than Book I, with nineteen laments of the thirty-one total chapters. The final psalm of Book II prays specifically for the king, that he reign with God's justice for the poor and needy (72:1–4,12–14), and that he live long as a blessing to God's people (72:5–6,15–17) with enemies bowing before him (72:8–11). Book III not only continues with lament (nine of seventeen psalms), but concludes with a psalm that verifies what we feared: the enemies have finally defeated God's king and the nation has fallen to Babylon (Ps 89). The conflict with the nations that began in Psalm 2 has come to a surprising climax. Despite God's promises to the Davidic dynasty (89:19–37), it has fallen and the nation has been crushed (89:38–45).

Book IV begins with a lament for the brevity of life—or what might be regarded as a funeral song for the death of the nation (Ps 90). But from this point forward, the Book of Psalms turns back toward the LORD with praise—not for a human king or kingdom, but for the LORD's reign over his people. The death of the nation reveals the truth, lost through many years and battles to keep the nation alive: the LORD reigns—always has and always will. Psalms 93–99 declare this news with force (all citations from the NRSV):

> The LORD is king, he is robed with majesty (93:1a)

> For the LORD is a great God,
>> and a great King above all gods. (95:3)

> Say among the nations, "The LORD is king!
>> The world is firmly established; it shall never be moved.
>> He will judge the peoples with equity." (96:10)

> The LORD is King! Let the earth rejoice;
>> let the many coastlands be glad! (97:1)

> With trumpets and the sound of the horn
>> make a joyful noise before the King, the LORD (98:6)

> The LORD is king; let the peoples tremble!
>> He sits enthroned upon the cherubim; let the earth quake! (99:1)

> Mighty King, lover of justice,
>> you have established equity;
> you have executed justice
>> and righteousness in Jacob. (99:4)

The recognition of the LORD's reign, with its commitment to judgment and justice (e.g., 90:10–13), changes everything for Israel and the world, even if Israel remains subject to Babylon, Persia, Greece, or Rome. Despite appearances, the LORD reigns.

At the end of Book IV, the psalmist confesses Israel's sins, and prays: "Save us, O LORD our God, *and gather us from among the nations*" (Ps 106:47, emphasis mine). In response, the first psalm of Book V urges those set free by the LORD to give thanks (107:1–3). Because of the recognition of Israel's true King and the LORD's intervention to free the captives, Books IV and V lead the reader back to enormous, thundering praise: eleven praises of seventeen psalms in Book IV, twenty praises of forty-four psalms in Book V (thirty-one total praise songs in Books IV and V, while Books I through III only have a total of ten). This enormous swing from lament (Books I–III) to praise (Books IV–V) in the Book of Psalms matches the movement within laments that takes their readers from complaint and request to renewed praise and confidence in the LORD.

This storyline within the Book of Psalms suggests that the book is far more than just a collection of randomly placed psalms. Instead, the editors tell the same story that we have been following throughout this book, from the introduction of sin and Israel's failure to be what God called them to be, to the LORD's refusal to give up on Israel or the world. The LORD still reigns, now and forever, and refuses to give up hope that someday our relationship will be mended.

The Message of the Old Testament

Psalms 104–105

Psalms 104 and 105 are a *psalm pair*—two psalms from one poet, or two psalms the editors deliberately placed side by side.

The opening lines praise the LORD in terms of a great King who emerges in the morning clothed with light (as the sun) and rides on the clouds across the sky, with the wind carrying messages and "fire and flame" (lightning), standing nearby, ready to serve (104:1–4). The next five verses establish the theme: God's mighty work in creation, as God established the earth on strong foundations and brought order to the chaotic waters (104:5–9). But there is more than praise for events in the distant past. Phrases and lines leap from the page: the LORD makes "springs gush forth in the valleys" (104:10 NRSV); the LORD waters the mountains (104:13) and makes grass grow for cattle (104:14a); and plants grow for people to turn into food, wine, oil, and bread (104:14b–15). The LORD "makes darkness," (104:20) so young lions come out looking for the food God gives them (104:21). In fact, everything on earth and in the seas "look to you to give them their food in due time" (104:27).

We may struggle with the claims of Psalm 104. After all, we have science on our side—we can explain how everything works that Psalm 104 claims for the LORD. A spring may be the result of **karst topography** or a confined aquifer. It becomes dark because of the earth's rotation. We don't need God to explain anything in works that Psalm 104—as did those in ancient Israel. So, maybe if this psalmist lived today, he or she might change the psalm, maybe even take it all back. Or not. The LORD did not wind up the earth, pull the string to set it spinning, or light the fuse on the *Big Bang*, and walk away. No—the one responsible for this world continues to support it; and, should the LORD decide to walk away, all creation will collapse. True three thousand years ago and still true today. So the poet hopes the LORD will rejoice in the world—enjoy his ongoing work so that he will stay (104:31). The psalmist vows to worship this God (104:33–34), and wishes those who oppose God's work would be dealt with quickly; they are the one thing that doesn't belong in a world, graciously upheld by God's love (104:35).

Psalm 105 also extends an elaborate call to praise the LORD (105:1–4) and summons for God's people to remember "all his marvelous works" (105:5–7). Specifically, the LORD's people need to *remember* that God *remembers* the covenant made with their ancestors (105:8–10). More specifically, they need to *remember* that the LORD *remembers* the covenant promise to give them the land of Canaan (105:11). There's a lot of *remembering* to do in Psalm 105.

The poet begins the story when the family of Abraham (as well as Isaac and Jacob) was small and an easy target to harass. The LORD would not allow anyone to touch them (105:12–15). The LORD sent Joseph to Egypt ahead of the family so, when famine hit hard, they could safely move to Egypt (105:16–23). The LORD brought a drastic increase in the number of his people, and then turned Pharaoh's heart to fear and hate them (105:24–25). If allowed, Pharaoh would have worked the LORD's people into the dust of Egypt. But the LORD would not allow it, instead sending Moses and plagues so that, by the time they left, Egypt was relieved to see them go, even though they took Egypt's gold and silver with them (105:26–38). Travel through the wilderness was no walk in the park, no food truck to visit every night with water for the next day. But for Israel, the LORD spread a cloud over them during the day, hung a fire in the sky for light at night, and brought quails and rained food from heaven when they asked. The LORD even opened up a rock so that a spring would gush out clean, cool water—like a river in the desert (105:39–41).

Why? Why would God, or any god, be so protective of a small family, think and work for their survival for years ahead of time, make them multiply like—well—rabbits, intervene with fireworks when they are oppressed by Pharaoh, lead them through no-man's land with shade, light, food, water, and . . . ? *Why?* The answer is simple: "Because God remembered his holy promise to Abraham his servant" (105:42). God remembers, and God keeps promises. That's why God gave them the land (105:43–45). When the LORD makes a promise, the LORD keeps the promise—and you (reader of Psalm 105) must *remember* that (105:5).

5. Psalms and Other Ancient Near Eastern Hymns

Egypt: Psalm 104 and the Egyptian "Great Hymn to the Aten" (The Sun Disk)

In Chapter Fourteen, we observed how the Egyptian Instruction of Amenemope stands behind Proverbs 22:17–24:22. So, it should come as no surprise that we find the same phenomena taking place between Egyptian hymns and the Book of Psalms. One of the strongest examples discovered is the connection between the "Great Hymn to the Aten" (The Sun Disk—see Figure 15.3) and Psalm 104. The "Great Hymn to the Aten" comes from a tomb built by Ay for his wife. Ay was a high official during the reign of Akhenaten and advisor to the next Pharaoh,

Figure 15.3. The Aten Disk

the famous Tutankhamun. After the young Pharaoh's death at age eighteen, Ay became Pharaoh (1327–1323 BCE). In Table 15.5 below, you will find selections from the "Great Hymn to the Aten" on the left, with space on the right for you to write all the similarities you can find from Psalm 104.

"Great Hymn to the Aten"[8]	Psalm 104
Beautifully you appear from the horizon of heaven, 　O living Aten who initiates life— For you are risen from the eastern horizon 　and have filled every land with your beauty; For you are fair, great, dazzling 　and high over every land, And your rays enclose the lands 　to the limit of all you have made . . .	
When your movements vanish 　and you set in the western horizon, The land is in darkness, 　in the manner of death . . .	

---

[8]Translation by William Nurnane, *Texts from the Armana Period in Egypt*, SBL Writings from the Ancient World, Series 5 (Atlanta: Scholars Press, 1995): 113–115. I have formatted the lines to fit the available column space.

"Great Hymn to the Aten"	Psalm 104

Every lion is out of its den,
    all creeping things bite.
Darkness gathers, the land is silent.
The one who made them is set in his horizon.
(But) the land grows bright when
    you are risen from the horizon,
Shining in the orb (= *Aten*) in the daytime,
    you push back the darkness
    and give forth your rays . . .	

The whole land, they do their work:
    All flocks are content with their pasturage,
    Trees and grasses flourish,
    Birds are flown from their nests,
        the wings adoring your Ka;
    All small cattle prance upon their legs.
All that fly up and alight,
    they live when you rise for them.
Ships go downstream, and upstream as well . . .	

[You] who gives breath to animate all he makes
    When it descends from the womb to breathe
    on the day it is born—
You open his mouth completely and make what he needs . . .	

How manifold it is, what you have made,
    although mysterious in the face (of humanity),
O sole god, without another beside him!
You create the earth according to your wish, being alone—
    People, all large and small animals,
All things which are on earth, which go on legs,
    which rise up and fly by means of their wings . . .	

"GREAT HYMN TO THE ATEN"	PSALM 104
You have granted an inundation [rain] in heaven, that it might come down for them And make torrents upon the mountains, like the Great Green [the Mediterranean Sea], to soak their fields in their locales . . .	
While your rays nurse every field: When you rise, they live and flourish for you. You make the seasons in order to develop all you make . . .	
Every eye observes you in relation to them, for you are Aten of the daytime above the earth . . .	
When you have risen they live, (but) when you set they die. You are lifetime in your (very) limbs, and one lives by means of you.	

Table 15.5. "Great Hymn to the Aten" and Psalm 104

Hopefully, you will have taken the time in class, or in preparation for class, to work carefully through the text of Psalm 104 (which is much younger than the "Great Hymn to the Aten") and are ready to wrestle with key compositional issues:

- How would you describe the relationship between the two hymns? Has Psalm 104 borrowed from or rewritten the "Great Hymn to the Aten"? Or is the relationship looser, only a matter of common ideas in the air of both cultures (but no direct relationship)?
- If Psalm 104 has rewritten or made use of the "Great Hymn to the Aten," what are the key ideas that Psalm 104 has challenged or changed from the Egyptian hymn?

Canaan: Psalm 29 and the Ugaritic Hymns to Baal

Our second example of how the Psalms may interact with the songs of other cultures is somewhat different than the example of Psalm 104 and the "Great Hymn to the Aten." Here, it appears that Psalm 29 may have been a hymn to Baal, now edited to be a hymn to the LORD. In support of this hypothesis are features of Psalm 29 that are similar to poetry from **Ugarit** and/or ideas in the psalm that sound like worship of Baal. Tremper Longman III identifies five of these commonalities:

- the repetitive nature of the lines
- the geographical locations are in the north, even beyond northern Israel
- the presence of the "divine beings" (29:1) is similar to the divine assembly of Ugaritic literature

- the final picture, "the LORD sits enthroned over the flood" (29:10), sounds like Baal's defeat of the sea at creation
- the LORD as the power of the storm "evokes a connection with Baal, the Storm god."[9]

Consequently, Longman points out that many scholars either see an intentional link between Psalm 29 and Ugaritic/Canaanite worship of Baal or they regard Psalm 29 to have originally been a hymn to Baal. In fact, the editing may have been little more than substituting the name Yahweh in place of the name Baal. Try it out and see if you think it works. Read the name Baal where "the LORD" appears in the psalm, e.g., "You divine beings! Give to Baal—give to Baal glory and power! Give to Baal the glory due his name! Bow down to Baal in holy splendor!" (29:1–2, modified). Once you read the psalm with Baal's name, consider the following questions:

- Does the substitution work? Does the psalm read well with Baal's name?
- With the substitution in place, do the claims made for Baal match what you learned about the Baal myth in Chapter Seven, page 140?
- Does it seem more likely that the psalmist reworked a prior Baal hymn or merely took claims made for Baal from many different sources to create Psalm 29?
- Finally, what consequence or result comes from what the author/editor of the psalm has done? What do you think the psalm writer was trying to say or accomplish?

Questions of literary dependence or borrowing are difficult to demonstrate three thousand years after the event; for that matter, it is almost impossible to prove anything after so much time has passed. So we look at the evidence and make our best judgment. Most important, whether borrowing or not, Psalm 29 speaks to its time, to people who believe all the claims made for the LORD are supposed to be true for Baal. The writer is daring, brave, and unafraid to challenge the status quo.

Conclusion

If Israel's world was anything like ours, we could confidently say that her psalms did more to shape her faith and her life than anything else. And maybe it's true that the power of music transcends culture and time. One hundred and fifty chapters of psalms, a book filled with love songs (the Song of Songs), and another of overwhelming grief (Lamentations), along with other songs scattered throughout the Hebrew Bible (catch Hannah's solo in 1 Samuel 2, or Deborah's fiery song in Judges 5, just to get started)—all these tend to make me think that Israel's music not only shaped her faith more than anything else, but expressed her faith best.

If true, then life with the Lord takes more than the worrisome lyrics and music of the contemporary praise songs that flood our sanctuaries and auditoriums. Life with the Lord, we have come to know through the pages of the Old Testament, calls for praise, but not just praise. The life of faith is not some dance from one *Praise the Lord!* to another *Hallelujah!*—God help us from

---

[9] Tremper Longman III, *Psalms*, in *Tyndale Old Testament Commentary* (Downers Grove, IL: InterVarsity Press, 2014), 155.

spreading such an image of the Lord who saves. Though it is God who saves, but faith-life is not so simple—never has been, never will be. Our faith-walk requires many different languages, many tones, many songs, and many singers. We need the praise songs, and we need the visceral cries of lament that choke back tears to ask, "How long will it last?" (Ps 89:46), or "My God! My God, why have you left me all alone?" (Ps 22:1). And we need the language of reversal, unexpected joy—one of those *you just had to be there* surprises when the Lord changes everything, including our clothes: "You have changed my mourning into dancing. You took off my funeral clothes and dressed me up in joy" (Ps 30:11). So the singers open our mouths to speak the many different languages vital—crucial—for a life-walk with the Lord. Ah, God—may we be people who see and sing the lyrics of those who live all of life with the God who saves.

To Discuss

1. Just how powerful are music and the combination of lyrics with music? How much does it matter what we listen to or sing? How much do the songs we listen to or sing shape our character?

2. See the discussion questions on Psalm 38 in this chapter. Did your work on the psalm raise additional questions?

3. Use the template for Lament as a guide to study other psalms. Change the list of basic elements in the far left-hand column to match the type of psalm you are reading. Good examples to study are, for Praise or a Hymn, Psalms 148 and 146; for Lament, Psalms 54 and 44; for Thanksgiving, Psalms 116 and 124. What elements are emphasized or omitted in the psalm? Do any verses in the psalm not fit within one of the elements? What do these verses contribute to the psalm? How does the recognition of form help or change your understanding of a psalm?

4. Read Psalm 136 as an antiphonal song. Beware: those responding with the same words over and over will tend to start fading by the middle of the psalm—don't fade away! What do you notice in the process of reading? Does it seem likely to you that Psalm 136 might have originated as a table prayer? If so, what strikes you as significant?

5. Does the short tour of Psalms as a book convince you that it carries a message above that of the individual psalms? What reservations do you have? What additional support do you notice?

6. In what way are Psalm 104 and 105 a psalm pair? How do they bring one another to new life by being together? What are the connections? What would be lost, not just to one but the other, if we didn't read these psalms as a pair?

7. See the discussion questions on Psalm 104 and "Great Hymn to the Aten." What additional questions do you have?

8. See the discussion questions on Psalm 29 and the Canaanite god Baal. Do you think the similarities merit recognition that the psalm was once a hymn to Baal? What additional questions does the study raise for you?

9. Does the same type of borrowing or reworking of ideas we find in Psalm 29 and Psalm 104 occur today? Do Christians adopt non-Christian songs and change their words or meanings? If so, make a list of specific examples.

To Know

1. The significance of the following in the assigned reading:

   Antiphonal   Parallelism (general idea)
   Antithetic Parallelism   Synonymous Parallelism
   Lament   Synthetic Parallelism

2. The number of books into which the Book of Psalms is divided and why.

3. Define each of the three forms of psalms introduced in this chapter and the basic elements of each type: Hymn of Praise, Song of Thanks, and Lament Psalm.

4. The theme of Psalm 136 and how this theme is established.

5. The message of the Book of Psalms (as introduced in the chapter). Briefly explain how this message is developed in Psalms.

6. The relationship between Psalm 104 and the "Great Hymn to the Aten."

7. The reflection of Canaanite beliefs and praise of Baal in Psalm 29.

To Dig Deeper: Research Topics

1. Further research one of the three forms (types) of psalms. What else can you learn about the form in research-level sources? Identify other examples of the form.

2. Select a type of psalm and write a psalm that includes the basic elements of the form/type you have selected. Can you include each of the three types of parallelism studied in this chapter? Write a paragraph that explains your psalm.

3. Dig deeper into the power of song, especially the combination of music and lyrics. What research has been conducted on this topic? What has been found or learned?

4. Study a favorite psalm more rigorously. Identify its form and use a chart similar to that for Lament Psalms to identify the elements of its form. Are any elements missing or especially strong?

5. Dig deeper into the concept of reading the Book of Psalms as book. Begin with sources listed below for further reading.

6. Research the types of songs that exist(ed) among the native population of your country, e.g., American Indians. What do you find? Are there any similarities to Israel's songs? How do they differ?

For Further Reading

Coogan, Michael D., ed. *A Reader of Ancient Near Eastern Texts: Sources for the Study of the Old Testament*. New York: Oxford University Press, 2013.

deClaissé-Walford, Nancy L., ed. *Reading From the Beginning: The Shaping of the Hebrew Psalter*. Macon: Mercer University Press, 1997.

Longman III, Tremper. *Psalms: An Introduction and Commentary*. Tyndale Old Testament Commentaries 15–16. Downers Grove: InterVarsity Press Academic, 2014.

McCann Jr., J. Clinton, ed. *The Shape and Shaping of the Psalter*. JSOTSup 159. Sheffield: JSOT Press, 1993.

Pemberton, Glenn. *After Lament: Psalms for Learning to Trust Again*. Abilene: Abilene Christian University Press, 2014.

———. *Hurting with God: Learning to Lament with the Psalms*. Abilene: Abilene Christian University Press, 2012.

The Books of the **Hebrew Scriptures** and the Old Testament

By 100 CE, the Jews living in Palestine had a generally recognized canon of books they regarded as Holy Scripture, authoritative for instruction in living by faith in the LORD and for ordering the life of the faith community. How they came to accept these books and not others is a question with little positive evidence, i.e., what happened, as opposed to what did not happen. So, we begin with what did not happen: (1) there was no vote by the faith community or their leaders as to which books to accept, (2) there was no prophet who spoke for the LORD and announced which books made the list, and (3) there was no clearly-identifiable moment in time before which there was no canon and after which a canon existed. The creation of the Jewish Bible was, instead, a long process.

So what did happen? How did a book become part of Jewish Scripture, and, in time, become the first half (or first three-quarters) of the Christian Bible? The answer may be too simple: survival and use. The books or scrolls that became part of Jewish Scripture were the scrolls that synagogues prized and kept in a time when a copy of a text was a sizeable investment (copied by hand, no quick copies or scanning) and storage space was limited (no storage space in "the cloud"). In time, a complete Hebrew Bible would take up to seventeen scrolls at an average cost of five months' worth of wages per scroll for a middle-class worker. For books to make it into this all-star status, the faith community must have heard something different in them: e.g., they spoke with authority about the life of faith or the community

KEY TERMS

Apocrypha: books and additions to books that are part of the Catholic Bible, but excluded from Jewish and Protestant Bibles

Canon: an official list of books (for any subject, e.g., the canon of major British authors); for the Bible, the canon is the list of books constituting the Bible

Deuterocanonical: the term Catholics use to refer to the extra books and additions to books they accept as canonical; these texts are excluded by Jews and Protestants

Qumran: the location of a Jewish community that flourished from c.a. 200 BCE–70 CE and left behind many of the Dead Sea Scrolls

Septuagint: Greek translation(s) of the Old Testament made for Jews living in the Greek-speaking world, beginning in ca. 200 BCE

TANAK: an acronym for a Jewish Bible made from the first letter of its three major sections: *Torah, Nebi'im,* and *Ketubim*

recognized the voice of God in these texts. Consequently, only the texts that survived the test of time and the test of usefulness for guiding the community in its faith-walk moved toward inclusion in the Hebrew Scriptures.

The Hebrew or Jewish Bible consists of three divisions (see Figure AI.1), most likely developing and finding acceptance in the order that they now stand in the Bible: 1st *Torah* (Instruction or Law), 2nd *Nebi'im* (Prophets), and 3rd *Ketubim* (Writings, a catch-all category). By the first century CE, the *Torah* and *Nebi'im* are clearly recognized as Scripture. Jesus and others frequently refer to "the Law and the Prophets" as Scripture (Matt 7:12, 22:40; Luke 16:16, Acts 13:15, Rom 3:21), yet only once does Jesus refer to "The law of Moses, the Prophets and the Psalms" (Luke 24:44, "Psalms" likely denotes the *Ketubim* or Writings). Nonetheless, it is safe to say that in the first century CE, most Jews had some sense of a canon with three parts or divisions. Most likely, the five books of the *Torah* were well established, and had been for some time. However, precisely which books or which editions of certain books (e.g., different editions of Samuel and Jeremiah existed at **Qumran**) belonged to the *Nebi'im* and *Ketubim* remained unsettled, and would remain so for some time.

Any motivation that may have existed for settling these issues in the first century would have come from two sources. First, the destruction of the temple in 70 CE made Judaism a religion founded on the LORD's book and no longer based on the LORD's place—the Jerusalem temple. As a result, it was important to know what constituted authority for the faith (their canon) as more and more Jews migrated throughout the world. Second, while Christianity began within Judaism, as time went by, the Christians began making books and regarding their books to be part of the *Ketubim*, the Writings of the Jewish canon. Whether or not, or even how much, this threat led Judaism to define what did and did not belong in their canon, it certainly helped motivate Jews to divorce the Christian movement and reject its literature as heresy—a sect that no longer belonged within Judaism.

The Jewish Scriptures consists of twenty-four books in three divisions (counting the twelve shorter prophetic books as one book). The first letter of each division put together spells the acronym **TANAK**:

Torah (Teaching or Law)	Nebi'im (Prophets)	Ketubim (Writings)
• Genesis	**Former Prophets**	• Psalms
• Exodus	• Joshua	• Proverbs
• Leviticus	• Judges	• Job
• Numbers	• 1–2 Samuel	• Song of Songs
• Deuteronomy	• 1–2 Kings	• Ruth
		• Lamentations
	Later Prophets	• Ecclesiastes
	• Isaiah	• Esther
	• Jeremiah	• Daniel
	• Ezekiel	• Ezra–Nehemiah
	• Book of the Twelve	• 1–2 Chronicles

Figure AI.1. The Canon of the Jewish Scriptures

Some Jews, whose primary language was Greek instead of Hebrew or Aramaic, had a more inclusive list of books and additions to existing books in the **Septuagint**. This canon of Scripture was rejected by Jewish leaders in Palestine, but kept by early Christian churches as they separated from Judaism. The Christian church adopted different categories (groups or divisions of material) and also rearranged the order of the books to suit their own purposes (see Figure AI.2). Today, the most accessible representative of this canon is the Catholic Old Testament.

The Catholic Old Testament has a different order from the Jewish Bible and includes more material—additional books (underlined) and additions to existing books (also underlined):

Pentateuch
- Genesis
- Exodus
- Leviticus
- Numbers
- Deuteronomy

Historical Books
- Joshua
- Judges
- Ruth
- 1–2 Samuel
- 1–2 Kings
- 1–2 Chronicles
- Ezra–Nehemiah
- Tobit
- Judith
- Esther (and additions)
- 1 Maccabees
- 2 Maccabees

Books of Poetry
- Job
- Psalms
- Proverbs
- Ecclesiastes
- Song of Songs
- Wisdom of Solomon
- Sirach

Prophets
Major
- Isaiah
- Jeremiah
- Lamentations
- Baruch (with the Letter of Jeremiah)
- Ezekiel

Prophets
Minor
- Daniel (with the Prayer of Azariah, Song of the Three Jews, Susanna, and Bel and the Dragon)
- Hosea
- Joel
- Amos
- Obadiah
- Jonah
- Micah
- Nahum
- Habakkuk
- Zephaniah
- Haggai
- Zechariah
- Malachi

Figure AI.2. The Catholic Old Testament

The Protestant move away from the canon of the Catholic Church did not occur until some time later. One claim of the Protestant Reformers was that all translations of the Old Testament should come from the original languages (i.e., Hebrew and Aramaic). Consequently, as Martin Luther translated the Old Testament from its original Hebrew and Aramaic, he set the "extra books" and "additions to books" that were in Greek into a separate section and entitled it "secret" or **Apocrypha**—an opening bid to remove these books and texts from the Old Testament. (Of note, recent scholarship suggests at least some of these Greek texts may have been originally composed in Hebrew.) More troublesome, the reformers saw that these extra books and additions gave support to the doctrine of purgatory, masses for the dead, and other practices they disliked and believed to be at odds with the rest of the Bible. So, the reformers went back to the Jewish canon, while keeping the arrangement of books in the categories that they already knew from their Catholic Bibles, continuing to include the Apocrypha as a separate section in their Bibles, at least for a while. Meanwhile, in response to the moves made by the Protestant Reformers, the Catholic Church declared the Apocrypha to be part of their Christian canon at the Council of Trent (April 8, 1546). The first known printing of the King James Version that officially rejected the Apocrypha appeared in 1640 (see Figure AI.3).

The Protestant Old Testament has the same content as Jewish Bibles, but uses the categories and arrangement of the Catholic Bible. The Protestants count the Book of the Twelve as twelve different books, place Daniel and Lamentations with the Prophets, and move Ruth and Esther into the Historical Books.

Pentateuch
- Genesis
- Exodus
- Leviticus
- Numbers
- Deuteronomy

Historical Books
- Joshua
- Judges
- Ruth
- 1–2 Samuel
- 1–2 Kings
- 1–2 Chronicles
- Ezra-Nehemiah
- Esther

Poetry/Wisdom
- Job
- Psalms
- Proverbs
- Ecclesiastes
- Song of Songs

Prophets
Major (4)
- Isaiah
- Jeremiah
- Lamentations
- Ezekiel

Minor (13)
- Daniel
- Hosea
- Joel
- Amos
- Obadiah
- Jonah
- Micah
- Nahum
- Habakkuk
- Zephaniah
- Haggai
- Zechariah
- Malachi

Figure AI.3. The Protestant Old Testament

To be sure, there are more than just Jewish, Catholic, and Protestant canons of the Old Testament. Various Orthodox traditions use other variations of the canon of the Old Testament—a topic worthy of further study, but far beyond the scope of this introduction.

At the end of our review we are left with many questions, two with special urgency. First, does the canon of the Old Testament matter; or, does it really matter which canon of the Old Testament a person accepts? The reformers certainly thought it mattered, at least for them. But what about us? Ultimately, the reader will have to make this decision, hopefully after much study and prayer. For a place to start, a reader might compare the end of a Jewish Bible (2 Chron 36:22–23) to the end of a Protestant and Catholic Old Testament (Mal 4:4–6) and take careful note of the theme of each: How do these Bibles or Old Testaments conclude? What are they looking for or hoping for? What is the significance of their different conclusions? Second, how is a person to decide which canon to accept? And third, can a person decide which books he or she believes belong, or is the canon closed for all time and not open for review and change? At this point, our choice turns into a matter of faith and a matter of which faith community we belong to (though, I am unaware of any church that considers the canon to be open for debate). To be a member of the Catholic church means to accept the canon of the Catholic church, to be a Jew means to accept the Tanak, and to be a Protestant means to accept the Protestant Old Testament.

For Further Reading

Brettler, Mark Zvi. *How to Read the Bible.* Philadelphia: Jewish Publication Society, 2005. See chapter twenty-seven, "The Creation of the Bible," 273–278.

Sanders, James. "Canon. Hebrew Bible." Pages 837–852 in volume 1 of *The Anchor Bible Dictionary.* Edited by David Noel Freedman. New York: Doubleday, 1992.

Translation and **Translations** of the Old Testament

W e begin with a question: Does it really matter which English translation of the Old Testament I use? And we can respond with an absolute and undeniable answer: no and yes. On the one hand, every English Bible in print today uses the same Hebrew manuscript as its foundation or primary source: the Leningrad Codex, the oldest complete Hebrew Bible (1109 CE). On the other hand, yes, it matters—perhaps the least when the difference is obvious and the most when the difference is slight and may escape our notice. For example, study the examples on the next page, all translations of Psalm 2, from three of the most popular English translations in use today. In addition to the many insignificant differences that do not change the meaning of the psalm, can you spot the differences that change the psalm's meaning? Take at least ten minutes, without giving up, then go to the next page for your first clue.

Figure AII.1. Thirteenth Century Hebrew Manuscript. This manuscript, open to Psalms 6:7–9:19, was used as a schoolbook in the first half of the thirteenth century. At least three Christians annotated the Hebrew text extensively in Latin and French.

KEY TERMS

Codex: a bound volume or book with hand-written pages on papyrus or vellum (animal skin)

Denomination: a united group of Protestant churches that believe in similar doctrines (e.g., Baptists and Methodists are each a denomination)

Evangelicals: Protestants who share a high regard for Scripture and stress that the Bible contains no errors of any type or that the Bible is trustworthy in matters of faith (among other characteristics)

Paraphrase: a translation that summarizes the meaning or ideas of the biblical text, usually prepared by one person

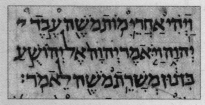

Figure AII.2. The Aleppo Codex. The beginning of Joshua in the Aleppo Codex, a Hebrew manuscript slightly older than the Leningrad Codex, but incomplete. This manuscript has a fascinating history (one that a student might want to explore).

Translation #1

Why do the nations conspire
and the peoples plot in vain?
[2] The kings of the earth take their stand
and the rulers gather together
against the LORD
and against his Anointed One.
[3] "Let us break their chains," they say,
"and throw off their fetters."

[4] The One enthroned in heaven laughs;
the LORD scoffs at them.
[5] He rebukes them in his anger
and terrifies them in his wrath, saying,
[6] "I have installed my King
on Zion, my holy hill."

[7] I will proclaim the decree of the LORD:

He said to me, "You are my Son;
today I have become your Father.
[8] Ask me,
and I will make the nations your inheritance,
the ends of the earth your possession.
[9] You will break them with an iron scepter;
you will dash them to pieces like pottery."

[10] Therefore, you kings, be wise;
be warned, you rulers of the earth.
[11] Serve the LORD with fear
and rejoice with trembling.
[12] Kiss the Son, lest he be angry
and you be destroyed in your way,
for his wrath can flare up in a moment.
Blessed are all who take refuge in him.

Translation #2

Why do nations assemble,
and peoples plot vain things;
[2] kings of the earth take their stand,
and regents intrigue together
against the LORD and against His anointed?
[3] "Let us break the cords of their yoke,
shake off their ropes from us!"

[4] He who is enthroned in heaven laughs;
the LORD mocks at them.
[5] Then He speaks to them in anger,
terrifying them in His rage,
[6] "But I have installed My king
on Zion, My holy mountain!"
[7] Let me tell of the decree:

the LORD said to me,
"You are My son,
I have fathered you this day.
[8] Ask it of Me,
and I will make the nations your domain;
your estate, the limits of the earth.
[9] You can smash them with an iron mace,
shatter them like potter's ware."

[10] So now, O kings, be prudent;
accept discipline, you rulers of the earth!
[11] Serve the LORD in awe;
tremble with fright,
[12] pay homage in good faith,
lest He be angered, and your way be doomed
in the mere flash of His anger.
Happy are all who take refuge in Him.

Translation #3

Why do the nations conspire,
and the peoples plot in vain?
[2] The kings of the earth set themselves,
and the rulers take counsel together,
against the LORD and his anointed, saying,
[3] "Let us burst their bonds asunder,
and cast their cords from us."

[4] He who sits in the heavens laughs;
the LORD has them in derision.
[5] Then he will speak to them in his wrath,
and terrify them in his fury, saying,
[6] "I have set my king on Zion, my holy hill."

[7] I will tell of the decree of the LORD:

He said to me, "You are my son;
today I have begotten you.
[8] Ask of me, and I will make the nations
your heritage,
and the ends of the earth your possession.
[9] You shall break them with a rod of iron,
and dash them in pieces like a potter's
vessel."

[10] Now therefore, O kings, be wise;
be warned, O rulers of the earth.
[11] Serve the LORD with fear,
with trembling [12] kiss his feet,
or he will be angry, and you will perish in
the way,
for his wrath is quickly kindled.

Happy are all who take refuge in him.

Figure AII.3. Comparison of Three Translations of Psalm 2

Clue 1: In the Hebrew text, there are no capital letters. Consequently, all decisions regarding special capitalization in an English translation are made by the translators.

Clue 2: So that you do not accidentally see this clue when you read Clue 1, the second clue is provided after this useless sentence. Now, here is the clue: I teach my students to turn in papers with standard capitalization of all pronouns (e.g., he, you, my, his); normally only proper nouns should be capitalized. Some translations, however, use capitalization of pronouns to help the reader recognize when a pronoun refers to God (or Jesus and the Holy Spirit). So look at the pronouns; what do you see?

Answer: Can you see the incredibly small detail that changes the meaning of the psalm? Two more wasted lines so those reading Clue 2 will not accidentally find the answer until they are ready. The difference is in the capitalization of the pronouns in verses 2, 5, 6, 7, 8, and 12, and the capitalization of words not normally capitalized in verses 2, 4, 6, 7, and 12. In Translation 1, specific words are capitalized: the term "Anointed One" (2:2), "One" (2:4), "King" (2:6), "Son" and "Father" (2:7), and "Son" (2:12). Through these capitalized words and pronouns, the translators convey the message they see in Psalm 2. The "Anointed One" (2:2) is Jesus or the Christ, whom the father—the "One" in heaven (2:4)—has installed as "my King" (2:6). This "King" is "my Son" and God is "your Father" (2:7). So, the kings of the earth had best be wise and kiss "the Son" (2:12). Translation 1 is a Christian reading of Psalm 2 from an early edition of the New International Version (NIV), a translation produced by Protestant scholars.

Translation 2 takes the psalm in a different direction. Here, the terms capitalized in the first translation are not capitalized: anointed, king, son, father. Instead, many pronouns are capitalized against normal rules: "His" (2:2); "He" (2:5); "His" (2:5); "My" (2:6); "My" (2:7); "Me" (2:8); and "He," "His," and "Him" (2:12). The message of the psalm, consequently, is the opposite of the first translation. The son who is made or anointed to be king is not divine (not capitalized). Instead, the one who anoints the king, speaks to the king, and warns the nations is divine—God (recognized as such with capital letters). Translation 2 comes from the TANAK, a translation of the New Jewish Publication Society (NJPS 1985), the work of Jewish scholars.

Translation 3 avoids the capitalization of both the pronouns and terms that are not typically capitalized, choosing instead to follow common English conventions as well as the lack of capitals in the Hebrew text. The translation sweeping up to this high middle ground is the New Revised Standard Version (NRSV 1989), the work of an ongoing committee of mostly Protestant and Catholic scholars, with the inclusion of an Eastern Orthodox member and a Jewish member.

Our simple exercise demonstrates one factor that inevitably affects translation of the Bible: theological commitment—what a scholar believes and the faith tradition to which he or she belongs. As hard as we may try, we cannot jump outside our own skin to a purely objective point of view when we translate. So, one factor to consider in selecting a Bible translation is the faith commitment of those doing the work. If you are unaware of who translated the text, normally the "Introduction" or "Preface for the Reader" will provide an answer. We may also identify a few of the most obvious cases below:

- From a single denomination: the Holman Christian Standard Bible (HCSB, primarily Southern Baptist scholars, 2003)
- From evangelicals: the New American Standard Bible (NASB 1971, update in 1995)
- From one or two schools: the New Living Translation (NLT, Trinity Evangelical Divinity School and Asbury Seminary, 2007)
- From mostly Catholic scholars: the New American Bible (NAB, 1986)
- From a single translator: the Living Bible (LB, Kenneth Taylor, 1971), and *The Message* (MSG, Eugene Petersen, 2001)

The final example is obviously the most prone to being influenced by the two independent translator's beliefs since these works come from a single person and lack review by other scholars.

A second factor that makes a difference in translation is the translator's method or theory. Most translators understand and accept the claim, "To translate is to lie." It's true. Languages are not alike and no translation will ever be able to say exactly the same thing with the same breadth of meaning, and with the same nuance as the original language. It's impossible. Nor does it seem possible for theorists to agree on terminology to describe the different types of translations. So we must decide how we will translate and define our own terminology. Will we attempt to provide a literal, word-for-word translation ("Formal Equivalence") that keeps as much of the original word order, grammar, and figures of speech as we possibly can without our English translation becoming impossible to understand? In this case, we keep the word-for-word phrases "son of man" (Ezek 3:1–3 NASV and most other English translations) and "cover his feet" (1 Sam 24:3 KJV). Or do we go to the other extreme ("Free Translation") and translate the idea of the Hebrew using an idea that best communicates in our culture? So we might translate 1 Samuel 24:3, which KJV has as "Saul went in to cover his feet," as "Saul went in to go to the toilet" (NIV Reader's edition), or "Saul went in to the cave to use the restroom" (CEB). Both extremes have obvious problems. The extreme literal nature of "Formal Equivalence" may leave the reader without a clue as to what Saul is doing in the cave. And an extreme "Free Translation" may lead the reader to think that Saul stopped at a public toilet in the wilderness. In the middle, between the extremes is a "Dynamic Equivalent" which tries to avoid the worst of each extreme. Although, trying to walk the line takes the risk of falling either direction. So in a "Dynamic Equivalent," Ezekiel 3:1–3 might be translated as "human" (NCV) or "mortal" (NRSV, NJPS), and 1 Samuel 24:3 to "relieve himself" (NRSV, CEV, MSG, HCSB).

One last note regarding theory: some translations move so far in the direction of "Free Translation" that they become a **paraphrase** (a restatement of the message in the translator's own words), not a translation. The Living Bible of 1971 by Kenneth Taylor was obviously a paraphrase, but other cases are not so easy to decide, such as *The Message* by Eugene Peterson, 2001. So at the far right of our diagram, there is an invisible breaking point between translation and paraphrase set by each reader or group.

Finally, a third factor related to translation theory, but not the same, is the reading level of the translation. Do the scholars use vocabulary and grammar that first graders could read or only high school seniors could understand? Naturally, the tendency is for "Free Translations" to work toward lower reading levels and "Formal Equivalence" translations to be written for higher reading levels. But it is possible for a beautifully written "Free Translation" to use the vocabulary and grammar of a college graduate. And while the reverse is not as likely to occur, some with generally low reading comprehension may understand a "Verbal Equivalence" Old Testament if he or she has been reading the same translation (e.g., KJV) all their life.

A diagram or chart plotting translations requires at least two dimensions: First, theory of translation, and second, reading level, with a third dimension (theology of the translators) left for the reader to investigate and watch for as he or she reads:

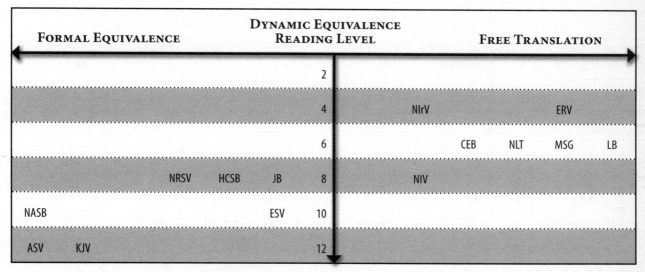

Figure AII.4. Translation Theory and Translations of the Old Testament

Conclusion

I am frequently asked the same questions about Bible translations: *Which translation should I use?* And I can openly answer this question: read the Bible that you can best understand. In all likelihood, if you try to read a Bible you don't understand you will not keep reading for long. Why would you? Then, after you have been reading the same translation for a long time, try a new translation that you can understand.

A second question, which is like the first: *What about newer translations that make use of gender neutral terminology instead of the traditional third person masculine pronouns (he, his), and the term "man"?* And I really can answer this question too (I am on a roll): it is quite obvious that many times when the Hebrew of the Old Testament uses the third person masculine, the pronoun refers to males and females, not just males. Thus, it would seem odd to me that we would even consider translating such a term with a misleading "he" or "his" when we can avoid confusion by using a more inclusive and accurate term. The same is true for the term "man" when it is clear that the Hebrew refers to males and females.

One last recommendation: when you are engaged in the study of a specific text or topic, use multiple translations, some from each end of the spectrum (available for free on websites such as BibleGateway.com) so that you can compare translations to discover if there is anything in the Hebrew text that translators are understanding in very different ways.

For Further Reading

Read the "Translator's Preface to the Reader" in the Bible you presently use. Look for answers to the basic questions raised in this appendix: What is the translation theory? What is the reading level of their translation? What is the theological commitment of the translators? (Do they come from the same denomination or school?).

Fee, Gordon, and Douglas Stuart. *How to Read the Bible for All Its Worth*. Third Edition. Grand Rapids, MI: Zondervan, 2003. See chapter 2, "The Basic Tool: A Good Translation."

Schulte, Rainer, and John Biguenet, eds. *Theories of Translations: An Anthology of Essays from Dryden to Derrida*. Chicago: University of Chicago Press, 1992.

The **Millennials**
Genesis 1–11 and Would You Like to Be a Thousand and Three?

Two lists boggle the mind (not to dismiss others) in Genesis 1–11. First, in Genesis 5, we are given a linear genealogy of Adam's family for ten generations with their life span or age at death stretching the limits of the imagination: Adam died at 930 years of age, Seth at 912, Enosh at 905, Kenan at 910, Mahalel at 895, Jared at 962, Enoch at 365 when God "took him" (5:23), Methuselah at 969, Lamech at 777, and Noah at 950 (5:1–32, 9:29). Second, in Genesis 11 we are presented with another linear genealogy of ten generations from Shem to Abraham: Shem died at 600 years of age,[1] Arpachshad at 438, Shelah at 433, Eber at 464, Peleg at 239, Reu at 239, Serug at 230, Nahor at 148, Terah at 205, and Abraham at 175 (Gen 11:10–26,32, 25:7). In this second list, the ages fall sharply to near-believability. We express our sympathy to poor Nahor who lived only 148 years, just in the prime of his life compared to old Methuselah, who holds the record at 969.

The most famous use of these lists comes to us through the calculations of James Ussher (1581–1656), Archbishop of Armagh in the Church of Ireland. Ussher worked carefully with these lists moving backward in time to establish the date of creation: the night preceding Sunday, 23 October 4004 BCE. Of course to do this, he took the years literally and the connection between each man to be that of a literal father and son. Other sources work in the same way to date the great

KEY TERMS

Book of Enoch (1 Enoch): an ancient Jewish book regarded as canonical by only a few Eastern Orthodox churches (cited in the New Testament book of Jude)

Book of Jubilees: an ancient Jewish work accepted as canonical by only Ethiopian Orthodox Churches, an abbreviated rewriting of Genesis ("Little Genesis")

Linear Genealogy: a genealogy that names the father and the son, then the son's first son, and so forth

Samaritan Pentateuch: a different form of the Pentateuch accepted by the Samaritans as their Bible (they exclude other books)

Segmented Genealogy: a genealogy that fans out like a family tree, including all members of the family

Septuagint: Greek translation(s) of the Old Testament made for Jews living in the Greek-speaking world, begun in ca. 200 BCE

---

[1] We arrive at the total age for those in Genesis 5 by adding the year when each man has his first son to the number of years he lives after this event (e.g., Shem is 100 when his son is born, and lives an additional 500 years after this event = 600 years).

flood: 2242 *a.m.* (*anno mundi* or years since creation) according to the Septuagint, or 1307 *a.m.* according to the Samaritan Pentateuch. These and other similar calculations undermine the Bible's credibility in the eyes of many contemporary readers: not only do we have unbelievably long human life spans, but we also have a young earth of seven thousand years or less. Scientists and critical thinkers in the twenty-first century may well close their Bibles and never move beyond these "outrageous" claims.

The biblical lists, however, do not stand alone in the ancient Near East. If we glance at the *Sumerian King List*, we no longer feel sorry for Nahor—we feel sorry for Methuselah. The *Sumerian King List* begins with A-lulim who ruled for 28,000 years, Alalgar who ruled for 36,000 years, En-men-lu-Anna 43,200 years, En-men-gal-Anna 28,800 years, then the god Dumu-zi ruled for 36,000 years. Eventually, the reigns become shorter and shorter: Mes-Anne-pada ruled 80 years, Mes-kiag-Nanna ruled 36 years, Elulu 25 years, and Balulu 36 years.[2]

Allow me to begin with several observations about what we know, what we don't know, and what close reading provides us. Then, I will review how different scholars read these genealogies:

1) The numbers (alone or in combination) may have had a symbolic or even astrological meaning. Enoch, for example, lived 365 years, the number of days in a solar calendar. This is an interesting life span for a man who "walked with God" and "disappeared" (Gen 5:23–24, CEB; or "he was no more" NRSV) because God took him. But, what his 365 years meant, if anything, is lost to us.

2) The names may have had rich traditional materials associated with them, perhaps long stories about the person or about their families. In other words, their name stands as the front page to a web site or as the title of a book, inviting the reader (or hearer) to go in and explore all that became of this person's family. But again, if these stories once existed, they are no longer in existence today. Later traditions did develop on the basis of these references in the biblical text, but they came well after, not before, these genealogies (see the Book of Jubilees, chapters 4–23, and the book of Enoch, especially chapters 37, 64–66, 75–90, and 105).

3) Each list consists of ten generations: the first from Adam to Noah (through Seth, not sinful Cain) and the second from Noah's son Shem to Abraham. The number ten likely suggests some sense of completion, a complete route finished from creation to the flood and from the flood to God's new work in Abraham.

4) The second list makes the transition from incredibly long ages to more reasonable human life spans (as does the *Sumerian King List*), although the ancestors in Genesis 12–50 continue to live well beyond today's average life expectancy: Abraham lived 175 years (25:7), Isaac 180 years (35:28–29), Jacob/Israel 147 years (47:28–29), and Joseph 110 years (50:26). This reduction in life span may suggest another consequence of humans trusting themselves over God. Rather than enhancing their lives through fully trusting God, they have only destroyed themselves by taking life into their own hands: what could have been (long life) has deteriorated into a shorter (and

---

[2] "The Sumerian King List," trans. A. Leo Oppenheim (in *Ancient Near Eastern Texts*, 256–266). The spelling of names found here are based on Oppenheim's translation of the text.

harder) life. One problem with this idea, however, is that the incredibly long ages in Genesis 5 also come after the introduction of sin in chapters 3 and 4.

4) Each list is preceded by another genealogy. The list in Genesis 5 that traces the line of Seth (third son of Eve and Adam) is preceded in chapter 4 by a linear genealogy of Cain. Some names are similar or the same, but in a different order: from Genesis 4 we find Cain, Irad, and Mehujael (4:17–18), in Genesis 5 we find Kenan (5:9–10), Mahalalel (5:12–13), and Jared (5:15–16). We also find the names Enoch (4:17–18, 5:22–24) and Lamech (4:18–19, 23–24, 5:25–31) in both lists. We take this moment to acknowledge that different people sometimes share the same or similar names. The list in chapter 11 that traces Shem to Abraham is preceded by a segmented genealogy in Genesis 10. The lists agree, except that Genesis 10:22–31 traces only five generations whereas Genesis 11 has a total of ten generations. Of some interest to our study, close comparison of these lists shows that the man who appears to be the firstborn of Shem in chapter 11 (Arpachshad, 11:10), is listed in chapter 10 as Shem's third son (after Elam and Asshur, 10:22).

Although some readers and scholars do take these high numbers as historically valid and claim that people once lived for nine hundred years or more,[3] most do not. On the one hand, many of those who do attempt to accept these numbers as correct do so with some explanation. For example, some writers point out that the formula "X became the father of Y" does not necessarily denote a literal father/son relationship. Genealogies in ancient societies often skip generations to go from one important figure to the next important figure. The genealogy of Jesus in the Gospel of Matthew drops three generations—Ahaziah, Joash, and Amaziah—between Joram and Uzziah (compare Matt 1:18 to Table 11.2, "The Kings of Southern Judah"). Thus, it is not necessary to accept a "young earth" as calculated by Ussher and others, because there may have been many generations skipped between the names on each list. This solution does not, however, deal with the incredibly long lives.

Others, who accept these numbers, suggest that at one time people counted ages or years differently. So the numbers are correct, we just don't know the system for counting (though this hypothesis works better with chapter 5 than chapter 11, given the age at which these men become fathers). Finally, some also explain that a name may stand for a tribe—so, the first number is the actual years the founder lived and the second number is the total life span of the tribe. This is still problematic for chapter 5: the first number ranges from 65 to 500 years before the tribal ancestor would have had his first son. In chapter 11, tribal founders lived between 29 and 100 years before having their first son.

On the other hand, many other scholars do not regard these numbers as any more scientifically valid than the ancient view of a flat earth with water below and a dome above holding more water back (Gen 1:1–2:4, see Chapter One, Figure 1.2). It is historically valid to say people once had this view of the cosmos, and to say that Scripture uses this view to say things about the true God. But this is not the same as demanding that all believers accept Genesis 1 to be an accurate

---

[3] See Henry Morris, *The Genesis Record: A Scientific and Devotional Commentary on the Book of Beginnings* (Grand Rapids: Baker, 1976), 153–162, 278–290.

description of the universe. God and Scripture work within culture to convey truth, just as competent missionaries do today. So unless we doubt the literary ability of the author or editors, we may be certain that he, she, or they had some reason for including these lists with these numbers, just as we may be certain that we don't understand why. And just as we read Genesis 1, we may read these lists as reflections of ancient Near Eastern society and beliefs without demanding that we take these numbers to be scientifically valid.

Ultimately, this question boils down to another more fundamental question: *What type of literature am I reading?* This inquiry does not doubt that Genesis 1–11 is part of Scripture and inspired. Instead, with integrity, it asks, what is the most faithful way to read what is before me? The Bible contains many different types of literature—psalms, parables, historical literature, and more—and the genre (or type of literature) determines which questions a text will answer and which questions will only mislead or frustrate the inquirer. When one question after another comes back with no answer because the writer doesn't tell us (or doesn't care), we have most likely misidentified the genre of the text. So what is the genre of Genesis 1–11? Some answer historical literature, others claim legend or myth (both of which can teach truth about God). The question, or questions, are now yours to answer.

For Further Reading

Brueggemann, Walter. *Genesis*. Interp. Atlanta, GA: John Knox Press, 1982.

Halton, Charles, and Stanley Gundry, eds. *Genesis: History, Fiction, or Neither? Three Views on the Bible's Earliest Chapters*. Grand Rapids: Zondervan, 2015.

Morris, Henry. *The Genesis Record: A Scientific and Devotional Commentary on the Book of Beginnings*. Grand Rapids: Baker, 1976.

von Rad, Gerhard. *Genesis*. Revised Ed. OTL. Philadelphia: Westminster Press, 1972.

Sibley Towner, W. *Genesis*. Westminster Bible Companion. Louisville: Westminster John Knox Press, 2001.

The LORD and Pharaoh's
Heart Disease

The purpose of this appendix is to provide information or data regarding the subject of Pharaoh's heart and the LORD's role in hardening Pharaoh's heart (see Chapter Four). The difficulty is of a theological nature. In other words, the problem has to do with God and what God does, or at least appears to do, with Pharaoh, and what that means for us. To be specific, let's formulate this problem as a question: Does the LORD harden Pharaoh's heart so that Pharaoh has no free will to make decisions for himself and no ability to do what he wants to do; instead, he can only do what the LORD wants or makes him do? And if the question is answered in the affirmative: *yes, Pharaoh can only decide what the* LORD *has already determined*, then what does that mean for our own ability to make decisions? Do any of us have free will to decide what we want to do? These are the questions that orbit around the central issue of what happened to Pharaoh's heart.

I. Definitions of Key Terms

We begin with definitions: when we talk about Pharaoh's heart, what are we talking about? In the Pentateuch, the term "heart" (Heb. *leb* or *lebab*) takes three clusters of meaning or function. First, much like our own use of the term, a person's heart may feel emotion. The heart may grieve (Gen 6:6, Deut 15:10), become discouraged (Gen 42:48, 45:26; Num 32:7, 9; Deut 1:28, 20:3, 8), or be glad (Exod 4:14). It may also be stirred up so that a person does something special (Exod 35:21, 26, 29). Second, the heart may function like what we call our mind. The heart thinks (Gen 8:21, Deut 15:9) and speaks to itself (Gen 27:41, Deut 8:17), just as it may contain wisdom (Exod 36:2) and may teach others

(Exod 35:34–35). Third, a person's heart is the center or core of a person's being. When we speak of our hearts, we speak about who we are at our most fundamental level. So, to do something with all our hearts means to do it with every ounce of energy that we possess: we must seek the LORD with all our hearts (Deut 4:29), just as we love (Deut 4:29, 6:5–6, 13:3, 30:6) and serve the LORD with all our hearts (Deut 10:12, 11:13).

Our second definition is the verb "to harden," which we soon discover comes from not one, but three different Hebrew verbs in Exodus 4–12—*kabed, hazaq,* and *qasha*—each with a slightly different nuance of the idea "to harden." The first term, *kabed,* expresses the idea of becoming heavy or dull—eyes become dim; ears hard of hearing; a tongue slurred, inarticulate speech . . . and a heart that doesn't work well anymore. The second verb, *hazaq,* means to be strong or to overpower. Hamilton suggests the closest English equivalent is "bullheaded."[1] Finally, the third term, *qasha,* expresses a range of meanings that include to have hard labor in childbirth, to become stubborn (stiff-necked), or to make something hard or heavy. The combination of these verbs with the concept of the heart from our work above (center of emotion, thought, and core of being) suggests an array of meanings in which hardening Pharaoh's heart means the presence of strong emotional responses, a breakdown in cognitive function, and Pharaoh losing his grip on his core being to the point where he is no longer in control of himself and his decisions. What a rational person would do in view of the evidence, a hard heart/mind no longer does. That person is stubborn, bullheaded, irrational, fiercely angry, and unpredictable—beyond the help of any psychotherapy or medical intervention.

II. Describing Pharaoh's Problem

Next, we observe three groups of texts that contain three different ways the text describes Pharaoh's heart problem (all examples are from the NRSV, emphasis mine). In the first group, sometimes Pharaoh's heart is the subject of a passive verb:

> Still *Pharaoh's heart was hardened,* and he would not listen to them, as the LORD had said. (Exod 7:13)

> But the magicians of Egypt did the same by their secret arts; so *Pharaoh's heart remained hardened,* and he would not listen to them, as the LORD had said. (7:22)

> And the magicians said to Pharaoh, "This is the finger of God!" But *Pharaoh's heart was hardened,* and he would not listen to them, just as the LORD had said. (8:19)

> Pharaoh inquired and found that not one of the livestock of the Israelites was dead. But *the heart of Pharaoh was hardened,* and he would not let the people go. (9:7)

In these texts, and others with the same grammatical construction, we are left with no answer as to who or what is causing Pharaoh's heart to harden. We only know that on these occasions

---

[1]Victor Hamilton, *Handbook on the Pentateuch,* rev. ed. (Grand Rapids: Baker Academic, 2005), 161.

his heart is not functioning in a sane manner. He has become so irrationally stubborn that he refuses to comply with the LORD's request.

In a second group of texts, the subject of the verb is Pharaoh:

> But when Pharaoh saw that there was a respite, *he hardened his heart*, and would not listen to them, just as the LORD had said. (8:15)

> But *Pharaoh hardened his heart* this time also, and would not let the people go. (8:32)

> But when Pharaoh saw that the rain and the hail and the thunder had ceased, he sinned once more and [he] *hardened his heart*, he and his officials. (9:34)

In these texts, we know who or what is causing Pharaoh's heart to become hard: it is Pharaoh. Pharaoh is the one who hardens his heart to the point where he "would not listen" (8:15) and he "would not let the people go" (8:32, and 9:34–35). The problem is Pharaoh.

Finally, in a third group of texts, the subject of the verb is the LORD:

> And the LORD said to Moses, "When you go back to Egypt, see that you perform before Pharaoh all the wonders that I have put in your power; but *I will harden his heart*, so that he will not let the people go. (4:21)

> But *I will harden Pharaoh's heart*, and I will multiply my signs and wonders in the land of Egypt. (7:3)

> But *the LORD hardened the heart of Pharaoh*, and he would not listen to them, just as the LORD had spoken to Moses. (9:12)

> Then the LORD said to Moses, "Go to Pharaoh; for *I have hardened his heart and the heart of his officials*, in order that I may show these signs of mine among them." (10:1)

> But *the LORD hardened Pharaoh's heart*, and he would not let the Israelites go. (10:20)

As in the second group, these texts identify the person or force causing Pharaoh's heart to become irrational, hard, or stubborn: it is the LORD. And as a result, Pharaoh will not let the people go (4:21, 10:20) while the LORD continues to multiply the signs and wonders he does in Egypt (7:3, 10:1).

III. Diagnosis and Prognosis

Careful analysis of the texts that speak of Pharaoh's heart and their placement in the narrative reveals a pattern: First, the LORD announces to Moses at the burning bush (4:21) and then again in Egypt (7:2) that he, the LORD, *will* (future tense) harden Pharaoh's heart. Second, a series of texts explain that either Pharaoh's heart was hardened (the first group of texts above: 7:13, 14, 22; 8:19; 9:7) or Pharaoh hardened his heart (the second group of texts above: 8:15, 32). Third, at the end of the sixth plague, for the first time, the narrative states the LORD hardens Pharaoh's heart (9:12, present tense); and from this point forward, only twice—in the same passage—does the narrative mention that Pharaoh hardened his heart or that his heart was hardened (9:34–35). Instead, the Lord takes control (the third group of texts above: 10:1, 20, 27; 11:10; 14:4, 8, 17). In fact, at this point, the Lord explains why he has stepped in to take control:

> For this time I will send all my plagues upon you yourself, and upon your officials, and upon your people, so that you may know that there is no one like me in all the earth. For by now I could have stretched out my hand and struck you and your people with pestilence, and you would have been cut off from the earth. But this is why I have let you live: to show you my power, and to make my name resound through all the earth. (9:14–16)

Only in retrospect does chapter 13 say that in the future the Israelites are to tell their children that, "By strength of hand the Lord brought us out of Egypt, from the house of slavery. When *Pharaoh stubbornly refused* to let us go, the Lord killed all the firstborn in the land of Egypt . . ." (13:14–15, emphasis mine).

The recognition of this pattern is a common solution or answer to the problem of the hardening of Pharaoh's heart and human free will. In this hypothesis, the Lord knew Pharaoh's character well enough to know that the only way he would ever let Israel leave would be if the Lord forced him. So, while the Lord gives Pharaoh the chance to do the right thing, when he refuses to cooperate, each refusal causes his heart to become a little harder, less reasonable, and more stubborn, until finally the Lord takes over and explains his purpose in the plagues. Without knowing it, Pharaoh has played directly into the Lord's plans.

Another solution has to do with the inner qualities of a substance and how we describe the reaction of the substance to an outside force. Follow along as I give two examples and then explain the hypothesis: 1) Under the great pressure of a mountain, a lump of coal will become a diamond. We may then say the coal was hardened into a diamond, or that the mountain hardened the coal into a diamond. We could even say the coal turned into a diamond and all of these statements would be correct. Ultimately, however, what caused the coal to become a diamond was the coal's character or molecular structure. 2) Under the tremendous pressure of a mountain, water will not turn into a diamond, but create fissures; and, with enough water, the fissures will lead to a spring of water coming out of the mountain. Again, we may describe what has happened in various ways: the water was made into a spring, or the mountain produced a spring, or simply, a spring came out of the mountain. The important issue, however, is the molecular quality of water that causes it to create fissures and springs, as opposed to becoming a diamond. These examples point toward a simple solution regarding Pharaoh's heart: it's what's on the inside that counts. His heart was of such a nature (because of a lifetime of choices) that when subjected to pressure regarding Israel, it became hard, stubborn, and irrational. We can describe this process in a number of different ways—Pharaoh hardened his heart, the Lord hardened his heart, or his heart hardened—but ultimately, what made the difference was the nature of Pharaoh's heart. When subjected to the same forces, other people may have acted in a different way, perhaps even softening their hearts.

Now you have the basic data regarding the problem of Pharaoh's heart and two of the most common responses to the problem—either of these may work fine until one turns to the New Testament Book of Romans (9:14–18). But it is here that I must stop and allow you to consider how this text plays into your resolution of the mystery of Pharaoh's heart.

For Further Reading

Hamilton, Victor. *Handbook on the Pentateuch*. Rev. ed. Grand Rapids: Baker, 2005. See pp. 161–167.

Steinmann, A. E. "Hardness of Heart." Pages 381–383 in *The Dictionary of the Old Testament: Pentateuch*. Edited by T. Desmond Alexander and David Baker. Downers Grove: InterVarsity, 2003.

The Incredible, **Amazing**, Growing Israelites

At the beginning of Exodus, Pharaoh is terrified by Israel's numbers and continued growth (Exod 1:8–9), so he implements the first of many attempts to destroy Israel. Based on the number we are given a few chapters later, who could blame him for thinking Israel could take over Egypt? With six hundred thousand men—a number which does not include the women (+600,000?), children (+1,200,00?), and "a diverse crowd" (+??)—somewhere over two million people leave Egypt in the Exodus story (Exod 12:37). This enormous number is confirmed at the end of the Book of Exodus: 603,550 men twenty years old and over, those able to join the army (38:26). The same number is given after the first census in the Book of Numbers (1:46), slightly more than the second census at the end of the Book of Numbers (601,650 men, 26:51). The testimony is as consistent as it is overwhelming. One can certainly understand why Pharaoh would be afraid of the Israelites. At over two million in number, the Israelites could have staked claim to Egypt and saved all that time traveling in the wilderness. For that matter, Israel would have had an army large enough to select the nation of their choice, write a letter, and tell them to leave. They would make them an offer they couldn't refuse.

But as we continue to read, we find claims that make little sense if Israel is over two million strong. If Israel is so large, why would the LORD say that he will drive out the Canaanites "before you little by little, until your numbers grow and you eventually possess the land" (Exod 23:30)? Or just prior to that, "I won't drive them out before you in a single year so the land won't be abandoned and the wild animals won't multiply around you" (23:29)? Why would the LORD say to Israel, when she is about to enter the land, that he is about to drive out "the Hittites, the Girgashites, the Amorites, the Canaanites, the Perizzites, the Hivites, and the Jebusites: seven nations that are larger and stronger than you" (Deut 7:1)? Then, in the same conversation, the LORD adds, "It was not because you were greater than all other people that the LORD loved you and chose you. In fact, you were the smallest of peoples!" (7:7).

Something doesn't seem right here, even more so if we allow comparative evidence into the conversation. Estimates suggest that in 2000 BCE, the largest cities in the ancient Near East had only 60,000 residents: Memphis (in Egypt) and Ur (in Iraq).[1] By 1200 BCE, nearer to the time Israel leaves Egypt, Babylon and Thebes (in Egypt) may have had as many as 80,000 residents.[2] Or to speak of the military, at the battle of Kadesh-on-the-Orontes in the thirteenth century BCE, the two super-powers of their time, the Egyptians and Hittites each fielded as many as 20,000 men, with numerous chariots.[3] And there is one other "minor" detail missing from the world of archaeology. Archaeologists have yet to find anything in the Sinai wilderness or elsewhere that would mark where Israel traveled and camped. For over two million people to cross the wilderness and not leave any trail behind would require a miracle, especially when they lived for nearly a year at Mount Sinai (Exod 19:1, Num 10:11–12). And, so that we have a face on the number, imagine leading the city of Houston (2,100,263 in the 2010 census) or Chicago (2,695,598). The logistical nightmare is staggering, especially in a time without modern communications, modern sanitation, or modern anything.

The last problem to do with Israel's enormous size is that, in all likelihood, Israel was never anywhere near the population suggested by most, if not all, English translations.[4] The problem itself is rather simple and revolves around a single issue: What does the Hebrew term *eleph* mean? We may translate this term in at least three different ways: First, *eleph* may mean "thousand," as in the texts and translations above. Second, *eleph* may mean "troop" or a "fighting unit" of various sizes. If so, the census totals in Numbers 1 change in a dramatic manner. The tribe of Reuben has 46 *eleph* that consist of 500 men total (technical note: understanding the Hebrew *waw* as epexegetic). So too for others on the list: Simeon,

CENSUS OF THE ARMY IN NUMBERS 1		
Tribe	*Eleph* (Troops)	Total Men
Reuben	46	500
Simeon	59	300
Gad	45	650
Judah	74	600
Issachar	54	400
Zebulun	57	400
Ephraim	40	500
Manasseh	32	200
Benjamin	35	400
Dan	62	700
Asher	41	500
Naphtali	53	400
Totals	598	5,550

Table AV.1. Census of the Army in Numbers 1

[1] Ian Morris, *Why the West Rules—For Now* (New York: Farrar, Straus, and Giroux, 2010), 632.
[2] Ibid.
[3] See Hector Avalos, "Kadesh-on-the-Orontes," in *Anchor Bible Dictionary* 4:3–4.
[4] In fairness to the translators, they probably know that the number is misleading, but they are caught between the proverbial rock and hard place when they translate these texts. If they change the numbers, they will be charged with being liberals who change God's word and their translation will rot in warehouse bins.

59 *eleph*, 300 men; Gad, 45 *eleph*, 650 men; Judah, 74 *eleph*, 600 men (Num 1:22–27); and so forth, until we reach a total of 5,500 men in 598 eleph or "fighting units" (see Table AV.1). The total in Numbers 1:46, however, appears to be the result of scribal error, a misunderstanding of the text by a copyist. In Hebrew, the phrase says six hundred *eleph waw* (and) three *eleph waw* (and) five hundred *waw* (and) fifty: 603,550. This total comes as the result of running together an original 598 *eleph* and 5 *eleph* to arrive at 603 thousand (normally, we would expect a writer to just say "six hundred and three *eleph*"), instead of recognizing that the final number is 598 *eleph* (fighting units) at a total of 5,550 men (a number confirmed by counting the *eleph* and number of men from the preceding list).[5]

Suddenly, Israel's size has taken on proportions that make sense of the LORD's statements in Exodus 23 and Deuteronomy 7. Two million has fallen to less than thirty thousand total Israelites: 5,550 men over 20 years old + 5,550 women (?) + 11,100 children (?) + 3,000 diverse crowd (?) = +/-25,200 (see Exod 12:37); a number still large enough to cause Pharaoh concern (Exod 1:8–9), but small enough to work with other texts as well as ancient Near Eastern population estimates.

A third possible way to translate *eleph* is "clan, family unit." Several texts use *eleph* with this meaning, as translators recognize. Numbers 1:16 identifies those "appointed from the community, chiefs of their ancestral tribes and leaders of the divisions (*eleph*) of Israel." In Judges 6:15, Gideon complains to the LORD's messenger, "With due respect, my Lord, how can I rescue Israel? My clan (*eleph*) is the weakest in Manasseh, and I'm the youngest in my household." And the final example comes from the selection of Saul by casting the holy lots (Urim and Thummim). Samuel tells the people to "assemble yourselves before the LORD by your tribes and clans (*eleph*)" (1 Sam 10:19). It seems fairly obvious that in all these texts, the CEB is correct to translate *eleph* as "division" or "clan," rather than misleading and confusing the reader with the literal "thousand" or "thousands." "Clan" or "division" is not likely to be the meaning of *eleph* in the context of a military census (Num 1, 2, 26), but the fact that *eleph* can and does take a meaning other than the literal translation "thousand," further opens the path for us to read the term in other non-literal ways, e.g., "troop" (Num 1:17–46).

---

[5] See G.A. Klingbeil, "Historical Criticism," in *Dictionary of the Old Testament: Pentateuch*, ed. T. Desmond Alexander and David Baker (Downers Grove: InterVarsity Press, 2003): 407–410.

For Further Reading

Humphreys, C. J. "The Number of People in the Exodus from Egypt: Decoding Mathematically the Very Large Numbers in Numbers i and xxvi." *Vetus Testamentum* 48 (1998): 196–213.

Klingbeil, G. A. "Historical Criticism." Pages 407–410 in *Dictionary of the Old Testament: Pentateuch.* Edited by T. Desmond Alexander and David Baker. Downers Grove: InterVarsity Press, 2003.

Beginning
Old Testament **Research**
Methods and Resources

Research begins with a question, a text, or a topic that a student finds especially interesting—or at least interesting enough to spend the necessary hours in investigative work until the matter is resolved. Obviously, this exploration will also be determined by the nature of the study. On one side, if the study is personal—only what we want to know for ourselves—then we may stop when we have found our own satisfactory answer. On the other side, if the research is for a paper, presentation, or other class assignment, the nature of the project will dictate the extent of research. This appendix recommends a path for those who are beginning Old Testament studies, whether for personal interests, class assignments, or perhaps for preparation that will lead toward public presentation in a Bible class or sermon.

I. The Primary Text

How a student's research will progress depends on several variables: the nature of the study (text or topic), familiarity with the Old Testament, and, in some cases, the ability to work with original languages (Hebrew and Aramaic, or even Greek). Most important for any type of research, however, is use of the primary resource: the Bible. Nothing can replace reading the text or texts selected for closer study. Read the text over and over again in many different translations and give your mind time to think about the text (meditate), even when you are not actively engaged in reading or research. Let the text become a part of you so that you think about it when you have a spare moment of free time.

In addition, as you read, compile a list of questions on key issues you need to know more about in order to understand the biblical text better. For example, if your text or topic includes the concept of "the heart" (as in Appendix IV), make a note that you need to find information about what "the heart" refers to or means in Exodus or in the Pentateuch. The notes and questions that you compile while you are reading will set the direction of your initial research. Then, as you move forward, you may add to your list as you learn more and as you discover more questions that demand answers.

II. Bible Dictionaries

In most cases, the notes from your initial reading will identify key words, persons, ideas, social practices, or other items for which a Bible Encyclopedia or Bible Dictionary will be most helpful. Depending on the required depth of your research, a quick glance at a single-volume Bible dictionary may be sufficient. In most cases, however, a one-volume Bible dictionary will lack the detail you will need to develop a research paper or presentation. Whereas a single volume will provide one or two paragraphs of summary information on a topic, a multi-volume Bible dictionary will often provide two or three pages of information, including evidence that supports any claims made and a short bibliography for further exploration of the topic. I encourage my students not to waste their time reading three or four one-volume dictionaries that will repeat the same summary of information, when they could read the entry in one up-to-date multi-volume encyclopedia and gain the detailed information they need for their papers.

Of the multi-volume Bible dictionaries or encyclopedias available today, the two best, by far, are the *New Interpreter's Dictionary of the Bible* (*NIDB*, 5 volumes, edited by Katharine Doob Sakenfeld, Samuel E. Balentine, and Brian K. Blount. Nashville: Abingdon, 2009), and the *Anchor Bible Dictionary* (*ABD*, 6 volumes, edited by David Noel Freedman, New York: Doubleday, 1992). The predecessor of the *NIDB* still retains significant value, *The Interpreter's Dictionary of the Bible* (*IDB*, 4 volumes, edited by George Arthur Buttrick, Nashville: Abingdon Press, 1962), as does the *International Standard Bible Encyclopedia* (*ISBE*, 4 volumes, Grand Rapids: Eerdmans, 1979–1988, a complete revision of the original 1939 edition).

Sometimes less information and fast summaries are all that we need. For this purpose, some of the multi-volume dictionaries come in trimmed down one-volume sizes. See the *Common English Bible Dictionary* (Nashville: Abingdon, 2011), the *HarperCollins Bible Dictionary, Revised and Updated* (New York: HarperCollins, 2011), and the *Eerdmans Dictionary of the Bible*, edited by David Noel Freedman, Astrid B. Beck, and Allen C. Myers (Grand Rapids: Eerdmans, 2000).

Finally, within the category of Bible encyclopedias and dictionaries are the reference works devoted to the Hebrew language. The most accessible of these for the non-Hebraist (non-Hebrew reader) is the *New International Dictionary of Old Testament Theology and Exegesis* (*NIDOTTE*, 5 volumes, edited by Willem A. VanGemeren. Grand Rapids: Zondervan, 1984). For example, if a student wishes to read about "the heart," he or she first looks up the term in the index of English words (in volume 5). Here the index refers to entries #4213 and #4222. We find both entries in volume 2: articles are written in English for students who know little or no Hebrew. The other major Hebrew reference work will require the assistance of someone who reads Hebrew to help you find the correct entry to read: *Theological Dictionary of the Old Testament* (*TDOT*, 15 volumes, edited by G. Johannes Botterweck and Helmer Ringgren, Grand Rapids: Eerdmans, 1974–2006). Alongside these dictionaries, students should also use a concordance to read and study the various ways in which a word is used and its range of meaning in the Old Testament. Thankfully, more and more of these tools are available online and are easy to use.

III. Bible Commentaries

All too often, students race to their favorite commentaries before doing their own work of reading the text and exploring their own initial set of questions. When this happens, students short-circuit the research process. Instead of reading, exploring, and thinking for themselves, they limit their thoughts to the conclusions others have already made—conclusions that sometimes lack solid evidence or careful, balanced research. Commentaries should be conversation partners later on in the path of research—partners who may point out features of the text that students have overlooked, or who present a compelling argument that opposes the students' present position. In these cases, commentaries help students bolster or rethink their hypothesis; this is an ideal use of commentaries.

Commentaries vary widely in the tasks they take on and the methods they use to accomplish their work. Some commentaries are highly technical, working through Hebrew, Greek, Aramaic, Coptic, and Latin manuscripts (just to name a few) in order to determine the best or most authentic Hebrew words that belong in every verse of the book or books they are writing about. These commentaries also include significant notes about the translation of the words in the text and proceed verse by verse in an analytical fashion intended only for those who are prepared to read slowly and carefully. Frequently, the scholars who produce these books spend decades in study, if not a lifetime, to produce just one commentary on one biblical book. Their contribution to our knowledge is enormous, and yet, despite all their study, they cannot guarantee 100 percent correct conclusions. Others, who have also spent decades in study may disagree, as may the student. At all times, what matters is the evidence and the persuasiveness of the argument, not the writer's fame in the public or scholarly world. This prestigious top tier category includes volumes in the following series (note: because individual volumes in these sets are written by different scholars, some are stronger than others):

- The Anchor Bible
- Word Biblical Commentary
- International Critical Commentary
- Hermeneia Commentary
- Old Testament Library
- Continental Commentary

Commentaries in the second tier are less intense in detail, generally shorter, and easier to read. Nonetheless, the volumes in these series are still representative of excellent scholarship:

- New International Commentary on the Old Testament
- Berit Olam: Studies in Hebrew Narrative and Poetry
- New Century Bible Commentary
- Baker Commentary on the Old Testament Wisdom and Psalms
- Interpreter's Bible
- New Interpreter's Bible

Finally, a third tier of commentaries are even shorter, deal less with individual verses and more with thought units (paragraphs), and typically place more emphasis on the theology or message of the text. Don't be fooled, however, by their smaller size. These commentaries are also based on careful research.

- Abingdon Old Testament Commentaries
- New International Biblical Commentary
- Westminster Bible Companion
- The Two Horizons Old Testament Commentary
- The NIV Application Commentary
- Interpretation: A Bible Commentary for Teaching and Preaching

Many other commentary series exist, as do individual volumes published outside of a series. As a general rule, it is best to use commentaries that have assigned different authors to the different books (as opposed to a single author for all of the Old Testament). For a complete list and brief description of each volume, see Tremper Longman, III, *Old Testament Commentary Survey*, 5th ed. (Grand Rapids: Baker, 2013).

IV. Academic Journals

Bibles are indispensable for research, the alpha and omega (beginning and end) of all biblical study. Dictionaries and encyclopedias help us acquire information on specific words, practices, or ideas, and commentaries provide a sustained interpretation of a biblical book. All of these books—dictionaries, encyclopedias, and commentaries—take years to research, write, and edit, and finally go to press. To some degree, by the time these books are published, they are already out of date. Other discoveries may have been made, new insights may have been developed, and some readings of a text may have been discredited—all in the time between the writing of a commentary and its publication. So, filling the gap for pioneering research are academic journals: academic "magazines" that feature papers with new ideas, new evidence, or new readings of a text (e.g., *Journal of Biblical Literature*, or *Journal for the Study of the Old Testament*, saving *Christianity Today* and *Time Magazine* for more general reading and information, but not for research purposes). Ideally, journals publish the most recent, cutting-edge research in the field—and do so in a manner much faster than a book. Journals also publish specific research on unique topics that may not appear in any other form. Consequently, another stop for students doing research is a search for relevant journal articles through the online catalog of the American Theological

Library Association (ATLA). More and more articles are becoming available in an online format. Beware, however, of waiting until midnight the night before your paper is due, only to find the perfect journal article (even written by your teacher) that requires a trip to the library (or an inter-library loan)—so much for earning an excellent mark on your paper.

The purpose of journals still remains; however, for many top-tier journals, the backlog of accepted papers causes a wait of one, two, or even three years (as long as for some books). Like the proliferation of commentary series, there is almost no end to the number of journals that publish work in Old Testament studies and related fields. One very helpful resource for reviewing the most recent work is *Old Testament Abstracts* (*OTA*, a product of the Catholic Biblical Association of America, an organization of Catholic, Jewish, and Protestant scholars of the Old Testament.) Incredibly up-to-date, *OTA* includes a brief summary of every scholarly publication (books, journal articles, essays in books, and more). For the student's reference, some of top-tier journals for Old Testament research are listed below (with my apologies to those I have inadvertently omitted):

> *BA—Biblical Archaeologist*
> *BASOR—Bulletin of the American Schools of Oriental Research*
> *BSAC—Bibliotheca Sacra*
> *BZAW—Beihefte zur Zeitschrift für die alttestamentliche Wissenschaft*
> *CBQ—Catholic Biblical Quarterly*
> *Int—Interpretation*
> *JBL—Journal of Biblical Literature*
> *JBQ—Jewish Bible Quarterly*
> *JBR—Journal of Bible and Religion*
> *JSOT—Journal for the Study of the Old Testament*
> *VT—Vetus Testamentum*

V. Additional Guides to Research

Many other monographs devoted to a single subject, collections of essays on one topic or a wide variety of topics, critical introductions to the Old Testament, Old Testament theologies, collections of translated documents from the ancient Near East, and other types of books are indispensible for advanced Old Testament research. As a student moves deeper into research, more detailed guides are necessary. I recommend Douglas K. Stuart, *Old Testament Exegesis: A Handbook for Students and Pastors* (4th ed.; Louisville: Westminster John Knox Press, 2009) and Gordon D. Fee and Douglas Stuart, *How to Read the Bible for All Its Worth* (4th ed.; Grand Rapids: Zondervan, 2014). May God bless your efforts to learn more about Scripture and its witness to God and the life of faith.

Epilogue

If you are wondering what happened to all the other books in the Old Testament, I hope you will understand and forgive me. It was never my intention to offer an introduction to the Old Testament that included every book. So in our study, I have given little more than a book's name for several texts, even less for others. The plan all along has been to build a foundation and basic framework, providing enough instruction that a student may return to and more confidently read the books we have passed by or touched on only a little. I hope you will be interested enough in what you have found in the Old Testament to decide that you want to read more.

While a number of texts provide an excellent summary of Israel's story (e.g., Neh 11, Ps 78, 105–106, 136), behind the story stands Israel's God—the One to whom the story testifies, and the One for whom the story exists. As interesting as the story may be, and as many details as we may now know, if we have missed the story's testimony to God, then we have missed the very purpose of the Old Testament. Israel told stories to talk about God:

> *Want to know about God's love?*
>   *Let me tell you a story.*
> *Want to know how God feels about and treats widows? . . .*
>   *Let me tell you another story.*

Scholars call it Narrative Theology; we might call it the heart of the Old Testament. And as we walk away from our study my greatest fear is that, after all our work and study, we may have failed to see the Lord and be fascinated by a God so terribly misunderstood by those who know little of the Old Testament: a God who is desperately in love with all people (not just Israel), who wants nothing less than an intimate relationship with all of us. Patient, forgiving, responsive to every need (as opposed to all our wants), a God who honors us by placing us as partners over creation and gives us the integrity of choice—to trust the Lord or to trust ourselves.

As your course concludes and you close this textbook, my hope for you moves from the academic to the personal and spiritual. I hope the God of the Old Testament (and the New Testament) has captivated your heart and your imagination, so that for the rest of your life you will return to these books and their testimony over and over again. I hope you have fallen in love with the God who always has and always will love you—and that you will say "yes" to the Lord's proposal, "Will you be mine?"

The Lord bless you and keep you;
the Lord make his face to shine upon you, and be gracious to you;
the Lord lift up his countenance upon you, and give you peace.
(Num 6:24–26 NRSV)

Glenn Pemberton
Abilene, Texas
July 2015

Glossary of Key Terms

Acrostic: a Hebrew poem that begins each line with the next letter of the alphabet, from the first letter (*aleph*) to the last (*tav*)

Alien: a person living in a foreign country where they are not citizens

Ammon: a nation east of the Jordan river, descended from Abraham's nephew Lot

Anachronistic: a chronological inconsistency, such as including an object in a story that did not exist until after the historical setting of the story

Ancient Near East: the land area roughly equivalent to nations from modern Egypt on the West to Iran in the East

Antiphonal: a song sung with call and response or back and forth between one person or group and another person or group

Annals of the King: the written record of the king's accomplishments for each year of his reign

Apocrypha: books and additions to books that are part of Catholic Bibles, but excluded from Jewish and Protestant Bibles

Apodictic Law: command law, absolute law without conditions: *you will* or *you must not*

Aram: the territory northeast of Palestine (modern day northern Syria and northwest Iraq), Nahor, Abrahams's brother and his family lived here

Asherah: the name of a goddess most often associated with Baal, represented by a wooden pole

Assyria: a kingdom in northern Mesopotamia that became a mighty empire at the beginning of the first millennium BCE, conquering North Israel (722 BCE) and sending its people into exile; Assyria fell to Babylon in the late-seventh century

Atonement: to make amends for a wrong or for causing ritual impurity; to cleanse what is polluted

Babylon: a kingdom in southern Mesopotamia that became a mighty empire for a brief time near the middle of the first millennium BCE, conquering South Judah (586 BCE) and sending its people into exile; Babylon fell to Persia in the second half of the sixth century.

Birthright: the inheritance typically given to the firstborn son, often twice the amount given to other sons

Blood: a ritual detergent for making objects and people clean

Book of Enoch (1 Enoch): an ancient Jewish book regarded as canonical by only a few Eastern Orthodox churches (cited in the New Testament book of Jude)

Book of Jubilees: an ancient Jewish work accepted as canonical by only Ethiopian Orthodox Churches, an abbreviated rewriting of Genesis ("Little Genesis")

Book of the Twelve: the books of the Hebrew Bible elsewhere recognized as the minor prophets, Hosea–Malachi

Canaan: essentially the "Promised Land"

Canon: an official list of books (for any subject, e.g., "the canon of major British authors"); for the Bible, the canon is the list of books constituting the Bible

Casuistic Law: case law, stated with conditions: *if . . . then . . .*

Census: either counting the number of people or determining the number of men available to fight in the army

Chaldeans: southern land area between the Tigris and Euphrates rivers, often associated with Babylon

Chronicler's History (CH): the books of 1–2 Chronicles, Ezra, and Nehemiah

Circumcision: the removal of the foreskin from a man's penis

Clean/Unclean: categories for objects and people; their ritual status

Codex: a bound volume or book with hand-written pages on papyrus or vellum (animal skin)

Collateral: property or goods given or promised as security for a loan

Concubine: a secondary wife, usually due to her family's lower economic status

Cosmogony: a story of the origins of the world and/or the universe

Covenant: an agreement between two parties, whether they are nations (e.g., a treaty), or individuals (e.g., marriage), that sets expectations, promises for obedience, and curses for disobedience

Cyrus: king of Persia who conquered Babylon (ca. 539 BCE) and proclaimed freedom for the captives from Judah as well as captives from other nations; instrumental in establishing the great Persian empire

Denomination: a united group of Protestant churches that believe in similar doctrines (e.g., Baptists and Methodists are each a denomination)

Deuterocanonical: the term Catholics use to refer to the extra books and additions to books they accept as canonical, excluded from the canon by Jews and Protestants

Deuteronomistic History (DH): the books of Deuteronomy through 2 Kings, excluding Ruth

Deuteronomistic Theology: the basic idea that God rewards those who do what is right, but punishes those who choose to do wrong (a theme nuanced in the DH and other books)

Deuteronomists (Dtr): the authors/editors of the Deuteronomistic History

Diaspora: the scattering of the Jewish population outside its homeland in Canaan

Doxology: praise of God, typically a short exclamation in praise of God's greatness

Dynasty: a succession of kings from a single family, normally from father to son or to the son's heir

Edom: a territory/nation southeast of the Dead Sea, descended from Abraham's son Esau (twin brother of Jacob)

Enuma Elish: the opening words of the Babylonian creation myth "The Epic of Creation," often used as title of this story

Ephraim: a tribe that becomes so large its name is used as an alternate name for northern Israel

Etiology: a story of how something began, e.g., how did the practice of marriage begin?

Evangelicals: Protestants who share a high regard for Scripture and stress the Bible contains no errors of any type or that the Bible is trustworthy in matters of faith (among other characteristics)

Exile: a forced migration away from a person's homeland to a foreign country

Festival of Booths (also known as *Sukkoth* or Tabernacles): a celebration of the last harvest of the year (grapes, olives, and nuts) and to remember and relive life in the wilderness by living in huts or booths

Former Prophets: the books of Joshua through 2 Kings (excluding Ruth), equivalent to the DH

Genre: the type or category of a written work, e.g., poem, novel, myth, or history

Glean: to pick up leftover crops after the harvest or pick fruit left on the vine

Grace: a gift, or kind and loving treatment instead of punishment

Hebrews: members of the nation of Israel whose native language is Hebrew

Herem: the Hebrew term translated as "the ban" (CEB), used to command total destruction in a battle

High place: a place of worship in villages or in the country, most often for idols

Holiness Code: instruction for living in God's presence, found in Leviticus 16–26

Horeb: another name for Mount Sinai

Israel: a family chosen by God to become a mighty nation and to bless the world; also the name God gives to Jacob, from whom the nation derives its name

Israelite: member of the family or nation of Israel (descended from Jacob/Israel)

Jew: the term for a follower of Yahweh after the Babylonian exile

Judaism: a term for the religion and culture of Israelites after the Babylonian exile; a movement of people who are devoted to following the teachings of Yahweh in the Hebrew Bible

Karst Topography: landscape formed by the dissolving of rocks such as limestone, creating underground streams and caverns

Lament: a form of prayer (or psalm) in which the person appeals to God regarding their troubles and asks for God's help

Latter Prophets: the Books of Isaiah, Jeremiah, Ezekiel, and the Book of the Twelve (excluding Daniel)

Law of Moses: most likely the Pentateuch, or some early form of the Pentateuch brought out by Ezra to read (Neh 8:1)

Law of Talion: punishment must fit the crime, e.g., *an eye for an eye* (Exod 21:23–25)

Leviathan: a mythological sea serpent, often represents chaotic forces that stand against life

Linear Genealogy: a genealogy that names the father and the son, then the son's first son, and so forth

Lord: a common substitution for the name of God revealed to Moses, *Yahweh* (Exod 3:14–15); a name Jews considered too holy to pronounce and they also did not want to break the third of the Ten Commandments: "You must not misuse the name of the Lord your God" (Exod 20:7a NLT)

Lyre: a small harp

Lyrical: song or songlike poetry

Mace: a club for combat that has one larger end often laced with metal spikes

Mesopotamia: the land between and closely surrounding the Euphrates and Tigris rivers

Midwives: women trained to deliver babies

Moab: a nation east of the Jordan river and south of the Jabbok river, descended from Abraham's nephew Lot (Gen 19)

Motif: a recurring idea or theme in a literary work

Oracle: a short speech unit prophets use to convey the Lord's word to people

Ordain: to appoint to a religious office or role

Ordeal: a physical challenge to demonstrate a person's guilt or innocence

Orthodoxy/Orthodoxies: adherence to accepted religious norms, holding a correct view of life with God

Parallelism: a term that helps to describe the relationship of one line of Hebrew poetry to the next, e.g., synonymous parallelism (the second line repeats the idea of the first to emphasize or nuance the first line)

Paraphrase: a translation that summarizes the meaning or ideas of the biblical text, usually prepared by one person

Patriarchy/Patriarchal: a family system in which the father controls and leads the family

Peace Offering: a type of sacrifice in which part of the meat is returned to the person who brought the sacrifice and to the priest who helps offer the sacrifice

Pentapolis: five city-states (of the Philistines) bound together as one entity or group by way of treaty

Pentateuch: the first five books in the Old Testament, also called the Torah or Law

Persia: a kingdom east of Babylon that established a vast empire (ca. 500–350 BCE) stretching from modern-day Iran to western Turkey and into parts of Greece, as well as Egypt

Pogrom: an organized massacre of helpless people (often Israelites or Jews)

Post-Exilic: refers to the time period after the exile of 587–536 BCE

Priest: an intermediary between the gods/God and people; Israel was to be a priest to the world (Exod 19:5–6), the sons of Aaron were priests for Israel (since God's presence was living with them in the tabernacle and the temple)

Promised Land: promised to Abraham and his ancestors, the land east of the Jordan from north of the Sea of Galilee to south of the Dead Sea (though the borders vary and more land was promised than that ever occupied); some Israelites also settled in the Transjordan area

Prophet: often, a person who conveys messages from the LORD to select person(s)

Province of Yehud: Persian province, roughly equivalent to the land of the former nation of Judah

Psalmist: the writer of a psalm

Psalter: a book that contains psalms, often used as alternate term for the book of Psalms

Puppet-King: a weak king from a dynasty set in place by a more powerful person who is not of the dynasty (not qualified to be king), but who controls the king

Queen Mother: a powerful political position; often, but not always held by the king's mother

Qumran: a Jewish community that flourished from ca. 200 BCE–70 CE and left behind many of the "Dead Sea Scrolls"

Reformation: a religious movement to revive or restore the spiritual life of a group of people

Sabbath: the seventh day of the week, a day of rest for Israelites

Sage: a wise person

Samaria: the capital of northern Israel and an alternate name for the country

Samaritan Pentateuch: a different form of the Pentateuch accepted by the Samaritans as their Bible (they exclude other books)

Sanctify: to make an object or person especially holy or set apart for God

Second Isaiah: Isaiah 40–55, chapters that address the end of the exile

Second Temple: the temple built by those who returned with Zerubbabel; also, the name given to an era or time period after the construction of this temple until its destruction by the Romans (ca. 516 BCE–70 CE)

Seer: a term for a prophet

Segmented Genealogy: a genealogy that fans out like a family tree, including all members of the family

Septuagint: Greek translation(s) of the Old Testament made for Jews living in the Greek-speaking world, begun in ca. 200 BCE

Shiloh: the first centralized place for worship in ancient Israel, with the tabernacle and the ark of the covenant

Sin: the name of the Babylonian moon god

Speech-Act: a message (from God) presented through some physical action (e.g., dressing like a person going into captivity to warn that captivity is coming)

Succession Narrative: 2 Samuel 11:1–1 Kings 2:11, a story about who will become the next king in David's dynasty

Synchronism: dating the beginning of one king's reign on the basis of another king's reign

Syncretism: merging the beliefs and worship practices of two or more gods

Tabernacle: a portable tent with a surrounding compound formed by a curtain fence; the Lord's dwelling place with Israel from Mount Sinai until Solomon builds the temple in Jerusalem

Tablet of Destinies: a tablet upon which the future is written, the god who holds this tablet has the authority to set laws and decree what will happen in the future

TANAK: an acronym for a Jewish Bible, made from the first letter of its three major sections: *Torah*, *Nebi'im*, and *Ketubim*

Theocracy: government led by God or by divinely inspired kings or priests

Theology: literally "words or talk about God," thus, our speech about God or life with God

Torah: the books of Genesis through Deuteronomy; also known as the Pentateuch

Tribe: an extended family group of one of Jacob/Israel's sons

Transjordan: the land on the east side of the Jordan River from the Arnon river in the south to north of the Dead Sea, settled by the tribes of Reuben, Gad, and half of Manasseh

Tribute: a tax imposed on a smaller or conquered nation by a superior nation or empire

Ugarit: an ancient kingdom on the Mediterranean coast (ca. 1400 BCE, now Ras Shamra)

Ugaritic: language of Ugarit; a large number of Ugaritic texts have been recovered giving insight to ancient Palestine and Baal worship

Vestments: the robes or clothing a priest wears

Wasf: a love poem that describes the lover's body from head to feet or feet to head, sometimes concluding on an object of great interest

Yahweh: see "Lord"

Zion (or Mount Zion): the hill on which Jerusalem sat; later came to denote the city of Jerusalem itself

Yoke: a wooden harness for joining animals (e.g., oxen) to plow the ground